ETHICS AND AESTHETICS IN EUROPEAN MODERNIST LITERATURE

David Ellison's book is an investigation into the historical origins and textual practice of European literary Modernism. Ellison's study traces the origins of Modernism to the emergence of early German Romanticism from the philosophy of Immanuel Kant, and emphasizes how the passage from Romanticism to Modernism can be followed in the gradual transition from the sublime to the uncanny. Arguing that what we call high Modernism cannot be reduced to a religion of beauty, an experimentation with narrative form, or even a reflection on time and consciousness, Ellison demonstrates that Modernist textuality is characterized by the intersection, overlapping, and crossing of aesthetic and ethical issues. Beauty and morality relate to each other as antagonists struggling for dominance within the related fields of philosophy and theory on the one hand (Kant, Kierkegaard, Nietzsche, Freud) and imaginative literature on the other (Baudelaire, Proust, Gide, Conrad, Woolf, Kafka).

DAVID ELLISON is Professor of French and Comparative Literature and Chairman of the Department of Foreign Languages and Literatures at the University of Miami (Florida). He is the author of *The Reading of Proust* (1984), *Understanding Albert Camus* (1990), and *Of Words and the World: Referential Anxiety in Contemporary French Fiction* (1993).

ETHICS AND AESTHETICS IN EUROPEAN MODERNIST LITERATURE

From the Sublime to the Uncanny

DAVID ELLISON
University of Miami

CAMBRIDGE UNIVERSITY PRESS
Cambridge, New York, Melbourne, Madrid, Cape Town, Singapore, São Paulo

Cambridge University Press
The Edinburgh Building, Cambridge CB2 2RU, UK

Published in the United States of America by Cambridge University Press, New York

www.cambridge.org
Information on this title: www.cambridge.org/9780521806800

First published 2001
This digitally printed first paperback version 2006

A catalogue record for this publication is available from the British Library

Library of Congress Cataloguing in Publication data

Ellison, David R.
Ethics and aesthetics in European modernist literature: from the sublime
to the uncanny / David Richard Ellison.
p. cm.
Includes bibliographical references and index.
ISBN 0 521 80680 1
1. Literature, Modern – 20th century – History and criticism. 2. Literature, Modern – 19th century – History and criticism. 3. Modernism (Literature) 4. Ethics in literature.
5. Aesthetics in literature. I. Title.
PN771 .E44 2001
809′.9112 – dc21 2001025769

ISBN-13 978-0-521-80680-0 hardback
ISBN-10 0-521-80680-1 hardback

ISBN-13 978-0-521-02516-4 paperback
ISBN-10 0-521-02516-8 paperback

Kierkegaard faces the problem, whether to enjoy life aesthetically or to experience it ethically. But this seems to me a false statement of the problem. The Either-Or exists only in the head of Søren Kierkegaard. In reality one can only achieve an aesthetic enjoyment of life as a result of humble ethical experience. But this is only a personal opinion of the moment, which perhaps I shall abandon after closer inquiry.

Franz Kafka (quoted by Gustav Janouch in *Conversations with Kafka*)

For Ellen, in the words of the poet

Ich hatt es nie so ganz erfahren, jenes alte feste Schicksalswort, daß eine neue Seligkeit dem Herzen aufgeht, wenn es aushält und die Mitternacht des Grams durchduldet, und daß, wie Nachtigallgesang im Dunklen, göttlich erst in tiefem Leid das Lebenslied der Welt uns tönt.

Contents

Preface *page* ix
List of abbreviations xiii

PART ONE KANT, ROMANTIC IRONY, *UNHEIMLICHKEIT*

1 Border crossings in Kant 3
2 Kierkegaard: on the economics of living poetically 24
3 Freud's "Das Unheimliche": the intricacies of textual uncanniness 52

PART TWO THE ROMANTIC HERITAGE AND MODERNIST FICTION

4 Aesthetic redemption: the thyrsus in Nietzsche, Baudelaire, and Wagner 87
5 The "beautiful soul": Alain-Fournier's *Le Grand Meaulnes* and the aesthetics of Romanticism 113
6 Proust and Kafka: uncanny narrative openings 133
7 Textualizing immoralism: Conrad's *Heart of Darkness* and Gide's *L'Immoraliste* 159
8 Fishing the waters of impersonality: Virginia Woolf's *To the Lighthouse* 185

EPILOGUE: Narrative and music in Kafka and Blanchot: the "singing" of Josefine 211

Notes 231
Works cited 265
Index 278

Preface

This book is an investigation into the historical origins and textual practice of European literary Modernism. My study does not extend to Spanish *modernismo*, but limits itself to the interpretation of selected writings from the cultural spaces of France, England, and Germany, including locations which, in their own individual ways, were in Germany's philosophical and literary orbit from the mid-nineteenth to the early twentieth centuries – Kierkegaard's Copenhagen and Kafka's Prague. My project is, at one level, comparative in the classical sense of that term, in that I pursue the categories of the sublime (*das Erhabene*) and the uncanny (*Unheimlichkeit*) across national borders, in the belief that the transition from the first to the second of these terms is a determining factor in the movement from Romanticism to Modernism. At the same time, however, the mode of my pursuit is not that of traditional intellectual history, in which individual texts are mustered to exemplify the general concepts under investigation, but rather the reverse: I begin and always remain with individual texts and find, within them, the points of emergence of the sublime and the uncanny, those areas that are inhabited or haunted by these categories.

Both the sublime, in its Kantian definition, and the uncanny as theorized by Freud via E. T. A. Hoffmann, are hybrid notions in that they are built upon the complex mixture and interplay of the aesthetic and the ethical. Whereas both Kant and Kierkegaard, in their stylistically diverse ways, set the aesthetic against the ethical as separate, cordoned-off areas equal in philosophical importance but dangerous to the integrity of each other's territory, imaginative writers from the period of German Romantic irony through what we call high Modernism have found it impossible not to break down the barriers separating the two heterogeneous domains. I shall be arguing that Modernist literature, from its earliest origins in the convoluted arabesques of Romantic irony, is the textual space in which uncanniness is both feared and desired, at times censored and prohibited from exerting its power but at others allowed to function freely, dangerously, diabolically.

The structure of my book has two dimensions. On the one hand, seen from the point of view of literary history, it is linear and (with pedagogical intent) straightforward in its presentation. I begin with a reading of selected passages from Kant's Second and Third Critiques with the purpose of uncovering those areas of rhetorical complexity in which the aesthetic and the ethical, despite the philosopher's considerable efforts to the contrary, do in fact overlap and contaminate each other's theoretical integrity. I continue with Kierkegaard, with an analysis of both *The Concept of Irony* and *Either/Or*, and concentrate on the difficulties inherent in the framing of the aesthetic by the ethical (this key notion of framing is viewed both philosophically and narratively, as will be the case throughout my study). And finally, the third essay of the book's first part is a close reading of Freud's essay "Das Unheimliche," with continual reference to the text underlying Freud's own: E. T. A. Hoffmann's "Der Sandmann." Chapter three is the theoretical center of my book.

With the literary-historical and theoretical backgrounds established in part one, I move on, in the next section, to five essays dealing with the heritage of Romanticism and the transition to Modernist textual practice. In chapter four I examine the Dionysian emblem of the thyrsus as it emerges in the late Romantic works of Nietzsche, Baudelaire, and Wagner. Chapter five is a reading of Alain-Fournier's *Le Grand Meaulnes* in the light of the notion of the "beautiful soul," a figure of considerable philosophical importance which incorporates or symbolizes the mixed mode of aesthetic morality. The universe of Alain-Fournier's novel lies at the threshold of Modernism, but does not cross over into it. Chapters six to eight are devoted to the interpretation of texts by what literary historians have designated as exemplary or canonical Modernist writers: Proust and Kafka; Conrad and Gide; and Virginia Woolf. In each of these chapters there emerges some form of textual uncanniness, and in each case my analysis focuses on the points of intersection or overlap between the categories of the aesthetic and the ethical. Throughout part two I combine a narratological perspective with psychoanalytic theory in my examination of intertextual linkages and uncanny textual echo-effects.

Following Flaubert's excellent advice – "l'ineptie consiste à vouloir conclure" – there is no conclusion to this book (no final totalizing frame) but rather an opening outward, in the form of an epilogue on Kafka and Blanchot. In this final essay I examine Kafka's Modernist redefinition of the sublime and his convergence with Blanchot in the conceptualization of death as unhomely home. If there were to be a conclusion, it would be, with apologies to Freud: "The aim of all texts is death." But "death" here is to be taken in the spectral neutrality with which it is given to us by both Kafka and Blanchot, as a place beyond places which we inhabit but which will have always inhabited us.

The second dimension of my book's structure is not based upon the perhaps deceptively clear chronological trajectory extending from Kant to Blanchot, but can be characterized as "musical." The book as a whole is a series of variations on the twin grand themes of the aesthetic and the ethical in which certain *Leitmotive* (the sublime, the uncanny, the diabolical, narrative framing, psychological ambivalence) and certain authors (notably Proust and Kafka as uncanny *Doppelgänger*) recur with some frequency, but change in their significance according to their insertion in new contexts. There is Kant's sublime but also Kafka's sublime; there is Freud's uncanny but also Woolf's uncanny; Kierkegaard and Gide are masters of a same-but-different narrative framing; the Proust of chapter five differs from the Proust who inhabits the depths of chapter eight; the Kafka twinned with Proust in chapter five is and is not the Kafka associated with Blanchot in the epilogue. This book, in other words, does not just describe the textual uncanny, but is pervaded by it. The chronological guard-rail running from Kant and Kierkegaard to Kafka and Blanchot is a framework of sorts, but by the time the book ends, the shortcomings of framing as such should have become abundantly clear. I leave it to the individual tastes of my reader to determine whether the first or the second structural dimension of my study is more appealing, more rhetorically convincing or enlivening.

Whether my reader's inclinations take him or her in the direction of literary-historical chronology or of structural musicality, in either case there is one fundamental tension inhabiting my book that will be constantly present, namely, the sometimes antagonistic pull or strain between conceptual generality and textual particularity. I have undertaken a project whose scope is vast (more than 150 years of literary and philosophical history) and whose intellectual effectiveness will depend upon how well my reader is convinced of my manipulation of large and notoriously slippery categories such as the sublime, the uncanny, Romanticism, and Modernism. The very nature of my project obliges me to deal with large generalities. Yet the interpretive method I have chosen is that of close reading, and, in particular, detailed scrutiny of the role of the signifier in the texts I analyze. It is precisely in the diabolical freeplay of the signifier that the upsetting or unsettling of the grand categories of the ethical and the aesthetic can be best observed. For this reason, I am asking of my reader a certain patience, a willingness to dwell within the signifier and its complex ramifications, a willing suspension of hermeneutical disbelief. My task will be to play Virgil to my reader's Dante, and to lead him or her through the textual "selva oscura" in the direction of the larger questions toward which the works examined here point. There will be signposts along the way, in which I remind the reader of the larger issues and problems; but it is my conviction that these issues, these problems, are only available, only ascertainable, after considerable interpretive labor. And the locus of this labor is the detail, the fragment, the word, sometimes the individual sound. To range between such smallness and such largeness is difficult. Perhaps it is the reader's active participation, even collaboration, in elaborating the meanings of my book, that will grant this study whatever value (aesthetic and ethical) it may contain.

The writing of this book was made possible by a generous sabbatical leave granted me by the University of Miami in 1997–98. My thanks go to Deans Paul Blaney and Kumble Subbaswamy, to Provost Luis Glaser, and to my colleague and friend Celita Lamar, whose willingness to assume the duties of department chairmanship during my absence is much appreciated. I would also like to express my appreciation to Greta West, whose clerical and computer expertise, as well as gracious encouragement, were most appreciated throughout the various compositional stages of this project.

I am grateful to Robert Norton and to the twist of fate that allowed for a certain lunchtime conversation to take place some years ago – a conversation that seems now to have produced two books. And there are those who deplore the lack of intellectual dialogue in our "benighted" times . . .

Finally, I would like to thank Dr. Linda Bree, Humanities Editor of Cambridge University Press, for her guidance and support throughout the final phases of the project. And my appreciation goes, as well, to the two subtle readers chosen by Dr. Bree to read the manuscript. Their comments and advice were both thought-provoking and of practical help to me in the revision process.

Earlier versions of three of the chapters of this study were published in *Poétique*, *MLN*, and *Yale French Studies* respectively. I wish to thank the editors of these journals for permission to reuse the material in revised form in my book.

Abbreviations

ALR	Marcel Proust, *A la recherche du temps perdu*
B	Franz Kafka, *Brief an den Vater*
BT	Friedrich Nietzsche, *The Birth of Tragedy*
C	Franz Kafka, *The Castle*
CI	Søren Kierkegaard, *The Concept of Irony*
CJ	Immanuel Kant, *Critique of Judgment*
CPrR	Immanuel Kant, *Critique of Practical Reason*
CS	Maurice Blanchot, "Le chant des sirènes"
D	Franz Kafka, *Diaries 1910–1913*
DS	E. T. A. Hoffmann, "Der Sandmann"
DU	Sigmund Freud, "Das Unheimliche"
DW	*The Diary of Virginia Woolf*
E/O	Søren Kierkegaard, *Either/Or*
F	Grimm brothers, "Von dem Fischer und seiner Frau"
GT	Friedrich Nietzsche, *Die Geburt der Tragödie*
GW	Sigmund Freud, *Gesammelte Werke*
HD	Joseph Conrad, *Heart of Darkness*
I	André Gide, *The Immoralist*
J	Franz Kafka, "Josefine, die Sängerin oder das Volk der Mäuse"
JMF	Franz Kafka, "Josephine the Singer, or the Mouse Folk"
KPrV	Immanuel Kant, *Kritik der praktischen Vernunft*
KU	Immanuel Kant, *Kritik der Urteilskraft*
L	Franz Kafka, *Letter to His Father*
L'Imm	André Gide, *L'Immoraliste*
RTP	Marcel Proust, *Remembrance of Things Past*
S	Franz Kafka, *Das Schloß*
SE	Sigmund Freud, *Standard Edition*
T	Franz Kafka, *Tagebücher*

TL	Virginia Woolf, *To the Lighthouse*
TS	E. T. A. Hoffmann, "The Sandman"
TU	Sigmund Freud, "The Uncanny"
VN	Maurice Blanchot, "La voix narrative, le 'il,' le neutre"
VW	Hermione Lee, *Virginia Woolf*

PART I

Kant, Romantic irony, Unheimlichkeit

CHAPTER 1

Border crossings in Kant

I CRITIQUE OF JUDGMENT

If Hegel is the thinker of overcomings and supersession whereby dialectical negation erases the boundaries between inside and outside, self and other in the synthetic unity of consciousness, Kant is the tracer of borders and limits, the thought-surveyor par excellence. Not only was Kant's critical enterprise a careful navigation between the extremes of empiricism and abstract metaphysical speculation in which clear limits were set for the capacities of human reason, but each of his three Critiques is characterized by the establishing of defining boundary-lines between it and the two others, such that cognition, morality, and aesthetic taste occupy, or seem to occupy, clearly delimited separate spheres.

Within Kant's system there is a very precise architectonics of interaction, an elaborate scaffolding of the "faculties" which, according to the treatise they happen to occupy, assume a dominant or subservient role. The three Critiques are "about" three different areas of human capability, and in this sense, up to a point, can be read as self-enclosed texts. The temptation to do so has long been a staple of Kant criticism, since, until relatively recently, scholarly consensus had it that the first and most massive of these volumes to appear, the *Critique of Pure Reason* (1781), was by far the most important of the three – that the other two might be viewed, despite their considerable intrinsic merit, as secondary or ancillary.[1] Yet it is apparent that Kant intended the three works to be a system, and that this intellectual goal of his was achieved once he found a way to integrate the Third Critique with the first two.

That it was, in fact, difficult for Kant to effect such an integration is of no small importance in the history of philosophy and of aesthetics as a branch thereof. Somehow the domain of the aesthetic (conceived of as the territory within which judgments of taste, *Geschmacksurteile*, are elicited) is problematic, its expanse difficult to measure with assurance.

For Kant, given the structure and terms of his system, the problem could be summed up in the following way: whereas in the first two Critiques one faculty held sway and "legislated" over another, subordinate faculty, in the *Critique of Judgment* (1790) there is no one faculty that dominates. This is because the attitude of aesthetic disinterest can only uphold itself in what might be called an initial suspension of all established categories – a suspension that presupposes the freeplay of the faculties among themselves. Gilles Deleuze puts it this way:

> The three Critiques present a complete system of permutations. In the first place the faculties are defined according to the relationships of representation in general (knowing [*Critique of Pure Reason*], desiring [*Critique of Practical Reason*], feeling [*Critique of Judgment*]). In the second place they are defined as sources of representations (imagination, understanding, reason). When we consider any faculty in the first sense, a faculty in the second sense is called on to legislate over objects and to distribute their *specific* tasks to the other faculties: thus understanding legislates in the faculty of knowledge [in the *Critique of Pure Reason*] and reason legislates in the faculty of desire [in the *Critique of Practical Reason*]. It is true that in the *Critique of Judgment* the imagination does not take on a legislative function on its own account. But it frees itself, so that all the faculties together enter into a free accord. Thus the first two Critiques set out a relationship between the faculties which is determined by one of them; the last Critique uncovers a deeper free and indeterminate accord of the faculties as the condition of the possibility of every determinate relationship. (*Kant's Critical Philosophy*, 68)

Just as Kant reversed the commonly accepted way of thinking about cognition (for him, we should think of objects as conforming to our modes of knowing rather than the other way around),[2] so Deleuze is inverting the usual way of reading the three Critiques as a philosophical unity. He is proposing that the *Critique of Judgment*, far from being a work that is merely rich and complex but, finally, not susceptible of integration into the critical system, is in fact the cornerstone, the "condition of possibility" of that very system. Without the Third Critique, the other two certainly would have constituted admirable argumentative structures on their own, but *the structure of the structure*, so to speak, would have remained blind to itself. The *Critique of Judgment*, in Deleuze's view, would be the work by which the system comes to know itself as system; the aesthetic would no longer be relegated to secondary or tertiary status, but would be that subterranean province that underlies the others, and, in the very indeterminacy of its freeplay, opens up the possibility of lawful relations, both theoretical and practical.

From an historical point of view, the *Critique of Judgment*, published in 1790, not only closes off Kant's system as the end toward which Enlightenment thought had always tended, but also, in Deleuze's interpretation, inaugurates Romanticism. In the preface to *Kant's Critical Philosophy*, Deleuze finds that the free and unregulated play of the faculties among themselves, "where each goes to its own limit and nevertheless shows the possibility of some sort of harmony with the others," represents nothing less than "the foundation of Romanticism" (xi–xii). He does not mean, in the context of French literature, the sentimental Romanticism of Lamartine, Musset and the early Hugo, but rather the revolutionary poetics of Arthur Rimbaud, whose evocation of "the disorder of all the senses" (*le désordre de tous les sens*) pushes Romanticism to its extreme limits and ushers in the movements of French Symbolism and European Modernism. The idea, then, is that whereas the first two Critiques position Kant as the grand synthesizer of the *Aufklärung*, the *Critique of Judgment* is a work of open boundaries whose complexity and polysemic possibilities make it a modern work.

What is intriguing, however, and of essential importance to any reader who wishes to respect the guidelines Kant himself traces between and among the three critical works, is the fact that the Third Critique also functions as an intermediary, as a bridge-text between the *Critique of Pure Reason* and the *Critique of Practical Reason* (1788), in that its primary agent, reflective judgment, is, in Kant's words, "the mediating link between understanding and reason" (introduction to the *Critique of Judgment*, 16).[3] More precisely, the faculty of judgment is capable of bringing about a "transition from the pure cognitive power, i.e., from the domain of the concepts of nature, to the domain of the concept of freedom, just as in its logical use it makes possible the transition from understanding to reason" (*CJ* 18). According to this formulation, aesthetics is not the endpoint of the system, but rather its articulating *middle*, its mediating drive, that which might be, or should be, capable of overcoming "the great gulf [*die große Kluft*] that separates the supersensible from appearances" (*CJ* 35; *KU* 33). The faculty of judgment is such a bridge because it, and it alone, furnishes the concept of the finality of nature, a teleological structure within which aesthetics as such occupies its appropriate place:

It is judgment that presupposes [the final purpose of nature] a priori, and without regard to the practical, [so that] this power provides us with the concept that mediates between the concepts of nature and the concept of freedom [*gibt den vermittelnden Begriff zwischen den Naturbegriffen und dem Freiheitsbegriffe*]: the concept of a *purposiveness* of nature [*einer Zweckmäßigkeit der Natur*], which makes possible the transition from pure theoretical to pure practical lawfulness, from lawfulness in terms of nature to the final purpose set by the concept of freedom [*von der Gesetzmäßigkeit nach der ersten zum Endzwecke nach dem letzten*]. For it is through this concept that we cognize the possibility of the final purpose [*die Möglichkeit des Endzwecks*], which can be actualized only in nature and in accordance with its laws. (*CJ* 36–37; *KU* 34)

In the original German text, Kant's argument is woven around a play on the word *Zweck* – goal or purpose. We are reminded that *Gesetzmäßigkeit*, or the lawfulness of nature, is the domain of the First Critique. *Zweckmäßigkeit*, or the purposiveness of nature, is developed in the Third Critique as a "bridge" toward the *Endzweck* of the Second Critique, the final purpose of man, which can only emerge in the supersensible territory of the law, of the "ought" which traces the boundaries of the province of morality and exercises its rule in accord with our freedom. In this scheme, which Kant elaborates carefully but quite confidently in the final section of his introduction to the *Critique of Judgment*, it is manifest that, in some fundamental sense, the aesthetic as such points toward the ethical, that the ethical stands as the *Endzweck* of the aesthetic. In this precise sense, then, the endpoint of the Kantian system is its middle, the *Critique of Practical Reason*, the place in which the moral law instantiates itself. As we proceed now to an analysis of the points of intersection between the Second and Third Critiques, it is important to keep in mind the double position of the aesthetic in Kant: it is, through the free and unregulated play of the faculties it allows, the limit toward which the Kantian system pushes and exhausts itself; and it is also, in its mediation between pure and practical reason, the passageway through which the ethical makes its appearance, shines forth.

There are three paragraphs in the *Critique of Judgment* which deal quite explicitly with the modality of the relationship between the beautiful or the sublime, on the one hand, and the ethical, on the other. They occur after the initial section, entitled the "Analytic of the Beautiful," in which judgments of taste per se are discussed and the domain of the beautiful is assigned its boundaries. They are: "On the Modality of a Judgment upon the Sublime in Nature" (par. 29); "On Intellectual Interest in the Beautiful" (par. 42); and "On Beauty as the Symbol of Morality" (par. 59). The first two of these paragraphs occur within the section called the "Analytic of the Sublime," and the third, which is the penultimate paragraph of the "Critique of Aesthetic Judgment," concludes the "Dialectic of Aesthetic Judgment." I think it is best to begin with paragraph 59, since it encapsulates the previous remarks Kant has made on the relation of the aesthetic to the moral or ethical (the domain of *Sittlichkeit*). It is both the clearest and the most complicated statement Kant makes in his writings about this relation.

On a first reading, paragraph 59 seems clear enough in that its argument leads toward a ringing assertion which defines the beautiful as "symbol of the morally good":

> Now I maintain that the beautiful is the symbol of the morally good [*das Schöne ist das Symbol des Sittlich-guten*]; and only because we refer the beautiful to the morally good (we all do so naturally and require all others also to do so, as a duty [*Pflicht*]), does our liking for it include a claim to everyone else's assent [*Beistimmung*], while the mind is also conscious of being ennobled [*sich . . . einer gewissen Veredlung und Erhebung . . . bewußt ist*], by this [reference], above a mere receptivity for pleasure derived from sense impressions, and it assesses the value of other people too on the basis of [their having] a similar maxim in their power of judgment. The morally good is the *intelligible* that taste has in view [*worauf . . . der Geschmack hinaussieht*], as I indicated in the preceding section; for it is with this intelligible that even our higher cognitive powers harmonize [*zusammenstimmen*], and without this intelligible contradictions [*lauter Widersprüche*] would continually arise from the contrast between the nature of these powers and the claims that taste makes. (*CJ* 228–29; *KU* 213)

The passage as a whole is characterized by two primary images: that of the harmonizing of voices (*Beistimmung, zusammenstimmen*) as opposed to the dissonance of contradiction (*lauter Widersprüche)*; and that of the ennobling elevation beyond the senses in the direction of the intelligible (*Veredlung, Erhebung*, and the expression *worauf . . . der Geschmack hinaussieht*). The notion of a harmonizing accord among the faculties confirms the position of the *Critique of Judgment* as endpoint of the critical enterprise, whereas the image of ennobling elevation places the aesthetic in a mediating role, defining it as that which *points beyond itself* toward the supersensible domain of the ethical. It would appear, in this strong declarative moment, that Kant wishes to grant to the aesthetic both a final and a mediating function, and that the interplay of imagery he uses here constitutes a stylistics of synthesis – in the image of a resolved harmony of elevation, where horizontal and vertical planes join each other in a logically arduous but rhetorically effective merger. Thus the superficial clarity of the declarative statement hides a complex rhetorical weave, in which the reader discovers Immanuel Kant as stylist, whose words function not merely as the transparent conveyors of a philosophical argument, but also as elements in a tropological discourse.[4] Such a passage does not simply "point beyond" the aesthetic in the direction of the moral; it points toward itself as text.

This involutedness serves to complicate considerably the overt message of the passage, which, in asserting that the beautiful tends toward the moral in "symbolizing" it, brings the text dangerously close to the frontier at which the beautiful effaces itself *in favor of* the moral, at which there is a moralization of the aesthetic. Kant's style, his poetics of harmonization and elevation, in which the ethical *becomes beautiful* in its "noble" loftiness, performs the opposite: namely, a rhetorically subtle aestheticization of the moral. In other words, Kant anticipatorily but only momentarily succumbs to the temptation to which Schiller will yield massively, perhaps completely: that of bringing together the aesthetic and the ethical in a dialectical play whereby "moral beauty" as such occupies the final, synthetic moment.[5]

It is not a coincidence, I think, that the declarative and somewhat emphatic passage I have just discussed exceeds, by its rhetorical complexity, the straightforward assertion it (also) makes. Preceding this excerpt in the earlier part of paragraph 59 is a development on the notion of symbolization per se in Kant's own technical terminology (we learn that symbolism is, along with schematism, one of the two types of what Kant calls *hypotyposis*), whose cryptic qualities have engendered reams of critical commentary. The central problem for an understanding of paragraph 59 as a whole lies in the problem of indirect language and, specifically, *analogy*. In differentiating between schemata and symbols, Kant writes:

> Hence, all intuitions supplied for a priori concepts are either *schemata* or *symbols*. Schemata contain direct, symbols indirect, exhibitions of the concept [*indirekte Darstellungen des Begriffs*]. Schematic exhibition is demonstrative. Symbolic exhibition uses an analogy ... Thus a monarchy ruled according to its own constitutional laws would be presented as an animate body [*durch einen beseelten Körper*], but a monarchy ruled by an individual absolute will would be presented as a mere machine (such as a hand mill); but in either case the presentation is only *symbolic*. For though there is no similarity between a despotic state and a hand mill, there certainly is one between the rules by which we reflect on the two and on how they operate [*ihre Kausalität*]. This function [of judgment] [*Dies Geschäft*] has not been analyzed much so far, even though it very much deserves fuller investigation; but this is not the place to pursue it. (*CJ* 227; *KU* 212)

An analysis of this passage may be helpful in shedding light on the critical debate surrounding the formula "the beautiful is the symbol of the morally good." Kant specialists from both the Continental and the Anglo-American tradition divide rather neatly into two camps: the "weak analogy" group, which finds in the comparison between the beautiful and the morally good a tenuous, inessential linkage;[6] and the "strong analogy" contingent, which considers that the comparison functions as a solid bridging device.[7] Underlying these critical divergences is a certain belief or non-belief in the capacity of the *analogon* to evoke its intended referent, of the image to translate its concept with clarity, as well as a trust or distrust in the epistemological possibilities of such a translational movement (*Übertragung*, or metaphorical transport, is the word Kant uses in par. 59, *CJ* 228; *KU* 213). Before one can ask the question "Is there a strong analogy *or* a weak analogy between the beautiful and the morally good," one needs to ask "What is an analogy?" Are analogies, in and of themselves, weak or strong? Are they capable, in their assigned role, of presenting the concept adequately, convincingly?

Perhaps the best way to undertake such an inquiry is to begin with Kant's own examples in this passage: the monarchical state as represented by a living body; and a despotic state as symbolized by a "mere machine" such as a hand mill. If the analogy is to function effectively, the representational images must conjure up, presumably without ambiguity or confusion, the concepts to which they refer: should they not succeed in doing so, they must be viewed as failed or improperly symbolizing symbols. Kant concedes that "there is no similarity between a despotic state and a hand mill," but he says, in a remarkably obscure statement, that "there certainly is one between the rules by which we reflect on the two and on how they operate." What are these rules? Where do they come from? Are they universal for all sentient beings? Is logic itself, and even that most slippery form of "logic," the rhetoric of analogy, a rule-bound domain? Kant not only does not answer these questions, but concludes the above passage with the brutal disclaimer: "this is not the place to pursue [this matter]." One wonders: what *better* place than precisely here, when so much is at stake? For the beautiful to be the symbol of the morally good, it is necessary that analogy as such function well and not be suspect in its structure or constitution. One is tempted to wonder if Kant was convinced by the validity of his own examples – and exemplarity, it goes without saying, is central to all philosophical discourse, since the example must stand in a relation of metaphorical synecdoche to that which it exemplifies, i.e., no part of it can exceed the bounds of the whole to which it belongs.

The basis or ground (one can speak of analogies only by using metaphorical language) of Kant's comparison, and of his comparative analogies, is the superiority of a monarchical state governed by laws over a despotic state ruled by one person's absolute (and therefore arbitrary) will. How can this concept of superiority in the territory of politics be represented in an image or images? Kant chooses an "animate body" for the law-based monarchy and a hand mill for the despotic system presumably because an animate body will be recognized by all readers of Kant's text as superior to (i.e., *nobler than*) a hand mill, and because a functioning that is merely mechanical and simply serves as a means toward a culinary end does not evoke the same kind of dignity as that of a living body (in the German, *ein beseelter Körper* – literally, a "soul-infused" body). Leaving aside for the moment that the analogy can only work given a traditional humanistic framework (once one undermines the "dignity of man," one can have surrealist imagery, in which a hand mill and a "soul-infused body" might appear as equally uncanny "objects"), it is necessary to remark that Kant's analogy works best when *we already know both terms of the analogical relation*. Unlike the poet, who only gives the reader an image, from which that reader must discover the represented concept, Kant gives us both sides of the *symbolon*, thereby de-activating the process of interpretation. Kant's analogy is, in fact, a logical illustration in the form of an image, not an image whose analogical structure invites disclosure in an interpretive reading.[8] His conclusion – that "this function [of judgment] [*dies Geschäft*] has not been analyzed much so far" – is, unfortunately, not just a general admission concerning the incomplete state of scholarship in the field of rhetoric, but an implicit admission of his own failure to confront directly and examine thoroughly the figural dimension of discourse, including that of philosophical exposition.

Kant retreats in the face of the aesthetic *as indirect discourse*. Indirection, which Kant himself says is the essential characteristic of the symbol, is also that which poses the greatest threat to his own critical enterprise, to his own *Geschäft* – a term we shall encounter later, in the context of his ethical writings. Could it be that there are, in fact, two *Geschäfte*, two forms of "business": that of philosophy, on the one hand, and that of literature, on the other? Philosophy, classically conceived, would be that discourse which avoids indirection even when encountering it and defining it, which flees the very territory (the figural minefield of aesthetics) it sets out to map. The philosophical transit and level are based upon clearly definable geometrical principles, upon mathematical laws, whereas what lies within aesthetics, the indirect realm of analogy, is subject to rules no one has discovered, rules that each work of art, on its own, must discover for itself. Could it be that between philosophical aesthetics and works of art in their praxis there resides a fundamental, foundational "antinomy" in the literal Greek sense (a conflict of laws or rules), an antinomy no amount of dialectical manipulation can overcome? This is the direction in which the indirection of analogy has led. Beyond the immediate Kantian context in question here, the problem is as follows: in what ways can a theorizing discourse, a discourse of generalizing concepts, contain what I should like to call the *inside of the aesthetic*, i.e., its elusive figural dimension, when that inside is the indirect translational movement of analogy, the tending-toward the to-be-discovered concept which the reader must pursue in a series of individual and repeated interpretive efforts?

What I am calling Kant's retreat from the territory of the aesthetic in paragraph 59 serves to clarify, retroactively, a number of his most important and celebrated propositions concerning the beautiful and the sublime. Thus, his observations on artistic design in paragraph 14 of the "Analytic of the Beautiful," which have led critics to attack him or defend him for his "formalism," can be seen as the philosopher's defensive reaction against the tortuous workings of art in its praxis: one attaches oneself to the outward form when the artwork's inner force is too strong, too threatening, to be encountered on its own terms. What is interesting in Kant, however, and also emblematic for formalist appreciations of art in general, is that the fear of what constitutes or founds the work in its innermost recesses – namely, its figural *déviance* – finds expression in the philosopher's manifest distaste for what he/she represents, metaphorically, as the farthest reaches of its "outside" – namely, the seductive raiment in which the work of art clothes its design (color, sound, rhetorical ornament).[9] Because the labyrinthine inside of the work of art is threatening in its very indirection, the philosopher/theorist *re-configures* the work of art, presenting it as an aesthetic object and emphasizing its form rather than its dangerous content. The philosopher then tells us that this form is enveloped in a pleasing outer envelope, which is deemed to be seductive in its appeal to the senses. It is easier to peal back the envelope and reveal the geometry underneath than it is to encounter seductiveness *as danger* within the workings of poetic language, in the byways of indirect discourse. Kant's most emphatic pronouncement on the fundamental importance of form, on the superiority of form over the "charm" of color, is to be found in paragraph 14:

In painting, in sculpture, and in all the visual arts – including architecture and horticulture insofar as they are fine arts [*sofern sie schöne Künste sind*] – *design* is what is essential [*ist die Zeichnung das Wesentliche*]; in design the basis for any involvement of taste is not what gratifies us in sensation, but merely what we like because of its form [*sondern bloß, was durch seine Form gefällt*]. The colors that illuminate the outline belong to charm [*Reiz*]. Though they can indeed make the object itself vivid to sense, they cannot make it beautiful and worthy of being beheld. Rather, usually the requirement of beautiful form severely restricts [what] colors [may be used], and even where the charm [of colors] is admitted it is still only the form that refines the colors [*und selbst da, wo der Reiz zugelassen wird, durch die erstere allein veredelt*]. (*CJ* 71; *KU* 64–65)

As was the case in paragraph 59, paragraph 14 also depends upon a rhetoric of *ennoblement* (*Veredlung*), whereby the enticing charms of the sensible, when given over to the disciplining power of design, are lifted above their own realm and are permitted entrance (*werden zugelassen*) into the domain of beautiful forms. Colors are allowable, but only insofar as they are muted by the rigors of form. It is difficult not to sense here a strong trace of Kant's Pietistic upbringing, a Protestant aversion to those forms of iconic figuration that purportedly convey a diabolical allure. One senses, in general, that Kant was not comfortable, not "at home" in the domain of the beautiful, largely because this province, in and of itself, remains too close to the merely sensual: it is in constant need of ennoblement and elevation, of disciplinary supervision.

Kant was able to recuperate the fine arts not so much in his theory of the beautiful per se, but rather in his original and multi-faceted meditation on the sublime.[10] To conclude my remarks on the crossings of aesthetics and ethics in the *Critique of Judgment*, I shall examine selected passages from paragraphs 29 and 42 of this work, in which the proximity of the sublime to the moral law is posited and somewhat cryptically developed.

In the long "General Comment on the Exposition of Aesthetic Reflective Judgments" that occupies the center of paragraph 29, Kant delineates, in an apparently simple contrast, the essential differences between the beautiful and the sublime as they arise from his earlier exposition on the two forms of aesthetic judgment:

Beautiful is what we like when we merely judge it [Schön *ist das, was in der bloßen Beurteilung gefällt*] (and hence not through any sensation by means of sense in accordance with some concept of the understanding). From this it follows at once that we must like the beautiful without any interest.

Sublime is what, by its resistance to the interest of the senses, we like directly [Erhaben *ist das, was durch seinen Widerstand gegen das Interesse der Sinne unmittelbar gefällt*].

> Both of these are explications of universally valid aesthetic judging and as such refer to subjective bases. In the case of the beautiful, the reference is to subjective bases of sensibility [*Sinnlichkeit*] as they are purposive for the benefit of the contemplative understanding. In the case of the sublime, the reference is to subjective bases as they are purposive [*zweckmäßig*] in relation to moral feeling, namely, against sensibility [*wider dieselbe (die Sinnlichkeit)*] but at the same time, and within the very same subject, for the purposes of practical reason. The beautiful prepares us for loving [*zu lieben*] something, even nature, without interest; the sublime, for esteeming [*hochzuschätzen*] it even against our interest (of sense) [*wider unser (sinnliches) Interesse*]. (*CJ* 127; *KU* 114)

It is important to respect the complexity of Kant's argument in this passage: he is positing that the beautiful and the sublime are both different and similar; their relation is not that of a simple binary opposition. They differ from each other in a subtle but essential way – the beautiful pleases "without any interest," whereas the sublime pleases "in resistance to the interest of the senses." The reader needs to take Kant's idea of opposition (*Widerstand*) to the seductions of the sensible in its full active sense, as a fight, a *résistance* planned and executed by a combatant. The sublime is morally elevated or "ennobled" by the fact that it stands its ground against the charm (*Reiz*) of the sensible, much as Odysseus braves the song of the sirens. At the same time, however – and herein lies the interesting difficulty of Kant's line of reasoning – both the beautiful and the sublime, in their specific and different ways, *tend toward* the goal of the ethical. In Kant's vocabulary, both are "purposive [*zweckmäßig*] in relation to moral feeling," a phrase that suggests an ethically grounded teleology for the aesthetic. The aesthetic has its territory, which can be surveyed by the aesthetician, but its borders are continually shifting toward the neighboring frontier occupied, inhabited, by the moral law. Art has its field, but if one views that field from the final perspective of the ethical, from the ethical downward, so to speak, one is obliged to note that art *as territory* is, in reality, a staging-ground, an area of "preparation" for the moral. And the reason Kant's own taste inclines him toward the sublime more strongly than in the direction of the beautiful, is that the former prepares us to *esteem* (*hochzuschätzen*) rather than "merely" to love (*zu lieben*). Resistance to charm is also resistance to love. Kant retreats from the beautiful as that area in which charm can lead to love, and chooses to emphasize the sublime, where esteem emerges from initial terror and places us in closest proximity to the moral good.

The sublime (*das Erhabene*) being that which lifts up or elevates (*das, was erhebt*), the question arises as to whether it might tend to lift the human being too high, beyond the finite limitations which are his or hers in the world. Kant's intellectual honesty compels him to address this problem quite directly, in a development on the role of the sublime in its elevation of one's mental disposition above the plane of the sensible into what might seem to be the threatening reaches of abstraction. Kant reassures his reader as follows:

> the sublime must always have reference to our *way of thinking* [*die Denkungsart*], i.e., to maxims directed to providing the intellectual [side in us] and our rational ideas with supremacy over sensibility.
>
> We need not worry that the feeling of the sublime will lose [something] if it is exhibited in such an abstract way as this [*durch eine dergleichen abgezogene Darstellungsart*], which is wholly negative as regards the sensible. For though the imagination finds nothing beyond the sensible that could support it, this very removal of its barriers also makes it feel unbounded [*fühlt sich doch auch eben durch diese Wegschaffung der Schranken derselben unbegrenzt*], so that its separation [from the sensible] is an exhibition of the infinite; and though an exhibition of the infinite can as such never be more than merely negative [*als bloß negative Darstellung*], it still expands the soul [*die aber doch die Seele erweitert*]. Perhaps the most sublime passage in the Jewish Law is the commandment: Thou shalt not make unto thee any graven image [*kein Bildnis*], or any likeness of any thing [*irgendein Gleichnis*] that is in heaven or on earth, or under the earth, etc.[11] (*CJ* 134–35; *KU* 122)

For Kant, unlike Burke, the important stage in the experience of the sublime occurs not during one's awe or terror at the immensity of nature, but rather in the final return to reason which takes place once the imagination has faced its limits. Yet the originality of Kant's theory consists not only in this emphasis on the enveloping force of reason as final resting-place of the sublime, but also in his description of the pathos of the imagination, which, even though it can "attach itself" to nothing beyond the realm of the sensible, feels the exhilaration of its own *boundlessness*. This is one of the rare moments in Kant's critical enterprise when all limits fall and all boundaries evaporate, the moment of the unsayable and unrepresentable infinite.

The concrete problem for art, for *mimesis* as such, becomes: how is it possible to render, to make visible, the sublime – that which, in its very infinite abstraction (or withdrawal: *Abgezogenheit*), can be nothing but a negative exhibition or presentation? How does one represent the unrepresentable? Kant's answer to this question places the sublime in such close proximity to the territory of the ethical that the frontier between the two areas seems to disappear altogether. This answer appears abruptly, just after the remarks on the "expansion of the soul" that is said to arise from the experience of the sublime. We are told that the biblical admonishment against the making of "graven images" is a quintessentially sublime passage, the very model for the textual sublime. The linguistic form of the sublime is that of the *command*, or, more precisely, of the command in a negative or privative mode. The sublime participates in the moral law in its earliest Old Testament guise, and shares with this law its categorical, unambiguous character: no images, no likenesses of anything, whether above or below the inhabited world. The command is absolute; the moral authority of the textual statement is unquestionable, since it emanates from the mouth of God. But within this austere environment, this sacred context, what remains of the aesthetic? No image or likeness: nothing representational or rhetorical remains (*Bildnis* can mean portrait as well as likeness; *Gleichnis* is a general term that can signify image, simile, allegory, or parable – all of this disappears under the privative power of the moral law). The negative imperative form is the closest thing in language to non-language: it puts a stop to the flow of narrative action, and in this particular case, to the process of figuration itself. The threat of the figural is removed in the command. The "expansion of the soul" which occurs within the sublime does so at the expense of the aesthetic, which contracts to nothing.

Kant's admiration for a certain Goethian form of "genius" (paragraphs 46–50) cannot hide from his reader the philosopher's profound distrust of art. In fact, Kant most often locates the aesthetic in nature rather than in works of artistic creation, and it is impossible not to sense that the "schöne Künste" are beautiful for him only insofar as they approach (but never reach) the loveliness or awesome power of the natural realm. Thus, near the conclusion of paragraph 42 in the "Analytic of the Sublime" entitled "On Intellectual Interest in the Beautiful," Kant associates authentic beauty with nature and art with deceit. He imagines a scene in which a "jovial innkeeper" fools his guests into believing that they are hearing the song of a nightingale when, in fact, a "roguish youngster" is imitating the bird's distinctive song with a reed or rush (*CJ* 169). Kant states the moral of his story before relating it: the kind of artistic playfulness which consists in such an imitation of nature ruins one's further appreciation of the thing imitated. In this case, it is no longer possible to enjoy the actual song of the nightingale once it has been thus counterfeited. In Kantian terms, the intellectual "interest" we take in the beautiful *must* be in the beautiful as it occurs in nature:

> But in order for us to take this interest in beauty, this beauty must always be that of nature; our interest vanishes completely as soon as we notice that we have been deceived, that only art was involved [*es verschwindet ganz, sobald man bemerkt, man sei getäuscht, und es sei nur Kunst*]; it vanishes so completely that at that point even taste can no longer find anything beautiful, nor sight anything charming. (*CJ* 169; *KU* 154)

Underneath the architectonics of the Third Critique, below Kant's theory of taste in the general sense, lies the philosopher's *distaste* for art as deception (*Täuschung*), for the non-natural aesthetic field as locus of a playfulness whose moral dimension is suspect. Art, for Kant, will have always been "mere art" (*nur Kunst*). Herein resides Kant's lifelong admiration for Jean-Jacques Rousseau, whose *Rêveries du promeneur solitaire* located beauty in nature rather than in "les tromperies de l'art" – the seductive aesthetic *Täuschungen* that characterized, in Rousseau's view, not only the French theater of his time, but also the frivolous *jeux de société* staged in the decadent Parisian salons. In the end, moral earnestness seems to have separated Kant from the aesthetic *in art.* I am suggesting that this is the conclusion one reaches on the basis of a rhetorical reading of the *Critique of Judgment*, a reading which locates personal tastes and distastes under the garb of a general *Theorie des Geschmacks.* In Kant, the aesthetic is a precarious, fragile, and shifting field that risks losing its own territory by annexation into the domain of the ethical. But the question remains: just how stable is the ethical itself, just how safe is it from the incursions of the aesthetic? Is the ethical a *terra firma*, or is it also subject to moments of instability? This point cannot be examined from within the Third Critique, but requires a brief foray into the *Critique of Practical Reason.*[12]

II CRITIQUE OF PRACTICAL REASON

Commonplace intellectual usage has long held that the "pure" is to be situated on a higher plane than the "practical," which, at best, is related to the former as its execution or application. Thus, in the domain of literary studies, a "pure" narrative theory would be capable of generating principles that are universal, that are valid for all individual stories; whereas applied or practical narratology would be the workmanlike verification, on individual texts, of certain hypothesized narrative laws. In Kant's philosophy, however, "practical reason" is not only not "lower" than pure reason as described in the First Critique; it is, rather, the *extension* of pure reason in the direction of the supersensible. The human being who is capable of comprehending the laws of causality within the sensible territory of nature – the domain staked out in the *Critique of Pure Reason* – discovers, upon reflection, that "pure reason alone must of itself be practical" (*CPrR* 23).[13] This practical pure reason, the intellectual agency of the moral law, functions within the carefully prescribed limits of the categorical imperative, of the universally legislating "ought" which, while establishing the moral dimension of our world, calls us all to live beyond the causality of the sensible, in freedom.[14]

Fundamental to Kant's conception of morality is the relation between the desires of each individual and the moral law in its universality. The author of the Second Critique distinguishes, from the beginning, between "maxims" (which a human subject establishes as "valid only for his own will") and "practical laws" (which are valid "for the will of every rational being") (*CPrR* 17). Maxims are, by definition, self-interested guidelines in which the force of personal desire has not been tamed. The most important of these is perhaps the maxim of self-love (post-Freud, we would call this narcissism), which Kant singles out to contrast with the moral law:

> The maxim of self-love (prudence) merely advises; the law of morality commands [*Die Maxime der Selbstliebe (Klugheit) rät bloß an; das Gesetz der Sittlichkeit gebietet*]. Now there is a great difference between that which we are advised to do and that which we are obligated to do. (*CPrR* 37–38; *KPrV* 43)

To advise someone is to open up a direction of conduct for that person, to lead him or her toward the obtaining of a certain advantage or final goal. Advice is a rhetorical strategy not uncommonly associated with deviousness and seduction: Mme de Merteuil gives Valmont much advice in Laclos's *Les Liaisons dangereuses*, to the peril of Mme de Tournon. Advice given either by the self to others or by the self to the self occupies the dangerous intellectual field of *Klugheit*, which does not mean the "prudence" (*Vorsicht*) of a merely reactive form of self-preservation, as in the cautious attitude one should manifest before crossing a street, but rather cleverness, shrewdness, cunning. To return for a moment to *Les Liaisons*: Valmont's seduction of Mme de Tournon is more interesting in its multiple strategies than in its final triumph, in its shrewd psychological manipulations than in its achieved goal. The seduction is not so much an accomplished action as an emerging (cruel) work of art, a cunning, duplicitous aestheticization of an increasingly undermined moral code.[15]

Unlike the advice-giving maxim of narcissistic self-gratification (which is the true final goal of all seductions, the goal behind the "goal"), the law of morality *commands*, which means that its message is univocal, understandable to all human beings. Everyone can obey an absolute order, meaning, at the close of the eighteenth century, not just the worldly-wise aristocracy. Just as *Les Liaisons dangereuses* is inconceivable as story outside the highest (and therefore, most decadent) levels of society, so the moral law would be inconceivable if it did not address itself, democratically, to all citizens. Kant's central notion of "duty," the expression of each person's adherence to the moral law in its universality, is thus characterized by clarity, whereas the maxims of self-love and the mere pursuit of happiness are hidden in obscurity:

> What duty [*Pflicht*] is, is plain of itself to everyone, but what is to bring true, lasting advantage to our whole existence is veiled in impenetrable obscurity [*in undurchdringliches Dunkel eingehüllt*] and much prudence [*Klugheit*] is required to adapt the practical rule based upon it even tolerably to the ends of life by making suitable exceptions to it. But the moral law [*das sittliche Gesetz*] commands the most unhesitating obedience from everyone; consequently, the decision as to what is to be done in accordance with it must not be so difficult that even the commonest and most unpracticed understanding [*daß nicht der gemeinste und ungeübteste Verstand*] without any worldly prudence [*Weltklugheit*] should go wrong in making it. (*CPrR* 38; *KPrV* 43)

The moral law must be easy to understand, but it can only be expressed in language. To express the moral law, therefore, one must render language unambiguous; one must free it from all semantic slippages; one must remove all its "veils" so that nothing but clarity remains. One can see, then, that the kind of moral perversity characteristic of Laclos's novel goes hand in hand with artfulness, understood as the devious, polyvalent behavior of persons or personages who possess no conscience, who refuse to engage in the economics of guilt and forgiveness, in the dialogic universe of the forgiveness of sins. To act deviously, in Kant's German, is *künsteln* (this term is used in the philosopher's discussion of the role of conscience in moral behavior [*CPrJ* 101; *KPrV* 114]) – a term that occupies the same semantic field as *Klugheit* or *Weltklugheit.* To act according to one's advantage is, finally, to *aestheticize life*, to live it as if it were a work of art, which is to say, a fictional universe of symbols in which meaning itself is "veiled in impenetrable obscurity." The worst imaginable enemy of moral certainty would be the symbolist aesthetic of Joseph Conrad's *Heart of Darkness*, the artfully fashioned domain in which the *Weltklugheit* of

Kurtz progresses through Enlightenment philosophy toward the extreme maxim-made-command: "Exterminate all the brutes!"

If we look (chronologically) forward now from the Second to the Third Critique, I think it is possible to risk a few general remarks. In the *Critique of Judgment*, we saw that the aesthetic tended toward the moral, especially in Kant's "Analytic of the Sublime." The moral could be seen as providing a ground, perhaps the final ground, of the aesthetic. The lifting upward of *Erhabenheit* as the sublime in nature, which is already massively present as a properly moral force in the *Critique of Practical Reason*,[16] provided an antidote to what the philosopher saw as the dangerous charms of the aesthetic in the sensuality of its ornamentation – in the colors and sounds that enveloped, and possibly obscured, the formal design beneath. The aesthetic is saved from itself, so to speak, by the pressure which the moral exerts on the aesthetic in the experience of the sublime. In the *Critique of Practical Reason*, we find that the moral must guard itself against the unwanted intrusions of the aesthetic. The moral law, in order to establish its universality, must suppress the primary danger lurking in human language – that of subtlety, of ambiguity, of "prudence" understood in the strong sense as the cunning of world-wisdom, *Weltklugheit*. But is this guarding against the aesthetic from within the watchtower of *Sittlichkeit* something that can be accomplished easily, in an act of the will accessible to all humans – including philosophers? Put differently: is it possible to write morally about morality, in such a way that literary style, with its own manifold forms of "prudence," does not aestheticize one's clear-sighted and straightforward purpose? To conclude my remarks on the points of intersection between the ethical and the aesthetic in Kant, I should like to look at one final passage from the *Critique of Practical Reason* in which the philosopher, in a rare moment of first-person confidential discourse, addresses the issue of the coherence of his critical project in an ethical register, but with an interesting, and in Kantian terms rather suspicious overlay, of self-involved, cunningly manipulated artfulness.

The rhetorically convoluted section to which I refer occurs in the final paragraph of the "Analytic of Pure Practical Reason," when Kant, having concluded this part of his argument, pauses for a moment to reflect upon how easily and naturally each structural articulation of the Second Critique "fits" or "attaches to" (*schließt sich an*) the grand architectural plan of the *Critique of Pure Reason*. This moment of Kant's text is properly self-congratulatory, with a tone verging on pride. The tending-toward-pride expresses itself in a very interesting methodological statement, in a theory of intellectual honesty and "openness" which is also a criticism of those writers who fall short of this ideal. The question is whether Kant's text, in developing his theory of honesty, is itself honest. Following is an excerpt from the final paragraph:

> Here [*bei dieser Gelegenheit*] I wish to call attention, if I may [*sei es mir erlaubt*], to one thing, namely, that every step which one takes with pure reason, even in the practical field where one does not take subtle speculation [*subtile Spekulation*] into account, so neatly and naturally dovetails [*sich . . . anschließe*] with all parts of the critique of theoretical reason that it is as if each step had been carefully thought out merely to establish this confirmation [*als ob jeder Schritt mit überlegter Vorsicht, bloß um dieser Bestätigung zu verschaffen, ausgedacht wäre*]. This agreement [*Eintreffung*] was by no means sought after . . . Frequent observation has convinced me that once one has seen through such business [*dieses Geschäfte*], that which, when half-finished, appeared very dubious in view of extraneous theories, is at last found to be in an unexpected way completely harmonious [*vollkommen zusammenstimmte*] with that which had been discovered separately without the least regard for them [*ohne Parteilichkeit und Vorliebe für dieselben*], provided this dubiousness is left out of sight for a while and only the business at hand is attended to until it is finished [*wenn ich diese Bedenklichkeit nur so lange aus den Augen ließ und bloß auf mein Geschäft acht hatte, bis es vollendet sei*]. Writers could save themselves many errors and much labor lost (because spent on delusions [*weil sie auf Blendwerk gestellt war*]) if they could only resolve to go to work with a little more ingenuousness [*wenn sie sich nur entschließen könnten, mit etwas mehr Offenheit zu Werke zu gehen*]. (*CPrR* 110; *KPrV* 123)

Kant's emphasis on the spontaneous character of the "dovetailing" between the architectural designs of the first two Critiques in their minutest details foreshadows a fundamental aesthetic tenet of literary Modernism – the superiority of instantaneous creative discovery over a merely planned, laboriously and artificially conceived intellectual construction (see Joyce's "epiphanies" and Proust's endorsement of *mémoire involontaire* over *mémoire volontaire*). Like Joyce and Proust, however, who may have based their novels on aesthetic theories of spontaneity but who certainly also lavished extraordinary attention on the necessarily voluntary constructedness of their respective fictional universes, Kant may be protesting too much, indulging in what Freud called *Verneinung*, when he tells his reader that he is agreeably surprised by the harmonious coming together of the two Critiques. The reason he gives for this purported surprise is of interest, nevertheless, whether one chooses to believe Kant's own "ingenuousness" at this point in the text or not: namely, that a domain of openness, honesty, and transparent communicability (the "practical," the moral) can attach itself so readily, so beautifully, to the territory of "subtle speculation" (that of "pure" or "theoretical" reason).

Much is at stake in this overlapping. First (logically): if the practical – which must be evident to all persons – could not be attached to or extended from the intellectual complexity inherent in the theoretical, there could be no community of thinking citizens, only a fragmentary assemblage of individuals separated by their variable talents rather than united by the ends of nature. Second (at a higher level of rhetorical complication): Kant, the author of the very subtle and speculative First Critique, as he reaches the final sentences of his confidential aside, makes it clear that, when he writes *about* morality, he does so morally (in the mode of *Offenheit*), and that many writers would do well to follow his example, instead of giving in to the "delusions" (*Blendwerk*) that are born of the intellectual's hubris-infused desire to erect theoretical systems in an act of precipitous distraction. Not only should one proceed to one's work with no prejudgment of its eventual outcome (*ohne Parteilichkeit und Vorliebe*), but one should concentrate on one's "business" (*Geschäft*) while closing one's eyes to extraneous difficulties. Thus, one could paraphrase the overt message of the passage as follows: "Writers, follow my example, my maxim; concentration on the here-and-now of work, avoidance of diversions, of Pascalian *divertissement*, will guarantee philosophical results imbued with moral probity."

But how does concentration, or focusing on one's "business," function textually? Kant is arguing for openness, which is the zero-degree rhetorical mode of morality and the very antithesis of the speculative subtlety one finds in theoretical knowledge (the First Critique) or in the labyrinthine movements of aesthetic symbolization (the Third Critique). Subtlety as such must be banished from the moral realm if the latter is to remain on solid ground. But how can one characterize the final stages of Kant's argument in the "Analytic of Pure Practical Reason" except by the term "subtle"? What happens, textually, as his argument unfolds, is the following: in attempting to demonstrate that concentration on one's work is a philosophical value in that it contributes to the lifting of "dubiousness" and the founding of clarity, he resorts, curiously and significantly, to the image of blindness. Indeed, in order for the philosophical *Geschäft* to be in order, the thinker must *close his eyes* to the outside, the "extraneous," all that risks calling into question the integrity of his system. The philosopher with closed eyes then immediately accuses an undefined group of *other writers* of basing their own ideas on "delusions" – in German *Blendwerk*, a term deriving from the verb *blenden*, to blind, meaning frippery, mockery, and hocus-pocus, and suggesting the kind of sleight-of-hand one associates with gaming houses, circuses, and other places housing the lowest forms of illusion-making. *Other* writers are the ones who are guilty of "blinding" their reading public with *trompe-l'oeil* devices, if one takes Kant's argument in its overt earnestness.

The text's rhetorical fabric glimmers in a different light, however, and shows that the integrity of the system – in this case, the Kantian critical system – rests upon the philosopher's blindness to his own devious argumentative strategies, to the self-blindness that allows *Offenheit* to mask a writerly strategy of closed-mindedness. I do not mean anything "negative" with this latter term. All systems of thought, whether they be conceived architecturally as grand unities (Kant, Hegel) or as self-annihilating and self-constructing fragmentary structures (Friedrich Schlegel and the Athenaeum group), must necessarily pose themselves in the very act of opposing the "outside" of their thought – namely, those "other writers" against whom they construct their models and their theoretical discourses. But it is important not to forget that the very act of intellectual decision-making, the tracing of categories and boundaries for thought, which the philosopher would like to conceive as a *resolution*, an *Ent-schließen*, is at the same time a closing-off, a seclusion, a roping-off of the frontiers, an *Ab-schließen.* Kant, in trying to convince us that his going-to-work is a *moral* "resolution," is practicing a little *Blendwerk* of his own, since the "ought" of the philosopher's "I ought to work" is the exterior form of his "I wish to work," "I aim to convince," and "I am driven to write because writing itself (not morality, not the law as supreme abstraction) compels me to enter the minefield of persuasive, that is, rhetorical, tropological, discourse."

If we now return to survey the landscape of the aesthetic and the ethical in Kant from a more distant perspective than my micro-readings have permitted, it becomes possible to reach some general conclusions. Kant presents the overlapping of these two fundamental areas in both the Second and the Third Critiques, and does so with considerable finesse and (despite his moralizing intentions) subtlety. In the *Critique of Judgment*, the aesthetic is in danger of encroachment from the ethical, from two sides: first, from Kant's elevation and ennobling of the province of the sublime, *das Erhabene*, which draw it, Icarus-like, dangerously close to the resplendence of the moral law in its supersensible domain; and second, from the philosopher's annexation and domestication of the hinterlands of the symbolical or analogical. These areas of aesthetic play, which belong most properly to Daedalus, labyrinth-constructor of infinite polysemic possibilities,[17] are robbed of their "irresponsible" freeplay through Kant's ethically motivated imposition of a stable and recuperative form onto the proliferation of seductive ornament. In the *Critique of Practical Reason*, the moral becomes subject to encroachment from the aesthetic from within Kant's own writing style. Kant postulates the unity, clarity, and transparence of *Sittlichkeit* (because the moral must be accessible to all and without "subtlety"), but his rhetoric, in its subtlety, introduces the aesthetic snake of seduction into the garden of good and evil. The turn toward the self in the final paragraph of the "Analytic of Pure Practical Reason," in which Kant, like God in Genesis, is well pleased with the beauty of his creation, presents itself as a paean to moral *Offenheit*. Yet this philosophical song of praise cannot erase manifest traces of an aesthetically articulated *Selbstliebe*, of the pride of an author who deserves, and receives, our respectful admiration for the edifice he has formed, but who also merits a skeptical survey of the fault-lines beneath his work's architectural splendor.

CHAPTER 2

Kierkegaard: on the economics of living poetically

> Man has just as great a claim upon the poetic as the moral has a claim upon him.
>
> (*The Concept of Irony*)[1]

I INTRODUCTION

The equilibrium between the aesthetic sphere and the domain of the ethical emerges as a founding theme in the earliest stages of Søren Kierkegaard's writing career. The thinker associated with a complex modern formulation of Christian existentialism needed to proceed through the aesthetic and ethical stages before encountering his most proper territory – that of revealed religion. And there is nothing perfunctory in this propaedeutic, this necessary rite of passage without which the religious as such would be ungrounded, abstracted from the combats and conflicts of the human mind. Indeed, Kierkegaard wrestles with the problematic interplay of the aesthetic and the ethical in both his theology dissertation, *The Concept of Irony* (1841), and the wittily earnest double work that first brought him intellectual notoriety, the twinned volumes of *Either/Or* (1843).

In this chapter I shall concentrate almost exclusively on these two works, since it is within their pages that Kierkegaard deals most explicitly with the aesthetic and the ethical per se. It should be noted, however, that the religious is present from the beginning in Kierkegaard, that his particular and unique conception of Christianity permeates all his writings, even those which, according to critical consensus, "pre-date" the creative explosion of his first religiously grounded works – *Repetition* and *Fear and Trembling* (1843); *Philosophical Fragments* and *The Concept of Anxiety* (1844). Thus, in the sentence quoted above from the penultimate chapter of *The Concept of Irony*, the use of the word "claim," in its association with the logic of debt and redemption, calls forth in the reader's mind the economics of guilt and forgiveness which undergirds the New Testament as a whole. In fact, the etymological origin of the word "claim" is the Greek *kalein* (later, Latin *clamare*), meaning "to cry out." There is an existential pathos of the claim whose riches Kierkegaard will mine with considerable force in his later works; but it is important to note that, as early as his dissertation, and within the limits of the poetic and the moral, the fundamental question is what one can claim (or call forth) by rights, and how one is claimed (or called upon) by a higher tribunal, an *instance supérieure*. The apparent equilibrium of Kierkegaard's formula (its rhetoric of "just as great as") serves to mask, or at least to attenuate, the possible imbalance between claiming and being claimed. Does the act of claiming, in and of itself, possess the same value as the moral claim on the individual, since the latter originates in the realm of the Law and instantiates itself in the mode of the categorical imperative? At what cost is a balanced harmony between the aesthetic and the ethical achieved?

Like all serious writers, Kierkegaard elaborates his thought *en situation*, and one could say, using his own terminology in the subtitle to *The Concept of Irony*, that he establishes his intellectual positions "with continual reference" to Hegel and Hegelianism on the one hand, and German Romantic irony on the other.[2] In the time that separates the *Critique of Judgment* (1790) from Kierkegaard's own works of 1841–43, there have been wild fluctuations not only in the exterior world of politics and governments (the French Revolution in its perplexing metamorphoses, the era of Napoleon, experiments with republicanism and the renewal of monarchies), but also in the realm of letters, music, and the plastic arts, where Kant's complex and problematic legacy – Romanticism – has reigned supreme for more than three decades. By the time Kierkegaard writes *The Concept of Irony* and *Either/Or*, however, Romanticism has passed through several phases (and several countries), and is now subject to critique, both from its adherents and its adversaries. Kierkegaard's views on the interplay between aesthetics and ethics are not only post-Kantian in that they presuppose Kant's critical system as a point of departure for modern thought, but also, in an important sense, post-Romantic, in that they build upon Hegel's often devastating attacks on Tieck, Solger, the brothers Schlegel, and Novalis (and behind Novalis, the figure of Fichte, whose influence on the theories and practice of Romantic irony should not be underestimated).[3]

Unlike Hegel, however, who so often accused the practitioners of irony of placing themselves above life in a position of arrogant superiority but who lambasted them from his own lofty stance of philosophical *suffisance*,

Kierkegaard descended into the ironical maelstrom and worked out his critique of Romanticism from within, assuming multiple masks and playing complicated narrative games with his readers. Kierkegaard's mode of writing is as important as the declarative statements he makes. Unlike Kant, Kierkegaard is not only quite consciously aware of the rhetorical deviousness that can creep into the thread of his conceptual argument, of the ways in which ethical seriousness can be undermined and aestheticized by his own figural discourse, but he revels in this confusion of categories, he delights in the perplexing overlap between the poetic and the moral. What has changed most fundamentally since Kant is that the aesthetic domain can no longer be imagined as a museum in which works of art present themselves in their unadorned transparency to the disinterested observer. One effect of the explosion of Romanticism was to move art from the confines of closed spaces (the museum, the theater, the recital hall, the salon) into the extensive and limitless sphere of lived existence. For Kierkegaard, there is, pace Kant, an aesthetic *interest*. For the Danish thinker, the crucial issue now is not so much how to appreciate or to judge works of the imagination, but rather how to live poetically. This is why what interests Kierkegaard, from his earliest writings, are certain exemplary figures – Don Juan, Faust, the Wandering Jew – whose legendary careers possess far more than a simple didactic function, and who incorporate various dimensions of the creative life-force which stands at the origin of artistic production in all its diverse manifestations. The problem of living poetically has its source in the aesthetics of Romanticism, which, according to Kierkegaard as well as Hegel, is an ironical aesthetics. But Kierkegaard, unlike Hegel, will try to argue (in the second volume of *Either/Or*) that it is possible to conceive of an ethically grounded poetic life. In order to follow the path that leads to the working out of this proposition, however, we need to begin with Kierkegaard's own point of departure: Hegel's unilateral condemnation of Romantic irony in the name of moral seriousness.

II HEGEL'S AESTHETICS

In the section of the introduction to his *Vorlesungen über die Ästhetik* [*Aesthetics: Lectures on Fine Art*] (1835) titled "Historical Deduction of the True Concept of Art," Hegel deals quite briefly and dismissively with the subject of Romantic irony. This development, however truncated, occupies an important narrative position within the *Aesthetics*, in that Hegel must eliminate the Romantics from serious consideration before he turns to his own systematic exposition. Indeed, the all-important section called "Division of the Subject" (in German, simply "Eintheilung"), in which Hegel performs a preliminary survey of the territories he will be exploring, follows immediately upon the passage on irony. This rhetorical gesture of philosophical domination (the perfunctory disarming of the enemy) repeats what Hegel had done in his earlier masterwork, the *Phenomenology of Spirit* (1807), in which the all-important transition to the chapter on religion was made possible by the philosopher's annihilation of the "beautiful soul" – the figuration of aesthetic morality which Hegel associated with what he judged to be the vapid evanescence of Romantic literature, especially Novalis's poetry.[4] In both works, the suspicious blending of the aesthetic with the moral needed to be shunted aside so that the Hegelian conceptual edifice could be constructed on a firm foundation.

Standing behind Friedrich Schlegel and the other practitioners of Romantic irony, according to Hegel, was the Fichtian philosophical system. Fichte is the primary villain in Hegel's conceptual psychodrama, the target at which he directs his most stinging barbs. Following is a stylistically complex passage from the "Historical Deduction of the True Concept of Art" in which Hegel critiques Fichte's key notion of the *ego*, qualifying it as "throughout abstract and formal" (*Aesthetics* 64) (the opposite, of course, of "concrete and substantial" – Hegel's own positively valued terms). It is the emptiness of the Fichtian *ego* which, in Hegel's view, allows for the development of irony as irresponsible freeplay:

The *ego* is a *living*, active individual, and its life consists in making its individuality real in its own eyes and in those of others, in expressing itself, and bringing itself into appearance. For every man, by living, tries to realize himself and does realize himself. Now in relation to beauty and art, this acquires the meaning of living as an artist and forming one's life *artistically* [*als Künstler zu leben, und sein Leben künstlerisch zu gestalten*]. But on this principle, I live as an artist when all my action and my expression in general, in connection with any content whatever, remains for me a mere show and assumes a shape which is wholly in my power [*nur ein Schein für mich bleibt, und eine Gestalt annimmt, die ganz in meiner Macht steht*]. In that case I am not really in *earnest* either with this content or, generally, with its expression and actualization. For genuine earnestness enters only by means of a substantial interest, something of intrinsic worth like truth, ethical life, etc., – by means of a content which counts as such for me as essential [*Denn wahrhafter Ernst kommt nur durch ein substantielles Interesse, eine in sich selbst gehaltvolle Sache, Wahrheit, Sittlichkeit, usw., – herein, durch einen Inhalt, der mir als solcher schon als wesentlich gilt*], so that I only become essential myself in my own eyes in so far as I have immersed myself in such a content and have brought myself into conformity with it in all my knowing and acting. When the *ego* that sets up and dissolves everything out of its own caprice is the artist [i.e., the Romantic ironist], to whom no content of consciousness appears as absolute and independently real but only as a self-made and destructible show, such earnestness can find no place, since validity is ascribed only to the formalism of the *ego* [*da nur dem Formalismus des Ich Gültigkeit zugeschrieben ist*]. (*Aesthetics* I, 65; *Vorlesungen über die Ästhetik* I, 101–2)[5]

The first two sentences in the passage appear, at first, unproblematic: what individual would not wish to express himself or realize herself? The fundamental idea that the goal of life is self-realization or self-actualization ("actualization" being also a grounding concept in Kierkegaard's writings) does not seem iconoclastic or in any way unusual. Although Hegel is purportedly expounding the views of Fichte throughout this section of his treatise, the introductory part of this passage does not fly in the face of philosophical *sensus communis*. The problems begin with the third sentence, in which beauty and art are brought into the picture. Whereas expressing oneself and bringing oneself "into appearance" (*sich zu äußern und zur Erscheinung zu bringen*) are considered the natural activities of humankind, to live *as an artist* (as a Romantic ironist) is to indulge in arbitrary semblance and "mere show" (*nur ein Schein*). Hegel is playing on the difference between *Erscheinung* and *Schein*, in which the former designates the inevitable outward orientation of the human being into concrete reality, whereas the latter connotes vagueness and irreality. The Romantic ironist does not truly *express* (*äußern*) anything; his reveries and imaginings remain inner-oriented. In Hegel's line of reasoning, earnestness (*Ernst*) becomes associated with expression as concrete exteriorization and with "actualization," with what he calls a "substantial interest." Now this interest has intrinsic worth, since it concerns itself with the very highest philosophical values, such as truth and the "ethical life" (*Sittlichkeit*). Economically speaking, the genuine philosopher is the creator of value, whereas the ironist is a counterfeiter. The words *gelten* and *Gültigkeit* apply to the authentic thinker, never to the artisan of idle and fanciful dream-visions.

As the passage develops, it becomes clear that the Romantic ironist is, to use a good Nietzschean term, at the "antipodes" of the serious philosopher, who is, by definition, the servant of *Sittlichkeit*. If we reverse the qualities attributed to the ironist into their binary opposites, we obtain a portrait of the genuine thinker (whose resemblance to Hegel is perhaps not a matter of coincidence). Just as exteriorization and realization were emphasized over the arbitrary artistic "forming" (*Gestalten*) of a poetic life, in the same way, in the latter stages of the passage, the "immersion" of the self into an epistemologically sound or ethically grounded content is valued over the "dissolution" (a favorite chemical metaphor of Friedrich Schlegel) capriciously performed by the empty Fichtean *ego* upon his environment or world. The problem with the Romantic artist's *making* or *techné* is that it is unethical in its narcissism. In the terms of contemporary literary theory, we would say that the creations and performances of the Romantic ironist are self-referential, and that self-referentiality is the greatest threat possible to seriousness – that philosophical attitude or mood which determines and envelops the field of aesthetics as theoretical domain. The involuted quality of ironic art, its specularity, is, properly speaking, *disorienting* to the aesthetician. In Hegel's interesting metaphorical expression, earnestness "can find no place" (*kann . . . keine Stätte finden*) in the ironically conceived poetic universe. Irony is the "place" of the philosopher's exile.

Hegel's argument in this paragraph is not just that Romantic irony is frivolous and empty in its unfettered playfulness, but that its frivolity and its vacuity rest upon the inauthentically assumed and ethically suspect superior attitude of the ironist, whose aesthetic mis-demeanor consists in his arbitrary exercising of *power* (*Macht*). In political terms, the ironist is a tyrant, a despot, in that he rules over a territory which he, by rights, should carefully tend, nurture, and respect. One senses here that Hegel is conflating irony with wit (Schlegelian *Witz*) or even sarcasm, and that it is the *tone* of the writings of the Romantic ironists that is inimical to his (earnest) philosophical mind. The question, however, is whether what Hegel says about irony has anything to do with irony as it is practiced, not only by Tieck, the Schlegels, E. T. A. Hoffmann, and others, but also by Kierkegaard, both in his dissertation and in the first volume of *Either/Or*. Is the "essence of irony" or the "truth of irony" to be equated with power *over* exterior reality, or does the territory of irony lie at the antipodes of such a determined and mastered world? What is the *experience of irony*? How can one describe or even engage in the praxis of irony? What Kierkegaard has to say about these unwieldy but aesthetically central problems is developed "with continual reference to Hegel," but constitutes a subtle and complex overturning of Hegelian seriousness. As we move now to an examination of the final sections of *The Concept of Irony*, the Hegelian condemnation of Romanticism in its particular Germanic/ironic mode needs to remain in the background, as the horizon against which Kierkegaard establishes his own aesthetic theory.

III THE CONCEPT OF IRONY

Although the greater part of Kierkegaard's dissertation focuses on Socratic irony, the latter sections of the work are directed against Hegel's definition of irony as "infinite absolute negativity" (*CI* 259 and *passim*). According to Kierkegaard, Hegel confused the notion of "negativity" with what appeared to be the destructive or "dissolving" qualities of Romantic irony, and had no understanding for the social and political contexts that made the modern return to the ironic mode of writing possible, perhaps necessary. In his discussion of Tieck which occurs in the chapter entitled "Irony after Fichte," Kierkegaard, using his own distinct brand of irony, writes:

> But it must be borne in mind that Tieck and the whole romantic school stepped into or thought they were stepping into an age in which people seemed to be totally fossilized in finite social forms. Everything was completed and consummated in a divine Chinese optimism that let no reasonable longing go unsatisfied, no reasonable desire go unfulfilled. The glorious principles and maxims of habit and custom were the objects of a pious idolatry; everything was absolute, even the absolute. One abstained from polygamy; one wore a stovepipe hat. Everything had its importance. . . . Everything occurred according to the stroke of the hour. One reveled in nature on St. John's Eve [Midsummer], one was contrite on the fourth Friday after Easter [Great Day of Prayer]; one fell in love when one turned twenty, went to bed at ten o'clock. One married, one lived for domesticity and one's position in society; one acquired children, acquired family worries. (*CI* 303)

In this interesting foreshadowing of Flaubert's "bovine" universe[6] – Monsieur Homais, the *dictionnaire des idées reçues*, the apotheosis of *bêtise* in the figures of Bouvard and Pécuchet – Kierkegaard proposes that Romantic irony functions as a salubrious corrective to bourgeois mediocrity and the secular religion of Rationalism. His litany of what "one" does (a preliminary hint of what will become *das Man* in Heidegger) is, on one level, what Søren Kierkegaard the human being was incapable of doing. His final rupture with Regine Olsen occurred just days after his dissertation defense, and conformity to the expected social norms of marriage and family would never again become possible or imaginable for him. On another level, it is clear that Romantic irony as a critical and literary movement possessed, for Kierkegaard, the kind of imaginative freedom that could produce a universe in which the generalized "one" could be undermined and joyfully robbed of all pretense to dignity.

Yet Kierkegaard's elective affinities with this particular, socially grounded tendency of Romantic thought should not blind his reader to the reservations he shared with Hegel concerning the uncontrolled, unbridled quality of the ironists' conjectural flights of fancy. Digressing briefly in the chapter "The World-Historical Validity of Irony, the Irony of Socrates," the Danish philosopher, having at first accused Hegel of discussing irony "in a very unsympathetic manner," goes on to state:

> But just as the irony of the Schlegels had passed judgment in esthetics on an encompassing sentimentality, so Hegel was the one to correct what was misleading in the irony. On the whole, it is one of Hegel's great merits that he halted or at least wanted to halt the prodigal sons of speculation on their way to perdition. (*CI* 265)

The history of thought is, indeed, a history of progressive "corrections." The Schlegels correct aesthetic sentimentality; Hegel corrects the excesses of irony; and Kierkegaard, while apparently agreeing with Hegel on the importance of "halting" the wayward divagations of the Schlegels and their group, also proceeds with considerable subtlety to correct his philosophical master and adversary. He does so by asserting that Hegel may well have been on target in his condemnation of a particular kind of irony – that of the Schlegels – but that, in focusing myopically on post-Fichtian irony, he was wrong concerning (nothing less than) "the truth of irony, and by his identifying all irony with this [its post-Fichtian articulation], he has done irony an injustice" (ibid.). This fundamental distinction – between different forms of irony which can occur at different historical moments, and irony in its truth – allows Kierkegaard to give Hegel his due, but also to proceed on his own discursive path, as he moves, via post-Fichtian irony, toward his *telos*, the short and cryptic final chapter entitled "Irony as a Controlled Element, the Truth of Irony."

The difference between Hegel and Kierkegaard concerning the Romantic ironists can be expressed, in Christian terms, as the opposition between paternal harshness on the one hand, and charity on the other. Hegel's wish to "halt the prodigal sons of speculation on their way to perdition" expresses what might have been the first reaction of the father to his younger (prodigal) son's excesses in the New Testament parable (Luke 15: 11–32), had he known of that son's actions while they were taking place. According to the biblical narrative, however, the sins – disastrous "speculations" in the financial sense and immoral living – become known to the father only after the fact. It is too late to "halt" what has already taken place. Here, only condemnation or forgiveness are possible as responses. Like the biblical father, Kierkegaard reacts charitably: his dissertation as a whole is an effort to show the pedagogical power and ethical limitations of irony in its Socratic form as well as the unmastered speculative exuberance of post-Fichtian irony, all the while remaining within the universe of irony, including and enveloping it within his argument. The ironists have perhaps "spent too much" in their intellectual speculations, but for this they will not be cast into outer darkness by the writer of *The Concept of Irony*.

In the chapter "Irony after Fichte" Kierkegaard not only passes in review representative works of Friedrich Schlegel, Tieck, and Solger, but also attempts to characterize what one might call the poetics of Romantic irony – the sources and cultural traditions from which it draws, and its mode of literary representation. The first point Kierkegaard makes early in the chapter is that for irony "there really never was a past" because it springs from metaphysical speculation rather than from the concrete historicity of lived human existence (*CI* 277). This means that irony "can have a free hand" with history as such, and also, that ironical works will be grounded, of necessity, in legend, myth, and fairy-tale, and will partake of the symbolic or allegorical modes of narration (ibid.). The chronological focus of irony is ever-changing. It moves from the "beautiful Greek sky" to the "primeval forest of the Middle Ages," with no specific interest in either of these periods; and its involvement with philosophical schools or religious thought is perforce a matter of whim, of caprice rather than reasoned choice (ibid.). This is to say that irony is the realm of *fiction*, and, as such, is defined not by its relation, however distant, to exterior reality, but by its "hovering" quality: in the terms of German Romanticism, it is *das Schwebende*.[7] Kierkegaard expresses this idea in the image of Hercules (as figure of irony) successfully overcoming the terrestrial force of Antaeus (as representative of history). Irony is victorious over reality in that it suspends the actual in a generalized hovering.

Like Hegel, Kierkegaard sees the ethical danger of such a suspension. He accuses the Romantic ironists of living in a "totally hypothetical and subjunctive way," and of lacking all continuity in their inner lives: these writers constantly "succumb" to the power of moods (*CI* 284). Now it may be that living poetically is the essential project of Romanticism, but this kind of living, in its fictional or hypothetical mode, lacks all seriousness, all grounding (*CI* 279). But Kierkegaard, although he sounds very much like the author of the *Aesthetics* in these and other related passages, adds a dimension that had been lacking in his predecessor's analysis: namely, the transcendental framework of Christianity. Whereas Hegel's argument was structured according to the simple polar opposition whereby living poetically was the symmetrical, negatively valued opposite to the positivity of living earnestly, Kierkegaard makes a distinction between an inauthentic way of living poetically (that of the ironists) and an authentic manner (that of the devout Christian). To live poetically in the authentic sense is not to hover or be "placed in suspension," therefore, but to subject oneself to "an upbringing, an education" (*CI* 280). Thus, viewed in the light of Christianity, poetic action and what Kierkegaard will call throughout his career "upbuilding" or "edification" (*Opbyggelse*) can be the destiny of the same, ethically secure human being. Irony oversteps itself in its desire to compose itself poetically, whereas the Christian individual, in allowing himself "to be poetically composed . . . lives far more poetically than many a brilliant intellectual" (ibid.). By this formula Kierkegaard means that "the Christian comes to the aid of God, becomes, so to speak, his co-worker in completing the good work God himself has begun" (ibid.). The Christian does not hover *over* reality, but accomplishes his or her moral duty within the human environment yet in subservience to God, acting as a receptive vessel for the divine will. Here, Søren Kierkegaard sounds very much like Judge William, the writer of the edifying admonitions of *Either/Or*, Part II. One can see the stylistically dazzling project of *Either/Or* emerging from the serious-and-playful academic prose of *The Concept of Irony*.

In a digressive interlude during his critique of Friedrich Schlegel's *Lucinde*, Kierkegaard returns to the idea of living poetically, and makes clear what he means by the term *poetry* in its relation to the inwardness of religious feeling. In order to distinguish between poetry as practiced by the Romantic ironists and the religious experience as such, Kierkegaard contrasts the notion of transfiguration to that of transubstantiation. The following is an excerpt from the two-page passage on this point:

> If we ask what poetry is, we may say in general that it is victory over the world; it is through a negation of the imperfect actuality that poetry opens up a higher actuality, expands and transfigures the imperfect into the perfect and thereby assuages the deep pain that wants to make everything dark. To that extent, poetry is a kind of reconciliation, but it is not the true reconciliation, for it does not reconcile me with the actuality in which I am living; no transubstantiation of the given actuality takes place . . . Only the religious . . . is able to bring about the true reconciliation, because it infinitizes actuality for me. Therefore, the poetic is a kind of victory over actuality, but the infinitizing is more of an emigration from actuality than a continuance in it. To live poetically, then, is to live infinitely . . . But an infinity such as that must cancel itself. Only when I in my enjoying am not outside myself but am inside myself, only then is my enjoyment infinite, because it is inwardly infinite. (*CI* 297)

The passage as a whole is based upon a stark contrast between images of verticality (poetry as victory *over* actuality and as the opening toward a higher actuality) and of depth (religion as inward infinity). Poetry resembles religion in that it, like religion, seems to offer a kind of reconciliation. The subtle difference between an only apparent poetic reconcilation and the true and profound reconcilation of religion is mirrored in the fundamental distinction Kierkegaard makes between transfiguration and transubstantiation. Of these two profoundly mysterious events, the first is the more obvious in its dramatic staging and external effects. The first three books of the New Testament agree in depicting Jesus' transfiguration as a foreshadowing of his resurrection, and portray this moment as an *ascent*: Christ goes up into a mountain to pray with Peter, James, and John; his countenance is altered and his garments glow in dazzling white; Jesus converses with Moses and Elijah; the disciples propose to build tabernacles to these three chosen-of-God, but they refrain from doing so when God reveals to the disciples that Jesus is not just one of many anointed prophets, but rather His son; and Jesus asks the disciples to promise not to reveal what they have seen and heard in this episode of divine revelation (Matthew 17:1–13; Mark 9:2–13; Luke 9:28–36). As is often the case in the New Testament, the new scene, that of the transfiguration as ascent into glory, mirrors an older episode, Moses' climbing of Mount Sinai to receive the Ten Commandments (the presence of the burning bush can be interpreted as a prefigurative element signaling the brightness of Christ's face and clothing in the transfiguration; and in both cases, God's voice is heard).

The transfiguration has become one of those moments in the life of Christ most often chosen for pictorial representation, precisely because of its chiaroscuro theatricality. Therein lies a problem, however, which Kierkegaard diagnoses in a very Kantian vein: the exterior signs of the transfiguration draw so much attention to themselves that the moral content of the biblical passage risks going unnoticed. We as readers or viewers see too much on the outside, and may be tempted not to attend sufficiently to the message: i.e., what God is saying *through* the lighting of Christ's semblance. This is why Kierkegaard, following Kant (and anticipating Ruskin), calls attention to the seductiveness of figuration as such, its foregrounding of exterior ornament to the detriment of all ethical content. And this is why Kierkegaard, in preferring religion to poetry in its Romantic guise, prefers transubstantiation to transfiguration, since the former is purely internal and invisible: the bread and wine become the body of Christ within the individual Christian. This "act" or "event" is, in the strict sense, not available to artistic representation, and is subject to a purely mental and interiorized form of abstract figuration.[8] We cannot see the transubstantiation, but we must believe in it in the "blindness" of our faith, in the unillumined darkness of our *for intérieur*. Transubstantation is the promise of content and of infinite inner enjoyment, whereas in the moment of transfiguration only a deceptive infinity emerges to charm our benumbed and disoriented senses.

The concluding chapter of the dissertation, "Irony as a Controlled Element, the Truth of Irony," is a complex, truncated section in which Kierkegaard, within the space of a few pages, poses more questions than he is able to answer. Not only does the final paragraph open out quite brusquely toward the theme of humor, as if the candidate in theology were in great haste to leave the troubled shores of irony, but it would seem that, in order to control irony and convey to his reader the truth of irony, Kierkegaard has had to redefine his concept, eliminating from it its suspect irresponsibility and playful subjectivity. When he speaks of irony in the final chapter, he invokes the serene "objectivity" of Shakespeare and Goethe, praising them for having constructed imaginative worlds in which

> irony is not present at some particular point of the poem but is omnipresent in it, so that the irony visible in the poem is in turn ironically controlled. Therefore irony simultaneously makes the poem and the poet free. But in order for this to happen, the poet himself must be master over the irony . . . To be controlled in this way, to be halted in the wild infinity into which it rushes ravenously, by no means indicates that irony should now lose its meaning or be totally discarded. On the contrary, when the individual is properly situated – and this he is through the curtailment of irony – only then does irony have its proper meaning, its true validity. (*CI* 324, 326)

But how is it that irony as suspended disorientation, in its diverse metamorphoses from the speculative fragments of the Athenaeum group to the tales of Hoffmann and the carnivalesque dance suites of Robert Schumann – how does *this irony* become oriented or "situated" without losing its essence? Is it possible to affirm, with Kierkegaard, that irony in the disorienting sense can be uplifted (*aufgehoben*), transmuted into "controlled irony" with no uncanny residue being left behind or outside of the writer's all-enveloping poetic purview? What Kierkegaard has done, at the conclusion of his treatise, is to *transfigure irony* so that he can end his argument on the note of aesthetic redemption.[9] There is a final cleansing of the spirit made possible by irony in its second, situated and situating, sense. Irony, in the end, is not a destructive but a corrective mode of encountering the real; in it are united aesthetic freeplay and moral seriousness in the perfect harmony of genius (only Shakespeare and Goethe could be called upon here; no lesser figures would do). When Kierkegaard asserts: "Even though one must warn against irony as against a seducer, so must one also commend it as a guide" (*CI* 327), it is important to note that he is speaking of two different ironies here, the seductive mode being characteristic of Romantic irony, whereas irony as existential *Leitfaden* belongs to the ethical orientation and edification of controlled irony.

In fact, Kierkegaard's argument on irony is based on another poetic figure, that of *paradox*. It is indeed paradoxical that irony should attain its truth by no longer being itself, by leaving behind its multicolored garb and assuming the sober new clothing of objectivity. To agree with Kierkegaard's conclusion in *The Concept of Irony*, one must accept and live within his logic of paradox, which is not, in a strict sense, a dialectic, but rather a jump, a logical "leap of faith," which means a leap beyond scholastic/academic argumentation. The conclusion of the dissertation is quite disappointing in purely academic terms: it is too short and it turns beyond and away from its subject. But this is because, already in 1841, Kierkegaard was beginning his own turn toward the embracing of paradox as the true logic of Christianity – a turn that will receive its most elegant formulation in the "absolute paradox" of the *Philosophical Fragments*.[10] Irony as such will have been abandoned, but the process of that abandonment leads beyond *The Concept of Irony* and through *Either/Or*, where the discovery of religion as the chosen territory of the paradoxical can only occur after the combat between the aesthetic and the ethical is staged in its dramatic intensity.

IV EITHER/OR

The Preface and the Problem of Framing

The literary complexity of *Either/Or* has been universally acknowledged by Kierkegaard's readers, and any serious scholarly analysis of the work necessarily begins with the following cautionary point: since Part I (which contains the writings of an unidentified Romantic aesthete) is simply juxtaposed to Part II (the repository of corrective and edifying letters sent by the ethically serious Judge William to the enthusiastic but immature author of Part I), it becomes very difficult to interpret the relation between the twin tomes, especially if by interpretation one means choosing between and among conflicting semantic potentialities. With *Either/Or* Kierkegaard begins what will become a lifelong experimentation with pseudonyms. The title page of the book's first edition, published by Bianco Luno Press in Copenhagen in 1843, indicates that *Either/Or: A Fragment of Life* was edited by a certain Victor Eremita: the author's name does not appear. To complicate matters further, Victor Eremita, whom the reader is constantly tempted to identify with Søren Kierkegaard (we do know, don't we, that *Either/Or* is Kierkegaard's "first important work," so we can attribute it to him – or can we?), is merely the editor of the papers he has assembled, and so might or might not wish to claim responsibility for them. This, of course, by 1843, was a well-worn literary device which had experienced its most impressive elaboration in the eighteenth-century epistolary novel. Kierkegaard, like Jean-Jacques Rousseau in his preface to *La Nouvelle Héloïse* (1761), plays with the very notion of the editor's ethical responsibility toward the text he publishes, and, like Rousseau, amuses himself by simultaneously identifying with and distancing himself from the papers he is now offering for public view and consumption. There is, however, a difference in the degree to which the two writers face the problem of textual ethics and in the manner in which they assume and remove their editorial masks. In his typically emphatic and moralistically self-serving tone, Rousseau writes, in the third paragraph of his preface:

> Any person possessed of honesty should openly acknowledge the works he publishes. Therefore I name myself on the title page of this book [as editor], not in order to appropriate it for myself, but rather to accept responsibility for it. If the book is evil, that evil can be ascribed to me; if it is morally good, I do not wish thereby to honor myself. If the book is bad, I am the more obligated to acknowledge it: I do not wish to be regarded as better than I am. (*Julie, ou la Nouvelle Héloïse*, 3; my translation)

As is often the case in Rousseau, the writer is hardly self-effacing in his proclamation of virtue: even though he purportedly did not write the letters he publishes, he is magnanimous enough to accept responsibility for any "evil" they might cause, including the moral danger they pose to young virtuous girls, who should be strongly dissuaded from reading this powerfully seductive work (*La Nouvelle Héloïse*, 4). Although, unlike Rousseau, Kierkegaard does not place his own name on the title page of *Either/Or*, he makes clever use of the conditional mode of discourse when, at the conclusion of his own preface written under the assumed name of Victor Eremita, he not only asserts that it could be useful for the reader to hypothesize that the two volumes were written by the same person (and in this case, the temptation to read Kierkegaard, *en palimpseste*, under his false name is very strong), but further, that the reader should heed the admonitions of Judge William and follow the latter's "well-intentioned advice" (*E/O* I, 15).[11] Like Rousseau, who warns his public against reading only the first, erotically charged letters of Julie and Saint-Preux without pursuing the novel to its ethically secured conclusion, in the same way Kierkegaard (as Victor Eremita) frames his double work by suggesting, with no great ambiguity or subtlety, that Part II is a successful answer to and overturning of the passionate excesses of Part I. The lack of Kierkegaard's name on the title page thus in no way indicates a lack of moral guidance or (in Kierkegaardian language) "orientation" for any reader who might be subject to interpretive waywardness.

What is interesting, however, and quite characteristic of Kierkegaard's considerable wit, is that one page before concluding on the note of Judge William's "well-intentioned advice," he has Victor Eremita say:

> Whether A [the young Romanticist] wrote the esthetic pieces after receiving B's letters [those of Judge William], whether his soul subsequently continued to flounder around in its wild unruliness or whether it calmed down – I do not find myself capable of offering the slightest enlightenment about this, inasmuch as the papers contain nothing. Neither do they contain any hint as to how it went with B, whether he was able to hold fast to his point of view or not. Thus, when the book is read, A and B are forgotten; only the points of view confront each other and expect no final decision in the particular personalities. (*E/O* I, 14)

According to Victor Eremita's alternating comments, it would appear that there are two ways to read *Either/Or*: an ethically grounded way, which would privilege Judge William's response to the Romantic aesthete, and a more properly "literary" way, which would leave the question of semantic resolution open, without finite interpretive position-taking. To choose between these two forms of reading is to decide how much importance one should grant the notion of narrative framing per se. If Victor Eremita's preface is *merely* playful, *just* an hors d'oeuvre that can be easily digested before moving on to the "main course" (the victory of ethics over a certain irresponsible form of aesthetics), then narrative framing is simply a device, a technique in the service of effective storytelling. If, however, it should indeed prove impossible to decide between A and B; if we confine ourselves to purely textual evidence; then the multiple frames surrounding the work's existential drama assume importance in themselves – which means that the reader is in a world of *dis*-orientation, of *mise-en-abyme*, or, to use Eremita's own terminology, a dizzying maze in which "one author becomes enclosed within the other like the boxes in a Chinese puzzle" (*E/O* I, 9). This is not the world of ethical security, but of uncanniness, of *Unheimlichkeit*.

If, at this juncture, I mention the notion of *Unheimlichkeit* (which I shall develop at greater length, via Freud, in the next chapter), it is because the early pages of Victor Eremita's preface are characterized by that particular kind of disquieting strangeness in which the frontiers between inside and outside, the internal and the external, become subject to bizarre and unsettling manipulations. In the very first sentence of the preface, Eremita writes: "It may at times have occurred to you, dear reader, to doubt somewhat the accuracy of that familiar philosophical thesis that the outer is the inner and the inner is the outer" (*E/O* I, 3). This would appear to be nothing less than the "topic sentence" of *Either/Or*, and since it is directed against Hegel and his philosophical system,[12] should we not be ethically obliged as readers to take it seriously, to see it as the line of demarcation Kierkegaard is tracing in order to establish his own thought *contra* Hegel? Doubtless, one should indeed take this idea seriously (*im Ernst*), but one cannot avoid noting that the editor of *Either/Or* also treats it with considerable playfulness, in that the grand theme of the disjunction between the inner and the outer is mirrored by the material fact that the papers of A and B are found in a piece of furniture – a secretary which Victor Eremita purchases for its exterior beauty, but in which he finds the papers that he will publish under the title *Either/Or: A Fragment of Life*.

The thesis that the internal is not the external receives its most immediate confirmation not in a structured philosophical argument propounded by an author (or editor speaking for a reflective subject in control of the text), but rather in the uncanny material coincidence that the inner contents of the secretary bear no resemblance to, cannot be dialectically unified with, the stately external appearance of the object in which the papers are enclosed, but from which they spill out in chaotic profusion. The first pages of the preface read very much like Baudelaire's "Le Mauvais Vitrier" or Mallarmé's "Le Démon de l'analogie," ironically conceived prose poems in which weighty aesthetic issues are treated in terms of the interference between the spiritual level of the poem's allegorized content and a diabolically constituted materiality that resists being subsumed under any "higher level" of figural significance. In the case of *Either/Or*, the question becomes: can the ethical frame the aesthetic, or will the aesthetic in its unruly materiality and resistance to all enclosure constantly "spill out" and undermine the stability of *Sittlichkeit*? Is there a fundamental incompatibility between the ethical as such and the essence of narrative as framing machine? These questions cannot be avoided in any attempted interpretation of *Either/Or*; they also subtend the entirety of the book you, Dear Reader, are now perusing, my book, the book of David Ellison, which purports to enclose and frame Kierkegaard among other modern writers, and for which I take as much responsibility as the conventions of literary criticism allow.

Part 1: the value-free economics of seduction

Although the first volume of *Either/Or* is a veritable treasure-house of Romantic motifs, a hodge-podge of forms and genres ranging from fragmentary poetic reflections to pseudo-academic essays, satiric orations, literary criticism and an introspective and cynical diary, the theme that predominates is that of erotic seduction, with its protagonist being Don Juan in his ancient and modern incarnations. The two sections of the first volume that are clearly not just experimentations with Romantic style and parodic echo-effects of Schlegelian diction are the long essay "The Immediate Erotic Stages or the Musical-Erotic" (47–135) and "The Seducer's Diary" (303–445), where the former is a paean to Mozart's *Don Giovanni* and the latter a contemporary staging of a Don Juanesque seduction. These two textual blocks provide symmetry and solidity to the volume's construction, and they echo each other in obvious ways, but they also differ from each other in one important respect: the essay on *Don Giovanni* focuses on what A calls "immediacy," whereas the "Diary" is a grand series of variations on the theme of "reflection."

A's thesis is that Mozart's greatness as a composer rests on his ability to make opera *purely musical*, i.e., not dependent upon the spoken (or sung) word for its significance. The character Don Giovanni is a brilliant creation precisely because he exists uniquely in the realm of the musical, which A equates with the aesthetic in its essential, unalloyed form. Don Giovanni's seductive gestures and actions, his *modus vivendi*, are completely enclosed within the aesthetic realm, and therefore are not unethical, but pre-ethical. A describes the Venusberg[13] as the territory par excellence of Don Juan, the place in which he exercises his dominion:

> In the Middle Ages, much was told about a mountain that is not found on any map; it is called Mount Venus. There sensuousness has its home; there it has its wild pleasures, for it is a kingdom, a state. In this kingdom, language has

no home, nor the collectedness of thought, nor the laborious achievements of reflection; there is heard only the elemental voice of passion, the play of desires, the wild noise of intoxication. There everything is only one giddy round of pleasure. The firstborn of this kingdom is Don Juan. But it is not said thereby that it is the kingdom of sin, for it must be contained in the moment when it appears in esthetic indifference. Only when reflection enters in does the kingdom manifest itself as the kingdom of sin, but then Don Juan has been slain. (*E/O* I, 90)

According to this argument, it is not quite correct to call Don Juan a seducer, since seduction implies rhetorical deviousness – i.e., the mediate, reflective, and conscious power of words. This is why A, a few pages after the passage quoted above, states that the mythic Don Juan "does not fall within ethical categories." Since he lacks the consciousness "of craftiness and machinations and subtle wiles . . . he does not seduce. He desires, and this desire acts seductively" (*E/O* I, 98–99). In other words, there is no temporal distance between Don Juan's desires and their accomplishment, which means that his amorous career is pure repetition – as expressed, notably, in the famous list which Leporello unfurls in the opera.[14] And a list is the negation of narrative as temporality. Aesthetic immediacy in its musical purity is prior to narrative, before or beyond its chronological lawfulness, its *espacement différentiel*. To call Don Juan a seducer is thus to use language loosely or improperly, whereas in the "Diary" A will trace the evolution of a seductive story in which the elapsing of time as such is the medium in which seduction, properly (verbally, reflectively, diabolically) speaking, takes place.

"The Seducer's Diary," like the first volume of *Either/Or* as a whole, is framed by a prefatory passage in which the editor of the pages we are about to read expresses his moral reservations about the "calculated nonchalance" and "contriving heart" of one Johannes, the man who will organize the seduction of a certain Cordelia (*E/O* I, 303). We learn from this initial editorial commentary that Johannes's "life has been an attempt to accomplish the task of living poetically," and that his diary, in reflecting this ideal, "is not historically accurate or strictly narrative; it is not indicative but subjunctive" (*E/O* I, 304). This is why, in the end, his "punishment has a purely esthetic character, for even the expression 'the conscience awakens' is too ethical to use about him" (*E/O* I , 308). Thus Johannes, like Don Juan, is said to exist in a purely aesthetic realm, prior to ethics as such, and therein lie his dangerous qualities. He will be incapable of responding to any appeal emanating from the ethical realm, and his "subjunctive" or hypothetical plan and execution of the seduction are conducted in such a devious way as to leave no trace for any moral detective who might wish to apprehend him. Unlike Don Juan, however, who lived in aesthetic "immediacy" or transparency, Johannes calculates every strategic move of his with quasi-military foresight and depends upon the rhetorical power of his words and letters to stalk his prey with greatest efficacy. In Kierkegaardian terms, therefore, he occupies the territory of reflective and self-reflective discourse, which remains distant from reality.

Johannes's plan is to coerce Cordelia into an engagement with him, then conquer her, then abandon her immediately thereafter. He succeeds in this enterprise, and the process itself deserves far more scrutiny than the limited scope of my investigation allows. What needs to be noted, at least minimally, is that the goal is not marriage per se, but rather engagement, since marriage, according to Johannes himself, has "ethical reality," whereas engagement, in his view, can be made to be "only a simulated move" (*E/O* I, 367). Following is what amounts to Johannes's philosophy of life (and of seduction as the affirmation of life in its aesthetically delimited sense):

> The banefulness of an engagement is always the ethical in it. The ethical is just as boring in scholarship as in life. What a difference! Under the esthetic sky, everything is buoyant, beautiful, transient; when ethics arrives on the scene, everything becomes harsh, angular, infinitely *langweiligt* [boring]. But in the strictest sense an engagement does not have ethical reality [*Realitet*] such as a marriage has; it has validity only *ex consensu gentium* [by universal consensus]. This ambiguity can be very advantageous for me. (ibid.)

The challenge Johannes faces can be best conceptualized or visualized as the problematic encounter of two planes of existence that one normally finds in different frames of reference: the figural/fictitious (that of Johannes as seducer) and the concrete/real (that of Cordelia, her aunt and her entourage). The fictional and the real can interface only if Johannes can frame the real within the fictional, only if he can weave his web of seductive discourse around the concrete social situations in which the "rake's progress" must be undertaken. Whereas Paul de Man wrote of the manifold ways in which critics have attempted to "defuse" the force of irony,[15] one could say that Johannes is the master of defusing the force of reality *through* irony and his use of the hypothetical modality of living poetically. Self-reflectiveness is pure inwardness *as* conditionality. The internal envelops the external without engaging with its substance. The inside contains the outside through the self-consciousness of a fictional narration, a narration over which the protagonist has total control, as he states in the transitional moment after the successful engagement and before he progresses to the seduction proper:

The aunt gives her consent; of that I have never entertained the remotest doubt. Cordelia follows her advice. As for my engagement, I shall not boast that it is poetic, for in every way it is utterly philistine[16] and bourgeois. The girl does not know whether she should say 'Yes' or 'No'; the aunt says 'Yes,' the girl also says 'Yes,' I take the girl, she takes me – and now the story begins. (*E/O* I, 375)

The story of seduction passes through a number of theatrically organized scenes, only to culminate in the seducer's boredom "after the fact." Economically speaking, the seduction in all of its stages is based upon wasting, defrauding, cheating, and ultimate loss. One must take the expression "nothing is gained" in its strongest sense when applying it to the outcome of Johannes's considerable efforts. Yet early in the story, the protagonist relishes the apparent wasting of his time, realizing that time is the element of seduction, that nothing must happen before the important something comes to pass:

Everywhere our paths cross. Today I met her three times. I know about her every little outing, when and where I shall come across her, but I do not use this knowledge to contrive an encounter with her – on the contrary, I am prodigal on a frightful scale. A meeting that often has cost me several hours of waiting is wasted as if it were a bagatelle. I do not approach her, I merely skirt the periphery of her existence. (*E/O* I, 341)

Only a Philistine would confuse the generalized squandering characteristic of the text's early scenes with the frustration of a "true" waste of time. What is being squandered here is counterfeit – the fictitious, invented sentiments of Johannes, which are conjured up uniquely in view of their rigorous teleological purpose. Once the goal has been achieved, since there has been no real investment, no concrete capital expended, it is not surprising that there should be "nothing left" – hardly even a conclusion to a narrative that simply expires two paragraphs after the triumph of Eros. Johannes writes:

But now it is finished, and I never want to see her again. When a girl has given away everything, she is weak, she has lost everything, for in a man innocence is a negative element, but in woman it is the substance of her being. Now all resistance is impossible, and to love is beautiful only as long as resistance is present; as soon as it ceases, to love is weakness and habit. (*E/O* I, 445)

The cynicism of this inconclusive conclusion serves as a perfect theatrical foil for the earnestness and solid virtuous demeanor of Judge William, which are just around the narrative corner. At the same time, Johannes's insistence on Cordelia's absolute loss of innocence/value, coupled with the playful, guiltless tone in which the seducer describes his machinations, center the reader's attention on the economic metaphorics that subtend the text as a whole. The entirety of the "Diary" is constructed on the relation between debt and guilt, which languages have been known to conflate in one term (see the German *Schuld* and Danish *Skyld* for "debt" in the bank and in the Lord's Prayer; see the French *devoir* and the Spanish *deber* for financial and moral obligation). Since Johannes refuses to conduct his life on the terrain of the ethical, he cannot be guilty, he cannot "owe" anyone anything; and therein lies the nullity of his existence. In his case, *Schuld* cannot attach itself to anything substantial or real, and is therefore, of necessity, evanescent, without content. "Woman's" absolute guilt is the absolute guilt of any person, male or female, who falls under the category of the ethical. As we turn now to Part II of *Either/Or*, it is important to keep in mind the degree to which the question of ethics as such (one's obedience or disobedience to its call) falls under an economically expressed metaphorical discourse in which the question of value, in order to "ring true," must be posed seriously, that is, authentically.

Part II: rendering accounts

The passage from Part I to Part II of *Either/Or* confronts the reader with a radical discontinuity: one moves from the universe of polyphonic ironic verbosity to the straightforward presentation of moral values by the solidly grounded and not always imaginative Judge William. Although critical consensus has it that the second volume is a corrective to the excesses of the first, and that Kierkegaard's authorial intention is to give the final, authoritative word to Judge William and to his friend, the Jutland pastor of the "Ultimatum" (*E/O* II, 339–54), Judge William cannot be viewed as an unproblematically transparent spokesman for the text's author. There are numerous passages in Part II in which the judge sounds a little bit too much like Kierkegaard's philosophical opponent, Hegel – as, for example, when the upstanding married man attempts to undermine A's glorification of erotic love as passionate "first love":

> [Marriage] is in the instant, sound and powerful; it points beyond itself, but in a deeper sense than the first love, for the abstract character of first love is precisely

its defect, but in the intention that marriage has, the law of motion is implicit, the possibility of an inner history. (*E/O* II, 61)

Or later, in the same vein:

First love remains an unreal *an-sich* [in itself] that never acquires inner substance because it moves only in an external medium. In the ethical and religious intention, marital love has the possibility of an inner history and is as different from first love as the historical is from the unhistorical. (*E/O* II, 94)

In reading Part II, one must constantly keep in mind that Judge William is a character in a multi-framed fiction – honest, stodgy in his mimetic Hegelianism, a trifle boring in his unrelenting *Ernst* – who is certainly no match, stylistically speaking, for A's aesthetic pyrotechnics. But herein lies Kierkegaard's own intellectual honesty, which consists in recognizing that *from an aesthetic standpoint the ethical is boring.* Style itself is a turn, a tropological field of deviousness against which the ethical must construct a fortress of bland but powerful uniformity. As Johannes stated it in a late "Diary" entry, there is a simple and amusingly paradoxical mathematics of the aesthetic as it opposes itself to the ethical:

They say that it takes a bit more than honesty to make one's way through the world. I would say that it takes a bit more than honesty to love such a girl [Cordelia]. That more I do have – it is deceitfulness. (*E/O* I, 385)

Deceitfulness (duplicity) is "more than" honesty in the sense that 2 is greater than 1. The aesthetic is double, whereas the ethical is single in its focus; but one must *be single* (a bachelor) to indulge in aesthetic duplicity, whereas one must be a couple to remain within the single-minded purposefulness of *Sittlichkeit.* The ethical-serious is of necessity domestic, whereas the aesthetic emerges in the waywardness of continual displacement, in the wanderings of the Romantic traveler. Hence Judge William's repeated references to the fundamental contrast between the straight path or direct route (the ethical) and the detour (or, as the French call it, in a morally significant metaphor, the *déviation* – an aesthetically constructed signpost). See, for example, the biblical admonition, drawn from Sirach 36: 24–26, which Judge William appropriates for his scolding of A:

"He who acquires a wife begins to acquire his best possessions, for he has acquired a helper and a support to rest upon. Where there is no fence, the property will be plundered; and where there is no wife, a man will sigh and be as one who wanders about. For who will trust an armed robber who skips from city to city? So who will trust a man who has no home, and lodges wherever night finds him?" (*E/O* II, 80)

This is a curious, metaphorically mixed passage of ethical condemnation, in which the wife, who is viewed essentially as property, is also compared to the fence around property, and in which the bachelor, who "wanders about" aimlessly, is also conflated with the plunderer of the estate, a person presumably capable of pursuing and accomplishing a nefarious goal. What counts here is not the rigor of a logical argument, but rather the associative chain of the rhetoric: the ethical man will of necessity take a wife, who will ground his existence in domesticity and ward off all marauders; the aesthete, the wanderer, is, in his deepest being, an untrustworthy robber *because he wanders.* The guilt associated with being a bachelor – which Kierkegaard and also Kafka had to write into their creative fictions (are Regine Olsen and Felice Bauer ever absent from their works?) – is the negative face of the coin (as Camus would say: its *envers*) whose positive side, its *endroit*, is the stability of domestic enclosure. To have an *endroit*, a place to live, is the *conditio sine qua non* of the ethical life. Hence, as we shall see in chapter seven of this book, the figure of Ménalque in André Gide's *L'Immoraliste* (1902) is already suspicious for his peregrinations and his lack of material possessions before he actively assumes the role of Michel's anti-moral mentor, finally undermining the latter's bourgeois moral certainties.

The binary oppositions that organize the dramatic framework of *Either/Or* can be summarized in the following way: aesthetic freeplay portrayed as the irresponsibility of Romantic irony versus ethical responsibility as exemplified by the life and opinions of Judge William; the waywardness of wandering versus the straight path that leads toward marriage and the home; the antisocial behavior of the bachelor versus the social inclusion of the married couple. Yet Kierkegaard shows the modernity of his thought in refusing to characterize the aesthetic as merely or only the negative face of the coin, the "evil" which is overturned when the coin is turned over onto its "good" side. In a central passage of the text, when Judge William defines what he means by the expression "Either/Or," he explains that the aesthetic is not equivalent to evil, but rather to what he calls "indifference" or "neutrality":[17]

Rather than designating the choice between good and evil, my Either/Or designates the choice by which one chooses good and evil or rules them out. Here the question is under what qualifications one will view all existence and personally live. That the person who chooses good and evil chooses the good is indeed true, but only later does this become manifest, for the esthetic is not evil but the indifferent. And that is why I said that the ethical constitutes the choice. Therefore, it is not so much a matter of choosing between willing good or willing evil as of choosing to will, but that in turn posits good and evil. (*E/O* II, 169)

The aesthetic, in its Kierkegaardian formulation, is no longer the domain of beautiful forms as it had been in the theories of the Enlightenment period, but rather an "indifferent" territory whose boundaries are impossible to survey. The difficulty Judge William faces in his letters to A is that, in his Herculean task of attempted moral conversion, his opponent is not an earth-bound Antaeus, but a spirit of the air that may or may not be reachable by ethical argument. It is not by chance that we never learn whether the judge's letters have any effect whatever on their addressee. There is, in Kierkegaard's cryptic and not extensively developed notion of "indifference" an uncanny similarity to Maurice Blanchot's theory of *le neutre*, which is also based upon the field of the aesthetic (or, more precisely, of narrativity *as* the aesthetic domain par excellence) as that which possesses no reference-points, no *points de repère* – without which, of course, surveying becomes impossible. In Blanchot's words:

the neutral word [*la parole neutre*] neither reveals nor hides anything. That does not mean that it signifies nothing (by pretending to abdicate meaningfulness in the form of nonsense); it means that it does not signify according to the manner in which the visible-invisible signifies, but that it opens within language an other power [*un pouvoir autre*], foreign to the power of enlightenment (or obfuscation), of comprehension or of misunderstanding. It does not signify according to the optic mode. ("La voix narrative, le 'il,' le neutre," 183; my translation)[18]

Just as for Kierkegaard the aesthetic in its indifference or neutrality falls outside of Enlightenment theory, so *la parole neutre* for Blanchot opens up an uncanny area outside the boundaries of the theoretical as optical mode of thought. And Blanchot takes his "insight" to the limit in his prose fictions, where what is at stake in his world beyond or before lighting as such lies outside of classical ethical categories, in an area to which no Judge William can have access. In *Either/Or*, of course, although I am suggesting that Kierkegaard touches upon a Blanchot-like modernity, at the same time the ethical dimension of the text is all-pervasive, and the textual stakes are, finally, ethical. In other words: although Judge William may have no hold on the aesthetic in its essential neutrality, this will not stop him (or Kierkegaard) from positing the original act of choosing as *the* act that defines the humanity of man. Unlike the universe of Blanchot's prose fantasies, the world of Kierkegaard is suffused with the existential pathos that comes from making that choice which his narrator calls "the baptism of the will" (*E/O* II, 169).

The introduction of Christian terminology and Christian theological premises into Kierkegaardian ethics includes not only the "first act" of baptism as *analogon* to the inaugural decision-making of the will, but also the later phase of repentance, itself part of the transformative process that leads to final redemption. The ethical Christian subject is in continual self-reformation and metamorphosis; he or she, unlike the Romantic ironist, is constituted by activity.

> at the very moment he chooses himself he is in motion. However concrete his self is, he nevertheless has chosen himself according to his possibility; in repentance he has ransomed himself in order to remain in his freedom, but he can remain in his freedom only by continually realizing [*realisere*] it. He who has chosen himself on this basis is *eo ipso* one who acts. (*E/O* II, 232)

Or, in a variation on the same theme:

> The task the ethical individual sets for himself is to transform himself into the universal individual. Only the ethical individual gives himself an account of himself in earnest and is therefore honest with himself; only he has the paradigmatic decorum and propriety that are more beautiful than anything else. (*E/O* II, 261)

The ethical individual realizes his or her possibility through concrete moral action, and this action is, properly speaking, transformative. Kierkegaard expresses transformation in economic terms: one "ransoms" oneself, one buys oneself back by transmuting the negativity of guilt/debt (*Skyld*) into the positivity of self-realization in freedom. And this self-realization is itself not only good, but also beautiful. The honest individual possesses "decorum and propriety" and is therefore able to live poetically in a more authentic sense than the Romantic ironist. The central polemical point Judge William attempts to make in Part II of *Either/Or* is that the ethical stance is superior to the aesthetic position not only because the latter conceals nothing less than moral bankruptcy, but because the living of the ethical life contains the promise of a higher beauty than is available to the aesthete. At bottom, there are two kinds of *accounting*: the aesthetic, which bases itself upon a narrative account, or story, and which possesses only the surface attractiveness or charm (in Kantian terms, *Reiz*) of all seductive story-telling; and the ethical, a clear-sighted balancing of ledgers which allows a higher beauty to shine through its apparently straightforward mode of presentation. This higher beauty emerges most forcefully not in the ethical per se, but in the ethical as it is uplifted and metamorphosed into the religious, that sphere in which the rendering of accounts takes on the poetic beauty of liberated tropological play. The conclusion of *Either/Or*, which can also be viewed as a transition toward *Fear and Trembling* and *Philosophical Fragments*, is a sermon written by a pastor friend of Judge William, and which the judge includes as an "Ultimatum" to his wayward friend. The subject of the sermon possesses a rigorous Protestant tone: its thesis is that "In Relation to God We Are Always in the Wrong." But this thought, which appears so forbidding in its abstract formulation, in actuality contains the solace of the Christian economics of salvation. In the simplest terms:

> wishing to be in the wrong is an expression of an infinite relationship, and wanting to be in the right, or finding it painful to be in the wrong, is an expression of a finite relationship! Hence it is upbuilding always to be in the wrong – because only the infinite builds up; the finite does not! (*E/O* II, 348)

Kierkegaard's rhetoric of paradox retroactively transforms the entirety of *Either/Or*, and does so in its manipulation of the place of *Skyld* within the work viewed now as a signifying totality. Whereas the upstanding ethical man, unlike the spendthrift and speculative aesthete, is the man of the ledger, the careful but uninspired accountant who is ethical *in that he pays his debts on time*, the individual who transcends the ethical in the religious understands that infinite speculation, infinite debt/guilt, is the terrain on which the human as such can encounter the divine. We are, from the beginning, in debt/in guilt, because Jesus Christ has already died for the sins we shall surely commit. It is the terrible paradox of Christ on the cross that stands behind the textual string of paradoxes animating the sermon that concludes *Either/Or*. The irony of the paradox, so to speak, is that stage three (the religious) resembles stage one (the aesthetic) more than stage two (the ethical), at least in its figurative dimension. In stages one and three there is infinite spending and also a freedom of metaphorical discourse one does not find in stage two. In the religious stage, the polymorphic language of aesthetics is reintroduced; the same flowers of rhetoric are to be found, but in the context of man's redemption rather than decadent corruption. Thus, whereas Romantic "longing" (the *Sehnsucht* or *Længsel* of the poets) is condemned by Judge William in favor of domestic *belonging*, the mode of longing returns in the sermon, but in the figural garb of an infinite soaring:

> Every time the cares of doubt want to make him [the human being in his sinfulness] sad, he lifts himself above the finite into the infinite, because this

thought, that he is always in the wrong, is the wings upon which he soars over the finite. This is the longing with which he seeks God; this is the love in which he finds God. (*E/O* II, 352–53)

At the conclusion of *Either/Or* the opposed categories of the aesthetic and the ethical recede, in favor of a religious discourse based upon the tropology of paradox. The truth of *Sittlichkeit* is reached not within its own boundaries, not within its own univocal language of earnestness, but in a poetically constituted transcendental beyond, which is discovered as the individual makes the most significant of possible turns. In the words of the Jutland pastor to his flock: "Then your soul *turned away* from the finite to the infinite; there it found its object; there your love became happy" (*E/O* II, 350–51; my emphasis). The religious realm is that of the Baudelairian "transports de l'esprit et des sens" in which the final goal of the movement upward is nothing less than the communion between the lowest (man as sinner) and the highest (Jesus as redeemer and savior, God as forgiver of all sins). Despite his distaste for the Hegelian system, Kierkegaard presents his readers with an apparent dialectic: thesis: the duplicity of Romantic irony and the irresponsible freeplay of the aesthetic; antithesis: the singleminded *Ernst* of the ethical; synthesis: the *Aufhebung* of the preceding steps in the final truth of religion, which combines a higher form of tropological discourse with a solid grounding for morality.

What distinguishes Kierkegaard's logic from that of Hegel, however, is that this apparent dialectic conceals an unbridgeable disjunction within it, based upon a linguistic heterology. Each stage *has its own language*: the aesthetic is ironical; the ethical is purely discursive or constative (the unambiguous account-ledger); and the religious is paradoxical (the lowest meets the highest in the twists and turns of metaphoricity). The inexorable movement of sublation "works" in *Either/Or* (which means: Kierkegaard can be assimilated to Hegel in this work) *only if* we pass over the linguistic dimension in which each stage realizes itself, only if we treat Kierkegaard's rhetorical manipulations as accessory or ancillary to the logic of *Aufhebung*. If we respect the linguistic virtuosity and multidimensionality of the text, however, we are faced with three separate modes of discourse that remain, in their essence, disjunctively related among themselves. Although the religious of stage three "resembles" or mirrors the aesthetic of stage one in an analogical fashion (the longing for God reminds us of Romantic longing, but transported upward), one cannot simply substitute the paradoxical for the ironical in the same way that one substitutes spiritual for material elements within the same figure of speech.

The paradoxical is not a "higher level" of the ironical, but a mode unto itself; and it was the discovery of this particular mode, and its theorization in *Philosophical Fragments* just one year after the publication of *Either/Or*, that allowed Kierkegaard to become himself as writer. The religious contains both the aesthetic and the ethical at the level of content, but it supersedes both these categories in the language of paradox, which alone clears an access to the lofty ideal of Christian upbuilding, or edification, while preserving that "deep inner motion" within which resides the guarded yet accessible truth:

> Do not interrupt the flight of your soul; do not distress what is best in you; do not enfeeble your spirit with half wishes and half thoughts. Ask yourself and keep on asking until you find the answer, for one may have known something many times, attempted it – and yet, only the deep inner motion, only the heart's indescribable emotion, only that will convince you that what you have acknowledged belongs to you, that no power can take it from you – for only the truth that builds up is truth for you. (*E/O* II, 354)

CHAPTER 3

Freud's "Das Unheimliche": the intricacies of textual uncanniness

I TEXT AND CONTEXTS

Until fairly recently, Freud's essay "Das Unheimliche" ["The Uncanny"] (1919) did not receive as much attention as those works which had an undisputed importance for the evolution of psychoanalysis as a discipline, those writings that seemed to constitute major breakthroughs in theoretical insight, such as *The Interpretation of Dreams*, *Beyond the Pleasure Principle*, and *Inhibitions, Symptoms, and Anxiety*, to name just three obvious examples. "Das Unheimliche" is not only a short and, as we shall see, in many ways truncated text; it also seems to be somewhat marginal in the Freudian corpus, in that it deals with an issue whose aesthetic foundation would appear to be at least as important as its psychoanalytic resonance. It has the misfortune, as well, of preceding the genuinely revolutionary *Beyond the Pleasure Principle* (1920) by such a short time-span that Freud's interpreters have tended to "leap over" the essay on the uncanny so as to meet the later text, with its intriguing theorization of the "repetition compulsion" and the "death drive," head-on. This situation changed as of the 1970s and early 1980s, when both French and Anglo-American scholars began to see in "Das Unheimliche" far more than its surface argument exhibited. To use Sarah Kofman's terminology, critics of various methodological persuasions began to read the essay *symptomally*.[1] Rather than merely comment on Freud's arguments for the importance of the uncanny as a concept within psychoanalytic theory, the newer interpreters concentrated on the significant hesitations, contradictions, and impasses that seemed to vitiate Freud's efforts to control his own text. "Das Unheimliche" came to be read as a self-deconstructing work in which uncanniness as such was equated with the essence of the literary; and the literary was considered to be that destabilizing force which doomed to failure all "reductionist" psychoanalytical attempts to understand the uncanny.[2]

Since the mid-seventies, following the lead of Hélène Cixous and Sarah Kofman, critics have tended to see in "Das Unheimliche" not so much a discursive text about a subject of psychological interest as a "fiction" (Cixous) or "theoretical novel" (Kofman) that Freud constructs in the vain attempt to circumscribe his theme. Theoretical discourse as rationally conceived, analytically organized "speculative" thought in the classical sense[3] gives way to a text that borrows its arms from the very domain – that of the aesthetic – that it seeks to conquer. The Freudian text ends by imitating the object of its scrutiny: the text "about" the uncanny is itself uncanny. At stake, therefore, is the fundamental question of borders that has been the central preoccupation of my book thus far. The uncanny is that force, that *energeia*, which, in pushing beyond clearly established boundaries of all kinds, ends up possessing the naively unsuspecting would-be possessor (interpreter) just as the voice of the god penetrates the body of the oracle. Allegorically speaking, the uncanny stands for all texts exhibiting literariness, and Freud is one in a long line of readers, all of whom are condemned to repeat the same mistake: that of trying to master or control uncontrollable semantic proliferation, the *polysémie* characteristic of literature.

From being read as merely one of several essays on aesthetic issues by Freud, it is safe to say that "Das Unheimliche," as we enter the twenty-first century, has now achieved what might be called exemplary status. "The Uncanny" *is literature*, literature as such, the literary in its essence. Or, according to both Neil Hertz (*The End of the Line*) and Harold Bloom (*Agon: Towards a Theory of Revisionism*), the uncanny is an avatar of the sublime. The uncanny is the sublime for our age. Just as Romanticism is impossible to understand without the sublime as one of its cardinal points, in the same way Modernism (and beyond?) cannot be studied independently of its figuration in the uncanny. To read Freud's essay "Das Unheimliche," therefore, is not just any exercise: the stakes are high, and the penalties for misreading, as we shall see, are not minimal or inconsequential, even though misreading, in Bloom's sense, may be what the uncanny is necessarily and unavoidably "about."

II FREUD'S ESSAY "DAS UNHEIMLICHE"

The overt purpose of Freud's essay is to examine the strange territory of the uncanny in order to discover its meaning and deepest implications for psychoanalytic theory. The essay itself is a crossroads at which the uncanny, as aesthetic phenomenon, encounters the language of psychoanalysis. In this scheme, the uncanny is the foreign or other, while the (ever-developing) concepts of psychoanalysis are the familiar turf to which Freud repeatedly returns, Antaeus-like, to regain strength and comfort in his struggle with the elusive object of his scrutiny. At the same time, the very notion of the uncanny is based upon a concatenation of the foreign and the familiar, so that Freud's *agon* as writer mirrors or doubles the doubleness of the uncanny.

In concentrating my attention on selected passages of "Das Unheimliche," I am essentially interested in Freud's use of language and in the recurrence of certain key terms or phrases which emerge "symptomally" from his text. These expressions, in their turn, engage in a far-reaching intertextual web which I shall examine later in this chapter. Since the overall structure of "Das Unheimliche" has been analyzed painstakingly in the critical literature (the most detailed treatment being that of Cixous), I shall indicate only in passing some of its points of articulation as I proceed to my interpretation.

The essay is divided into three parts, each of which possesses, at the highest level of generality, a coherent focus. In the first part, Freud examines the linguistic field of "das Unheimliche," giving us a preliminary definition – "the uncanny is that class of the frightening which leads back to what is known of old and long familiar" (TU 220)[4] – followed by a remark on the ambiguity of the word *heimlich*: "In general we are reminded that the word '*heimlich*' is not unambiguous, but belongs to two sets of ideas, which, without being contradictory, are yet very different: on the one hand it means what is familiar and agreeable, and on the other, what is concealed and kept out of sight" (*SE* 224–25). And in the concluding paragraph of the first section, we have this synthetic statement: "Thus *heimlich* is a word the meaning of which develops in the direction of ambivalence, until it finally coincides with its opposite, *unheimlich. Unheimlich* is in some way or other a sub-species of *heimlich* [*Unheimlich ist irgendwie eine Art von heimlich*]" (TU 226; DU 257).

The following sections of the essay build upon the linguistic data furnished initially and, Freud hopes, illuminate with the "lenses" of psychoanalytic insight the curious complexity of *Unheimlichkeit.* The second part is a complex concatenation of examples of the uncanny taken from literature and from life experience (we shall return to the most important of these examples in due course). And in the third part, Freud, in attempting to respond to the objections his reader might have to his methodology, makes a final effort at circumscribing the domain of the uncanny by proposing a definition of it in psychoanalytical terms and by distinguishing its literary manifestations from its appearances in everyday reality.

Freud's confidence in his interpretive enterprise is not constant throughout the essay, however. The most consequential problem he faces is a logical one – how to subsume the "examples" (the words *Fall* and *Beispiel* recur with obsessive regularity) he chooses under the general laws of the psychoanalytic theory he has been developing until the year 1919. When he says that "Unheimlich ist irgendwie eine Art von heimlich," not only is his statement completely lacking in assertive tone, but the expression "eine *Art* von heimlich" – literarally, a "*kind* of *heimlich*" – is not as precise or as "scientific" a phrase as the English translation ("a *sub-species* of *heimlich*") would have us believe. What Freud would like to do is to make certain that all the examples of the uncanny he will cite in parts two and three can be encompassed, included within his psychoanalytic theory. Put the other way, the uncanny as such would be one of many phenomena that would illustrate the truth of his theory by not exceeding their status as "sub-species." But what if there are so many "kinds" of uncanny phenomena and situations that the very notion of uncanniness becomes resistant to subsumption? If this were the case, of what use is the psychoanalytic arsenal Freud brings to bear on the uncanny, which includes, most notably, the Oedipus complex, the repetition compulsion, and the omnipotence of thoughts? In strategic (military) terms, Freud attacks the uncanny with weapons borrowed from psychoanalysis, but is this very borrowing an innocent act of *Wissenschaft*, or does it, rather, proceed from the force of a desire – the impulse to dominate and reduce the enemy (here, the uncanny) to servitude, to the tight reins of the concept?

If we return to the beginning of part one we read in the very first sentence: "It is only rarely that a psycho-analyst feels impelled to investigate the subject of aesthetics [*Der Psychoanalytiker verspürt nur selten den Antrieb zu ästhetischen Untersuchungen*], even when aesthetics is understood to mean not merely the theory of beauty but the qualities of feeling" (TU 219; DU 229). From the start, we learn that Freud fears aesthetics as foreign territory and makes his incursion onto this unfamiliar area only because he is "impelled" or *driven* to do so (*Antrieb* is close to *Drang*, another term we shall encounter later). We are not dealing here with the disinterested, dispassionate search for knowledge (if such a thing exists outside of a certain rationalistic ideology of science), but with an impulse that carries its human subject beyond his or her own field. In Greek, this is called *hubris*, and not the least interesting feature of "Das Unheimliche" is Freud's ethical awareness of his hubris, his ambivalence about treading on foreign soil, the inextricable combination of modesty and aggressivity that fuels his speculative undertaking.

It is bad enough that Freud, to encounter the uncanny, must do so in a field (that of aesthetics) which is not his own. Compounding his sense of estrangement (and competitive *Drang*) is the fact that he is following in the footsteps of a previous explorer, E. Jentsch, whose "Zur Psychologie des Unheimlichen" had appeared in 1906. Since, as we later learn in Freud's essay, the uncanny manifests itself in the troubling phenomenon of *Doppelgänger*, the problem, from the outset, is that Jentsch, whether the author of the 1919 essay likes it or not, whether he acknowledges it or not, is Freud's own distorted image. Now in order to retain one's own ego-image when faced with an uncanny mirror-doubling, a rapid and definitive act of differentiation is necessary: the "I" must split itself forcibly and unambiguously from the other that resembles it too much for comfort. This Freud does by characterizing Jentsch's contribution as a "fertile but not exhaustive paper" (*inhaltsreiche, aber nicht erschöpfende Abhandlung*) (TU 219; DU 230). If Freud's own paper is to go beyond Jentsch's insights, it must not only be rich in content (which it certainly is), but, in some way, it must exhaust the field; it must not simply add incrementally to Jentsch, but it must take from the domain of the uncanny all of its rich nourishment. Here, of course, is an allegory of academic scholarship which, to use the vocabulary of *Unheimlichkeit*, is a bit "too close to *home*." Each scholar writing on the uncanny after Freud (or really, after Jentsch, or really, after E. T. A. Hoffmann, and so on in infinite regress) will be guilty of attempting to exhaust a field which their predecessor has not quite exhausted. There will always be something left, even in a field that has been as picked-over as that of the uncanny.

It is significant, I think, that the verb *erschöpfen* recurs near the conclusion of "Das Unheimliche," in a very interesting section where Freud has been indulging in what might be called "fiction envy." He has been describing the poetic license of storytellers in envious terms, contrasting the great freedom of the fiction writer with the limits imposed upon the psychoanalyst as man of science by the experiential framework of the uncanny as it is encountered within the confines of reality. With apologies for jumping forward somewhat in my analysis, I would like to quote the passage that concludes this line of reasoning so as to emphasize the problematic of "field exhaustion" in Freud's essay:

> We have clearly not exhausted the possibilities of poetic licence and the privileges enjoyed by story-writers in evoking or in excluding an uncanny feeling

[*Es ist offenkundig, daß die Freiheiten des Dichters und damit die Vorrechte der Fiktion in der Hervorrufung und Hemmung des unheimlichen Gefühls durch die vorstehenden Bemerkungen nicht erschöpft werden*]. In the main we adopt an unvarying passive attitude towards real experience and are subject to the influence of our physical environment. But the story-teller has a *peculiarly* directive power over us [*Für den Dichter sind wir aber in besonderer Weise lenkbar*]; by means of the moods he can put us into, he is able to guide the current of our emotions, dam it up in one direction and make it flow in another, and he often obtains a great variety of effects from the same material. All this is nothing new, and has doubtless long since been fully taken into account by professors of aesthetics [*Dies ist alles längst bekannt und wahrscheinlich von den berufenen Ästhetikern eingehend gewürdigt worden*]. We have drifted into this field of research half involuntarily [*Wir sind auf dieses Gebiet der Forschung ohne rechte Absicht geführt worden*], through the temptation to explain certain instances which contradicted our theory of the causes of the uncanny. And accordingly we will now return to the examination of a few of those instances. (TU 251–52; DU 266–67; translator's emphasis)

In looking back at the movement of his argument (in which, to add clarity to his analysis, he had attempted to distinguish between the uncanny in life and in literature), Freud is obliged to confess that he has not "exhausted the possibilities of poetic licence and the privileges [*die Vorrechte*]" of storytellers. In other words, in his examination of the practitioners of the aesthetic, he has been no more successful than was Jentsch in his survey of aesthetics as theoretical field: both readings end without closure, without conceptual envelopment. There is an unmistakable sense of melancholy, defeat, and perhaps even resentment (*Ressentiment*) as "Das Unheimliche" reaches its ending. What Freud envies in the fiction writer is his or her creative freedom, which he describes not as the result of a struggle with artistic expression, but rather as a given right, a *Vorrecht*, or right before all establishing of rights: Freud the commoner versus literary aristocrats. Freud expresses his grudging admiration for the literary artist by emphasizing the latter's "*peculiarly* directive power," which is said to contrast with our "unvarying passive attitude towards real experience." This is a most curious statement, since it would be easy to assert the exact opposite: that we live life, we struggle against it, we work to succeed in it; whereas we are free to resist the charms of aesthetic freeplay, which, after all, fall under the domain of our moods, the moods we ourselves possess.

The power of the storyteller resides in a certain animistic energy. When we fall under the spell of fictional narration, we participate in what aesthetic theory calls "the willing suspension of disbelief" – i.e., we are willing to be directed (*wir werden lenkbar*), we become passive, in order to enter the story, in order to transgress the boundary between the real and the fictional. The difference between Freud the psychoanalytical theorist and the writers he unwillingly admires is that he has attempted to make the uncanny an example, a case for inclusion within the field of psychoanalysis, while the tellers of tales *fall into the uncanny*. The uncanny is that which cannot merely be an example (*ein Fall*), but which is a fall (*ein Fall*) into literariness[5] – and which is also a trap (*eine Falle*) for the analytical thinker as fabricator of clear distinctions.

I am suggesting, therefore, that "Das Unheimliche" as (aesthetic) totality is framed by the problematic of the not-to-be-exhausted field. Between the initial confident comments on Jentsch's analytical insufficiencies and the concluding somewhat dispirited paragraphs, the large and rich middle section of the essay consists of manifold efforts to achieve this very exhaustive analysis. Freud's own essay is the compulsion to repeat – to repeat the military gesture of exhausting the adversary's (the aesthetician's) field. The best way to do so is to outdo the aesthetician on his or her very own turf. If literary criticism is a "sub-species" of aesthetics, and if criticism in its exegetical function serves to illuminate textual obscurity, then the best way for Freud to triumph in his account of the uncanny is to read an uncanny text (using the language of psychoanalysis) more illuminatingly than the aestheticians can with their own paltry science and insufficient vocabulary. Among the numerous examples (*Fälle*) of the uncanny in part two of the essay, certainly the master-example is that of E. T. A. Hoffmann's "Der Sandmann" (1817), a short story which Freud summarizes and, confining himself to a complicated footnote, ventures to analyze in a highly cryptic manner. Since "Der Sandmann" happens to be a prime instance, or, one might say, an exemplary example, of Romantic irony in its dizzying practice, an examination of the echo-effects it exhibits when juxtaposed to Freud's "Das Unheimliche" is of particular interest to my own argument in the first three chapters of this book. If the uncanny is the unruly descendant of Kant's sublime, it is also the mode of Romantic irony, thereby possessing strong elective affinities with Kierkegaard's early writings. In the following section, I shall discuss not only the way in which Freud used (or misused) Hoffmann's story to buttress his argument in "Das Unheimliche," but also the peculiar (uncanny) manner in which "Der Sandmann" anticipates, foreshadows, and undermines Freud's claims to analytic mastery and control, both in his temporary function as reader of Hoffmann, and in his larger role as clarifier of the uncanny.

III "DER SANDMANN"

E. T. A. Hoffmann's ironical tale, notwithstanding its convoluted plot and multiple narrative voices, is based upon one organizing polarity: the classical opposition between *physis* (nature and the natural world) and *techné* (cultural artifice and fictionality). The protagonist of the story, Nathaniel, continually hesitates in his affections between Clara, a clear-sighted (as her name indicates) orphaned young woman taken in by his family and living in his house, and a certain Olympia, a creature of exquisite but strange beauty who elicits his obsessive fascination but who turns out to be an automaton – the unnatural, fabricated product of her "father" Spalanzani, who made her body, and Giuseppe Coppola, who gave her her eyes. Coppola, in his turn, is possibly the same person as, or at least the "double" of a man named Coppelius, whom Nathaniel holds responsible for his father's death. The narrative is punctuated by a number of articulated moments in which Nathaniel turns, alternately, toward Clara or toward Olympia – which means, toward "real life" in its natural rhythms or toward a fanciful, unreal entity that merely reflects or instantiates Nathaniel's own erotic projections.

Although the final and literal dismantling of Olympia occurs near the end of the story, Hoffmann provides enough clues early on in his narrative to indicate to the reader that the "mechanical" strangeness of Olympia – her dead gaze, her stiff bearing, her "conversation" composed only of exclamatory monosyllables – may reveal a mechanism in the technological sense, a clockwork precision proceeding from her very inhumanity. The uncanniness of "Der Sandmann" resides, first of all, in the human-but-not-really-human appearance of Olympia. Nathaniel's hesitation between Clara and Olympia is a hesitation between clearly defined nature on the one hand, and a nature-*like* artifice on the other. Artifice (and art as such) owes its power not to its structural design (only scientists / literary critics are interested in the inner mechanism of a doll/text), but to its capacity to mimic the living, to adopt a deceiving mask which allows it to pass as real. In the second half of the story, there is a multiplication of subjunctive and conditional expressions: Olympia inhabits the domain of the "as if" in that she exists only in the deluded eyes of Nathaniel. Her eyes are, in fact, dead, but, as Nathaniel views her through his own telescope (or point of view, *Perspektiv*), they "change":

> He [Nathaniel] had never in his life before handled a glass which brought objects to the eyes so sharply and clearly defined. Involuntarily he looked into Spalanzani's room: Olympia was, as usual, sitting before the little table, her

arms lying upon it and her hands folded. Only now did Nathaniel behold Olympia's beautiful face [*wunderschön geformtes Gesicht*]. The eyes alone seemed to him strangely fixed and dead, yet as the image in the glass grew sharper and sharper it seemed as though beams of moonlight began to rise within them [*als gingen in Olimpias Augen feuchte Mondesstrahlen auf*]; it was as if they were at that moment acquiring the power of sight [*als wenn nun erst die Sehkraft entzündet würde*]; and their glance grew ever warmer and more lively [*immer lebendiger und lebendiger flammten die Blicke*]. Nathaniel stood before the window as if rooted to the spot [*Nathanael lag wie festgezaubert im Fenster*], lost in contemplation of Olympia's heavenly beauty. (TS 110; DS 36)[6]

R. J. Hollingdale's smooth and readable translation passes over some details of the German text that deserve emphasis. Olympia's "beautiful face" is, in fact, a "wunderschön *geformtes* Gesicht," which introduces into the portrait of her lovely appearance the suggestion of artifice: the face has been formed, made, but by whom, and for what purpose? The cascade of "as if" clauses centers not just on the theme of light in general, but on fire in particular, and on the mesmerizing quality of Olympia's flaming glances. Nathaniel does not so much stand at the window as lie at its edge, incapable of movement, blinded by the brilliance of what he sees as the power of her sight (*Sehkraft*). We are in the domain of magic or of the fairy tale here, of sorcery and spells: Hollingdale's "as if rooted to the spot" renders the physical influence of Olympia on her admirer, but does not convey the magical element which inhabits "lag wie *festgezaubert*."

This descriptive passage is important not just in showing that Olympia is an empty vessel into which Nathaniel pours a fanciful and literarily inspired "life," but also in providing a subtle echo of the story's beginning. The allusions to fire and to the forming of inert matter into the false beauty of man-made artifice remind the reader of the early scene in which Nathaniel's father and the repulsive Coppelius labor over an "alchemical" fire in a secret and terrifying Promethean project. Nathaniel hides to observe the night-time activities of his father and companion (whom he identifies with the dreadful Sandman of a nursery-story), but is caught by Coppelius. The latter, imitating the children's story, first threatens to tear out Nathaniel's eyes, but respects the father's entreaty to spare them. Then, in Nathaniel's words: "And with that he seized me so violently that my joints cracked, unscrewed my hands and feet, and fixed them on again now in this way, now in that" (TS 91–92). Not only is Nathaniel's life, like Olympia's mechanical "body," constructed around the problem of the presence and absence of eyes and the attendant thematic of vision in general, but the grotesque scene of the detachment and rearrangement of his limbs foreshadows Olympia's fate in the latter stages of the tale, when Spalanzani and Coppola, in fighting over her, finish by tearing her apart, by reducing her to *membra disjecta* that can never be recombined into a totality, never be made whole again. Thus, Nathaniel, who admires and thinks he loves Olympia, who has her as the object of his deluded affection, is also quite like her. The resemblance between a young poet and an automaton is not the least of the story's ironically turned uncanny effects.

This resemblance is of no particular interest to Freud, however, who, as recent interpreters of "Das Unheimliche" have demonstrated, turns his own gaze resolutely away from Olympia (and also Clara, and all other female characters in the story) and focuses upon Nathaniel as a kind of modern-day tragic hero. The theme of threatened sight, of removable eyes and of blindness is, for Freud, a literary transposition of the dread of castration, and therefore a sign of the protagonist's Oedipal anxieties at the hands of the text's father-figures. In this scheme, Olympia is reduced to "nothing else than a materialization of Nathaniel's feminine attitude towards his father in his infancy. Her fathers, Spalanzani and Coppola, are, after all, nothing but new editions, reincarnations of Nathaniel's pair of fathers" (TU 232). The short story as a whole inscribes itself in the Oedipal triangle, or more precisely in the father–son conflict, while the mother and the other women are shunted aside, shoved outside the narrative with the imposition of Freud's rigid and self-justifying interpretive framework.

In the paragraph following his short and partial summary of the story's plot, Freud makes clear that "Der Sandmann" is being used to score points in his polemic against Jentsch. Freud argues that the idea of being robbed of one's eyes ("really" castration, as only the knowledge of the insightful psychoanalyst can show) is a more significant example of the uncanny than "intellectual uncertainty" (Jentsch's central thesis):

> Uncertainty whether an object is living or inanimate, which admittedly applied to the doll Olympia, is quite irrelevant in connection with this other, more striking instance [*Der Zweifel an der Beseeltheit, den wir bei der Puppe Olimpia gelten lassen mußten, kommt bei diesem stärkeren Beispiel des Unheimlichen überhaupt nicht in Betracht*]. (TU 230; DU 242)

A "symptomal" reading of Freud's prose in this passage inevitably uncovers a large dose of aggressivity which the author of "Das Unheimliche" allows to well up against the earlier explorer of the uncanny's territory, his *frère ennemi.* The problem for Freud is that the uncanny manifests itself in various guises (perhaps *dis*guises) throughout Hoffmann's tale, and the psychoanalyst has the audacity to call his own example – the eye motif and its association with castration – stronger (*stärker*) than the uncertainty between the living and the inanimate, which Jentsch had emphasized and which Freud must grudgingly admit to have *some* (small) value: "Der Zweifel an der Beseeltheit, den wir bei der Puppe Olimpia gelten lassen *mußten.*" If Freud is not aware of the violent gesture with which he pushes aside his predecessor and arbitrarily prefers his own example (*Beispiel*) to that of Jentsch, his prose style conveys this awareness and exhibits it as a symptom. It would appear that the only way to control the proliferation of examples (*Fälle, Beispiele*) is to cast some out, dictatorially, and choose others which illustrate more convincingly the already "proven" theories of psychoanalysis in its evolution up to 1919.

The theme of intellectual uncertainty, which looms large in Hoffmann's "Der Sandmann," whether Freud likes it or not, is a stumbling-block for the psychoanalyst who attempts to deny its significance. Freud states that this theme, which in his view belongs to Jentsch but in fact belongs to Hoffmann, and before him to the textual uncanny in its multiple historical apparitions, "kommt bei diesem stärkeren Beispiel des Unheimlichen *überhaupt nicht in Betracht.*" Intellectual uncertainty does not "come into view" because Freud hides it from us, and he does this because there is so much intellectual uncertainty in "Der Sandmann" and in the uncanny that his own efforts at analytical mastery and control will have been undermined, from the beginning. The uncanny is a hidden bomb which detonates each time an interpreter armed only with the defusing device of his theory (in this case, psychoanalytical) makes his naively unprotected entrance onto the mined territory. Freud's theoretical "lenses" do not guarantee him from blindness any more than Nathaniel's telescope protects him from falling into delusion, and finally, madness. The text Freud summarizes briefly and "analyzes" only in the space of one highly concentrated footnote is far more dangerous than he would let us latecomer-readers think; and it must have been perceived as dangerous by Freud's unconscious mind, given the extraordinary efforts he makes to mask and bury its perilous qualities.

But what is it, then, about "Der Sandmann" as literary text, as example of the uncanny, that is so threatening to Freud's interpretive enterprise? First, the uncanny, as exemplar of Romantic aesthetics, is a series of disparate fragments that can be totalized only by an act of violence (as we have seen: Freud's preference of one form of the uncanny over another; his battle with Jentsch). There are doubtless many instances of the uncanny, but the field of *das Unheimliche* cannot be fully or definitively surveyed. Each time one example of the uncanny is encountered, others follow, uncannily – just as in "Das Unheimliche," having demonstrated to his satisfaction the ubiquitous insistent presence of the eye/castration theme in "Der Sandmann," Freud simply and blithely moves on to a discussion of the "double," which is, of course, another instance of the uncanny. In a nutshell: Freud is trying very hard to write an analytical essay in the classical sense, while the object of his scrutiny undoes his efforts at conceptual clarity. Just as the multiplication of the old gentlemen in Baudelaire's Parisian poem "Les Sept Vieillards" causes the poet to lose his bearings and cling to the remnants of his reason, the unwinding of the string of uncanny examples in Freud's essay exceeds the compass of analytical discourse as conceptual envelopment.

Second, the threat Hoffmann's story poses to Freud is not merely that it ironically anticipates his every enveloping move, thus defeating him in an intellectually refined game of hermeneutical chess; but it also "speaks" to him and through him on a personal level about the value of psychoanalysis as method of interpretation. "Der Sandmann" is uncanny from a temporal perspective: it furnishes an anticipatory critique of the very psychoanalytical tools which Freud brings to bear upon it. It speaks through Freud in an act of marvelously strange ventriloquism. The father of psychoanalysis becomes the dummy (a new Olympia) whose brilliant insight is revealed to be as false and mechanical as the dazzling but dead eyes of the automaton.

In what follows, I shall first emphasize certain areas of "Der Sandmann" which Freud passes over in silence; then I shall proceed to examine the ways in which Hoffmann's story, in these very areas, uncannily, bridges the gap between the self-referential fictionality of Romantic irony and Freud's own existential situation in 1919. The story says far more about Freud than Freud says about the story. Whereas Freud's conscious motivation was to illuminate a small corner of the field of aesthetics with psychoanalytical insight, it is my contention that his fascination with Hoffmann's text, at the unconscious level, is grounded in the analyst's narcissism. Freud sees himself in "Der Sandmann," and beyond the ironic tale he sees Oedipus – not the theorized "Oedipus complex," but Oedipus before theorization, a most dangerous and diabolical antagonist who comes back to haunt his interpreter and rock the foundations of the psychoanalytical edifice itself.

IV "DER SANDMANN" AS MIRROR

At first glance, the narrative structure of Hoffmann's tale bears no resemblance to the logical organization of Freud's analytical discourse on the psychoanalytical significance of the uncanny. As we have seen, "Das Unheimliche," when viewed at a distance and at the highest level of generality, possesses a tripartite structure (indicated quite explicitly by the Roman numerals I, II, and III in the text) which I have described as follows: I. examination of the linguistic peculiarities of the words *heimlich* and *unheimlich* in their interrelation; II. examples of the uncanny from literature and from life, the most important of which is "Der Sandmann"; III. Freud's responses to possible objections to his methods and conclusions, along with a series of fine distinctions on the origins and types of the uncanny. There is no apparent similarity between this quite classical scheme of discursive presentation and the broad outline of the Romantic novella, which Sarah Kofman describes concisely:

> The complexity of the tale: it begins with an exchange of letters between Nathaniel, Lothario and Clara (two characters to whom Freud pays hardly any attention); it continues with a direct address by the author to the reader; finally it unfolds according to the most banal narrative conventions. ("The Double is/and the Devil," 132)

In Kofman's view, Hoffmann also opted for a tripartite organization, but it is much more "complex" than that of Freud, in that there is a mixing of heterogeneous narrative modes which follow each other in a purely metonymic juxtaposition. We have, first, what appears to be an epistolary novella, followed brusquely by the intervention of the "author" (let us say, more prudently, the playfully omniscient *narrator*), and concluding with what Kofman calls a final unfolding of the story "according to the most banal narrative conventions." (I shall leave aside, for the moment, the important question of the "banality" of the conventions Hoffmann makes use of, a "banality" which seems to disappoint Kofman but which cannot be shunted aside with the *désinvolture* she allows herself here. To make use of banal conventions is not necessarily to fall into banality, as the works of Flaubert and Kafka consistently demonstrate.) Freud, in writing about the uncanny, seems to be adopting a "simpler" form of narrative presentation than Hoffmann, and in this sense, the form of his essay confirms what he says in his essay about the greater freedom enjoyed by the creator of fictions, whose poetic license allows him or her to spin a convoluted web which can trap and hold a multiplicity of disparate personages, actions, and voices.

Once one descends beneath the bird's-eye view, however, once one adopts a *Perspektiv* allowing a closer evaluation of both Freud and Hoffmann, one finds a properly uncanny similarity between the two texts at the level of what I shall call *unconscious motivation*. Both writers are obsessed by the problem of narrative framing and closure, and both strive relentlessly to enclose the uncanny within a logical structure. In Freud's case, we have the dogged efforts, in part three of "Das Unheimliche," to distinguish between and among possible forms of the uncanny. To classify a phenomenon properly and definitively is to neutralize the unsettling power of that phenomenon. Yet Freud begins his essay with an elaborate precautionary move (to paraphrase: "I as psychoanalyst now enter a foreign territory, am impelled to do so, and the field is in any case small, just a small bit of the aesthetic"), and concludes by evoking the "ghastly multiplication" of trap-doors in Nestroy's farce *Der Zerrissene*, and the theme of ghosts in general as they relate to "the factors of silence, solitude and darkness." The final sentence of "Das Unheimliche" reads:

Concerning the factors of silence, solitude, and darkness, we can only say that they are actually elements in the production of the infantile anxiety from which the majority of human beings have never become quite free. This problem has been discussed from a psycho-analytic point of view elsewhere. (TU 252)

The conclusion closes nothing, but, like Nestroy's trap-doors, opens outward to the large general problem of the human being's imprisonment in infantile anxiety, and, as the editors of the *Standard Edition* inform us in a footnote to the passage (ibid.), to Freud's own *Drei Abhandlungen zur Sexualtheorie* (1905), the textual "elsewhere" which contains further (previously stated) remarks on the theme rapidly alluded to in the final lines of "Das Unheimliche." The desire to solve the analytical problem of the uncanny expresses itself, metaphorically, as the unrealizable impulsion to close doors, to shut off that which escapes logical containment.

Uncannily, this desire to close, to conclude by closing, this impulsion (*Antrieb*, *Drang*) toward logical control, is also the driving force of "Der Sandmann." Hoffmann's tale begins with the word "gewiß" ("certainly") and concludes, after Nathaniel's death, with what appears to be a "banal" happy ending, in which the narrator describes the domestic happiness of Clara in the following terms:

Several years later, you could have seen Clara, in a distant part of the country, sitting with an affectionate man hand in hand before the door of a lovely country house and with two lovely children playing at her feet, from which it is to be concluded that Clara found in the end that quiet domestic happiness which was so agreeable to her cheerful disposition and which the inwardly riven Nathaniel could never have given her. (TS 125)

Nach mehreren Jahren will man in einer entfernten Gegend Klara gesehen haben, wie sie mit einem freundlichen Mann Hand in Hand vor der Türe eines schönen Landhauses saß und vor ihr zwei muntre Knaben spielten. *Es wäre daraus zu schließen*, daß Klara das ruhige häusliche Glück noch fand, das ihrem heitern lebenslustigen Sinn zusagte und das ihr *der im Innern zerrissene Nathanael* niemals hätte gewähren können. (DS 49; my emphasis)

Just as the first line of "Der Sandmann" begins with the notion of certainty, with the word "gewiß," in the same way the last sentence contains the verb "schließen," which, in this context, means "to conclude," but which, used in the concrete setting of doors and windows, signifies "to close." This is, without a doubt, a "banal," conventional ending to a story that is far from banal. It presents itself as a quite deplorably weak ending to an otherwise entertainingly upsetting narrative (which, I think, explains Kofman's critical remark). But has Hoffmann fallen into the trap of conventionality, or has he used conventionality as a trapping, the better to *en*trap his earnest interpreters (even the most astute students of Freud)? A close reading of the German text cannot help but highlight the conditional mode in which the vision of happy domesticity is represented: "Nach mehreren Jahren *will mann* in einer entfernten Gegend Klara gesehen haben," and "Es *wäre* daraus zu schließen." One might, if one wished, if one should have such a wish, envision such happiness. Hoffmann is as cautious in his final picture of fecund calm (and of the home, the *Heim*) as is Freud in the beginning sentences of "Das Unheimliche." Hoffmann is just as doubtful about containing the dispossessing effects of *Unheimlichkeit* as is Freud upon entering the remote corner of the forbidden territory of the aesthetic which "houses" the uncanny.

Freud's problem – and it is no small problem – is that Hoffmann already knew that the uncanny could be contained only by the arbitrary imposition of a worn-out narrative convention. In a story permeated with death and ghastliness, the final "triumph of life" can only be read ironically, in the same way that in Kafka's "The Metamorphosis" the concluding family outing into the countryside, with the revelation of Grete Samsa's blossoming womanhood, constitutes an ironical counter-image to Gregor's abjection and death. Hoffmann knew, in other words, that the uncanny is the territory of death, of uncontainable, repetitious dying. This is the territory into which Freud entered in 1919, after the death-trance of World War I, but which the psychoanalyst and interpreter of texts also discovered, literarily transposed, in a Romantic fantasy written one century before his time.

If, to use Freud's own vocabulary, one might say that the conscious purpose of his essay "Das Unheimliche" was to remove the uncanny from the domain of the aesthetic and reterritorialize it within the field of psychoanalytic theory, its unconscious motivation would seem to be the instantiation of the repetition compulsion in a literary mode. Freud's writing style follows the impulse, the drive, to say again, and repeatedly, what the uncanny has already said through a multitude of texts, including, most strikingly, "Der Sandmann." And what the uncanny says or testifies to, ceaselessly, is death. *Beyond the Pleasure Principle* becomes the retroactively deferred theoretical justification for the praxis of "Das Unheimliche." Beneath narrative appearances, beneath the contrasting tripartite structures of Freud's "theoretical fiction" and Hoffmann's fiction *tout court*, lies *the* pattern of narrative, which is the uncanny repetitiousness of the *Antrieb* or *Drang*.[7]

Freud's multiple hesitations, definitions, and redefinitions, his ambivalent rhetoric of caution and aggressivity, in short, the intellectual uncertainty emanating from the analyst's inner divisions concerning his elusive theme, mirror the articulated pattern beneath the overt structure of Hoffmann's tale. It is a pattern that can only strike fear into the heart of a medical practitioner whose domain is the human mind: namely, the falling in and out of health, the repeated apparent but deceptive "cures" of the "patient" Nathaniel, which end in analytical failure and the analysand's death. It is perhaps no coincidence that Freud concludes his description of the uncanny with an allusion to a work of literature entitled *Der Zerrissene* [The Torn Man], since the last words of "Der Sandmann" describe the unfortunate protagonist as "der im Innern zerrissene Nathanael" – the man who loved an automaton rather than the clear-sighted and "lebenslustige" Clara. It is precisely the inner division of Nathaniel, a split which tempts other characters in the novella to make him whole, but which is, in fact, incurable, that provides "Der Sandmann" with its narrative locomotion – a movement of fits and starts that is uncontainable within any macro-structure, whether tripartite or otherwise delimited.

Nathaniel's first active intervention in his domestic environment occurs when he decides to spy upon his father and Coppelius. This intervention proceeds not from the clarity of a calm, conscious choosing, but from an "irresistible urge": "At length, impelled by an irresistible urge, I decided to conceal myself within my father's room and there await the sandman" (*Endlich, von unwiderstehlichem Drange getrieben, beschloß ich, im Zimmer des Vaters selbst mich zu verbergen und den Sandmann zu erwarten*) (TS 88; DS 14). Like the *Antrieb* that motivated Freud to enter the foreign territory of aesthetics, the impulse to discover the unknown is at the origin of Nathaniel's assumption of his role as protagonist. Like Freud the theorist, Nathaniel is in fact poised between two contrary forces: on the one hand, an urge or drive coming from outside his conscious mind that forces him to make an incursion into a hitherto protected domain; on the other, the conscious power of decision-making, which is expressed in the verb "to conclude" – *beschließen.* Just as Freud attempts, with monotonous regularity, to conclude his essay on the uncanny, only to be caught up in an ever-widening spiral of illustrative examples, in the same way Nathaniel, despite his stated desire to solve the mystery of his father's evening occupations, will end his fantasy-existence spinning out of control into madness. Hoffmann's initial juxtaposition of the verb *treiben* in the passive voice to the decisive *beschließen* establishes the tension out of which the novella in its entirety will evolve, as an alternation between moments of calm and lucidity and the inevitability of the protagonist's progression toward folly and death. When Freud read "Der Sandmann" he not only found, at the conscious level of his analytical thinking, a confirmation of his ideas on the fear of castration and the Oedipus complex, but he also discovered a psychodrama that could only heighten his anxiety about the real-world medical effectiveness of his new discipline: namely, the story of a young man who, despite the loving care and analytical lucidity of his best friends, cannot be cured.

If Freud's essay imitates Hoffmann's novella in its hesitation between logical mastery and uncontrollable fragmentation, it is because Freud sees himself in the story and cannot extricate himself from Hoffmann's narrative logic and from the fascinating power exercised over the twentieth-century thinker by fictional characters from the previous century. Freud is possessed by Hoffmann's text: he can only repeat, but never truly alter, the oracular obliqueness of the "example" he uses, among others, in his discourse on the meaning of the uncanny. Freud is *in the text*, and he is "already Freud," one might say, in the character of Clara, whose clear-sightedness prefigures the analytical lucidity of the father of psychoanalysis. This prefiguration is not based merely on the abstract notion of lucidity or clarity, however: it inscribes itself into the very style with which Clara speaks to her beloved Nathaniel, which is unmistakably the style of the psychoanalyst. It is uncanny indeed to be quoted one century *before* one has written about the uncanny, but this is what happens in "Der Sandmann," when Clara seeks to reassure Nathaniel about his fears of Coppelius. The logic of her argument is based upon an unwavering distinction between the "inside" of Nathaniel's brooding mind and the "outside" of external reality. Nathaniel can find solace and be cured of his anxious fantasies if he is able to recognize that his fears are merely imaginary, that what he "saw" when he hid in his father's workroom had no basis in the real, but was the result of his own fanciful projections:

> Let me say straight out what it is I think: that all the ghastly and terrible things you spoke of took place only within you, and that the real outer world had little part in them. Old Coppelius may have been repulsive enough, but it was because he hated children that you children came to feel an actual revulsion for him.
>
> The frightening sandman in the nursery tale naturally became united [*verknüpfte sich*] in your childish mind with old Coppelius; although you no longer believed in the sandman, Coppelius was still to you a spectral monster especially dangerous to children. The uncanny night-time activities with your father were no doubt nothing more than secret alchemical experiments they were making together [*Das unheimliche Treiben mit Deinem Vater zur Nachtzeit war wohl nichts anders, als daß beide insgeheim alchimistische Versuche machten*], and your mother could hardly have been pleased about it, since a lot of money was undoubtedly wasted and, moreover, as is always supposed to be the case with such laboratory experimenters, your father, altogether absorbed in the deceptive desire for higher truth [*ganz von dem trügerischen Drange nach hoher Weisheit erfüllt*], would have become estranged from his family. (TS 95–96; DS 21)

Like the psychoanalyst whose methods and vocabulary she anticipatorily borrows, Clara sets out to demonstrate that the "ghastly and terrible things" in her patient's mind do not correspond to facts and events in the outer world, but have their origin in a union or "knotting" (*Verknüpfung*) of affective imagery deriving from the frightening nursery tale of the Sandman. This story has since become associated, in Nathaniel's mind, with the purportedly diabolical activities of the repulsive Coppelius, who has seduced his father into pursuing certain strange night-time "experiments." Clara's argument is a discourse of demystification in which the uncanny quality of these nocturnal researches, *das Unheimliche*, is reduced to "no doubt nothing more than secret alchemical experiments." Uncanniness is explained away as *mere alchemy* – in Kantian terms, *bloß Kunst*, simply artfulness, a play with the elements that has no effect on external reality, since, as we all know, alchemy, as pure wastefulness, *never works*. As pure and irresponsible freeplay, and as a false promise of transmutation of base reality into a higher essential form, alchemical experimentation impels its adepts toward a deceptive higher truth. There is a *Drang* toward truth, but the uncanny urging [*das unheimliche Treiben*] destroys the family and the home [*Heim*]. Clara and Nathaniel's mother are enlisted to protect domestic tranquillity in the battle against male hubris, which, in "Der Sandmann," takes the form of a compulsion to create artificially, to rob the gods of their fire in order to make something outside of or beyond nature. In this sense, the male union of Spalanzani and Coppola, like that of Nathaniel's father and Coppelius, can only "produce" pure artifice – an automaton who bears no more resemblance to a real woman than the "brightly gleaming substances" (TS 91) in the father's chimney do to real gold. The domain of *techné* is that of the male artificer, whose "deceptive" (*trügerisch*) labyrinthine labor poses a threat to ethical stability, to the straight path of nature and nurture.

The central dramatic conflict of "Der Sandmann," the conflict that gives rise to the story's narrative energy, is Nathaniel's hesitation between the clear-sighted Clara and the doll Olympia, whose eyes are a lifeless reflective surface. In terms of literary representation, the male protagonist cannot at first decide between an ethically constructed world in which the "inside" of the imagination is allotted a finite and restricted space, and the universe of Romantic irony, in which the unbounded power of the imagination's projective capacities causes the young man to find beauty and even life where there is, or has been, only a ghostly resemblance to life. At the beginning of the story, before Nathaniel assumes his role as protagonist, while he is still only a child among children within the family, the choice between ethical stability and aesthetic artifice is posed, significantly, in the form of two different "readings" of the sandman fairy tale – one provided by his mother, and the other elaborated by the old woman who cares for his sister.[8] The phrase "the sandman is coming" is used by the mother on those evenings when the father appears gloomy and when a stranger's footsteps are eventually heard in the house: it is a signal for the children to go to bed. Before Nathaniel has his first encounter with Coppelius (before he can make his first association of this man with the sandman), he asks the question: "Mama, who is this sandman who always drives us away from Papa? [*Ei, Mama, wer ist denn der böse Sandmann, der uns immer von Papa forttreibt?*]" (TS 86; DS 12). The mother's answer is as follows:

> "There is no sandman, my dear child," my mother replied. "When I say the sandman is coming, all that means is that you are sleepy and cannot keep your eyes open, as though someone had sprinkled sand into them [*als hätte man euch Sand hineingestreut*]." (TS 87; DS 12–13)

Unhappy with his mother's prosaic answer, Nathaniel seeks another interpretation from the old servant woman, whose folk-wisdom reply contrasts sharply with maternal rationality:

[The sandman] is a wicked man who comes after children when they won't go to bed and throws handfuls of sand in their eyes, so that they jump out of their heads all bloody, and then he throws them into his sack and carries them to the crescent moon as food for his little children, who have their nest up there and have crooked beaks like owls and peck up the eyes of the naughty children. (TS 87)

Hoffmann's novella begins at a crossroads. Nathaniel must choose between a demystified version of the folk story that "sees through" its crude imagery, purifying it of all threatening violence, and the unsettling version of the servant, which makes of the same "primitive" material a cautionary tale for disobedient children. In linguistic terms, the difference between the two readings resides in the interpreter's skepticism or belief in metaphorical transport as such. The mother's neutral lucidity derives from her linguistic agnosticism: she knows that the tale of the sandman is to be read conditionally or subjunctively, in the "as if" mode of the *Konjunktiv* ("als hätte man euch Sand hineingestreut"). She, like Kierkegaard's Judge William, sees clearly the artifice of figural discourse and is not taken in by it. Much to his misfortune, however, Nathaniel does not find his mother's skepticism convincing or appealing, but is swayed by the verbal picture painted by the servant woman – a picture that now places itself within his consciousness: "Gräßlich malte sich nun im Innern mir das Bild des grausamen Sandmanns aus" (DS 13). For Nathaniel, there is no "as if." Like the young Romanticist in Part 1 of *Either/Or*, the protagonist of "Der Sandmann" chooses to *live aesthetically*, which means that he lives in and among figural discourse, believing in its transformative power. The carrying up of the children's eyes is metaphor as transport (*Übertragung*), as the bridging of the distance between earth and moon and the transmutation of dead eyes into nourishment by what Rimbaud called *l'alchimie du verbe*. Unfortunately for Nathaniel, he, like his father, is an alchemist, unable or unwilling to hear the reassuring advice of his mother or the subsequent psychological admonitions of Clara. Nathaniel's fall into aesthetics as the realm of unmastered figuration is also a straying from the laws of nature and from human sociability in its ethically centered domestic expression.

Throughout the novella Nathaniel is surrounded by what one might call representatives of the ethical life, whose function is to bring him back to a sense of boundaries, constraints, and his responsibilities as a member of society. Clara and Lothario play this role most obviously, and do so from the beginning of the story until its tragic conclusion. They are not alone, however. When Nathaniel leaves his home for the last time, thinking that he will return one year hence to find his mother and to resume his happy relationship with Clara, he finds that his student lodgings have burnt down (the alchemical fire of the father figures seems, uncannily, to have contaminated the son's life), and, providentially, moves into a new dwelling directly opposite Spalanzani and Olympia.[9] It is at this point in the narrative, when Clara is no longer physically present for Nathaniel, that Hoffmann introduces, quite brusquely, a new character into his tale – a young man who, in his lucidity, his ethical demeanor, and common-sense grasp of reality, is Clara's male *Doppelgänger*. His name is Siegmund. The reader first encounters him at a crucial juncture in the text, when Nathaniel, while writing a letter to Clara, feels compelled to look up from his desk, seize his newly acquired telescope, and observe Olympia. At this very moment Siegmund intervenes and takes Nathaniel away from his compulsive voyeuristic activity:

> Now he sat down to finish his letter to Clara, but one glance through the window convinced him that Olympia was still sitting there, and in an instant he sprang up, as if impelled by an irresistible power [*wie von unwiderstehlicher Gewalt getrieben*], and seized Coppola's telescope; he could not tear himself away from the seductive sight of Olympia until his friend and fellow-student Siegmund called him to come to Professor Spalanzani's lecture. (TS 111; DS 37)

The leitmotiv of the *Trieb* or *Drang* appears once again later in the same paragraph, and reaches its culminating point when Nathaniel, frustrated at not being able to see Olympia behind the drawn curtain of her window, "driven by burning desire" (*getrieben von Sehnsucht und glühendem Verlangen*) (TS 112; DS 37), flees into the countryside, where Olympia's image blots out all memory of Clara and erases all traces of physical/natural reality. From a clinical perspective, Nathaniel's problem can be summed up as follows: when he is accompanied (the French would say *encadré* – "framed") and kept under control by Clara, Lothario, or now Siegmund, the text holds out the possibility that the protagonist can be coaxed back to a reasonable view of his circumstances and reintegrated into the community. But when he escapes such control, when left to his own devices, he succumbs to the unmediated power of poetic vision, a power that leads toward final madness.

Siegmund not only replaces Clara as lucid interpreter of psychological phenomena, but he also speaks for the community and for its sense of decorum. It is Siegmund who, after Olympia's "débutante ball," speaks in the name of the other guests at that event and declares:

We have come to find this Olympia quite uncanny [*Uns ist diese Olimpia ganz unheimlich geworden*]; we would like to have nothing to do with her; it seems to us that she is only acting like a living creature, and yet there is some reason for that which we cannot fathom. (TS 116; DS 42)

The uncanny is diabolical not just in the sense of aesthetic complexity (narrative framings and unframings, the strange anticipatory mirroring of "Das Unheimliche" performed by "Der Sandmann," Freud as Hoffmann's *Doppelgänger*), but also in the ethical sense. Uncanniness is a destabilizing threat to social norms and conventions, as Siegmund is the first to recognize. One of the most humorous passages in "Der Sandmann" occurs in Hoffmann's description of the days following the revelation that Olympia was, after all, only a doll. The consensus of public opinion is that Spalanzani's now dismantled artificial creation was "an altogether impermissible piece of deception" (TS 121). Even members of the legal profession become involved in the retrospective judging of Spalanzani, finding his "cunningly conceived" (ibid.) automaton unacceptable in the deviousness of its human-but-not-human appearance. We find here the same register of moral outrage that obtained in Kant's critical reaction to the innkeeper who deceived his guests into believing they had heard the call of a nightingale when in fact a young boy was imitating the bird's song on a reed or pipe (*CJ*, par. 42). Unlike Kant, however, Hoffmann frames the expression of moral disapproval with what might be described as "the revenge of the artificial over the real." The Olympia case is not closed with the mere enunciation of a harsh verdict against Spalanzani's artistic "crime." Hoffmann concludes his digression on the ethical implications of the automaton's entry into society with some observations on the "detectable mistrust of the human form" (TS 121) that has now insinuated itself into many townspeople, especially those engaged in courtship. In post-Olympia society, men wish the female objects of their attention to dance with some irregularity, to yawn intermittently rather than sneeze at clockwork intervals, in short, to exhibit the imperfection of the human.

Spalanzani has effected a properly uncanny reversal: rather than evaluate the doll's beauty by the closeness of its resemblance to the human form, after Spalanzani one is obliged to redefine feminine beauty in terms of its non-mimetic relation to the doll's perfection.[10] Imitator and imitated exchange positions, and in so doing introduce an aesthetic indeterminacy or *indécidabilité* into the community's attempts to drive away (*forttreiben*) the artificial, to make Olympia and her "progenitor" into scapegoats. Even when banished, Olympia lives on as a ghost among the living, an obstacle to the finality of ethical reasoning, which can control her only by equating her dismantling with the absolute absence of death. But the problem, as Hoffmann knows and Freud is repeatedly learning as he writes "Das Unheimliche," is that an automaton can never die. Perhaps what we call death itself in its unmastered *Trieb* – death beyond the individual residing domestically in his or her ethical/social frame – does not die, but is structured as an eternal/infernal repetition, a *Teufelskreis*: that would be *das Unheimlichste*; that would be the lesson of the uncanny.

If the uncanny, in its ghostly appearance, can be provisionally defined as an unmastered force which passes between life and death, crossing the boundary human rationality establishes between these two domains, it represents that which exceeds the control of the agents of reason, that which blinds those who possess even the strongest "lenses" with which to observe and classify the world and its inhabitants. Thus it is not surprising that even the faithful Siegmund cannot control Nathaniel's madness when the latter discovers that Olympia is an artificial creature: "Strong though he was, Siegmund was unable to restrain the madman [*Siegmund, so stark er war, vermochte nicht den Rasenden zu bändigen*], who continued to cry in a fearsome voice 'Spin, puppet, spin!'" (TS 120; DS 45). This is the moment in Hoffmann's story which must have been the most fearsome for Freud, and the most uncanny, in the sense that a fictional character possessing his own prized qualities – analytical insight, ethical demeanor, the capacity for male friendship – is not able to control his "patient," is not capable of substituting for the "spinning" words of Nathaniel a logical line of reasoning that would reestablish the boundaries of the real for a young man falling into madness. The uncanniness is all the more uncanny, so to speak, in that the fictional character and the distinguished practitioner of the healing arts *possess the same name*, the only difference being that the fictional Siegmund has all the letters necessary to enunciate the symbolic value of Freud's name: namely, the man who achieves victory (*Sieg*) through the mouth (*Mund*). This, of course, is the dream of Freud the psychoanalyst – to gain victory over the dangerous fragmentation of the human mind, to put back together the dismantled psyche, through the power of the word, through the "talking cure." But Freud's problem in 1919, just as he is about to make what he thinks is an important theoretical breakthrough (the discovery of the repetition compulsion, of the death instinct), just as he is about to achieve another intellectual victory, is that the very text which anticipates his essay "Das Unheimliche" (and in many ways also, *Beyond the Pleasure Principle*) inscribes within its pages the final defeat of the analyst, his undoing when faced with a mental complexity and instability that threaten the foundation of his scientific project.

V THE OUTERMOST FRAME AND THE INNERMOST FRAMED

Put succinctly, one could conclude that the most striking result of a close reading of "Der Sandmann" is a reversal of narrative frames. Whereas Freud set out to use Hoffmann's novella as one example among several of the uncanny, thereby enclosing it within his own conceptual framework, the textual uncanniness of "Der Sandmann" consists in anticipating, ironizing, and enclosing Freud within its own strange narrative logic, mirroring him in the figures of Clara and his eponymous *Doppelgänger*, Siegmund. Like *Der Zerrissene* with its trap-doors, "Der Sandmann" contains depths below depths into which the psychoanalyst gazes, only to discover a distorted image of himself. There is, in a general sense, a relation of analogy that obtains between the defeated would-be victor Siegmund and Sigmund Freud, and this relation, at the unconscious level, is at the origin of the seismic disruptions and hesitations that characterize "Das Unheimliche" as an essay attempting but not succeeding to master its own logical movement. But the uncanny linkages are not limited to textual generality: they extend into the realm of the particular and the real, into the real-world context in which Freud sat down to write "Das Unheimliche." To be more precise: the problem of victory and defeat which emerges from a confrontation of "Das Unheimliche" with "Der Sandmann" is *also* the problem that haunts Freud in his life and at the farthest margins of his 1919 essay, at the edges of the frame that encloses his meditation on the uncanny within the *Gesammelte Werke* and the *Standard Edition* as they appear to us today, in their bound and definitive forms. I refer to the presence, at the end of both the German and English volumes within which "Das Unheimliche" appears, of two necrologies, two homages to adherents of Freud's new discipline who died during the Great War, and who are praised for their respective contributions to the emerging field of psychoanalysis. They are James J. Putnam and Victor Tausk. They, like Hoffmann's Siegmund, mirror Freud, but from the referential sphere, from an extra-textual area that impinges, uncannily, on Freud's essay and on his double obsession with death and with victory.

The outermost frame: Putnam, Tausk, and Freud

The "Gedenkworte" ("memorial words") devoted to Putnam and Tausk were contributed, unsigned, by the editorial committee of the *Internationale Zeitschrift für Psychoanalyse* and were included in the fifth volume of that periodical (1919) before being placed at the conclusion of volume XII of the *Gesammelte Werke* (1917–20) (hereafter *GW*) and volume XVII of the *Standard Edition* (1917–19)(hereafter *SE*). Putnam and Tausk appear as similar-but-different *Doppelgänger.* They are said to have possessed the same essential qualities, as representatives of the new science of psychoanalysis (they were both compulsive achievers; they were lucid in their analytical insight; they contributed to the diffusion of psychoanalysis through distinguished publications and faithful membership in international organizations). They were, in a sense, brothers in the faith, separated by geography but brought together by a common belief in a no-longer fledgling discipline. At the same time, however, the writer(s) of the necrologies make clear that Putnam was the good brother, while Tausk was the black sheep. In the most general terms, here are the differences between the two men:

1. Putnam died a natural death at age 72, while Tausk committed suicide at 42 (in 1919, Freud himself was 62, closer in age to Putnam, closer to the time at which one might expect or fear a natural death).
2. Putnam's career was characterized by a smooth progression. He began as a neurologist, then gradually embraced the new science of psychoanalysis, and became the esteemed president of the "pan-American psycho-analytic group" (*SE* XVII, 271). Tausk's life was a series of fits and starts. He was, successively: a magistrate in Bosnia, a journalist in Berlin, an M.D. in Vienna, a participant in the War on the German side, and finally, a mentally unstable person whose idiosyncratic nervosity was seen as disruptive at the 1918 Budapest Congress on Psychoanalysis, and as a harbinger of his suicide one year later.
3. The word "Würdigung" appears twice in the homage to Putnam (*GW* XII, 315), once to describe the esteem in which he was held by his colleagues, and another time to foreshadow the appreciation or evaluation of his writings on psychoanalysis which would be contributed soon to the *Internationale Zeitschrift* by Ernest Jones. The clarity and richness of his thought, the decisiveness of his engagement in the international movement around Freud, go hand in hand, therefore, with an "unimpeachable character" (*SE* XVII, 271). Tausk was valued

for "his straightforward character, his honesty towards himself and towards others," but his "passionate temperament found expression in sharp, and sometimes too sharp, criticisms" (*SE* XVII 275). In the ethical balance, Tausk thus falls short of his *Doppelgänger*'s calm and judicious demeanor.

4. Putnam's homage is shorter than Tausk's, partly because Jones's forthcoming evaluation of the former's works renders a detailed discussion of his ideas in the context of the "Gedenkwort" superfluous, and partly because Putnam is pictured as a "man of one piece," whereas the divided (i.e. *zerrissene*) Tausk requires a more subtle, more differentiated, description. There is one passage in Tausk's necrology which stands out as particularly *nuancé*, and which relates uncannily to the central problematic of "Das Unheimliche" and to the driving narrative force (*Trieb, Drang*) of Hoffmann's novella as well. It concerns Tausk's ambition to combine philosophy with psychoanalysis, to give a philosophical grounding to psychoanalytic observation:

> His [Tausk's] strong need to establish things on a philosophical foundation and to achieve epistemological clarity compelled him to formulate, and seek as well to master, the whole profundity and comprehensive meaning of the very difficult problems involved. Perhaps he sometimes went too far in this direction, in his impetuous urge for investigation [*In seinem ungestümen Forscherdrang*]. Perhaps the time was not yet ripe for laying such general foundations as these for the young science of psycho-analysis. (*SE* XVII, 274; GW XII, 317)

Once again, we find the leitmotiv of the "impetuous urge" with which Freud initiated his essay on the uncanny (the *Antrieb* to explore the foreign territory of aesthetics) and which punctuates the entirety of "Der Sandmann." As reader of the two necrologies, Freud had to wonder whether he resembled Putnam or Tausk – which is to say, *either* a man of maturity and ripened insights whose death, at 72, provided natural closure to a life of manifold scholarly and ethical contributions; *or* an individual whose multiple careers, divided allegiances, premature drive toward theoretical founding or grounding, and eventual suicide at 42, conjure up a picture of incompleteness, of unredeemable fragmentation. *Victor* Tausk, like Hoffmann's *Siegmund*, is named for victory; yet he "achieves" only defeat.[11] He is the failed would-be philosopher of psychoanalysis, the man guilty of what could be called *theoria praecox*. In this sense, his is a most uncomfortable image for Freud to contemplate at the precise moment the founder of psychoanalysis is about to initiate a complex and counter - intuitive new theory – that of the "death instinct." In 1919,

Freud had to wonder whether this new theory was destined to enjoy the same eventual *Würdigung* by his disciples as his revolutionary conception of dreams and his ground-breaking re-evaluation of the significance of human sexuality in its earliest stages. What if the grand theory of the "repetition compulsion" and the "death instinct" were to be formulated, in 1919 and 1920, in a precipitous manner? What if Freud was about to go too far and act before the time was ripe ? If this were the case, he would most certainly resemble the failed non-victor Tausk more than the successful and mature Putnam. Freud's discomfort could only have been exacerbated by the fact that Tausk, in his *Forscherdrang*, in the repetitiousness of his immature and premature drives, in his final suicide, *also resembles Nathaniel.* Looking deep into the necrologies, Freud therefore finds himself, in double form: as a failed analyst and as a madman.

We know, from the biographical evidence, that Freud's relation to Tausk was delicate from the first, convoluted in its development, and highly troubled in the end. In "Freud and the Sandman," via a concise summary of Paul Roazen's *Brother Animal: The Story of Freud and Tausk*, Neil Hertz addresses the issue of Freud's possible guilt feelings vis-à-vis his younger colleague, feelings which could have arisen from Freud's refusal to be Tausk's analyst, from his decision to entrust the latter's care to a less experienced disciple, Helene Deutsch, who, it so happened, was being analyzed by Freud at the time. A not-so-salubrious situation ensued, wherein Freud's sessions with Deutsch were consumed with talk of Tausk, while Deutsch and Tausk talked about Freud. In the end, Freud convinced Deutsch to terminate Tausk's treatment, and it was not long thereafter that Tausk committed suicide. Roazen is intrigued by the possible crossover between Freud's theoretical ideas in 1919 and the real-life conflict between Freud and Tausk. He wonders whether Tausk might have been "acting out Freud's newest, or even just barely burgeoning idea," or whether "the notion of a death instinct represented another way for Freud to deny any responsibility for Tausk's situation."[12] At this juncture, Hertz intervenes judiciously, with the following observation:

> Well, we know the notion of a death instinct represents considerably more than that in the economy of Freud's thought, and we may find it easier, at this point, to pull free: there is nothing like a reductive interpretation to break the spell of a fascinating anecdote. (117)

At one level, Hertz's comment is well taken and of fundamental importance for literary studies. Roazen's naively formulated idea that there could be a direct causal relation between a fact or event in Freud's life and a complex theoretical statement is, of course, "reductive" and dangerous, in that it establishes a simple and crudely mimetic one-to-one correspondence between the real and the process of theorization: Freud was interested in the strange notion of a "death instinct"; Tausk succumbed to an impetuous death drive; Freud felt guilty about Tausk's death; therefore the *Todestrieb* as such derives from Freud's guilt about Tausk. Such a pseudo-syllogistic pattern of "reasoning" is quite reductive indeed, and in this respect one can only agree with Hertz. At the same time, however, if one confines oneself to the way in which the referential sphere impinges upon the textual without succumbing to the temptation of using Freud's "guilt" as an all-encompassing explanatory foundation, one is compelled (!) to note that the unsettling resemblance of Freud to Tausk *mirrors*, in an uncanny way, the discomforting resemblance of Freud to Nathaniel, and in this sense, *das Unheimliche* in its most diabolical form would be the odd, distorted, but spell-binding *extension* of the real into the depths of the textual. Although Hertz is quite convincing in his argument against interpretive reductiveness (and one is certainly in more secure territory, hermeneutically speaking, with Hertz than with Roazen), his desire to "break the spell" of the "fascinating," however admirable in its ethical intention, imitates the gesture of conceptual purification with which Freud attempts, repeatedly, to reduce *das Unheimliche* to a "sub-species" of *das Heimliche*, to bring it back to a clearly delineated, theoretically circumscribed haven. We will never know with any degree of certainty about Freud's feelings of guilt (or lack thereof) for Tausk's death; but I am suggesting that the Putnam-Tausk paratext, in its function as frame for "Das Unheimliche," brings the real perilously and diabolically close to Freud's unconscious anxieties as reader of "Der Sandmann," thereby adding a layer of resonance to what is already a textual echo-chamber of uncontrollable uncanny effects. In sum: Freud is everywhere implicated, everywhere involved and inscribed. Everywhere he looks, he sees himself; and the mirrors point both beyond the texts he reads and writes and deep into them. Both far outside and abysmally deep inside, he finds multiple brothers, a procession of real and fictional associates from whom he would like to dissociate himself, but whose "spell" entrances him into an unsettling connivance.

The innermost framed: Oedipus before theory

Outside the borders of "Das Unheimliche" as theoretical essay lies the territory of real-world fraternal resemblance-and-difference, in the form of the *Doppelgänger* Putnam and Tausk. Inside the essay one finds two sets of brothers as well: Lothario–Nathaniel, and Siegmund–Nathaniel. Lothario provides active resistance to Nathaniel's threatening violence by saving Clara from death in the tower scene; and Siegmund furnishes an intellectually formed, clear-sighted analytical opposition to Nathaniel's poetic excesses and eventual folly. As I now conclude, I would like to take a final interpretive step toward that which, in my view, resides farthest inside Freud's unsettled essay: namely, the figure of Oedipus, a personage also accompanied by a *Doppelgänger*, an infamous and tragic literary hero whose legendary territory is that of the deceptively homelike non-home – precisely and terrifyingly the unwelcoming realm of the uncanny.

Like many ancient dramas, Sophocles' *Oedipus the King* (c. 425 B.C.) is based upon what, in today's terminology, we would call a "conservative" message: the necessity of counteracting the faithlessness of a people, of restoring its belief in the prophecies and oracles of the gods. The fall into unbelief has spawned the gods' anger, which manifests itself in natural disasters of all kinds, in the barrenness of the land and of its inhabitants. It is in this situation of desolation that the play begins. The plot in its unfolding reveals that Oedipus is the cause of these calamities, and he will be the scapegoat whose expulsion beyond the city walls allows for a return to normalcy – which means adherence to religion as the ultimate guarantor of fertility and of political and social continuity. The Chorus, with its collective "I," expresses the problem cogently as it bemoans the current sad state of affairs (as things stand before Oedipus's entry into the paradoxical darkness of blind self- knowledge):

> No longer to the holy place,
> to the navel of earth I'll go
> to worship, nor to Abae
> nor to Olympia,
> unless the oracles are proved to fit,
> for all men's hands to point at.
> O Zeus, if you are rightly called
> the sovereign lord, all-mastering,
> let this not escape you nor your ever-living power!
> The oracles concerning Laius
> are old and dim and men regard them not.
> Apollo is nowhere clear in honour; God's service perishes. (48–49)[13]

The Chorus's plea is for the god of gods, Zeus, to restore the central place of religion in the people by rendering manifest, in plain intelligible signs, the meaning of his prophets' oracular pronouncements. What has been lacking of late is the kind of sign "for all men's hands to point at" – i.e., a message that does not lend itself to misinterpretation and to confusion. In *Oedipus the King* there are two moments of special hermeneutic intensity. The first occurs before the action of the play proper, when Oedipus deciphers the riddle of the Sphinx; and the second takes place when the protagonist finally understands the meaning of the "oracles concerning Laius" and his own tragic deeds as his father's murderer and his mother's incestuous spouse. From the beginning of the play Oedipus is an agnostic as far as traditional oracular wisdom is concerned. He does not give credence to what he considers to be the superstitious beliefs of established religion, the pronouncements of seers who rely upon the entrails of animals to signal future events in the world. It is precisely in his role as decipherer of riddles that Oedipus opposes himself to the tradition, in that he uses only his reason, his rational clear-sightedness, to discover that the animal that walks on four "legs" in the morning, two at noon, and three in the evening, is man. His mistaken preconception, as the drama begins, is that this same capacity for reasonable thought will allow him to discover clues that will lead to apprehending the man whose crime has polluted the city. As Alain Robbe-Grillet wittily demonstrated in his experimental novel *Les Gommes* [*The Erasers*] (1953), Oedipus, before his self-revelation, is essentially a detective.

But what gift of intelligence does it take, in fact, to decipher the Sphinx's riddle? Not so much reason, that mental capacity which permits one to proceed naturally and inevitably from cause to effect, as a kind of imagination or poetic intuition that allows one to understand the nature of metaphorical language – in this case, the fact that the third "leg" referred to in the riddle is a cane, a false, artificial appendage, an *Anhang* that is added on to the human body, that is attached to it metonymically, that resembles it but does not share its organic properties. Rather than heed the resonance of signs at the gods' dwelling in Olympia, Oedipus is an artificer who, like Spalanzani and his creation of a false doll named Olympia, is possessed of the hubris of the scientist, of the human who reaches too far in his intellectual agon with the gods. Within every would-be scientist, every rational being, within every Sigmund Freud, there resides a poetic gift which, if taken too far or developed before its time, can lead far beyond rational/theoretical knowledge and toward the abyss of madness.

What is it that Oedipus does not know at the beginning of the play? His crimes, of course, but also, most crucially, his origins. He is a man who has found his home prematurely, before his time. He has made an unfortunate, criminal incursion into a territory that is more familiar than his clear consciousness recognizes. His *Doppelgänger*, Tiresias, the man who is blind but sees (whereas Oedipus is the one who, in his initial ill-conceived rationality, sees but is blind), reveals to him quite early in the proceedings that the man who needs to be punished for the city to regain its health is a Theban-but-also-foreigner, a man who is, uncannily, both at home and away from home in his current place:

> I tell you, King, this man, this murderer,
> (whom you have long declared you are in search of,
> indicting him in threatening proclamation
> as murderer of Laius) – he is here.
> In name he is a stranger among citizens
> but soon he will be shown to be a citizen
> true native Theban, and he'll have no joy
> of the discovery: blindness for sight
> and beggary for riches his exchange,
> he shall go journeying to a foreign country
> tapping his way before him with a stick.
> He shall be proved father and brother both
> to his own children in his house; to her
> that gave him birth, a son and husband both;
> a fellow sower in his father's bed
> with that same father that he murdered.
> Go within, reckon that out, and if you find me
> mistaken, say I have no skill in prophecy. (30)

The last two lines of Tiresias's speech establish, with evident irony, a clear dichotomy between the "reckoning out" (unriddling) of which Oedipus is capable and the art of prophecy, which the unfortunate protagonist, unlike his blind interlocutor, is far from possessing. What Oedipus cannot understand is uncanniness, *Unheimlichkeit* in its various diabolical forms: a son who is also a father; a mother who is also a lover; a "sowing" which repeats, but in the mode of the unnatural, the very "sowing" that begot him; an adopted land (Thebes) that is, in fact, a native land (which replaces a false native land [Corinth] that turns out, in retrospect, to have been an adopted land). And underlying all these doublings, all this complicated and unsettling interchange of curiously related elements, is one small and haunting detail. Oedipus's imaginative "discovery" of the meaning of the third leg as cane, which allowed him to escape death in the claws of the Sphinx, *belongs to a prophetic self-understanding at the unconscious level* in that, when he is driven from Thebes, he will "go journeying to a foreign country / tapping his way before him with a stick," accompanied by his faithful daughter Antigone. The cane which was necessary for the solving of a riddle worthy of a parlor-game was meant for Oedipus himself, as an individual. The person who finds an answer as noble as "man" to the riddle of existence is himself subject to dark laws that exceed his ability to reason, that inscribe his destiny in an eternal wandering.

The true home of Oedipus is neither Corinth nor Thebes: it is Mount Cithaeron, where he was abandoned by his parents, who, fearing the oracle, left their son alone to die. Oedipus' life, between the moment of his abandonment and his discovery of the truth, is a long reprieve, a life-in-death which is ghostly, uncanny. This reprieve has allowed him to participate in human activities – to reign as king, to have children – but his is a usurped crown and his are unnatural progeny, destined for rejection by society, for deprivation and eternal exclusion. Antigone can only accompany the blind-but-lucid man as he taps his way, on three legs, toward the next city.

In conclusion, then, beneath "Das Unheimliche," "Der Sandmann," and the theme of blindness/castration is *Oedipus the King* and the self-blinding of a man whose faith in reason alone ran up against the uncanniness of death-in-life. Freud's "Oedipus complex" is a cornerstone of his theoretical edifice, and, in his capacity as theorist, Freud is in a position to abstract himself from the human condition, to step momentarily outside its bounds and show what he believes to be its psychological truth: that all of us, as members of families, belong to, suffer from this "complex," which proves to be a fecund explanatory model. At the same time, however, while about to contribute further theoretical insight into human behavior – by laying bare the presence of a "repetition compulsion" and a "death instinct" – Freud could no longer keep his distance, and *fell into* the *Dränge* and *Triebe* that he himself was attempting to delimit conceptually. Reading through and beyond "Der Sandmann," Freud could only find himself, again, back with Oedipus. But this time, at the unconscious level, he had to identify with the Greek tragic hero, a figure whose rational abilities are undone by uncanniness and who, having found what he thought was his home, was un-homed by final exile. When, in his own years of English exile, Freud would compare himself to Oedipus and his daughter Anna to Antigone, he experienced more than the small pleasure others derive from literary allusion.[14] Freud, through "Das Unheimliche," "Der Sandmann," and *Oedipus the King*, here evoked something far more terrifying than the mind of a scientific thinker would like to face: namely, the fear that the unriddling investigation of nature or human nature is itself a pact with the devil, a form of unnatural meddling which will call forth the revenge of the supernatural in its most primitive and devastating form – in the lifeless barrenness, the fruitless artifice ushered in by the uncanny, that strange but familiar place where only death is at home.

PART II

The Romantic heritage and Modernist fiction

CHAPTER 4

Aesthetic redemption: the thyrsus in Nietzsche, Baudelaire, and Wagner

I POETRY AND IMAGINATIVE SYMPATHY

In the first three chapters of this book, I have presented the interplay of the ethical and the aesthetic as a series of envelopments and overlappings whereby now the one field, now the other achieves (temporary) dominance. In the Kantian system, although the aesthetic occupies its own distinct space as the self-standing Third Critique, the ethical inhabits it and haunts it, most obviously in the theory of the sublime. And even within the austere pages of the Second Critique, where the ethical holds sway, the aesthetic emerges at the moment at which Kant pauses to contemplate the structural beauty of his conceptual edifice. In Kierkegaard's *Either/Or*, the ethical and the aesthetic are set up as equally powerful alternative domains: it is up to us as readers to make the difficult, perhaps impossible decision, as to which of these two territories should engage our final assent or adhesion. Reading through E. T. A. Hoffmann into the depths of the Oedipus myth, Freud, like Kierkegaard, finds the ethical located in nature and in the domestic sphere, whereas the aesthetic erupts in the uncanny and sterile manipulations of *techné*. In each of these cases, the aesthetic appears as that subterranean and potentially diabolical force which constitutes a danger for the ethical; on this view, the ethical expresses itself in lawful, Mosaic injunctions and acts as a control mechanism working against the disruptions of the aesthetic.

The pattern I am describing will emerge, in various forms, throughout this book, and constitutes one of the principal *leitmotive* of my textual analyses. Yet it would be a sin against the complexity of intellectual history to assert that the relations of the ethical to the aesthetic can be reduced to the alternating rhythms I have just evoked, and that the two domains necessarily coexist agonistically, in a never-ending movement of narrative framings and unframings. There are moments in which either the ethical or the aesthetic is foregrounded with such power that the other territory tends to disappear altogether, or to be in some way subsumed. The most obvious example of this is when all pretense to the achievement of artistic form is cancelled by a heavy-handed didactic or moral message, as in the oxymoronic "Nazi art" of Hitler's period, or in Soviet Realism. When the boot of moral violence tramples the aesthetic and kills it, it is not difficult, for readers unblinded by the political system that produces such kitsch, to recognize and lament the demise of art as such. The opposite situation – in which the territory of the aesthetic is said to constitute, in and of itself, a more fundamental morality than the morality of laws and commandments – is more interesting, more complex, and worthy of critical scrutiny. This is precisely what occurs during the maturation of Romanticism, when the theme of the poetic imagination takes center-stage in the reflections of that period's theoretically inclined writers.

Conceived as a rejoinder to Thomas Love Peacock's *The Four Ages of Poetry* in 1821, but not published until 1839, Shelley's *A Defence of Poetry* presents the creative imagination as a form of sympathy that binds the poet to his fellow humans, to nature, and to his social environment, and in so doing enriches him morally. Shelley asserts that this form of enrichment *precedes* the codification of ethical precepts and laws and is more fundamental to the moral improvement of the individual than are these retroactively imposed rigid codes. On this view, Kant would doubtless appear as a Prussian schoolmaster, as formidable in his cold rationality as the frosty compass-wielding Urizen in Blake's imagined universe. This is Shelley's conception of the primordially constituted ethical dimension of the aesthetic:

> The whole objection, however, of the immorality of poetry rests upon a misconception of the manner in which poetry acts to produce the moral improvement of man. Ethical science arranges the elements which poetry has created, and propounds schemes and proposes examples of civil and domestic life; nor is it for want of admirable doctrines that men hate, and despise, and censure, and deceive, and subjugate one another. But Poetry acts in another and diviner manner. It awakens and enlarges the mind itself by rendering the receptacle of a thousand unapprehended combinations of thought. Poetry lifts the veil from the hidden beauty of the world ... The great secret of morals is love; or a going out of our own nature, and an identification of ourselves with the beautiful which exists in thought, action, or person, not our own. A man, to be greatly good, must imagine intensely and comprehensively; he must put himself in the place of another and of many others; the pains and pleasures of his species must become his own. The great instrument of moral good is the imagination.[1]

The awakening of the mind by poetry thus stands at the beginning of the moral education of the human being: the rationally organized laws and negative commandments come afterward, and can be seen as a perversion of the sympathy one human feels for another through the power of poetic discourse. Implicit in Shelley's argument is a notion that will be developed at some length in the works of Nietzsche and Heidegger: namely, that the *language of poetry* is ontologically prior to the language of concepts – which is to say, the language of philosophy in its classical idiom. As we shall see later in this chapter, in *The Birth of Tragedy* (1872) Nietzsche attempts to uncover the original *Bildersprache* that tells the story of Apollo and Dionysos before Socratic philosophy repressed and covered over this metaphorically elaborated story with a conceptual veneer. In the same way, in his "Letter on Humanism" (1947), Heidegger reflects on the necessity of "a thinking more rigorous than the conceptual" (235) that would open up to the individual the hermeneutical possibility of questioning the truth of Being, of initiating a fundamental inquiry in a language that would be uncontaminated by the scholastic accretions of philosophical discourse in its academic-disciplinary form. What is being postulated, in both cases, is a return to the intimacy and immediacy of poetic discourse (in Shelley's terms: the particular discourse born of the sympathetic imagination), to the strange-but-familiar place that resides prior to the elaboration of ethics as a philosophical system and prior to the theoretical reduction of the aesthetic to the benign stasis of the disinterested gaze.

When Shelley states that the poet "must put himself in the place of another and of many others," he is not just enunciating an ethical theory based upon sympathy, but is, in fact, delineating one of the primary ways in which Romantic intertextuality functions. The era of Romanticism sees a multiplication of homages, dedicatory prefaces, and artistic salutes directed from one maker of texts to another, along with a remarkable development of collaborative writing and composing.[2] Throughout the nineteenth century writers, painters, and musicians allow themselves to be inhabited or haunted by their immediate predecessors and contemporaries; the notion of sympathy is not some vague formula, but amounts to the very *état d'esprit* that presides over artistic creation as such. Yet in the very act of paying homage, at the very moment in which one author points outside him- or herself toward the human community, one finds also a critical reflection on what *separates* the second creator of texts from the first. In other words, in Romanticism there is also a thorough development of what we now call literary *theory*. The tension between poetic sympathy and critical distance can be expressed, with some economy, by the juxtaposition of statements made by an early Romantic and a late Romantic writer, each of whom created works of fiction and also wrote important theoretical essays: Friedrich Schlegel and Charles Baudelaire. In the passages that follow, both writers seek to describe what the act of criticism should be, and both see criticism as occupying an important position within literature. There is, however, a subtle difference in emphasis and in tone in the two texts. Schlegel, like Shelley, underlines the necessary sense of sympathetic identification between the latecomer and the poet he seeks to understand. Baudelaire, on the other hand, asserts that the act of criticism originates in a rupture or "crisis," in a moment of disassociation of the interpretive reader from the creative writer he scrutinizes. Schlegel writes, in 1797:

> Poetry can be criticized only through poetry. A critique which itself is not a work of art, either in content as representation of the necessary impression in the process of creation, or through its beautiful form and in the liberal tone in the spirit of the old Roman satire, has no right of citizenship in the realm of art.[3]

And this is Baudelaire in 1861:

> It would be a novel event in the history of the arts if a critic should become a poet, a reversal of all psychological laws, a monstrosity; on the contrary, all great poets become naturally, inevitably critics. I pity those poets who are guided only by instinct; I believe them to be incomplete. In the spiritual life of the former [great poets] a crisis invariably occurs, in which they desire to reason about their art, to discover the obscure laws by means of which they have created, and to draw from this study a series of precepts whose divine goal would be infallibility in poetic production. It would be prodigious for a critic to become a poet, and it is impossible for a poet not to contain within himself a critic.[4]

In this chapter, I shall turn my attention toward the period of late Romanticism, when the Wagnerian *Gesamtkunstwerk* dominated continental Europe not only in concert halls, but also in theoretical discussions about the interrelations of the arts. I shall examine selected writings of Nietzsche and Baudelaire that originated in an act of sympathetic literary homage – Nietzsche toward Wagner, and Baudelaire ostensibly toward Liszt, though on a deeper level also toward Wagner. At the center of my analysis will be Wagner and Liszt as human figures toward which the texts of Nietzsche and Baudelaire direct their intentional energy.[5] At the same time, however, I shall be concerned with the poetic figure of the *thyrsus*, which is evoked by Nietzsche, Baudelaire, and Wagner at crucial points of articulation in their respective works. The thyrsus – a staff tipped with a pine cone and entwined with ivy or vine leaves – is the emblem of Dionysos. The thyrsus conjures poetry in an act of the sympathetic imagination, but it also engenders theoretical discourse on and in poetry. It is to this double function of the thyrsus, and to a further investigation of the sense of theory as it emerges from within poetic discourse, that this chapter will be devoted.

The thyrsus, which Dionysos agitated so that his followers might congregate around him orgiastically, becomes an emblem of Romantic discourse (both philosophical and literary) and is used to bring together a community of like-minded aesthetically inclined acolytes. The thyrsus figures the notion of *aesthetic redemption*. The territory of the aesthetic is no longer the Kantian domain of contemplation at a distance, but rather a field of passionate encounter between work and reader, or music and performer, in which art promises nothing less than release from phenomenal reality and earthly travail.

II NIETZSCHE'S VARIATIONS ON THE THEME OF REDEMPTION

Nietzsche's first book, *The Birth of Tragedy*, is an overt act of homage to the genius of Richard Wagner. The complex dialectical play of the Apollonian and Dionysian forces which Nietzsche sees as engendering Attic tragedy is directed teleologically toward the figure of Wagner, who, in his *Gesamtkunstwerk*, has synthesized these forces and afforded them a "rebirth" in the fusion of the visual and musical arts. Nietzsche's labyrinthine demonstration, which borrows a great deal of its conceptual ammunition from the philosophy of Schopenhauer, is, however, framed by a short introductory essay written in 1886 and entitled "Versuch einer Selbstkritik" ["A Critical Backward Glance"]. Here, Nietzsche concludes that his youthful enthusiasm for Wagner was misdirected, that the music of Wagner is nothing but German Romanticism (both of these words possess uniquely negative connotations in the vocabulary of the late Nietzsche), and that the question of how modern music might become truly Dionysian remains unresolved.[6] The reader of *The Birth of Tragedy* is in a somewhat unenviable position from the outset, in that he or she is about to embark upon a dizzying dialectical journey with the foreknowledge that this journey's goal is false, that the god adored in 1872 has become (to use good Nietzschean terminology) a mere idol in 1886.

Nietzsche's rejection of Wagner is not the simple result of a change in musical taste (the emphatic praise of Bizet's *Carmen* in the opening lines of

The Case of Wagner [1888], for example, is to be taken with several grains of salt).[7] I shall argue that Nietzsche's turn away from Wagner, which Heidegger, in 1938, called "the necessary turning point of our history,"[8] was, in fact, a rejection of synthesizing dialectical reasoning as such. What is "wrong" in *The Birth of Tragedy* is not just that the admiring Nietzsche fell into the trap of idolizing a master of masks and theatrical deception whose narrow Germanness and strident anti-Semitism he grew to detest, but that the young philosopher's own mode of argumentation was in itself, and from the beginning, fundamentally flawed. Nietzsche's critical backward glance allows him to see that, despite his polemic against Socrates in his early work, he was himself proceeding far too Socratically – that is, dialectically. He was attacking the enemy using the enemy's arms, and he was succumbing to the great temptation of all dialecticians: that of reconciling opposites in a final, uplifting synthetic unity.

Like Nietzsche, I have framed my discussion with a proleptic indication of the direction in which my own argument is to proceed. However, before moving too far ahead in the direction of Nietzsche's rejection of Wagner, I propose to concentrate my attention on two passages from *The Birth of Tragedy* that are constructed on the kind of reasoning that Nietzsche was later to find suspect: the very first paragraph of the work, in which the Apollonian–Dionysian duality is introduced, and the conclusion of section 20, which relates the triumph of the Dionysian spirit while invoking the figure of the thyrsus. Let us begin with the beginning, with the paragraph that foreshadows and encapsulates the remainder of the treatise:

Much will have been gained for esthetics once we have succeeded in apprehending directly – rather than merely *ascertaining* [*wenn wir nicht nur zur logischen Einsicht, sondern zur unmittelbaren Sicherheit der Anschauung gekommen sind*] – that art owes its continuous evolution to the Apollonian–Dionysiac duality, even as the propagation of the species depends on the duality of the sexes, their constant conflicts and periodic acts of reconciliation [*Versöhnung*]. I have borrowed my adjectives from the Greeks, who developed their mystical doctrines of art through plausible *embodiments* [*Gestalten ihrer Götterwelt*], not through purely conceptual means [*in Begriffen*]. It is by those two art-sponsoring deities, Apollo and Dionysos, that we are made to recognize the tremendous split, as regards both origins and objectives, between the plastic, Apollonian arts [*zwischen der Kunst des Bildners, der apollinischen*] and the non-visual art of music inspired by Dionysos [*und der unbildlichen Kunst der Musik, als der des Dionysus*]. The two creative tendencies [*Triebe*] developed alongside one another, usually in fierce opposition [*im offnen Zwiespalt*], each by its taunts forcing the other to more energetic production [*zu immer neuen kräftigeren Geburten reizend*], both perpetuating in a discordant concord that agon which the term *art* but feebly denominates: until at last, by the thaumaturgy of an Hellenic act of will [*durch einen metaphysischen Wunderakt des hellenischen "Willens"*], the pair accepted the yoke of marriage and, in this condition [*in dieser Paarung*], begot Attic tragedy, which exhibits the salient features of both parents [*das ebenso dionysische als apollinische Kunstwerk der attischen Tragödie erzeugen*]. (*BT* 19; *GT* 25–26) [9]

The primary tension (in Nietzschean terms: *Zwiespalt*) that inhabits *The Birth of Tragedy* emerges clearly in this first paragraph. The problem is that Nietzsche wishes not to conduct a logical argument in the usual style of classical philosophy (with concepts, *in Begriffen*), but to arrive at an unmediated certainty, using the "plausible embodiments" he derives from the ancient Greek world – figures of the gods which, in an important sense, antedate concepts as such. According to the Nietzschean view of historical development, before there was dialectics (before the advent of Socratic philosophy, Socratic irony, and the Platonic dialogue) there was mythology; and the central mythic figures that interest him here, Apollo and Dionysos, can be seen to engage in a primary struggle out of which Greek tragedy will arise. In the simplest schematic terms, the progression of the treatise as a whole runs as follows: 1) the world of myth, of Apollo and Dionysos, begets Attic tragedy, notably the dramas of Aeschylus and Sophocles; 2) authentic tragedy degenerates into the merely representational (no longer mythic, no longer religiously profound) theater of Euripides, who has fallen prey to the rational perspective of Socratic philosophy; and 3) the moribund mimetic arts are finally uplifted, *aufgehoben*, by Wagnerian opera, which rediscovers the force and value of myth in its newly created fusion of the arts. This movement is, of course, that of classical dialectics: thesis, antithesis, synthesis, in which the movement (or work, or "strain") of negation – in Hegel's vocabulary, *die Anstrengung des Begriffs* – culminates in a final reconciliation (*Versöhnung*) of contraries at a higher level. Wagner's *Gesamtkunstwerk* recapitulates the values of Greek tragedy and synthesizes them at the advanced level of our modernity (which is, of course, in its most authentic dimension, a rediscovered antiquity).

One sees Nietzsche's problem, which is a consequential one. In the first paragraph of his work he tells his readers that he will be delving into a mythic world, which is, in its essence, pre-logical, pre-philosophical. To describe this world, Nietzsche resorts to metaphor, notably the metaphor of sexual union (propagation, the "pairing" of masculine and feminine principles, the "begetting" of tragedy). But he envelops his metaphorical discourse within the framework of an overarching dialectical scheme.

Apollo and Dionysos, figures of myth and of metaphor, become trapped within philosophy, within the kind of "logical insight" which Nietzsche wished to supersede in an unmediated vision of mythic truth. Apollo and Dionysos, initially *Gestalten* or *Bilder* in the Greek realm of myth, become convenient illustrations, allegorical pseudo-concepts in a rational argument.

Nietzsche's dialectical method is further complicated by the fact that the second, antithetical stage of the process (the degeneration of tragedy into the mere representation of the "life-like," an art of *trompe l'oeil* and of rational clear-sightedness) *resembles*, in a degraded form, the category of the Apollonian. In one of his most cogent juxtapositions of the Apollonian to the Dionysian, Nietzsche makes the following distinction:

> [Apollo and Dionysos] represent to me, most vividly and concretely, two radically dissimilar realms of art. Apollo embodies the transcendent genius of the *principium individuationis*; through him alone is it possible to achieve redemption in illusion [*Erlösung im Scheine*]. The mystical jubilation of Dionysos, on the other hand, breaks the spell of individuation and opens a path to the maternal womb of being [*während unter dem mystischen Jubelruf des Dionysus der Bann der Individuation zersprengt wird und der Weg zu den Müttern des Sein's, zu dem innersten Kern der Dinge offen liegt*]. (*BT* 97; *GT* 103)

What has happened with the advent of Socratic philosophy and Euripidean drama is that the "principle of individuation" which, at the transcendent level of the Apollonian, is said to lead to "redemption in illusion," has been counterfeited and brought down to the level of simple mimesis, to the status of imitative characterization. Socrates becomes an *unheimlich* double of Apollo, and his usurpation of the Apollonian principle of individuation leads to the near-disappearance of Apollo in the middle sections of *The Birth of Tragedy*. Indeed, although Apollo returns in the final paragraphs of the treatise, the moment of greatest rhetorical intensity occurs when Dionysos, by himself, triumphs over Socrates as pseudo-Apollo. This passage, from the conclusion of paragraph 20, is of particular importance to the argument of *The Birth of Tragedy* both in its message and in its emphatic tone:

> Indeed, my friends, believe with me in this Dionysiac life and in the rebirth of tragedy! Socratic man has run his course; crown your heads with ivy, seize the thyrsus [*nehmt den Thyrsusstab zur Hand*] and do not be surprised [*wundert euch nicht*] if tiger and panther lie down and caress your feet! Dare to lead the life of tragic man, and you will be redeemed [*Jetzt wagt es nur, tragische Menschen zu sein: denn ihr sollt erlöst werden*]. It has fallen to your lot to lead the Dionysiac

procession [*dionysischen Festzug*] out of India into Greece. Gird yourselves for a severe conflict, but have faith in the thaumaturgy of your god! [*aber glaubt an die Wunder eures Gottes!*] (*BT* 124; *GT* 132)

In this passage, Nietzsche uses the term "redemption" (*Erlösung*) not in reference to Apollo's "Erlösung im Scheine," but to the ultimate release that can be obtained by the believer in Dionysos, by the practitioner of the tragic life. It is through the defeat of Socrates and his rational philosophy that the rebirth of tragedy can take place; it is through a decisive victory over the father of Western philosophy as "man of theory" (*theoretischer Mensch*) (*BT* 108; *GT* 115) that the procession from east to west, from India into Greece, can begin. This procession is, of course, the *Festzug* of Dionysos, the parade of Maenads congregated around the god of wine and the thyrsus, symbol of Bacchic frenzy.[10]

It is only too easy to imagine the pilgrimage to Bayreuth as a modern-day equivalent of the Dionysian voyage, except that the Londoner or Parisian would be travelling in the wrong direction, from west to east (Nietzsche himself had great difficulty with this voyage, and was unable to "stomach" day after day of Wagner's music[11]). Most importantly for our purposes, according to the universe of *The Birth of Tragedy*, Richard Wagner *is* the new Dionysos leading a cast of pilgrims upward, toward the temple of his "total art." Like Dionysos, Wagner is a god: if one believes in him and his power, one will be redeemed, and this redemption will occur, not as the effect of some ascertainable cause, but as an unforeseeable, marvelous occurrence. It is significant that in section 20 Nietzsche repeats the word *Wunder*, which he had used in the opening paragraph of the treatise. In section 20, tragic man (the man of aesthetic enthusiasm, of *Jubel*) defeats Socratic man through the marvels of Dionysos, whereas in the opening paragraph of the volume, using the Schopenhauerian lexicon, Nietzsche writes that the begetting of Attic tragedy through the "pairing" of Apollo and Dionysos will take place "durch einen metaphysischen *Wunderakt* des hellenischen 'Willens'". Although Apollo is notably absent in section 20, having been replaced by his shadowy double, Socrates, the meaning of *Wunder* is roughly the same in both contexts: the term conveys, in a mythical register, the religious phenomenon of the miraculous, that which transcends the bounds of the rational mind and of sense certainty. One sees, then, that the notions of *Wunder* and *Erlösung* are closely connected in Nietzsche's early vocabulary: they occur as expressions of the tragic and in opposition to mere "logische Einsicht." And the figure that instantiates the marvelous in the early Nietzsche is Wagner, himself the "redeemer" of the German arts.

The transitional period in Nietzsche's relation (or apparent discipleship) to Wagner occurred between 1874 and 1876. As his visits to the Wagner home multiplied, so did his reservations about the master's aesthetic and political views. As Giorgio Colli remarks in his endnotes to the first volume of the *Kritische Studienausgabe*, the fourth *Untimely Meditation*, entitled *Richard Wagner in Bayreuth* (published in 1876 on the occasion of the opening of the Festspielhaus), requires what amounts to a double reading. On the one hand, the published text itself appears to be an unequivocal panegyric; on the other hand, the numerous drafts of the "Meditation" contain clear indications of Nietzsche's growing distaste for a man whom he now considered to be an actor, a hypocrite, a master of masks rather than an authentic redeemer. Colli notes astutely that Nietzsche solved the problem of his ambivalence by citing the writings of Wagner as much as possible, so that, in fact, *Richard Wagner in Bayreuth* is less Nietzsche's praise of his mentor than Wagner's own appreciation of himself.[12]

It is safe to say that the figure of Wagner haunted Nietzsche until the end of his productive career. Indeed, the final year of the philosopher's sanity, 1888, begins and ends with reflections on Wagner: *The Case of Wagner* and *Nietzsche Contra Wagner*. Two other volumes written that year, *Twilight of the Idols* and *The Antichrist*, share the same thematics, the same recurring obsessions that originate in the problems posed by the works and beliefs of the musician who had died five years earlier. On one level, as Walter Kaufmann has observed, these final writings "are sometimes dismissed as mere products of insanity, and they certainly manifest a rapid breakdown of the author's inhibitions."[13] They are polemical pieces, *Streitschriften* in the strongest sense of the word, and their argumentative structures (if one can even use this term) are often based on simple, even crude dichotomies. Thus, in *Nietzsche Contra Wagner*, we have the following:

WAGNER AND WAGNERIAN AESTHETICS (−)	NIETZSCHE (+)
swimming	dancing
chaos	rhythm
decadence, decline	the ascending life

These primary polarities, which simply stage what is negative in Wagner in contradistinction to what is positive in Nietzsche, are then associated with other related opposites, such as:

PASCAL AND FLAUBERT (–)	GOETHE (+)
negators of life	affirmer of life

In this and other similar cases, one senses that Nietzsche has reduced the intellectual universe to a stark contrast between "good" and "bad" works, "good" and "bad" writers – according (unsurprisingly) to how close these works and these writers come to his own conceptions and tastes. At a certain level, then, *Nietzsche Contra Wagner*, which is a compendium of paragraphs lifted and modified from the author's previous works, is properly *unreadable*. It lends itself only to agreement or disagreement, not to the dialogic structure of an active interpretation. It is certainly not a dialectic; it moves disjunctively by the paratactic posing of one thesis after another. And yet there is, at the very end of this hybrid and meandering work, a cryptic epilogue which reintroduces a certain Apollonian dimension, and thereby a certain promise of a final synthesis, beyond the mere juxtapositions of Wagner and Nietzsche, negative and positive, bad and good. In this epilogue the philosopher takes one more "critical backward glance" at his life, and concludes that the pain he has suffered, the sickness (physical and metaphysical) that he has endured, are for a purpose, a higher (or, in his words, *more profound*) purpose. He confesses his *amor fati*, which is his "inmost nature."[14]

What does it signify to submit to one's fate, or rather, to espouse one's fate with joy? It means that, out of the pain, from within suffering, comes a rebirth. But this rebirth has nothing to do with Wagner, with redemption in the Christian sense, or with the reawakening of German culture: it is, rather, the discovery of what Nietzsche calls "a different taste – a *second* taste":

> Out of such abysses [*Abgründen*], also out of the abyss of great suspicion, one returns newborn [*kommt man neugeboren zurück*], having shed one's skin, more ticklish and sarcastic, with a more delicate taste for joy, with a more tender tongue for all good things, with gayer senses, with a second dangerous innocence in joy [*mit einer zweiten gefährlicheren Unschuld in der Freude*], more childlike and yet a hundred times more subtle [*hundert Mal raffinirter*] than one has ever been before . . . How the theatrical scream of passion now hurts our ears, how strange to our taste the whole romantic uproar and tumult of the senses [*der ganze romantische Aufruhr und Sinnen-Wirrwarr*] have become, which the educated rabble loves, and all its aspirations after the elevated, inflated, and exaggerated! [*sammt seinen Aspirationen nach dem Erhabenen, Gehobenen, Verschrobenen*]. No, if we who have recovered still need art, it is another kind of art – a mocking, light, fleeting, divinely

untroubled, divinely artificial light, which, like a pure flame, licks into unclouded skies! [*eine spöttische, leichte, flüchtige, göttlich unbehelligte, göttlich künstliche Kunst, welche wie eine reine Flamme in einen unbewölkten Himmel hineinlodert!*] Above all, an art for artists, *for artists only*! (*Nietzsche Contra Wagner*, 681–682; *Nietzsche contra Wagner*, 79–80)[15]

The newfound innocence to which Nietzsche refers here is not the result of a tripartite dialectical movement culminating in a final moment of sublation. It is a simple two-step scheme, in which initial pain is shed, in a natural, quasi-biological replacing of one "skin" by another. Just as the snake is still the same snake after shedding its skin, in the same way Nietzsche is still Nietzsche, but *more so*: the first part of the passage quoted above abounds in comparatives – "*more* ticklish," "*more* childlike and yet a hundred times *more subtle*," etc. The change is a matter of degree, not a matter of negation or of the overturning of opposites into a higher synthesis. It is because Nietzsche has discovered his "second," more refined taste (*Geschmack* in the physical as well as aesthetic sense) that he is now able to look back at his initial admiration for Wagner and discover in Wagnerianism a "theatrical scream of passion" and mere "romantic uproar." Having shed his first skin, Nietzsche now finds in Wagner a muddled aesthetic of the sublime (Nietzsche uses the Kantian term, *das Erhabene*, in this passage) that confuses the lofty with the hyperbolic, with mere hystrionics. What Nietzsche proposes, in the final words of his counter-statement to Wagnerian aesthetics, is an art for artists only – which is to be taken as an urbane (cosmopolitan or pan-European) art that is perforce *not* for the "people," that does not have the ambition to rekindle something like "essential Germanness" in the audience or public.

The Case of Wagner begins where *Nietzsche Contra Wagner* concluded: with praise for the "pure flame" of a serene, newly conceived Apollonian art, with an evocation of the *limpidezza* of Bizet's musical style (in contradistinction, of course, to the muddiness, the fogginess of Wagner's all-too-German false profundity). Once again, Wagner is targeted: first, for his badly executed aesthetics of the sublime (the sublime being a quintessentially German intoxicant, according to Nietzsche); second, for his theatricality (in this trait he is compared to both Victor Hugo and Franz Liszt, figures to whom we shall return in due course); and third, most emphatically, for his ethics of redemption, which, according to Nietzsche, pervades nearly all of his operatic works. I shall give in to the temptation of quoting an extensive passage on this point, since it is both central to my argument and quite typical of Nietzsche's mordant and somewhat outrageous late style:

The problem of redemption [*Erlösung*] is certainly a venerable problem. There is nothing about which Wagner has thought more deeply than redemption: his opera is the opera of redemption. Somebody or other always wants to be redeemed in his work: sometimes a little male, sometimes a little female – this is *his* problem. – And how richly he varies his leitmotif! What rare, what profound dodges! [*Welche seltenen, welche tiefsinnigen Ausweichungen!*] Who if not Wagner would teach us that innocence prefers to redeem interesting sinners? [*daß die Unschuld mit Vorliebe interessante Sünder erlöst?*] (The case in *Tannhäuser.*) Or that even the Wandering Jew is redeemed, settles down, when he marries? (The case in *The Flying Dutchman.*) Or that old corrupted females prefer to be redeemed by chaste youths? (The case of Kundry [in *Parsifal*].) Or that beautiful maidens like best to be redeemed by a knight who is a Wagnerian? (The case in *Die Meistersinger.*) Or that married women, too, enjoy being redeemed by a knight? (The case of Isolde.) Or that "the old God," after having compromised himself morally in every respect, is finally redeemed by a free spirit and immoralist? (The case in the *Ring.*) Do admire this final profundity above all! [*Bewundern Sie in Sonderheit diesen letzten Tiefsinn!*] Do you understand it? I – beware of understanding it [*Ich – hüte mich, ihn zu verstehn*]. (*The Case of Wagner* 616; *Der Fall Wagner* 11–12)

Although Nietzsche is never more explicit or more ironical in his condemnation of the notion of redemption than in this passage, this condemnation (if Wagnerian terms can be forgiven here) is nothing less than a leitmotiv in all the works he wrote in 1888.[16] In rejecting Wagner, especially the late Christian Wagner, apostle of chastity and obedience, creator of *Parsifal*, Nietzsche also necessarily rejects the dialectical move whereby the human subject as "sinner" is raised up, *aufgehoben*, through the power of redemption. With the deconstruction of the very notion of "sin" and with the overturning of dialectics, it would seem that Nietzsche has prepared the way for a final triumph of *limpidezza*, for a victory of "lightness of being" over the tragic view per se. However (and herein lies the complexity of Nietzsche's late thought), the figure of Dionysos, the procession of the Maenads around the thyrsus, which had been associated with the living of the tragic life, do not disappear entirely from view, but re-emerge, metamorphosed into a human figure – that of Goethe. Dionysos is no longer the symbol of tragedy, but of what Nietzsche calls "totality" – a notion that deserves some scrutiny. The following lines come from paragraph 49 of *Twilight of the*

Idols (in German, *Götzendämmerung*, a rather nasty play on the Wagnerian *Götterdämmerung*):

Goethe – not a German event, but a European one: a magnificent attempt to overcome the eighteenth century by a return to nature, by an *ascent* to the naturalness of the Renaissance [*durch ein Hinaufkommen zur Natürlichkeit der Renaissance*] – a kind of self-overcoming [*eine Art Selbstüberwindung*] on the part of that century. He bore its strongest instincts within himself . . . What he wanted was *totality* [*Totalität*]; he fought the mutual extraneousness of reason, senses, feeling, and will (preached with the most abhorrent scholasticism by *Kant*, the antipode of Goethe); he disciplined himself to wholeness, he *created* himself [*er disciplinirte sich zur Ganzheit, er schuf sich*] . . . Such a spirit who has *become free* stands amid the cosmos with a joyous and trusting fatalism, in the *faith* that only the particular is loathsome, and that all is redeemed and affirmed in the whole – *he does not negate any more* [*Ein solcher freigewordner Geist steht mit einem freudigen und vertrauenden Fatalismus mitten im All, im Glauben, daß nur das Einzelne verwerflich ist, daß im Ganzen sich alles erlöst und bejaht* – er verneint nicht mehr]. Such a faith, however, is the highest of all possible faiths: I have baptized it with the name of *Dionysus*. (*Twilight of the Idols*, 553–54; *Götzendämmerung*, 188–89).

It would be more correct to say that the same word – Dionysos – has been used in two different baptisms and has represented, has figured, two different "faiths." In the first instance, in *The Birth of Tragedy*, Dionysos was the mythic figuration, the *Bild* or *Gestalt* of the contemporary "god" Richard Wagner evolving in the dialectical universe of the tragic. In the second instance, in the late works after the turn away from Wagner and dialectics, Goethe "becomes" Dionysos, takes on the features of the Greek god, instantiates him, not in an imagined return to antiquity, but in a reviving of Renaissance values. What has happened in the turn from Wagner, in the Nietzschean *Kehre*, is that the highest value is no longer that of the aesthetic in its proximity to local (i.e., German) political concerns, but rather a transnational valuation of "life" as movement of natural ascension [*Hinaufkommen zur Natürlichkeit*]. Kant, who had been cited with deference in *The Birth of Tragedy*, now becomes, to use Nietzschean terms, the *antipode* to Goethe: Kant, the master analyst, the philosopher who separated and defined the faculties, who particularized and pulled apart the domains of the epistemological, the ethical and the aesthetic, thereby destroyed the essence of life, which is totality. In the final form of his thought, Nietzsche replaces the process of negation with its opposite, affirmation, and reintroduces the notion of redemption into a non-dialectical framework, into the context of *amor fati*, of adherence to one's destiny and espousal of life in its alternations of bitterness and joy. In the end, Nietzsche alternatively offers the *limpidezza* of Apollonian serenity and newfound innocence, and the "fatalistic" totality of Dionysian freedom: the two ancient Greek figures appear in metonymic succession, not in the interplay of negation and supersession.

Despite the considerable differences between the author of *The Birth of Tragedy* and the late Nietzsche, there is one constant feature (one would be tempted to say, using a musical metaphor, a *Grundton*) that subtends the Nietzschean oeuvre from beginning to end: the rejection of rational or theoretical man, whether it be the Socrates of *The Birth of Tragedy* or the Kant of *Twilight of the Idols*. Just as the rebirth of tragedy through Wagner is predicated on a victory over Socratic philosophy, in the same way Goethe as modern Dionysos, as figure of totality, as genius, stands over Kant and the "scholastic" dissection of the particular. The questions that remain, however, are the following: in attacking Kant's supposed scholasticism in the name of totality, does not Nietzsche use Kant's own definition of genius to depict and define that totality? While he attacks Wagner's Romanticism, does not Nietzsche represent Goethe's genius *in Romantic terms*? Is there something more to be said about theory itself? Might it be possible to refine on Nietzsche's conception of the theoretical as merely the opposite of "Goethean" creativity? It is to these questions that I turn now, as I move to a discussion of Baudelaire's late poetic praxis.

III BAUDELAIRE'S "LE THYRSE": THE DOUBLE SENSE OF THEORY

I have suggested that an understanding of the fundamental shifts between the styles of the early Nietzsche and the late Nietzsche – the passage through and beyond dialectics – is best achieved by an examination of how the figure of Richard Wagner metamorphoses between *The Birth of Tragedy* and *The Case of Wagner*. Wagner is initially admired because his musical drama lends itself to a dialectical overcoming, a final merging of antithetical forces that remains unquestioned by Nietzsche in 1872. Wagner is later rejected because Nietzsche associates the seductions of Wagner the histrion with the seductions of reconciliation and redemption, those enslaving false rewards imposed on the freedom of man by the "priestly caste" and the Christian religion as such. Of primary interest to my argument is the fact that Nietzsche's evolution as thinker and writer originates with the *turn toward Wagner*, and ends with the *turn away from Wagner*; without Wagner as a figure toward whom one turns, there would be no evolution at all, no writing. Nietzsche's writing, in its essence, is to be understood as a tropic or tropological movement, a turning-toward which turns into its opposite.

In the case of Charles Baudelaire, whose poetic praxis is often considered to inaugurate European literary modernity, I would like to suggest that his later poetry (the "Tableaux parisiens" in *Les Fleurs du Mal* and the *Petits Poèmes en prose/Le Spleen de Paris*), which is, in many cases, self-reflective (poetry about poetry, exercises in allegorical mirroring, in *mise-en-abyme*[17]), is also based upon a turning-toward, a properly intentional movement whereby the Baudelairian text constructs itself in the very process of its referring to an outside figure, either a person or a symbolic representation. Thus, one of the most important and complex poems of the "Tableaux parisiens" series, "Le Cygne," points to Victor Hugo in exile: this pointing, and the political implications of a dedication to the exiled Hugo in 1859, situate the poem, establish its horizon of readability.[18] In the same way, I shall argue that the prose poem "Le Thyrse" must be read in and through its dedication to Franz Liszt. The thyrsus, itself at one level a figuration of poetry as such,[19] also addresses itself to the figure of Liszt. Just as, in an important sense, Goethe is Dionysos for Nietzsche, for Baudelaire Liszt is associated with the emblem of Dionysos, the thyrsus. In both cases, what is being represented is genius, but how genius is defined and put into play differs from Nietzsche to Baudelaire; it is the nature of this difference (as well as the relation of genius to theory) that stands at the center of my reading of the poem.

Much has been made in the critical literature of the dedicatory letter to the editor of *La Presse*, Arsène Houssaye, which frames *Les Petits Poèmes en prose*. It is accepted practice to place this witty and double-edged letter at the very beginning of the volume, doubtless because it contains what seems to be a theoretical introduction to the works themselves, formulated in unforgettable metaphorical terms. The series of poems is compared to a serpent possessing "neither head nor tail" and that can be cut up at will: "Remove one vertebra, and the two pieces of that tortuous fantasy will reunite without difficulty."[20] The problem with this playful comparison is that too many critics have taken it too literally: the poems are most often read without respect for their narrative ordering;[21] and even within a particular poem, it would seem that Baudelaire's letter to Houssaye has been used to dispense critics from following the movement of the text, from adhering to its structural constraints.

I shall be suggesting an interpretation of "Le Thyrse" that is based upon the sequentiality of the poem, its rhythm, its hesitations and interruptions as it progresses from the initial question, "What is a thyrsus?" to the final praise of Liszt's genius. The poem as it appears on the printed page is divided into two paragraphs of unequal length: the first one, fairly long, is devoted to a complex series of definitions and redefinitions of the thyrsus, while the second, much shorter, is an effusive panegyric to Liszt. The central interpretive problem posed by the poem is the nature of the relation between the two paragraphs – between a symbolic figure, the thyrsus, and a human figure evoked for his representative qualities, Franz Liszt. Because my argument is based upon a detailed reading of the poem, I shall quote the poem in its entirety, first in French, then in Edward Kaplan's English translation.[22] So that the reader of this chapter can anticipate the direction in which my interpretation will proceed, I have included parenthetically within the poem numbers (1 through 6) which indicate where I find that the text begins to move in a new direction. I divide the first paragraph into five parts, and consider that the final paragraph constitutes part six:

LE THYRSE

A Franz Liszt

(1) Qu'est-ce qu'un thyrse? Selon le sens moral et poétique, c'est un emblème sacerdotal dans la main des prêtres et des prêtresses célébrant la divinité dont ils sont les interprètes et les serviteurs. Mais physiquement ce n'est qu'un bâton, un pur bâton, perche à houblon, tuteur de vigne, sec, dur et droit. (2) Autour de ce bâton, dans des méandres capricieux, se jouent et folâtrent des tiges et des fleurs, celles-ci sinueuses et fuyardes, celles-là penchées comme des cloches ou des coupes renversées. Et une gloire étonnante jaillit de cette complexité de lignes et de couleurs, tendres ou éclatantes. Ne dirait-on pas que la ligne courbe et la spirale font leur cour à la ligne droite et dansent autour dans une muette adoration? Ne dirait-on pas que toutes ces corolles délicates, tous ces calices, explosions de senteurs et de couleurs, exécutent un mystique fandango autour du bâton hiératique? (3) Et quel est, cependant, le mortel imprudent qui osera décider si les fleurs et les pampres ont été faits pour le bâton, ou si le bâton n'est que le prétexte pour montrer la beauté des pampres et des fleurs? (4) Le thyrse est la représentation de votre étonnante dualité, maître puissant et vénéré, cher Bacchant de la Beauté mystérieuse et passionnée. Jamais nymphe exaspérée par l'invincible Bacchus ne secoua son thyrse sur les têtes de ses compagnes affolées avec autant d'énergie et de caprice que vous agitez votre génie sur les coeurs de vos frères. – Le bâton, c'est votre volonté, droite, ferme et inébranlable; les fleurs, c'est la promenade de votre fantaisie autour de votre volonté; c'est l'élément féminin exécutant autour du mâle ses prestigieuses pirouettes. (5) Ligne droite et ligne arabesque, intention et expression, roideur de la volonté, sinuosité du

verbe, unité du but, variété des moyens, amalgame tout-puissant et indivisible du génie, quel analyste aura le détestable courage de vous diviser et de vous séparer?

(6) Cher Liszt, à travers les brumes, par-delà les fleuves, par-dessus les villes où les pianos chantent votre gloire, où l'imprimerie traduit votre sagesse, en quelque lieu que vous soyez, dans les splendeurs de la ville éternelle ou dans les brumes des pays rêveurs que console Cambrinus, improvisant des chants de délectation ou d'ineffable douleur, ou confiant au papier vos méditations abstruses, chantre de la Volupté et de l'Angoisse éternelles, philosophe, poète et artiste, je vous salue en l'immortalité!

THE THYRSUS

To Franz Liszt

(1) What is a thyrsus? According to its social and poetic meaning, it is a sacerdotal emblem to be held by priests and priestesses celebrating the divinity whose interpreters and servants they are. But physically it is only a staff, a mere staff, a vine pole for hops, a vine support, dry, hard, and straight. (2) Around that staff, in capricious meanderings, stems and flowers play and frolic, some sinuous and elusive, others tilted like bells or overturned cups. And an astonishing glory bursts from that complexity of lines and colors, tender or dazzling. Doesn't it seem that the curved and spiral lines are courting the straight line and dance around it in mute adoration? Doesn't it seem that all those delicate corollas, all those calices, explosions of odors and colors, are executing a mystical fandango around the hieratic staff? (3) And yet what foolhardy mortal would dare decide if the flowers and vines were formed for the staff, or if the staff is but the pretext for highlighting the beauty of the vines and flowers?

(4)[23] The thyrsus is the representation of your astonishing duality, powerful and venerable master, dear Bacchant of mysterious and impassioned Beauty. Never did a nymph frenzied by the invincible Bacchus shake her thyrsus over the heads of her crazed companions with as much power and caprice as you wave your genius over your brothers' hearts.

The staff, it is your will, straight, firm, and unshakable; the flowers, the rambling of your fancy around your will: the feminine element executing around the male its prodigious pirouettes. (5) Straight line and arabesque line, intention and expression, tautness of the will, sinuosity of the word, unity of goal, variety of means, all-powerful and indivisible amalgam of genius, what analyst would have the hateful courage to divide and to separate you?

(6) Dear Liszt, through the mists, beyond the rivers, above the cities where pianos celebrate your fame, where printing presses translate your wisdom, in whatever place you may be, in the eternal city's splendors or the mists of the dreamy lands consoled by Gambrinus, improvising songs of delight or of ineffable sorrow, or confiding your abstruse meditations to writing, singer of

Voluptuous Pleasure and Anguish eternal, philosopher, poet and artist, I honor you in immortality!

Before suggesting an overall interpretation of this playful and complex poem, I would like to follow it in its movement, step by step, according to the six "vertebrae" of its serpentine sinuosity:

(1) Contrast between the dictionary definition of the thyrsus and its physical appearance

In his own attempt to describe the thyrsus, the poet at first refuses to accept the *given definition* – that is, what the thyrsus has come to mean to humankind through the centuries. He gives us a first "moral and poetic" meaning of the object, but then calls it into question, in his insistence that we consider the object's materiality. We move then in the opposite direction of Baudelaire's early poetics (the ascending passage from the material to the spiritual that characterized the lyrical mode of *correspondances*): in "Le Thyrse," we pass from the spiritual down to the material. The description offered in the poem's third line is simple and apparently univocal: the thyrsus is, materially, a stick and only a stick, dry, hard, and straight. There is, however, an interesting subtle suggestion of duality that appears alongside this simplicity: the thyrsus can be either a "perche à houblon" or "tuteur de vigne." This difference does not appear significant at first, but once we have read the poem in its entirety, we see that one of its organizing polarities is that of Germania versus Romania, beer versus wine (in (6) Liszt is evoked both as Roman pilgrim and citizen of the climes "consoled" by the inventer of beer, Gambrinus). Thus, from the beginning, *sotto voce*, that which is straight and uncomplicated already participates in a world of polar opposites.

(2) Poetic interruption on the possible meanings (connotations) of the thyrsus's dual construction

Here we have what might be called an explosion of polarities in freeplay, with the feminized elements (flowers, vines) "dancing" around the straight line of the stick. The dance itself has both religious and erotic elements: the flowers move seductively around the stick, but they do so in "mute adoration." Although duality is almost uniquely emphasized here, the poet does affirm that the dance of the meandering flowers around the straight stick produces "*an* astonishing glory" (une *gloire étonnante*). Within the "complexity" of the flowery figuration bursts forth (*jaillit*, a verb with strong sexual connotations, here suggesting ejaculation) a singular energetic and creative force. There is, within this sentence, the promise (but here, only a promise) of a possible combining of the contraries into some final unity.

(3) First theoretical interruption

Here, in an ironical "aside," the poet alludes to the philosopher or literary critic of analytic persuasion (whom Baudelaire will derisively call, in his own critical essays, a *professeur-juré d'esthétique*, and whom Nietzsche designates by the emblematic names of "Socrates" or "Kant"), that unfortunate "man of theory" who would be *imprudent* enough to *decide* whether the flowers were made for the stick or vice-versa. It would seem that the poet is attacking the act of critical dissection and implying that the play of polarities that constitutes the poem should be left untouched, unanalyzed. It is important to note here that the critic is referred to as a "*mortel* imprudent," whereas in (6), in the closing line of the poem, the poet salutes Liszt "*en l'immortalité*" – something to which we shall return in a moment.

(4) The poet's definition of the thyrsus: the center of the poem

Here the poet provides us with a first synthesis of the elements he had introduced in the previous sections, lifting his description to a higher level of abstraction – words like "représentation," "dualité," "fantaisie," and "volonté" replace the metaphorical language of the text's first half. It is clear that the poet's own definition of the thyrsus is, at one level, merely a restatement of the conventional definition in (1), in that it emphasizes the priestly function of the symbolic object and renders explicit its Bacchic origins. But there is also an important shift. To use Baudelairian terminology, the poet "peoples his solitude" by introducing an interlocutor: the thyrsus is not simply the representation of an abstract duality, but of the duality possessed by a figure, a *master figure*, who, we learn in (6), is Franz Liszt. All the metaphorical elements in (2), notably the central comparison between floral filigree and straight stick, now point to their transcendental signified: the *genius* of Liszt. The stick is not merely a stick, a material object; it is now lifted up to the spiritual level and given the symbolic meaning of "votre volonté, droite, ferme et inébranlable." In the same way, the flowers are not merely evanescent decoration, they are "la promenade de votre fantaisie autour de votre volonté." All elements have been raised up to symbolic abstraction, and they all refer to the focal point of Liszt's genius.

One would be tempted to say that, like Goethe for Nietzsche, Liszt *is* Dionysos for Baudelaire, and that the genius of Liszt, like that of Goethe, is characterized by totality, by a subsuming of all particulars within its significant unity. But if one reads carefully the second sentence of (4), one notes that the comparison goes as follows: Liszt is not being compared directly to Dionysos, but rather to the nymph "frenzied [*exaspérée*, another term with strong sexual connotations in French] by the invincible Bacchus." Liszt's genius is compared to the thyrsus; his genius is "waved" over the "hearts" of his brothers in the same way that the nymph shakes the thyrsus over her sister Maenads. But if the comparison is to hold, if the analogy is to function fully, Liszt must himself be "frenzied" by some master-figure like Dionysos; his genius is not in itself a totality, but the emblem of a greater force that traverses him. It may be that this force is that of Dionysos, but Liszt is, after all, a figure of Baudelairian modernity. Could it be that his genius is "exasperated" by another figure, one that participates in that modernity? This is another point to which we must return.

(5) Second theoretical interruption

Here the poet repeats the idea expressed in (3) using the same form of rhetorical question. Just as previously he had asked "what imprudent mortel" would dare decide whether the flowers were made for the stick or vice-versa, in the same way now he asks "what analyst would have the hateful courage to divide and to separate" the masculine and feminine elements in their oppositional freeplay. Each of the binary opposites – arabesque line and straight line, intention and expression, etc. – would appear to melt into the "*amalgame* tout-puissant et indivisible du génie." One should be careful with the term "amalgame," however. Whereas in English "amalgam" is generally taken to mean a "mixture of different elements" without there being a negative connotation attached to the notion of "mixture," in French the figurative sense of the word is "mélange d'éléments différents qui ne s'accordent guère."[24] Thus, the question with which we are left as we move from the first to the second paragraph of the poem is: what is the nature of the unity or totality to which the thyrsus in its duality corresponds? Is there a unity beyond frenzy, beyond metaphorical chaos, which offers more than a mixture of discordant elements – a crucial question in a text which represents the genius of a musician.

(6) Second paragraph: a salute to Liszt as musician and writer

The poem concludes in a lyrical flight (*une envolée lyrique*) – and the term "flight" needs to be taken in a near-literal sense: we as readers are invited to hover over the cities where pianos play Liszt's works, where printing-presses turn out his prose; we are alternately in Rome and in Germanic regions, in a vertiginous atmosphere calling to mind the paintings of Marc Chagall. Once again, the play of dualities, of polar opposites, builds the entirety of the poetic structure: piano versus printing-press (music versus writing); Rome versus the "pays rêveurs que console Cambrinus"; songs of delight on the one hand, of sorrow on the other; voluptuous writings on the one hand, anguished writings on the other. The only element that introduces a slight change in this otherwise monotonous series of dualities is the triadic characterization of Liszt as "philosopher, poet and artist."

The second paragraph is one long sentence (one remarkably flexible "serpent") beginning with "Cher Liszt" and ending with the exalted words "je vous salue en l'immortalité!" The play of polarities occupies the long central section of the sentence, and is subsumed by the warm, even affectionate address to Liszt. The dualities form themselves within a properly dialogic structure. The poem has moved, gradually, from a series of definitions and rhetorical interruptions to a profound sense of identification between the poet and the subject of his praise. What unifies the poem appears to be, on the one hand, the genius of Liszt, and on the other, the act of dialogue itself, in which both the interlocutor and the poet receive the promise of "immortality" – the promise of the duration of their respective works of art. The appearance of a triumphant *Aufhebung* could not be clearer or more seductive than in this final paragraph, in which the two artists, addressor and addressee, rise "above death."

If one were to remain within the confines of "Le Thyrse" as individual text, this conclusion would seem to impose itself as logical, irrefutable. However, it happens that "Le Thyrse" is also an act of citation. The poem originates in an earlier work of Baudelaire we encountered briefly at the beginning of this chapter, entitled "Richard Wagner et *Tannhäuser* à Paris." To be precise, it originates in a paragraph Baudelaire quotes in that article from Liszt's book on Wagner, *Lohengrin et Tannhäuser de Richard Wagner* (1851). At a critical juncture of his essay, when Baudelaire wishes to characterize the Wagnerian leitmotiv, he borrows from the language of Liszt, prefacing the quotation itself by the following remarks: "Here I humbly allow Liszt to speak [*Ici je laisse humblement la parole à Liszt*], whose book *Lohengrin and Tannhäuser* I take this occasion to recommend to all admirers of profound and refined art. Despite his rather bizarre language, a kind of idiom composed of fragments of several languages [*espèce d'idiome composé d'extraits de plusieurs langues*], he manages to translate with infinite charm the rhetoric of the master [Wagner]" (801; my translation). Aside from the interesting slight difference in tone between the "méditations abstruses" of "Le Thyrse" and the "langue un peu bizarre qu'il affecte" of "Richard Wagner et *Tannhäuser*" (in which one sees that Baudelaire may have had to force his admiration for Liszt as writer somewhat in composing the prose poem), it is important to note that the "espèce d'idiome composé d'extraits de plusieurs langues" is an excellent definition of *amalgame* in the French sense of that word. Although it is tempting to see in Liszt's genius as characterized in the poem the force permitting a final reconciliation of opposites in eternity, in the prose piece we find that Liszt combines *bizarrely* Romance and Germanic traits within the discordance of his style. Beer and wine do not "marry" well.

Even more striking is the fact that Baudelaire seems to have borrowed from Liszt's vocabulary in *Lohengrin et Tannhäuser de Richard Wagner* for the creation of "Le Thyrse" as a play of straight and meandering forces. In the passage quoted by Baudelaire, Liszt writes that Wagner, "by means of several principal phrases, has tied a melodic knot which constitutes the drama as a whole. The folds (*replis*) made by these phrases, in binding and intertwining themselves around the poem's words [*en se liant et s'entrelaçant autour des paroles du poème*], provoke a stirring effect in the audience." And later, in the same vein: "There are phrases . . . that traverse the opera like a poisonous serpent, twining around the victims and fleeing their saintly protectors [*comme un serpent venimeux, s'enroulant autour des victimes et fuyant devant leurs saints défenseurs*]" (801, 802; my translation). In describing the genius of Wagner, which consists of the merging and melding of the arts, Liszt resorts to the metaphor of the serpent, which is not only the prime metaphor of the dedicatory address to Arsène Houssaye, but also the figure that subtends the meandering movement of the flowers around the stick in "Le Thyrse" (one thinks, farther back in time, of the serpent in Eden seducing Eve, then of the seductive Eve "dancing" her temptation of Adam). It would be no exaggeration to say that "Le Thyrse" is a series of brilliant variations on the theme proposed by Liszt.

But what is this theme? It is not sufficient to say, abstractly, that it is the "marriage of contraries," because these contraries refer to and express metaphorically the unity of genius. But whose genius? Who stands behind Liszt? Whose "rhetoric" is Liszt attempting to *translate* in the *amalgame* of his own "bizarre" language? The figure behind the agitation of the thyrsus is Richard Wagner, who represents (emblematizes) for Baudelaire what Goethe represents for Nietzsche – the god Dionysos. Wagner is the protagonist behind the meandering, serpentine figurations of "Le Thyrse"; Liszt is the interpreter of the god, his translator, his *porte-parole.* It is Wagner who appears through the veil of Liszt's genius.

There is, in this positioning of the god behind his priest, an uncanny structural similarity between the delicate microcosm of "Le Thyrse" and the portentous macrocosm of Wagner's own *Tannhäuser.* In Act III, scene 3 of the opera, when Tannhäuser relates his travails as pilgrim to Wolfram – the sufferings he endured in what at first appears to have been a failed effort at redemption for his sins – he describes the reaction of the pope to his entreaties as follows:

> "Hast du so böse Lust getheilt,
> dich an der Hölle Glut entflammt,
> hast du im Venusberg geweilt:
> so bist nun ewig du verdammt!
> Wie dieser Stab in meiner Hand
> nie mehr sich schmückt mit frischem Grün,
> kann aus der Hölle heissem Brand
> Erlösung nimmer dir erblüh'n!"
>
> "If thou hast shared the joys of Hell,
> If thou unholy flames hast nursed
> That in the Hill of Venus dwell,
> Thou art forevermore accurst!
> And as this barren staff I hold
> Ne'er will put forth a flower or leaf,
> Thus shalt thou nevermore behold
> Salvation, or thy sin's relief!" (28–29)[25]

Despite his immediate intention, after the papal refusal, to return to the Venusberg and finish his life in sensual oblivion, Tannhäuser, following the death of Elisabeth (a martyr to "true love"), will obtain redemption (*Erlösung*) in his own death. At the very end of the opera, a chorus of pilgrims sings:

> Heil! Heil! Der Gnade Wunder Heil!
> Erlösung ward der Welt zu Theil!
> Es that in nächtlich heil'ger Stund'
> der Herr sich durch ein Wunder kund:
> den dürren Stab in Priesters Hand
> hat er geschmückt mit frischem Grün:
> dem Sünder in der Hölle Brand
> soll so Erlösung neu erblüh'n!

Hail! Hail! the Lord hath marvels wrought!
Redemption He to all hath brought!
One night in bless'd, propitious hour,
He left a sign of His dread power;
The barren staff of priestly rule
He made to bloom with summer's green!
Now man's curse doth the Lord annul,
His pitying love shall make us clean! (32)

The decision of the pope to condemn Tannhäuser is overturned by God. Redemption is granted at the last moment by the supreme power, whose omnipotence cancels the arrogance of his priest (in an act that could only please German Evangelicals, it is presumed). The flowering of the staff, which Baudelaire may have had in mind in his flowering thyrsus,[26] is made possible only through an act of God (or of a god in the pagan context). Redemption is not a matter for priests (representatives, mediators, Franz Liszt), but for the power that shines through them in transcendental (Wagnerian) totality.

The differences between Baudelaire and Nietzsche can be summed up as follows: Nietzsche's career evolves as a turning-toward and turning-away from Wagner. When Wagner is praised in *The Birth of Tragedy*, Nietzsche exhorts his readers to seize the thyrsus and follow the god in his procession from east to west. When Wagner becomes an object of scorn in the later works, an "antipode" to Nietzsche, Goethe replaces Wagner and becomes Dionysos, symbol of genius, of totality. Goethe's all-encompassing works of the "ascending life" represent the ideal of artistic expression, whereas Kant's analytic disposition, his stance as "man of theory" mark him as inferior, dry, stifling. Baudelaire shares Nietzsche's interest in the creative power of the Dionysian temper. His prose poem "Le Thyrse" is in praise of genius – genius understood in the Nietzschean sense, as totality. However, whereas Nietzsche is content to juxtapose genius to theory in an unequivocal contrast of positive to negative, Baudelaire creates a poem that stages *the inevitable fall into theory within poetry itself.* Baudelaire includes, within the rhetorical sinuosity of his prose poem, the moment of analytical decision and division. What Barbara Johnson calls Baudelaire's "second revolution" is based upon the *amalgame* of poetry as imaginative sympathy and as theoretical reflection *within* the prose poem, and "Le Thyrse" illustrates this mixing of modes as well as any text in *Les Petits Poèmes en prose.* Through my reading of "Le Thyrse" I am proposing, however, that Baudelaire's second style (fragmentation, *amalgame*) is not merely the "antipode" of his first style (*Aufhebung* of the sensual in the spiritual). I have suggested that the figure of Wagner stands behind that of Liszt, that the god stands behind and illuminates his priest. This would mean that the first style of the poet, based on the reconciliation of opposites and the promise of a final redemption, *haunts* the second style, shines through it as in a barely visible palimpsest. "Le Thyrse" addresses itself to Liszt's genius, but it is traversed by the mute voice of Wagner, Baudelaire's absent interlocutor.

Perhaps the superimposition of two styles in one poem renders the very distinction of first from second style problematic. Nevertheless, it is useful, if only for pedagogical (theoretical) purposes, to make such distinctions. The critic is, after all, a species of "man of theory." But the reading of "Le Thyrse" as *both* a poem of fragmentation (readable only through analytic division) *and* a poem of redemption (emblem of a final totality) may correspond to the antithetical sense of the primal word *theoria*. Indeed, the first meaning of the Greek verb *theorein* is "to look at, view, behold, observe; especially to be a spectator at the public games and festivals"; it is only in its second, derived acceptation that the verb came to be equated with the Latin *contemplari* in the philosophical sense. Also, the noun *theoros* means "a spectator, observer, one who travels to see men and things; an ambassador, sent by the state to consult an oracle."[27] Thus, at its origins, the notion of the theoretical is associated not with the disinterested gaze of aesthetic man, not with what will become the presuppositions of Kantian philosophy, but with travel, discovery, and the difficult deciphering of obscure meanings. In fact, in the most fundamental sense, *theoria* is not contemplation per se, not what Nietzsche dismissively calls "theory," but rather the sending of people abroad for the purpose of a final understanding of the world. Thus, the thyrsus in its Baudelairian guise is the theoretical – as the *procession of devotees of the god*.

Perhaps the best way to understand "Le Thyrse" as a coexistence of the fragmentary and the redemptive is to follow the serpentine procession of the faithful, who, like readers of poetic texts, accompany the meanderings of significance as *amalgame*, but also sense, in the space that separates speaker from interlocutor, the pilgrim from his or her goal, the path of the literary – which is so often directed toward absent figures that haunt our strivings.

CHAPTER 5

The "beautiful soul": Alain-Fournier's Le Grand Meaulnes *and the aesthetics of Romanticism*

> And has not form two aspects? Is it not moral and immoral at once: moral in so far as it is the expression and result of discipline, immoral – yes, actually hostile to morality – in that of its very essence it is indifferent to good and evil, and deliberately concerned to make the moral world stoop beneath its proud and undivided sceptre?
>
> Thomas Mann, *Death in Venice*[1]

I BEAUTY AND MORALITY AT THE DAWN OF THE TWENTIETH CENTURY

In the second chapter of *Death in Venice* (1912), when describing the artistic evolution of the protagonist, Gustav von Aschenbach, the narrator emphasizes the increasing importance of formal rigor and discipline in the writings of an author who has been canonized before his time by an admiring public. This meditation on the creative act not only establishes the foundation of our future appreciation of Aschenbach's psychodrama (the protagonist will undergo a progressive undermining of the aesthetic order he has imposed on his life), but merits, in itself, the scrutiny of the contemporary literary theorist. In the passage quoted above, Thomas Mann raises a question which stands at the center of modern aesthetics and at the center of this book: namely, what is the relation between the work of art viewed as formal construction and the focus of that same work on moral or ethical matters? In Mann's metaphorical conception, form has a Janus-like "double face." As the result of the labor of transformation which the artist imposes on his materials, form seems to express or incorporate a certain discipline. At the same time, however, the narrator of *Death in Venice* affirms that it is in the very nature of form to be "indifferent" (*gleichgültig*) to the moral ideas that it envelops and encloses in beautiful semblance, that it forces to bow under its all-powerful "scepter." The rhetoric of the passage makes clear that literary art can be considered dangerous insofar as it can tend or turn toward the "second face," that of moral indifference. This observation has a prophetic value in the specific case of *Death in Venice*, a cautionary tale that carries within its formal elegiac beauty a story of complex moral significance. This work, whose surface mirrors the brilliant light of the Venetian cityscape, rests on an interior drama, a darkly illumined stage where Apollo and Dionysos struggle over the mastery of the protagonist's mind and body.

Of especial interest is the fact that the content of Aschenbach's story, the evolution of his life in Venice, consists of the revenge of the subterranean moral drama over the beautiful forms he had previously imposed on his carefully choreographed existence. In other words, one might wonder whether it is in the nature of form to master *only apparently* – that is, by the *trompe l'oeil* of beautiful appearance – that force which emerges in the combat between the moral and the immoral, and whose principal quality is to *always return*, to call into question the aesthetic stability of the text. One must ask whether the moral as such (the force of moral ideas in their difficulty, their complexity) allows itself to be subsumed within the aesthetic. This question will be at the center of the reading I am proposing in this chapter for Alain-Fournier's *Le Grand Meaulnes* and its intertextual relations to Romantic and pre-Romantic texts.

II LE GRAND MEAULNES: A FIRST LOOK

Since this "novel of adolescence" is no longer as widely read in the English-speaking world as it once was, I offer the following summary and commentary:

Le Grand Meaulnes is set in the region of Sologne, an isolated area of central France best known for its hunting and fishing, at the antipodes of Parisian culture and decadence. The story begins with the arrival of Augustin Meaulnes at the country schoolhouse which is also the home of François Seurel (the narrator) and his parents. Meaulnes and François are depicted as opposites throughout the narrative: Meaulnes is active and adventurous; François is the passive observer. In part one, Meaulnes has his most important adventure. Purely by chance, he discovers an old château in which a curious festivity is taking place. It is in this "Mysterious Domain" that Meaulnes meets not only Yvonne de Galais, the woman he will eventually marry, but also, fleetingly, Frantz de Galais, her eccentric brother, whose fiancée (Valentine) is strangely absent from the carefully orchestrated *fête étrange*.

The two loose strands of the narrative – Meaulnes's pursuit of Yvonne, and Frantz's pursuit of Valentine – do not come together until the third and final part of the novel, when we discover retrospectively that Meaulnes, in his search for Yvonne, encounters Valentine and has an amorous liaison with her. This relationship is described by Alain-Fournier as sordid and disillusioning. When Meaulnes finally marries Yvonne toward the middle of part three, his happiness is interrupted by Frantz, who, appealing to an oath made by the friends during their adolescence, asks Meaulnes to leave his wife and domestic tranquillity in order to find Valentine. Meaulnes does so, no doubt in expiation of his "sin." When he returns, having accomplished his mission, he finds that his wife has died in childbirth, leaving behind a daughter, who then becomes Meaulnes's companion for possible future adventures.

The central interpretive difficulty of *Le Grand Meaulnes*, which is also the focus of the present chapter, is that of the considerable stylistic differences between part one (the daydream atmosphere of the Mysterious Domain, its melancholy charm) and parts two and three (a "fall" into commonplace reality). The novel seems to change from romantic quest to mere adventure: the modal identity of the work vacillates; and the story divides itself into two apparently irreconcilable sections. This division, or "faultline," is the point of departure for my analysis.

The only novel completed by Alain-Fournier is in many ways problematical, in large measure because of its success. Ever since its publication in 1913 it has been categorized as a "novel of adolescence," and it is often among the first literary works read by the youth of France: it is what one might call a *classic*, but a classic judged suitable for novices, for readers who have, in an important sense, no experience at reading. Its classification as a classical or even canonical early twentieth-century novel has become a good excuse for adult readers to not (or no longer) read it. Those critics who have made the effort to return to *Le Grand Meaulnes* during the last three decades have done so (if I my simplify somewhat but not very much) for three essential reasons: first, because they have found in the form of the novel either a more complex structure than had been uncovered previously, or else the repetition of a grand archetypal form;[2] second, because Alain-Fournier's novel shares certain aesthetic tenets with other works of the Modernist period;[3] and third, because the novel exasperates the critic to such a degree that he finds it necessary to unburden himself by writing ironically, nastily (*méchamment*) against Alain-Fournier and his art.[4] One should add to these three categories one other, more recent approach, which is that of genetic criticism (*critique génétique*) – a method which underlies, to differing degrees, the editions by Claude Herzfeld (Nizet) and Daniel Leuwers (Classiques Garnier) as well as the critical edition by Claudie Husson entitled *Alain-Fournier et la naissance du récit.*[5] If one takes into consideration the respectable number of articles still being published on *Le Grand Meaulnes* and the editions and re-editions of Alain-Fournier's correspondence,[6] it is easy to conclude that this "novel of adolescence" continues to exert considerable charm among informed contemporary French readers.

But against the background of this rich variety of methods and critical approaches, at the very heart of the interest with which *Le Grand Meaulnes* is greeted, the reader is compelled to face one aesthetic issue in particular which seems to arise from the novel's weakness – an issue one must either ignore if one wishes to love the work and be its loyal defender, or else illuminate with critical scrutiny if the love of the text is not to be a criterion for the analysis of its meanings. This problem is that of the major divergence – of tone and of generic character – between the first part of the novel (centered on the quasi-magical, dreamlike discovery of the Mysterious Domain by Meaulnes) and the second and third parts, which are essentially an adventure novel set in the precise and prosaic milieu of recognizable geography: the isolated stretches of Sologne in central France. André Gide noted the problem in his *Journal* in January 1933:

> One loses interest in *Le Grand Meaulnes*, which extends over too many pages and too much time, whose design is uncertain and whose most exquisite qualities exhaust themselves within the first hundred pages. The remainder of the book strives in vain to recapture this first virginal emotion. . . . I know that this vain striving is the very subject of the book; but it is also its fundamental weakness, so that it was not, perhaps, possible for the novelist to achieve a greater "success" in his project.[7]

Gide's commentary has a double thrust. On the one hand, the author of the *Journal* informs us of his displeasure as reader when confronting a text that foils his expectations: the "exquisite" qualities of the novel, those features that originally captivated him, do not manage to last. On the other hand, however, he is forced to admit that the loss of the ideal, the effacement of the exquisite and the virginal are the subject of the book, and this subject, in being narrated, in assuming a properly diegetic movement, can only lead to the reader's sense of deception. Did Alain-Fournier's aesthetic error consist of attempting to make of one poetic instant – the meeting of Meaulnes and Yvonne de Galais – the evanescent center of a novel of disillusionment? Does *Le Grand Meaulnes* necessarily appear to the attentive reader as an awkward mixture of two incompatible genres – the poetic novel (or even a kind of long prose poem) and the adventure novel, Baudelaire/Laforgue and Dickens/Stevenson?[8]

This question of the fundamental difference between the beginning of the novel and its succeeding sections has come to the surface once again, and in highly dramatic fashion, in a book by Alain Buisine entitled *Les Mauvaises Pensées du Grand Meaulnes* (1992). In a subtle and original psychoanalytical reading which should be taken seriously despite its voluntarily outrageous style,[9] Buisine asserts that *Le Grand Meaulnes* is an "idealizing software package" (15) that "functions like a machine to suppress and efface its second part" (21). Buisine's interpretive efforts are directed toward the deconstruction of this machine, toward the uncovering of its idealizing effects: the critic takes great pains to exhibit the latent sexual content which makes of the text a vast tableau depicting the anxious avoidance of female sexuality. Making numerous parallels between Alain-Fournier's novel and the real life of Henri Fournier, Buisine arrives at the following general statement: "Fundamentally, *Le Grand Meaulnes* is a novel about the impotent impossibility of assuming reality" (42).

Like Gide, Buisine places at the center of his critical preoccupations the separation between the initial meeting of Meaulnes and Yvonne de Galais in the Mysterious Domain and the protagonist's subsequent efforts to rediscover the lost world of this encounter. What Buisine adds to Gide's remarks is that the construction of an ideal dreamworld in the first part of the novel is, in fact, a mask hiding reality rather than a "virginal" image which the reader might feel justified in admiring for its aesthetic purity. Unlike Gide, Buisine seems insensitive to the poetic qualities of the first part, and much more attentive to certain passages where the text's "unconscious" manifests itself, where the text reveals the fundamental ambivalence on which it is constructed.

Now it is worth noting that in one of the most convincing analytic sections of his study, where Buisine emphasizes the conflict between the apparent "Frenchness" of the novel (its nostalgic attachment to provincial reality, to the *terroir*) and an unmistakable German or Germanic thematics (47–58), he repeats, without acknowledgment, pertinent observations made thirty years previously by the distinguished critic of Romanticism, Léon Cellier, in his study entitled '*Le Grand Meaulnes' ou l'initiation manquée* (1963). Cellier, who is closer to Gide than to Buisine in his appreciation of the novel's beginning section, reaches different conclusions from those of Buisine, in that he accuses the novel's characters not of not having assumed their existential responsibilities, but rather of not having remained faithful to the ideal as it appeared in the Mysterious Domain. But, like Buisine, he is interested in the stratum of the text in which a certain historically determined drama, originating in the Romantic era, plays itself out between France and Germany. Despite obvious differences in methodology and vocabulary – Buisine speaks in Freudian language of "drives" (*pulsions*) whereas Cellier emphasizes literary "models" – in both cases the critics feel they have reached the center of the novel's interpretation once they have isolated and illuminated the France–Germany dichotomy.

With an ironical verve equal in intensity to that of Buisine, Cellier enacts what might be called, *avant la lettre*, a "deconstruction" of the novel, subjecting Alain-Fournier's text to a double reading. In a first section, he shows that the archetypal scheme of the text, the fundamental form that subtends it, is that of the *quest novel*: in this perspective, Alain-Fournier's modern work would be a rewriting of Chrétien de Troyes's *Perceval*. Meaulnes would be an initiate; his task would be to decipher the mystery of the Domain; his adventures would constitute a series of mystical ordeals on the path toward final understanding. But in a second section Cellier attempts to demonstrate that the narrative progression of quest and initiation stalls and stagnates: *between* the discovery of the Domain and the pages that follow the novel undoes itself; it metamorphoses from quest novel to simple adventure novel, in which the theme of remorse (or of sin, of Meaulnes's moral waywardness) takes center stage.

Cellier's erudition and reading experience allow him to discern in *Le Grand Meaulnes* a novel that reprises not only the most ancient archetypes, but also certain Romantic themes, and it is here, in the context of the period he knows so well, that the critic's judgment is particularly severe:

> As concerns the novel's Romanticism, it is of the cheapest sort. How can the reader not be disappointed at the conception of Romanticism the novel implies? *Le Grand Meaulnes's* Frantz [one of the three major male characters] is but a caricature of the author of *Sylvie*; infantile behavior is not equivalent to a childlike spirit; the extravagance of Frantz has nothing in common with moral complexity; the hero of *Sylvie* does not marry Sylvie. As far as Meaulnes is concerned, who would confuse this perverted, *parvenu* peasant with a Romantic hero? (41)

If Cellier condemns the novel, it is because Meaulnes has not been equal to his task as would-be initiate, and because Frantz is but a pale imitation of a Romantic hero. *Le Grand Meaulnes*, which is, at its deepest level, an imitation of *Perceval*, is also, more visibly but no less unfortunately, a rewriting of Gérard de Nerval's evocative and elliptical *Sylvie*. But here as well, the modern novel runs aground, because Alain-Fournier allowed Meaulnes to possess his dream, whereas, as Cellier remarks, Nerval does not commit the aesthetic (and moral?) error of giving Sylvie as wife to the narrator-protagonist of his novella. For Buisine, therefore, the characters of *Le Grand Meaulnes* do not live enough; for Cellier, they do not dream enough; in both cases, they fail, and their failure turns our reading into an exercise in frustration and disillusionment.

If I have permitted myself to follow the interpretive paths of readers as different as André Gide, Alain Buisine, and Léon Cellier, it is to indicate that a reading of Alain-Fournier's text necessarily passes through and acknowledges the faultline that divides it at its center. Unlike Proust's novel, which appears to unfold or uncoil itself from the initial concentrated skein of the *petite madeleine* episode, *Le Grand Meaulnes* is divided, disjointed, dismembered: its two sections can never meet. On the one hand there is the momentary, ephemeral image of Meaulnes's encounter with Yvonne de Galais in the Mysterious Domain, characterized by an atmosphere of purity and perfection; on the other hand we have the desperate travels of the protagonist, his impossible search for an irremediably lost purity.

But how can one explain this structural dichotomy, and what is the origin of the novel's incapacity to reach its own synthesis, its narrative reconciliation? It is at this juncture, it seems to me, that one ought to proceed beyond a simple declaration concerning the novel's "failure" toward an investigation that places *Le Grand Meaulnes* in its particular historical context. Now this context, as Cellier has demonstrated, is that of European Romanticism. To be more precise, one should say that those texts that lie before and "underneath" *Le Grand Meaulnes* belong to that brief period that immediately precedes and makes possible Romanticism as such. Alain-Fournier's early twentieth-century novel follows in the wake of a number of fundamental texts which provide the basis and critical accompaniment to Romanticism. A textually grounded interpretation of *Le Grand Meaulnes*, notably of its central faultline, has a greater chance of reaching a place other than that of the reader's disillusionment and anger if we follow those traces in the novel that indicate its aesthetic provenance. I propose to initiate my own reading by citing and commenting upon a passage from *Le Grand Meaulnes*, before beginning an intertextual voyage which will first lead us far away in time and space before returning us to our point of departure – the interpretive difficulty inherent in this double, divided, schizoid work.

The passage I shall be citing is taken from the penultimate chapter of the novel, from the moment at which the reader learns, thanks to

François's transcription of Meaulnes's schoolboy notebooks, the nature of Meaulnes's adventures during his absence from the text (essentially, his liaison with Valentine, the young woman he encountered while searching for Yvonne de Galais – a liaison which is at the origin of the protagonist's remorse). In the pages that precede the passage we learn that Meaulnes, having discovered the letters from Frantz in Valentine's possession, and having thus discovered that she is the "fiancée" from the Mysterious Domain who was unable to believe in Frantz's extravagant projects and hopes, separates himself from her and, in a certain sense, sends her to her ruin. In his desire to find Valentine after this brutal separation, Meaulnes rents a bicycle and rides to Bourges, but his efforts are in vain. He does not find her, and returns home, discouraged:

> The long voyage that remained for him was to be his last recourse against his suffering, his last forced distraction before succumbing to unending anguish.
>
> He departed. Next to the road, in the valley, he saw lovely farmhouses between the trees, at the edge of the water, which exhibited their pointed gables decorated with green trelliswork. No doubt, over there, on the lawns, attentive young girls spoke of love. One could imagine, over there, beautiful souls [*de belles âmes*].
>
> But for Meaulnes, at that moment, nothing existed except one particular love, the unsatisfied love that had just been extinguished so cruelly, and the young woman among all others [Valentine] whom he should have protected, saved, was precisely the one he had sent to her ruin. (272)[10]

This return to Bourges, this voyage of disillusionment, is all the more significant in that it has a rather curious narrative motivation. At this moment in the story, François has strayed well beyond his role of editor of Meaulnes's diary: here, he grants himself the privileges of a third-person omniscient narrator to relate not only the actions of Meaulnes, but also the latter's most intimate thoughts and desires. The phrases "*no doubt*, over there, on the lawns, attentive young girls spoke of love," as well as "*one could imagine*, over there, beautiful souls," are the narrator's projections, notions with which he fills the mind of the protagonist. François, in examining the presumed fantasies of his culpable friend, has become (to borrow from Nerval's vocabulary), the creator of Meaulnes's *chimères*. And in the detailed scenic representation of the bicycle trip, François places Meaulnes in the position that he, as secondary character and narrator, usually occupies: that of passive and melancholy observer. The dramatic contrast on which the passage is based rests on the absolute distance or difference between the imagined purity of the "attentive young girls," of the "beautiful souls" engaged in a discourse on love, and the moral fall of the protagonist, who has "sinned" in appropriating for himself a woman not destined for him, in showing himself to be incapable (as Cellier would say) of rising to the level of the ideal.

This passage concentrates or distills the essence of the text's fundamental conflict at the very moment that the narration reaches its conclusion. There can be no more "distractions" for Meaulnes, since his spirit hesitates between two visions of the world, two *Weltanschauungen* that share no common element: either he can think of these young women discussing love in an atmosphere of reflective calm, or he is condemned to relive the remorse of his dalliance with Valentine. It is evident that the *jeunes filles en fleurs* of Alain-Fournier, in their virginal simplicity, repeat, in an ironic mode, the founding image of Yvonne de Galais as she appeared in the Mysterious Domain. The fact that the young women are properly inaccessible to the protagonist is rendered by the repetition of the expression "over there" ("là-bas") – which emphasizes the distance between Meaulnes and these daydream-creatures. But it is important to dwell on one detail in the text that gives it a particular historical resonance: the use of the term "beautiful soul" (*belle âme*) to designate the young girls. This term is not a simple variation or substitution for the phrase "attentive young girls." One should say, rather, that the passage from "attentive young girls" to "beautiful souls" constitutes what one would call in German a *Steigerung*, a tonal amplification through the use of a parallel, but stronger, expression. Now the notion of the beautiful soul is historically and culturally marked, and carries with it the historical baggage of Romanticism, or rather, as I have suggested, of the rich period that precedes and renders possible the Romantic movement per se. I propose now to survey the various transformations of the notion of the beautiful soul during the last part of the eighteenth century and the first years of the nineteenth, in order to return to *Le Grand Meaulnes* and better interpret its constitutive break, its faultline. In the end, my goal is to situate Alain-Fournier's novel in the crucial transition that occurs, in the period around 1913, between the decline of Romanticism and the explosion of new forms which constitute what is generally called European Modernism.[11]

III THE GERMAN INTERTEXT OF *LE GRAND MEAULNES*: THE "BEAUTIFUL SOUL" AND ITS HISTORY[12]

The English expression "the beautiful soul" is the exact equivalent of the term "die schöne Seele," whose evolution in the writings of the most important poets and thinkers of German Classicism and Idealism conveys, in microcosmic manner, a certain conceptual drama that played itself out in this period, notably concerning the problematic nature of the relations between the aesthetic and moral domains. I shall limit myself here to three authors – Schiller, Goethe, and Hegel – who write about the beautiful soul quite explicitly in their respective discourses. To be more complete, one would need to take into consideration the numerous variations on this theme that can be found in other writers – in Wieland, Kant, and Hölderlin, for example – but this would take us beyond the purview of the present analysis.

In the German-speaking world, the term "schöne Seele" has its origin in Protestant Pietism; it surfaces first in the religious literature of the late eighteenth century in Germany and Switzerland before being "reconverted" into secular and philosophical discourse by Schiller, in the clearest manner in his 1793 essay "Über Anmut und Würde" [Grace and Dignity]; Goethe, in his novel *Wilhelm Meisters Lehrjahre* [*Wilhelm Meister's Apprenticeship*] (1795–96); and Hegel, in *Die Phänomenologie des Geistes* [*The Phenomenology of Spirit*] (1807).

Schiller

Schiller wrote "Über Anmut und Würde" just one year before *Über die ästhetische Erziehung des Menschen in einer Reihe von Briefen* [*On the Aesthetic Education of Man in a Series of Letters*] and two years before *Über naive und sentimentalische Dichtung* [*Naïve and Sentimental Poetry*] – the two masterworks by which we know (and to which sometimes, unfortunately, we reduce) the theoretical thought of the writer. These three studies were written in the shadow of the critical philosophy of Kant, whose massive influence is discernible throughout Schiller's meditations. In a general sense, one can say that Schiller attempted to emancipate himself from his mentor especially in the elaboration of a new conception of moral duty. Whereas Kant made a categorical separation between the domain of art and the purview of moral decision and action, Schiller sought a synthesis of the two areas, emphasizing the possibility of a "moral beauty" at work in those human actions most worthy of our admiration.

It is against Kantian rigorism, therefore, against the notion of moral duty conceived as an order imposed by a principled conscience on purposeful human activity, that Schiller works out his dialectic of aesthetic grace (*Anmut*) and moral dignity (*Würde*). And to render this dialectic accessible to the reader's senses as well as intelligence, Schiller introduces the notion of the "die schöne Seele." The beautiful soul is characterized by the facility with which it submits itself to the most severe of moral imperatives:

The beautiful soul has no other merit except to be. With an admirable lightness [*Leichtigkeit*], as if acting only from instinct, the beautiful soul accomplishes the most painful moral duties [*Pflichten*] given to man; and the most heroic sacrifice to which it submits its natural drives [*Naturtriebe*] seems a freely chosen effect [*Wirkung*] of these very drives. Thus, the beautiful soul is never itself conscious of the beauty of its actions, and it never imagines that one could act and feel otherwise.[13]

In the context of Schiller's synthetic presentation, the beautiful soul is the figuration of the fragile reconciliation of human instincts or drives (the word *Trieb* will, of course, be used by Freud in his psychoanalytical theory) and moral duty (*Pflicht*). What distinguishes the beautiful soul, in this formulation, from the rigors of the Kantian system, is that its "sacrifices" are not equivalent to the abandonment of instinctual satisfaction under the boot of moral duty. These "sacrifices," in fact, appear as such only to a distant observer, someone who, unlike the beautiful soul, does not act with the ease or "lightness" (*Leichtigkeit*) of moral freedom.

Schiller inscribes the figure of the beautiful soul within a properly dialectical movement which is developed beyond "Über Anmut und Würde" in the more systematic essays included in *On the Aesthetic Education of Man in a Series of Letters*. It is in this work that Schiller, in an ambitious and sinuous argument, traces the history of human development through distinct stages, in which he establishes a tripartite hierarchical scheme. Beginning with primitive or "physical" man, who is characterized only by a sensual drive [*sinnlicher Trieb*], we move to aesthetic man, who possesses a form instinct or impulse [*Formtrieb*], and finally to moral man, who synthesizes sensual drives and the form impulse in a unifying "instinct to play" [*Spieltrieb*], guarantor of human liberty. One should not underestimate the seriousness of the argument advanced by Schiller when he pleads for a central place for art and aesthetic sensibility in society. The beautiful soul figures the ease with which one should be able to pass from the aesthetic to the moral. In "Über Anmut und Würde" Schiller depicts what one might call a graceful feminine "character" that incorporates and renders visible the reconciliation of conceptual opposites toward which the poet's aesthetic philosophy is aimed. In the passage from the physical to the aesthetic and then to the moral, the first step is by far the more difficult: in other words, once one reaches the aesthetic stage, morality is not far away. This is because the aesthetic stage *predisposes* human beings to moral action: such is the conclusion Schiller reaches in the twenty-third *Letter*, which is essentially an abstract repetition of what he had said about the beautiful soul in "Über Anmut und Würde":

> It is therefore one of the most important tasks of culture to subject man to form even in his purely physical life, and to make him aesthetic as far as ever the realm of Beauty can extend, since the moral condition can be developed only from the aesthetic, not from the physical condition . . . In a word, in the realm of truth and morality sensation [*Empfindung*] must have nothing to determine; but in the sphere of happiness form may exist and the play impulse [*Spieltrieb*] may govern.[14]

Goethe

Goethe develops the notion of the beautiful soul in the sixth book of *Wilhelm Meister's Apprenticeship* which is entitled "Confessions of a Beautiful Soul" ["Bekenntnisse einer schönen Seele"]. Already Schiller had made use of the feminine gender of the word "Seele" to grant the beautiful soul traditionally feminine attributes – lightness, grace, formal beauty – but Goethe goes a step farther, in bestowing upon his "schöne Seele" the gift of speech. The Beautiful Soul is a character in Goethe's *Bildungsroman*, and rather than being part of what I called a conceptual drama, as was the case for Schiller, she now plays a central role in a fictive psychodrama. The sixth book of *Wilhelm Meister* has always posed problems for critics, for two related reasons: first, this section of the text is a departure from the novelistic frame, in that it introduces a character, the Beautiful Soul, who does not participate in the plot of the story (although her niece will marry Wilhelm at the end of the novel, and it is through this family relation, no doubt, that Goethe could placate lovers of verisimilitude); and second, an attentive reading of this book runs up against Goethe's irony, an irony that does not manifest itself in occasional bursts, but rather extends throughout the entirety of the "Confessions." In a word: what should one think of a figure whose purity, whose "moral beauty" is such that she does not participate any longer in what one generally designates by the word "life"? It is true that some of the first readers of the sixth book were seduced by the purity of the character, and saw in the Beautiful Soul a direct representation of Susanna Katharina von Klettenberg, a Pietist friend of Goethe's mother whose correspondence with Lavater remains an excellent testimony to the religious currents of the period.[15] Since it seems that Katharina von

Klettenberg helped Goethe overcome a "spiritual crisis" in his youth,[16] it was tempting to read the "Confessions" as a pious and unambiguous homage to this extraordinary woman. Not only did Goethe's mother fall into this interpretive trap, but it would appear that Schiller himself was taken in: perhaps he could only be insensitive to a pervasive irony that called into question his own eminently serious conception of the beautiful soul.[17]

The story of the Beautiful Soul seems to be that of a progressive elevation, of a purification and elimination of those affective links that bind the character to her environment. The "Confessions" tell of two ill-fated liaisons. The first of these does not work out because of the immaturity of the young suitor (named, significantly, Narcissus); the second ends abruptly when the rather mysterious "impurity" of a certain Philo is discovered (as this name implies, the character loves; but he is not loved in return). As the narrative progresses, the Beautiful Soul becomes less and less happy in polite society (at one point in the story, she had been a *Stiftsdame* (canoness) at the court), and, having had a mystical experience in which she believes she has communicated directly with Christ, she decides to retire from the world and its superficial pleasures. Throughout all this what I am calling Goethe's ironical point of view might still remain a matter of interpretation. One reader might find in the actions of the Beautiful Soul the proof of a superior morality; another could well see in the progressive self-denial of the protagonist unmistakable signs of a singular incapacity to live and even a pronounced fear of sexuality.[18]

There is in the sixth book, however, a character who seems to be Goethe's spokesperson and who serves as a foil to the Beautiful Soul – namely, her uncle, who plays a secondary but nevertheless crucial role in "The Confessions." His actions and moderate words contrast dramatically with his niece's pious and increasingly supersensible vocation. During a conversation in his castle, where he holds a distinguished collection of paintings, the uncle initiates a discussion on the question of aesthetic judgment and on the problem of the quality of works of art. Whereas the Beautiful Soul refuses to succumb to the "temptations" of the beaux-arts (the seductive beauty of color, harmony, and form), her uncle demonstrates that creative genius, which evolves in the cultivation of beautiful shapes and structures, is itself perhaps closer to moral perfection than the naïve hymns and devotional literature that provide the Beautiful Soul with her limited inspirational sustenance. In the remarks that follow, one may well hear, filtered through the uncle's discourse, Goethe's own corrective voice:

[My uncle] then drew my attention to some pictures that had not struck me particularly, and tried to make me understand that only study of the history of art can give us a proper sense of the value and distinction of a work of art. One must first appreciate the burdensome aspects of technical labor that gifted artists have perfected over the centuries, in order for one to comprehend how it is possible for a creative genius to move freely and joyfully on a place so high that it makes us dizzy.

With this in mind he brought together a number of pictures, and when he explained them to me, I could not avoid seeing in them images and symbols of moral perfection. When I told him this, he said: "You are absolutely right, and one should not pursue the cultivation of one's moral life [*der sittlichen Bildung*] in isolation and seclusion. We are more likely to find that a person intent on moral advancement will have every cause to cultivate his senses [*seine feinere Sinnlichkeit*] as well as his mind, so as not to run the risk of losing his foothold on those moral heights, slipping into the seductive allurements of uncontrolled fancy and debasing his nobler nature by indulging in idle frivolities, if not worse.[19]

One can see here how Goethe's reflexions echo those of Schiller, but with some notable differences. Whereas for Schiller, in the *Letters*, the central point was to go beyond the level of mere sensual instinct (*Sinntrieb*) in order to attain the infinitely superior and "noble" aesthetic and moral stages, in the "Confessions," Goethe suggests that one must always cultivate what he calls one's "more delicate sensibility" (*seine feinere Sinnlichkeit*). It is the harmonization of this sensibility and of moral culture (*die sittliche Bildung*) that produces the truly cultivated human being, in the sense of the German *gebildet*. In the context of such reasoning, it is clear that the mystical adventures of the Beautiful Soul can only represent one step in the *Bildung* of the novel's protagonist, who should see in the "Confessions" not a model of conduct, but rather a warning against the excesses of self-contemplation and self-involvement. Perhaps it is not a matter of coincidence that the activity chosen by Wilhelm once he has concluded his adventures, in *Wilhelm Meisters Wanderjahre* (1829), is that of medicine (surgery as *Handwerk*) – an art of healing and of aid to others, where science is allied with altruism. The error of the Beautiful Soul is double: on the one hand she neglected the aesthetic specificity of works of art and, in so doing, could not understand the moral content inhering in them; and on the other hand she lived in ethereal regions where the moral beauty she thought she perceived was nothing more than a pale aestheticization beyond all effective action and all concrete reality. To conclude, one might say that the error of the Beautiful Soul consists in not having made any errors: it is through the mistakes and mis-steps along the route of one's *Bildung* that apprenticeship take place.

Hegel

In a language quite different from that of Goethe in *Wilhelm Meister*, and with a quite different distribution of roles in his drama of the development of consciousness, Hegel nevertheless traces much the same story of *Bildung* in the conceptual architecture of his *Phenomenology of Spirit*. In both cases, the fundamental issue is that of evolution – whether it be that of a fictive character representing the strengths and weaknesses of humanity, or whether it be consciousness itself in its movement beyond sense certainty toward morality, religion, and absolute knowledge. And this evolution is told, takes on a properly narrative form. By coincidence, the "scene" played by the beautiful soul in the *Phenomenology*, a short but decisive one in the section concerning "Spirit that is certain of itself," can be found in the sixth section of eight, just as was the case in *Wilhelm Meister*. This is to say that the moment of the beautiful soul comes toward the end, but not at the end, of a process of refinement of consciousness. In Hegel's scheme, the stage of the beautiful soul must be overcome (*aufgehoben*, that is, sublated), and this overcoming operates in Hegel's construction in a manner philosophically analogous to the way in which the resonance of the Beautiful Soul is both negated and preserved in the seventh and eighth books of *Wilhelm Meister*.

According to Hegel, the beautiful soul is the poetic figure of absolute self-consciousness completely folded in upon itself and thus incapable of all effective action in the world. This involution of consciousness is a necessary moment of the spirit's progression, but a moment that must efface itself before the advent of a superior movement – that of "evil and its forgiveness" – which concludes the sixth section of the treatise. In brief: the beautiful soul is sublated at the moment at which consciousness seeks the *recognition* of its convictions by another consciousness. In simple terms, one might say that the human being cannot isolate him- or herself from others, and that the need for recognition, which is universal, causes one to leave the charming but restrictive enclosure of "moral beauty." In the same way that Wilhelm Meister, after the sixth book, will discover the society of the Tower and finally turn toward an altruistic *métier*, here the beautiful soul will dissipate in the movement of the recognition of alterity.

As Hegel's commentators have noted, it is probable that the passage on the beautiful soul constitutes a thinly veiled (if veiled at all) polemic against the poetry and poetics of Novalis (and therefore also against Fichte, whose philosophy, along with a certain kind of German Romanticism, had influenced this poet).[20] In any case, the rhetorical tone of the passage which concludes the section on the beautiful soul is that of irony – not Goethe's serene irony, but rather a ferocious debunking. The beautiful soul may be philosophically sublated, but it is then, in the lines that follow, effectively destroyed (*vernichtet*):

> Here, then, we see self-consciousness withdrawn into its innermost being, for which all externality as such has vanished – withdrawn into the contemplation of the "I = I," in which this "I" is the whole of essentiality and existence . . . [Consciousness] lives in dread of besmirching the splendour of its inner being by action and an existence; and, in order to preserve the purity of its heart, it flees from contact with the actual world, and persists in its self-willed impotence to renounce its self which is reduced to the extremes of ultimate abstraction, and to give itself a substantial existence, or to transform its thought into being and put its trust in the absolute difference [between thought and being]. The hollow object which it has produced for itself now fills it, therefore, with a sense of emptiness. Its activity is a yearning which merely loses itself as consciousness becomes an object devoid of substance, and, rising above this loss, and falling back on itself, finds itself only as a lost soul. In this transparent purity of its moments, an unhappy, so-called "beautiful soul," its light dies away within it, and it vanishes like a shapeless vapour that dissolves into thin air.[21]

IV RETURN TO *LE GRAND MEAULNES*: FROM ROMANTICISM TO MODERNISM

In the brief period of time that separates "Über Anmut und Würde" (1793) from *Phenomenology of Spirit* (1807), the notion of the beautiful soul underwent significant modifications. Schiller's point of departure was the desire to effect a dialectical unification of beauty and morality through the creation of a figure – that of the "schöne Seele" – which would combine aesthetic grace with moral dignity, thus overcoming the division Kant had striven to establish between the separate domains of aesthetic appreciation and ethical praxis. It seems in retrospect, however, that Schiller's dialectic was not rigorous enough, at least in the Hegelian sense, in that, with the creation of the figure of the beautiful soul, sensual instinct (*Sinntrieb*) was not *aufgehoben* in the triple sense of negated/preserved/overcome, but simply *abandoned and forgotten*, effaced by the more noble aesthetic and moral impulses. It is against this forgetfulness, this abandonment of human sensuality and concrete reality that Goethe and Hegel reacted, each in his own style, the former insisting on the necessity of error in *Bildung*, and the other emphasizing the fundamental role of negation/alienation in the development of human consciousness. Jean Hyppolite's description of the final goal of Hegel's *Phenomenology* can be applied also to Goethe's conception of apprenticeship: "It is not the subjectivity of the beautiful soul, which embraces within itself the entire substantiveness of spirit and reduces it to itself, that is the last word of philosophy, but rather both this universal subjectivity and the partiality of concrete action taken together."[22] What was lacking in Schiller's conception of the beautiful soul was precisely this "partiality of concrete action," and this partiality is at the center of Goethe's preoccupations in *Wilhelm Meister.*

In his own representation of the "belles âmes" holding court on a pristine meadow, Alain-Fournier echoes Schiller rather than Goethe or Hegel. When François Seurel enters into the mind of Meaulnes to say: "No doubt, over there, on the lawns, attentive young girls spoke of love. One could imagine, over there, beautiful souls," it is to contrast the irremediable moral degradation of the protagonist with the purity of the imagined young women. In other words, to use Hegelian vocabulary, these young girls who figure beautiful souls (and who, it must be emphasized, do not exist, are not real, are not in the visual field of Meaulnes) are simply the dreamed result of an empty "yearning," of a hollow nostalgia. Instead of creating a hero like Wilhelm Meister who moves through life and submits to its moral ordeals in order to transform himself, instead of giving his protagonist the capacity to navigate between the extremes of purity and defilement, Alain-Fournier divides his imaginary world into two irreconcilable parts – on the one hand, a beautiful but inaccessible realm of idealized love, and on the other hand, the domain of sin and remorse for which, unlike in Hegel's scheme, there is *no pardon.*

To return now to the question of Romanticism, one can see why *Le Grand Meaulnes* bothered Léon Cellier so much. Alain-Fournier's imagination borrowed from Romanticism only one of its aspects: its most obvious and overused theme, that of nostalgia for an impossible love. The universe of *Le Grand Meaulnes* is characterized by solipsism, and this solipsism is in reality the result of a bad or false reading of the first Romanticism, of Romanticism before the development of a literature of simple nostalgia. For Goethe and Hegel, writers who do not belong to the Romantic movement properly speaking, but who live it in meditating on Romanticism at the level of its most fundamental presuppositions, the insufficiency of the figure of the beautiful soul resides in its detachment from the human community, its separation from reality.

One of the most beautiful passages in *Le Grand Meaulnes* takes place when the protagonist, an intruder in the Mysterious Domain, fortuitously comes upon a scene which, in its aesthetic perfection, seems to escape from the contingencies of human temporality. I am alluding to the theatrical *tableau* in which the narrator shows Meaulnes listening to a young woman who is playing the piano in a room full of children:

> It was a kind of small parlor; a woman or perhaps young woman, with a large brown cloak thrown over her shoulders, her back to her audience, was playing quite softly melodies from roundelays and comic songs. On the couch nearby, six or seven young boys and girls all in a row as if portrayed in a picturebook, obedient as are all children when it is late, were listening . . .
>
> After this charming but frantic and loud evening . . . Meaulnes found himself submerged in the most tranquil happiness imaginable.
>
> Without noise, while the young woman continued to play, he went back to the dining-room and sat down, and, opening one of the large red books scattered on the table, he began, absentmindedly, to read.
>
> Almost immediately one of the little boys who was on the floor came up to him, leaned on his arm and climbed his leg to look on with him; another did the same from the other side. Then it was the same dream he had dreamt before. He could imagine for a great while that he was in his own house, married, on a beautiful evening, and that this charming and unknown being who was playing the piano nearby was his wife. (75–76)

What is striking in this lovely fixed image is the excessively immobile quality of its staging: there is an uncanny (*unheimlich*) tone to this fictitious domesticity, where the children are actors disguised in old-fashioned costumes, and where the young woman at the piano *turns her back to us*. Meaulnes's imagination is focused on a dead image, or even an image of death. Already here we have the figuration of the impossibility of the realization of love, the effacement of woman as concrete reality. The very rapid repetition of this scene in the seventh chapter of part three ("Le Jour de noces"), where François hears Yvonne de Galais playing the piano for Meaulnes, only adds to its fragile and melancholy character.

In the light of our discussion of the beautiful soul and its history, a first conclusion imposes itself: *Le Grand Meaulnes*, a novel published in 1913 just before World War I and the social, political, and artistic upheavals of that period, remains firmly attached to a certain Romantic aesthetic – that of melancholy, of nostalgia for a beautiful and irrecuperable past. But it must be noted, at the same time, that Alain-Fournier's novel does not participate (as do the most lucid works of the Romantic period) in a serious examination of the theoretical presuppositions on which it is constructed and the lovely figures it employs to seduce its readers.[23] The faultline at the center of the novel which preoccupied Gide, Buisine, and Cellier is not merely some lack of compositional talent on the part of the author, but rather a line of absolute separation between the domains of the aesthetic and the moral, and this separation undermines both areas equally. The beauty of the book masks its existential immobility; and the issue of moral complexity, the problem of choices and responsibility, as well as the passage to adulthood, are all eluded, bypassed. Poetic imagery (*das Bild*) covers up and stifles moral progress (*die Bildung*).

In the perspective of modern literary history, a second conclusion imposes itself: *Le Grand Meaulnes*, in being anchored to a merely nostalgic Romanticism, does not participate in the renewal brought about by European Modernism, which, in its strongest moments, enacts what Proust, in writing about the chronological distortions of the dreamworld, calls "un jeu formidable . . . avec le Temps."[24] What appears already in *Du côté de chez Swann*, published, like Alain-Fournier's novel, in 1913, is the transformation of memory from the handmaiden of impotent regret into a method of knowledge and a primary motor in the construction of narrative order. And the progression of the *Recherche* reveals that the content of memory (and of specific memories) is not always tinged with the alternation of euphoria and melancholy. The path of the novel's interiorized *Bildung* is punctuated by all the revelations concerning Albertine, revelations that destroy the linear temporality of the work and reveal its hidden and deviated byways. And this twisting of time has as its essential result an illumination of the complexity of human relations, which is made *by* the elaboration of a new aesthetic form but *in* an analysis of the moral labyrinth. Proustian memory is, in its deep structure, simultaneously aesthetic envelope and moral content.

Returning now to the liminary quotation from *Death in Venice* with which I began this chapter, I would like to offer a concluding comment on Thomas Mann's remarks concerning the interaction of the aesthetic and moral realms. It is certainly in the nature of artistic form to tend toward moral "indifference," since form *includes* the moral question by thematizing it. But one should add that it is in the nature of the moral question, when it is strongly problematized (for example, in *Wilhelm Meister* and

A la recherche du temps perdu, but not in *Le Grand Meaulnes*), to undo all efforts at aesthetic mastery, to return to the surface of the text at the precise moment of the greatest narrative transparency – as in the Proustian "intermittences du coeur," and as in the *Sinntrieb* Rainer Maria Rilke puts into action in the third Duino Elegy, written also, "by chance," in 1913.

What Rilke evokes in this poem dedicated to Neptune, "the blood's River-God," is the force of chaotic ancestral drives that reside below all formal constructions, all aestheticization of life, all beautiful flowerings. In a manner emblematic of Modernism, Rilke no longer shows aesthetic form modeling life, he no longer imagines a possible variation on the "beautiful soul," but traces the portrait of a man being thrust into existence (we are very close here to Heideggerian *Geworfenheit*) who, since time immemorial, is "entangled" (*verstrickt*) in his destiny. The human being is no longer the one who controls form from the outside, the one who dreams of an immobile perfection, but he or she who, living on the "fallen and mute ruins" of Time, is hurled into the dynamism of figures, a novice participating in the deployment of images ("jagende Formen") which model his reality and constitute the inner space of his moral drama (the luminosity of his "heart"):

Er, der Neue, Scheuende, wie er verstrickt war,
mit des innern Geschehns weiterschlagenden Ranken
schon zu Mustern verschlungen, zu würgendem Wachstum, zu tierhaft
jagenden Formen. Wie er sich hingab –. Liebte.
Liebte sein Inneres, seines Inneren Wildnis,
diesen Urwald in ihm, auf dessen stummen Gestürztsein
lichtgrün sein Herz stand.

So young and shy, how he entangled himself
in the spreading roots of events inside him,
twisted patterns, strangling tendrils, shapes
of preying animals. How he surrendered –. Loved.
Loved his interior world, the jungle in him, that
primal inner forest where his pale green heart stood
among the fallen and mute ruins.[25]

CHAPTER 6

Proust and Kafka: uncanny narrative openings

In the previous chapter I suggested that *Le Grand Meaulnes* stands at the juncture between a waning Romantic sensibility and the advent of Modernism, at a crucial crossroads in literary history just prior to World War I. My conclusion was that the narrative faultline in the novel between part one and parts two and three, between the domain of an aestheticized dreamworld and the territory of ethical responsibility, constitutes an unbridgeable gap for Alain-Fournier. The figure of the "beautiful soul" appears in a moment of moral crisis and cannot save the protagonist from his remorse. The universe of *Le Grand Meaulnes*, despite its initial promise of poetic charm, becomes mired in guilt and an unredeemable melancholy. The uncanny figure of the woman at the piano with her back turned to Meaulnes and to the reader serves as a negation of the "beautiful souls" discoursing on love in the meadow. In his description of the otherworldly calm in which Meaulnes listens to the woman at the keyboard amid theatrically costumed children, Alain-Fournier brings us close to, but not into contact with, the realm of *Unheimlichkeit*. We as readers do not cross the threshold into uncanniness, just as the novel itself does not cross over into Modernism.

In the three chapters that follow – on Proust and Kafka, Conrad and Gide, and Woolf – I shall be locating what might be called *the narrative emergence of uncanniness as territory* within representative works by these writers. As we have seen in earlier chapters of this book, *das Unheimliche* is the domain of death-in-life, a ghostly place or non-place in which the aesthetic and the ethical cross into each other's territories and disrupt the boundaries separating the one sphere from the other. What distinguishes the Modernist writers I am about to examine from Alain-Fournier is that each of them, in his or her own distinct way, discovers literature (the literary as such) while falling into the strange-but-familiar territory of the uncanny. For Proust and Kafka, narrative movement itself is inseparable from the uncanny reverberations present within the signifier: to open up the diabolical potential residing within the signifier is to liberate literary language and to release an infinite diegetic energy. For Conrad and Gide, *das Unheimliche* lies beneath and upsets the simple opposition between home territory (England, France) and the foreign "other" (North Africa, the Congo): uncanniness, for both writers, is conceived of as *the inhuman*, that area lying below and beyond all narrative frames and all ethical control. In Woolf's fictional universe, the uncanny is synonymous with *the impersonal*: the place of *das Unheimliche* is to be found in a watery blurring of distinctions, in a generalized narrative permeability that goes against the very logic of framing as such. The Modernist texts I am reading here undermine formal symmetries and moral certainties by opening themselves to the radical otherness of the uncanny, an otherness that is ontologically prior to the classical binary oppositions of self and other, home and foreign, *physis* and *techné*. Chapters six, seven, and eight of this book are designed to be read together, as variations on the theme of the uncanny in its unruly narrative manifestation, in its raising of the barriers separating ethical action from aesthetic form.

I PROUST AND KAFKA ON FICTIONAL ORIGINS: RHETORIC AND NARRATOLOGY

In traditional intellectual biographies of novelists, the central issue for the biographer is to discover at precisely what point the novelist becomes himself or herself. The formative events of childhood, the early readings and first attempts at writing, lead toward the moment at which the creator of fictions sheds external influences and discovers a personal style. This moment is represented, in the intellectual biography, as a threshold, a passageway between unrealized efforts and accomplished goals, between *juvenilia* and authentic artistic creation.[1] Of course, one might object that the extreme clarity with which many traditional accounts of authors' lives depict such a passage is achieved at the price of simplification: it is no doubt easier for the biographer to trace an orderly career from a retrospective point of view than it is for the writer to recognize, in life, the threshold-moment when it occurs. Nevertheless, it is a fact that those writers whose works have an autobiographical form or self-reflective focus often insist (with energy equal to that of their biographers) upon the absolute value of one moment, which they represent dramatically as a beginning, a birth, or an opening into the space of writing.

For the two writers I shall be examining in this chapter – Marcel Proust and Franz Kafka – the threshold-moment can be conceived, in psychological terms, as a liberation from childhood anxieties. George Painter, in his *Marcel Proust: A Biography*, sees the early stages of Proust's literary infatuations in cathartic terms, as the chapter headings "Salvation through Ruskin" (in volume I) and "Purification through Parody" (in volume II) indicate. Proust is free to write and "become himself" once he has shed the external literary influences of Ruskin and Sainte-Beuve, on the one hand, and once his father and mother have died, on the other. Proust lives once influences have been buried – and, Painter adds, once he no longer must submit to the pressures of the Oedipal triangle in which his psychological ambivalence has been nurtured.[2] Ronald Hayman's *Kafka: A Biography* is even more obviously centered in a transparent Freudian configuration. Hayman begins his book with a chapter entitled "The Turning Point: 1912," in which he describes the evening of the composition of "The Judgment" ("Das Urteil") – Kafka's first supposedly Kafkaesque narrative, where the all-determining relationship between son and father jumps upon the page with theatrical intensity. The maturity of Kafka's biological life is "really" the beginning of his creative life: for us readers of Kafka, the evening of 22 September 1912 slices like a blade between before and after, the inessential and the essential, non-writing and writing.[3]

It would be easy enough – I believe, too easy – to criticize both Painter and Hayman for their naïve, teleological "Hegelianism," while granting their studies a limited value as indispensable groundwork for the more sophisticated textual analyses that interest many readers today. The intellectual movement of classification/appropriation whereby the biographer determines exactly where the turning point is located in the life of the fiction writer is far more universal than it might at first appear: it is, after all, the expression of a desire widely shared by critics of divergent persuasions – the desire to penetrate beneath the plane of what is given to discover the source or origin of surface appearances. It is not difficult to find, within the pages of even those critics and theorists we consider to be the most sensitive to textual complexities, the same gesture of definition, the same peeling back toward origins, that strikes one as excessively simple and categorical in traditional intellectual biographies. The critic I have in mind, and the issues raised by his writing, will lead directly to the topic of my essay and to the problem of narrative *openings* in general: I am thinking of Gérard Genette, and specifically of the critical move he makes at the end of "Métonymie chez Proust" as he prepares his own transitional jump from the close analysis of rhetorical complexities that characterizes this magisterial essay to his "Discours du récit" – the methodical treatise of "narratology" that concludes *Figures III*.[4]

The final two pages of "Métonymie chez Proust" are doubly transitional: first, because Genette needs to justify the inclusion, within *Figures III*, of a first section containing short critical studies and a second, far more unified section on narrative theory. Secondly, on the level of subject-matter, Genette needs to demonstrate how metaphor and metonymy can coexist harmoniously within a literary text: this requires detailed demonstration since metaphor, according to Genette (via Jakobson),[5] is the pole of simultaneity, memory association as "frozen time," and ecstatic immobility; whereas metonymy, the mode of diachronic juxtaposition, is the pole of narration. In asking how the opposites of metaphor and metonymy can be reconciled within the higher unity of the text, Genette returns to the threshold-moment which Proust himself designates as the very matrix of his novel – the moment at which a series of involuntary memory associations generates *A la recherche du temps perdu* as narrative. I am referring to the well-known madeleine episode, which Genette describes as a *coupure* (cut) separating the first chapter of *Du côté de chez Swann* [*Swann's Way*] from the second:

There is indeed a striking cut [*coupure*], in the first part of *Swann*, between the first chapter, almost exclusively devoted to that originary and obsessive scene which Proust calls "my bedtime drama" [*le théâtre et le drame de mon coucher*], a scene that had remained for a long time in the narrator's consciousness as the only memory of Combray which had not sunken into forgetfulness, an immobile scene in which the narrative becomes enclosed and engulfed as if drained of all hope of disengaging itself; and the second chapter, where, replacing this vertical Combray of repetitious obsession and of "fixation" . . . arises the horizontal Combray, with its extensive space, its "two sides" [*"deux côtés"*], its alternating walks, its childhood geography and family calendar, which combine to form the point of departure, the veritable beginning of the novel's narrative movement. (*Figures III*, 62; my translation)

The madeleine section mediates between the vertical immobility of an instantaneous revelation and the horizontal extensiveness of an incipient narration. But it is important to note that for Genette the passage through the disjunctive space of the narrative *coupure* is itself fluid rather than disjunctive, metaphorical rather than metonymical. Indeed, he imagines the *Recherche* as a synthesis of lyric instantaneousness and narrative discontinuity in which the unravelling of the fictional story does not negate or complicate its point of origin in atemporal reflectiveness, but rather *substitutes* for it: narration does not destroy but merely *replaces* the poetry of memory. Thus, the transition from "le théâtre et le drame de mon coucher" to the telling of Marcel's story in its chronological sequence does not shock the reader's sensibility or invalidate the aesthetic unity of the novel. The wound in the text is only apparent; it is, paradoxically, within the narrative *coupure* that the novel takes its shape. Implicit in Genette's argument is the assumption that there is a higher unity than that of discrete textual fragments ("chapters"), under which these fragments can be subsumed. There must be a transcendental Text that provides the horizon for both vertical and horizontal, metaphorical and metonymical dimensions, in much the same way as traditional intellectual biographies appeal to higher units of meaning ("the *real* Proust, the mature author of the *Recherche*; the *essential*, post-1912 Kafka") within which the successive, chaotic writing-traces of an author are ordered in a hierarchical progression.

I do not make this comparison between the theoretician Genette and the biographers Painter and Hayman in order to blur the essential distinctions between differing methodologies, but to illustrate a general tendency of critical thought: the movement toward the closing of interpretive gaps through synthetic rhetorical manipulations. The two-page passage at the end of "Métonymie chez Proust" is an interesting piece of rhetorical writing that contains, on a lower level of poetic intensity, many of the same complexities to be found in the Proustian text it analyzes; but these complexities do not impinge upon the self-contained logical validity of the "Discours du récit" that immediately follows in Genette's own "narration." Indeed, Genette's "technologie du discours narratif"[6] stands on its own as a terminologically precise study of narrative definition, but by its self-sufficient metonymical extensiveness it distances itself from the rhetorical convolutedness of Proust's text. Narratology as literary theory/technology may be, according to Heidegger's description of *techné* in general, *a falling away* of thought from its element, an instrumental elaboration of systems destined to lose touch with its source.[7] My purpose in the following pages will be to return to that source – the knot of figural entanglement at the gateway to the novel – in order to study how the strategic opening of gaps and wounds in the text, the crossing of the narrative threshold, generates the construction of literary space.

II PROUST

Viewed as an interiorized *Bildungsroman*, *A la recherche du temps perdu* is the story of a consciousness that comes to itself in writing, that discovers, in a final act of retrospective understanding, an apparently simple "fact": that the fragmentary actions and reactions of its affective life can be molded into a narration. As in all *Bildungsromane*, however, the hero must traverse a wide space of inner and outer topography before he can understand the meaningfulness of what originally appeared without form or purpose. Perhaps the best place to start, if one wishes to measure or survey the distance that separates Marcel the "almost-novelist" of *Le Temps retrouvé* from his embryonic self is not the madeleine episode (in which the narrator is already middle-aged), but the section "Noms de pays: le nom" ["Place-Names: The Name"] that concludes *Du côté de chez Swann*. In this final chapter of the novel's first volume we encounter Marcel as a young boy fascinated with the evocative (or, more precisely, associative) power of place-names. Not yet having traveled himself, Marcel endows the outside world (which he knows through the images of books and photographs) with symbolic significance. He projects onto the unknown world all the grandeur he does not find within himself:

> I was curious and eager to know only what I believed to be more real than myself [*ce que je croyais plus vrai que moi-même*], what had for me the supreme merit of showing me a fragment of the mind of a great genius, or of the force or the grace of nature as it appeared when left entirely to itself, without human interference. (*RTP* I, 417; *ALR* I, 377)[8]

At this early stage in the development of the protagonist's consciousness, single words suffice to construct vast edifices of imagined reality. In Jakobsonian terms, we are in the domain of metaphorical substitution, of paradigmatic relations, in which names like "Balbec," "Venise," "Florence," "Quimperlé" are one-word lyric poems that freely replace each other according to the arbitrary whims of Marcel's mind. Here, we are as far as can be imagined from the structures and laws of narrative.

The metaphorical fusion that characterizes the section on place-names is based upon the possibility of uniting elements the adult (rational) mind might keep categorically separate. Thus, when Marcel dreams of Balbec, he combines two images of Normandy in one:

> Thereafter, on delightful, stormy February nights, the wind – breathing into my heart, which it shook no less violently than the chimney of my bedroom, the project of a visit to Balbec – blended in me [*mêlait en moi*] the desire for Gothic architecture as well as for a storm upon the sea. (*RTP* I, 418; *ALR* I, 378)

Balbec is the place where the magnificence of nature and the prestige of culture fuse, where Gothic art merges with tempestuous weather. It is also, in the exaggerated words of the nature *and* culture snob, Legrandin, the end of the Western world, the equivalent of Gibraltar in medieval literature, the point beyond which no civilization exists:

> "You still feel there beneath your feet," he [Legrandin] had told me, "far more than at Finistère itself... that you are actually at the land's end of France, of Europe, of the Old World. And it is the ultimate encampment of the fishermen, the heirs of all the fishermen who have lived since the world's beginning, facing the everlasting kingdom of the sea-fogs and shadows of the night." (*RTP* I, 417)

The two geographical poles that function within the associative logic of the protagonist's consciousness are Normandy (Balbec) on the one hand, and Italy (Venice and Florence) on the other. East and West, Saint Mark's and Bayeux, Byzantium and the Norman world, form a panoply of mixed images whose opposite origins are not initially felt to be in conflict, since the names "Balbec," "Venice," "Florence" are *just* names – signifiers dissociated from their referents. However, the narrator of "Noms de pays: le nom" is also the narrator of later episodes of the novel, and he does not hesitate to divulge to his readers how fragile the young Marcel's system of analogical, a-geographical poetic relationships is:

> But if these names thus permanently absorbed the image I had formed of these towns, it was only by transforming that image, by subordinating its reappearance in me to their own special laws; and in consequence of this they made it more beautiful, but at the same time more different from anything that the towns of Normandy or Tuscany could in reality be, and, by increasing the arbitrary delights of my imagination, aggravated the disenchantment that was in store for me when I set out upon my travels. (*RTP* I, 420)

Here, in a typically Proustian negation of suspense, the narrator foreshadows the reality of Normandy and Italy within the *Recherche* – a textual "reality" we do not discover until well after "Noms de pays: le nom." The highly enigmatic and truncated Venice episode occurs in *Albertine disparue*, two thousand pages after the section on place-names.[9] And the first trip to Balbec is separated from the original daydreaming *on* Balbec by a more modest but still very considerable textual space of three hundred pages. The important matter, the phenomenon worthy of examination, especially in the case of a novelist who so openly admired Flaubert's use of dramatic temporal *blancs*,[10] is the very existence of the spacing between the naming of Balbec (in "Noms de pays: le nom") and the visit to Balbec in "Noms de pays: le pays" ["Place-Names: The Place" – the second "chapter" of *A l'ombre des jeunes filles en fleurs*]. The decomposition of the associative, metaphorical, paradigmatic forms characteristic of the place-naming episode occurs when the protagonist *travels* for the first time – i.e., when he discovers the mysteries of topography. With the dramatically open *coupure* between name and place, episode and episode, begins the metonymical accumulative network of events we call narration. And the role of narration is to demystify the poetic charm of metaphorical play, to reveal the irresponsibility of the freely circulating signifier and its associative constructions. Indeed, when, after an exhilarating, aesthetically and erotically charged train-ride, Marcel arrives at Balbec, he finds that the dreamed word he presumed to denote a geographical unity in fact hides two radically different realities: Balbec-en-terre (Balbec-le-vieux) and Balbec-plage (*RTP* I, 708; *ALR* II, 19).

The two elements previously associated in the protagonist's mind – the cathedral and the ocean – are now revealed to exist in separate contexts. Thus the movement of referential testing, the narrative quest for the "truth" of Balbec, results in a splitting of signifier from signified, and in a doubling of the signified itself: narration takes place in a spatial disjunction (*coupure*) and itself enacts a *coupure* within signification. The cutting of the rhetorical knot "Balbec" causes the progressive disentanglement of associated images. In a first step, the capacity of names to contain or enclose the "idea" of a city ("these names thus permanently absorbed the image I had formed of these towns") is shown to be impossible, since the one designation "Balbec" is not monosemic. Consequently, the individuality or personality conferred upon the imagined city by the evocative power of the name no longer exists. What remains for the observer to see is not a system of subjectively postulated, necessarily related elements, but an amalgam of pure contingency, a group of arbitrarily juxtaposed objects whose chief attribute is resistance to synthetic understanding. Rather than rise above the waves of a storm-battered coast, the cathedral's belltower

> stood on a square which was the junction of two tramway routes, opposite a café which bore, in letters of gold, the legend "Billiards" . . . And the church – impinging on my attention at the same time as the café, the passing stranger of whom I had had to ask my way, the station to which presently I should have to return – merged with all the rest [*faisait un tout avec le reste*], seemed an accident, a by-product of this summer afternoon [*semblait un accident, un produit de cette fin d'après-midi*], in which the mellow and distended dome against the sky was like a fruit of which the same light that bathed the chimneys of the houses ripened the pink, glowing, luscious skin. (*RTP* I, 708–9; *ALR* II, 19–20)

It is significant that the accidental quality of the cathedral's presence on the town square, which indicates the unfounded nature of Marcel's dreams, is immediately negated and recuperated in the unified golden harmony of the afternoon. The decomposition of a fragile metaphorical system of resemblances yields, in the subtle transition from "accident" to "*produit* de cette fin d'après-midi," to a metonymic system of juxtaposed illuminated objects, whose beauty is the result of a spatial or contextual totalization. It is as if, for Proust, even in a moment of heightened critical lucidity, the tendency of the mind were to continue constructing associative frameworks as a defense against the threat of a significant void.

In the end, however, the closer the protagonist observes the individual detail of the mundane setting in which the cathedral is inscribed, the more he is depressed by what Proust calls "the tyranny of the Particular" (*RTP* I, 710). *In particular*, the statue whose reproduction the young Marcel had studied and admired in Combray, la Vierge du Porche, now appears "transformed, as was the church itself, into a little old woman in stone whose height I could measure and whose wrinkles I could count" ("métamorphosée, ainsi que l'église elle-même, en une petite vieille de pierre dont je pouvais mesurer la hauteur et compter les rides") (*RTP* I, 710; *ALR* II, 21). The depth of disillusionment emerges not only in the transparent reference to Baudelaire's superb ironic poem "Les Petites Vieilles,"[11] but also in a somewhat more hidden allusion to Proust's own previous writing: the essay "Journées de pèlerinage," written as part of the preface to his Ruskin translation, *La Bible d'Amiens*.[12] La Vierge du Porche at Balbec is the inverted, parodied version of La Vierge Dorée, the statue in the Amiens cathedral that, in the mind of the young Proust, represented the inseparable oneness of cathedral and city. What was celebrated with enthusiasm in "Journées de pèlerinage" – the "individuality" and "personality" of the humanized statue – has become degraded, transformed into grotesque caricature. Compare the "petite vieille de pierre" of Balbec to Proust's earlier formulation:

> I sense that I was mistaken in calling it [La Vierge Dorée] a work of art. A statue which belongs forever to a certain place on the earth, to a certain city, i.e., a thing which possesses a name like a person, which is an individual, the equivalent of which one can never find on the face of the continents, whose name railway employees cry out to us, telling us precisely where we had to come to find it, and which seems to say to us, without realizing it: "Love what you can never see a second time" – such a statue is perhaps less universal in significance than a work of art, yet it retains us by a stronger tie than that of the work of art itself, one of those permanent ties by which only people and countries can bind us. ("Journées de pèlerinage," 85; my translation)

In the final sentence describing Marcel's encounter with Balbec-en-terre, Proust inverts the *contenant–contenu* (container–contained) structure of *absorption* ("these names thus permanently absorbed the image I had formed of these towns") that characterized the dreamed images of places in "Noms de pays: le nom." Now, the name *opens* itself and releases its contents to the outside: Marcel's voyage of discovery culminates in the imprudent intrusion into a taboo space:

> but as for Balbec, no sooner had I set foot in it than it was as though I had broken open a name which ought to have been kept hermetically closed, and into which, seizing at once the opportunity that I had imprudently given them, expelling all the images that had lived in it until then, a tramway, a café, people crossing the square, the branch of the savings bank, irresistibly propelled by some external pressure, by a pneumatic force, had come surging into the interior of those two syllables which, closing over them, now let them frame the porch of the Persian church and would henceforth never cease to contain them. (*RTP* I, 710)

The name of Balbec is a Pandora's Box, a receptacle of illusory virtues and beliefs which, when released, can never be reappropriated; and yet the hope of a return to original harmony remains. The protagonist of the *Recherche* will continue to think that "other towns still remained intact for me, that I might soon, perhaps, be making my way, as into a shower of pearls, into the cool babbling murmur of watery Quimperlé" (*ibid.*), but the inexorable negativity of the novel will continue to demonstrate the arbitrariness of the relationship between sign and referent, between the poetically evocative "pearl" of *Quimperlé* and the actual appearance of the city in its geographic prison.

The Ruskinian echoes in the Balbec-en-terre episode are very deep; they transcend the level of superficial parody present in the Vierge Dorée and Vierge du Porche mimicry. One senses, in following the complex manipulations of *contenant* and *contenu*, the opening/closing of receptive/resistant surfaces, that the base structure underlying all these variations is the "Open Sesame" motif of *The Arabian Nights* – a constant theme in the *Recherche* that Proust borrowed from Ruskin's *Sesame and Lilies.*[13] The final sentence of the Balbec-en-terre section makes clear that the opening and shutting of mysterious doors is a magical process of brusque (sometimes painful) substitution, in which one *contenu* replaces another, or even drives it out. The childhood images of Balbec are forever gone: now the word "contains" its geographical reality; the word has become anchored in topography.

Yet it would be a simplification to assert that the *Recherche* "is" the movement of disillusionment from dream to reality, from vague poetic association, via an ironic narration, to a clear view of "things as they are." First of all, what *is* this strange split city of Balbec? What happens if we, like the young Marcel, pronounce its syllables and allow them to resonate with associations? Balbec sounds a lot like BAALBEK, the ancient city, now in Lebanon, whose name derives from Baal, the Phoenician sun god (the Greeks called the city *Heliopolis*, city of the sun). The congruence of names is so obvious as to be blinding.[14] The curious thing is that Marcel's travel west, toward the end of the known world, Legrandin's Finistère, is, simultaneously, a move toward the rising sun, the cradle of civilization, the world in which Scheherazade told her death-defying stories. What appeared strangely and inappropriately exotic in the architecture of Balbec's cathedral – its "Persian" style – becomes logical enough once we accept that Balbec/Baalbek is West *and* East, Normandy *and* the Orient.

This topographical conflation occurs more than once in the *Recherche*, and is typical of those moments in the novel that stage the protagonist's search for hidden truths. The Balbec episode is the first in a series of travel experiences, each of which compulsively repeats the same quest of referential verification. Despite his many disappointments, Marcel never ceases to believe that the world outside the self contains riches that the self can appropriate and store within its inner treasury. However, with each succeeding voyage outward, it becomes increasingly clear that the discovered places – "Balbec," "Florence," "Venice" – are, in fact, projections, interwoven images like those in a dream that radiate outward from a common source: the childhood scene of Combray. Indeed, when Marcel travels to Venice, in a second pilgrimage inescapably reminiscent of Ruskin,[15] he discovers not only that the city of the Doges, like Balbec, is the *point de rencontre* of East and West, of Roman Christianity and Byzantium, but also, perhaps even more uncannily, that Venice is a "transposition" of Combray:

> as beauty may exist in the most precious as well as in the humblest things – I received there [in Venice] impressions analogous to those which I had felt so often in the past at Combray, but transposed into a wholly different and far richer key. (*RTP* III, 637)

The entire Venice episode falls under the category of the "uncanny" as Freud defines it: "that class of the frightening which leads back to what is known of old and long familiar."[16] On the one hand, Venice is strange, exotic, "oriental," a series of illuminated pages from *The Arabian Nights*:

> My gondola followed the course of the small canals; like the mysterious hand of a genie leading me through the maze of this oriental city, they seemed, as I advanced, to be cutting a path for me . . . and as though the magic guide had been holding a candle in his hand and were lighting the way for me, they kept casting ahead of them a ray of sunlight for which they cleared a route. (*RTP* III, 641)

On the other hand, the more Marcel follows the path traced by the genie, the more he feels, spiritually, close to the revelation of a secret, the more he feels in possession of himself, the more he feels *at home*: "J'avais l'impression, qu'augmentait encore mon désir, de ne pas être dehors, mais d'entrer de plus en plus au fond de quelque chose de secret" ("I had the impression, which my desire only served to augment, of not being outside, but of entering more and more deeply into something secret") (*ALR* IV, 207).[17] Venice is thus *another* Combray. To travel from Combray to Venice is also, simultaneously, to travel back to Combray, back to the source, back to the *Heimat*, the native land. The liquid world of Venice harks back to the maternal, intrauterine world of origins around which Proust constructed his paradise: Combray.

In my analysis of the origin of narration in Proust, I have come up against an apparent paradox. On the one hand, I have pointed out how narrative spacing, as metonymical displacement, occurs with the disassociation of metaphorical images and the discovery of the split sign in Balbec. On the other hand, I have shown that this movement of temporal difference (différ*a*nce) is accompanied by the protagonist's belief in (desire of) the qualitative difference between the place from which he departs and the exotic place toward which he travels, the place that may contain a secret truth worthy of un-earthing. However, it turns out that this *other* place is really the *same*, or, to use Freud's terms, *das Unheimliche* (the uncanny, the non-home) is really *das Heimliche* (the familiar, the homelike). Narration in Proust – the movement away from lyrical sameness, through metonymical spacing, toward an un-settling, disjunctive reunion with the native land – reproduces the semantic displacements of the word *heimlich*, which Freud describes in this way: "Thus *heimlich* is a word the meaning of which develops in the direction of ambivalence, until it finally coincides with its opposite, *unheimlich*. *Unheimlich* is in some way or other a sub-species of *heimlich*" (TU 226). To probe further the structure of narration as development "in the direction of ambivalence," and to clarify the paradoxical definition of the *unheimlich* as "in some way or other a sub-species of *heimlich*," I shall turn to the uncontested modern master of the *unheimlich*, Franz Kafka.

III KAFKA

The uncanniness of Kafka's world may be the only major point of convergence in which critical studies of his works reach consensus. It is universally acknowledged that the protagonist's labyrinthine wanderings in the three novels, the bizarre bestiary of the short stories, and the extreme self-deprecation of the letters, all create the effect of *Unheimlichkeit*: that is, the reader of these writings feels far from home, uprooted, alienated. The problem is to interpret what this mysterious uncanniness *means*, and it is in the interpretation of the enigma of uncanniness that the Babel Tower of Kafka criticism has grown to its present awesome heights. Much of Kafka criticism can be described as an effort to allegorize the literal surfaces of the writer's stories, to bridge the gaps between fragmentary textual blocks, to find the appropriate exegetical key that would unlock the closed, crystalline surface of the author's style, in order to uncover, for lack of a better expression, "deep meanings." In the bazaar of Kafka criticism one can choose among theological, existential/philosophical, psychoanalytical, Marxist, and, more recently, literary self-referential interpretations[18] – a great diversity indeed; but in most cases, to varying degrees, the underlying assumption is that something exists "underneath the language" that lends Kafka's writings a far greater resonance than they exhibit on their fluid, flatly harmonious, outward envelope.

What does not emerge in the majority of studies is the relation between *Unheimlichkeit* and Kafka's play with language – a linguistically immanent uncanniness that has a great deal to do with the narrative construction of the author's works. Although much has been written, occasionally on a high level of theoretical abstraction, about Kafka's ambivalent (outsider's) position vis-à-vis the German language,[19] the specific, highly idiosyncratic way in which Kafka manipulated words and repeatedly combined certain privileged chains of signifiers needs more study. In the following pages I shall examine the problematics of Kafkan narrative through an analysis of certain key words and the variability of their contextual inclusion.

If, like Genette interpreting Proust, we wish to find in Kafka's writings the dramatization of the moment of passage from fragmentary daydreaming to narrative coherence, the most obvious equivalent of the madeleine episode in intensity (and in centrality for the whole of Kafka's literary production) is the section of the *Tagebücher* [*Diaries*] that includes "Das Urteil" – the work that Hayman and most critics consider to be Kafka's first "mature" piece of writing. In the midst of sometimes mundane, often aphoristic remarks on his daily life, Kafka set down the fictional story "Das Urteil," which, he tells us in the entry directly following the story, was written at one sitting from 10 p.m. on 22 September until 6 a.m. on 23 September 1912. In this entry, Kafka relates his elation at the continuity of his narration. Although his body had become stiff from sitting at the desk, the writing flowed: "The fearful strain and joy, how the story developed before me, as if I were advancing over water" ("Die fürchterliche Anstrengung und Freude, wie sich die Geschichte vor mir entwickelte wie ich in einem Gewässer vorwärtskam") (*D* 276; *T* 460).[20] The quasi-miraculous outpouring of "Das Urteil" convinced Kafka that his earlier writings were unimportant, invalid, mired in literary "lowlands":

> The conviction verified that with my novel-writing I am in the shameful lowlands of writing. Only *in this way* can writing be done, only with such coherence, with such a complete opening out of the body and the soul [*mit solcher vollständigen Öffnung des Leibes und der Seele*]. (*D* 276; *T* 461; translator's emphasis)

This opening of the body and soul is an openness within the act of writing itself. While composing his story, Kafka did not shut himself completely to all outside influences, but experienced "many emotions carried along in the writing," especially thoughts of other writers and writings, including "thoughts about Freud, of course" (*D* 276). It is tempting to take this parenthetical remark as an (open) invitation to read "Das Urteil" in a Freudian vein, as an Oedipal struggle between Georg Bendemann (Franz Kafka) and his father (Hermann Kafka). I think one may find it enriching to read the contextual frame of "Das Urteil" – the diary entries before and after the story – in a "Freudian" manner, certainly, but also in a Proustian manner, by allowing certain privileged words and sounds to reverberate. Remembering the key words of the ecstatic morning after writing, I now quote from Kafka's diary two weeks before the composition of "Das Urteil":

> It will be hard to rouse me, and yet I am restless. When I lay in bed this afternoon and someone quickly turned a key in the lock, for a moment I had locks all over my body [*und jemand einen Schlüssel im Schloß rasch umdrehte, hat ich einen Augenblick lang Schlösser auf dem ganzen Körper*], as though at a fancy-dress ball, and at short intervals a lock was opened or shut here and there. (*D* 269; *T* 433)

Clearly, the symbolism of opening and shutting, unlocking and locking, was for Kafka a concretization of the wide alternations between inspired writing and creative closure. This lying shackled in bed in a Houdini-like posture while, independently of one's conscious will, locks are opened and shut, provides a humorous mechanistic representation of what Freud called the "unconscious," and at the same time foreshadows Kafka's later coercive treatment of the human body – as in the stories "In the Penal Colony" and "A Hunger-Artist". But the symbolism of opening and shutting, the allusions to keys and locks, are more than illustrative metaphorical devices or thematic constructs: they structure an undercurrent-discourse, a *geheime Rede* that flows from work to work, from genre to genre, and that constitutes what might be called Kafka's *language of the source.*

To pursue this bifurcated language, I will turn now to the most concise and self-contained of Kafka's autobiographical writings, the *Brief an den Vater* [*Letter to His Father*] – an undelivered message[21] in which Kafka explains his personality, career, and life-sufferings as a struggle against his father. The *Letter* has always been a double-edged document for critics, since, by providing them with the most serviceable of possible (Freudian) keys to unlock the secrets of Kafka's writings, it robs them of any claim to original psychological insight. Kafka pre-empted his Freudian critics and set in motion the psychocritical interpretation of his work with the observation, located two-thirds of the way into the *Letter*:

My writing was all about you; all I did there, after all, was to bemoan what I could not bemoan upon your breast. It was an intentionally long-drawn-out leave-taking from you [*Es war ein absichtlich in die Länge gezogener Abschied von Dir*], yet, although it was enforced by you, it did take its course in the direction determined by me. (*L* 87; *B* 160).[22]

Important in this statement is the association of writing with the movement of flight. If Kafka could not struggle with his father on his father's terms, he could build and follow alternative paths, paths more complex and less real than those of everyday existence. Throughout the *Letter* Kafka describes the life of the writer in terms diametrically opposed to those that characterize "normal" people, i.e., people with socially useful occupations and with families. As is well known, the most dramatic and pathetic organizing principle of Kafka's life was his inability, despite repeated attempts, to marry. Unlike Proust, who knew his only permanent relationship could be with the book he was composing, Kafka seemed to be repeatedly drawn to and repulsed by the idea of joining with a woman to engender children. In the passage that follows, we can see how Kafka conceived of himself in relation to those people who, unlike the alienated writer, were pursuing in an unquestioning way their biological destiny:

Marrying, founding a family, accepting all the children that come, supporting them in this insecure world and perhaps even guiding them a little, is, I am convinced, the utmost a human being can succeed in doing at all [*das Aüsserste, das einem Menschen überhaupt gelingen kann*]. That so many seem to succeed in this is no evidence to the contrary; first of all, there are not many who do succeed, and secondly, these not-many usually don't "do" it, it merely "happens" to them; although this is not that Utmost, it is still very great and very honorable (particularly since "doing" and "happening" cannot be kept clearly distinct). And finally, it is not a matter of this Utmost at all, anyway, but only of some distant but decent approximation [*Und schliesslich handelt es sich auch gar nicht um dieses Aüsserste, sondern nur um irgendeine ferne, aber anständige Annäherung*]; it is, after all, not necessary to fly right into the middle of the sun, but it is necessary to crawl to a clean little spot on earth where the sun sometimes shines and one can warm oneself a little. (*L* 99–100; *B* 168)

The writer-bachelor is thus a man without *ground*, a man who can only hope, like the animals of Kafka's short narratives, to creep his way toward a limited place, a man of the cold who cannot hope to face the rays of the sun (the power of the father). Later in the same section of the *Letter* Kafka uses similar language in a more detailed account of his failures to marry:

I will try to explain it in more detail [*Ich will es näher zu erklären versuchen*]. Here, in the attempt to marry, two seemingly antagonistic elements in my relations with you unite more intensely than anywhere else. Marriage certainly is the pledge of the most acute form of self-liberation and independence. I would have a family, in my opinion the highest [*das Höchste*] one can achieve, and so too the highest you have achieved; I would be your equal [*ich wäre Dir ebenbürtig*]; all old and ever new shame and tyranny would be mere history [*bloss noch Geschichte*]. It would be like a fairly tale [*Das wäre allerdings märchenhaft*], but precisely there does the questionable element lie. It is too much; so much cannot be achieved [*Es ist zu viel, so viel kann nicht erreicht werden*]. It is as if a person were a prisoner, and he had not only the intention to escape, which would perhaps be attainable, but also, and indeed, simultaneously, the intention to rebuild the prison as a pleasure dome for himself [*die Absicht, das Gefängnis in ein Lustschloss für sich umzubauen*]. But if he escapes, he cannot rebuild, and if he rebuilds, he cannot escape. If I, in the particular unhappy relationship in which I stand to you, want to become independent, I must do something that will have, if possible, no connection with you at all; though marrying is the greatest thing of all and provides the most honorable independence, it is also at the same time in the closest relation to you [*in engster Beziehung zu Dir*]. To try to get out of all this has therefore a touch of madness [*Wahnsinn*] about it, and every attempt is almost punished with it. (*L* 113; *B* 175–76)

As in the previous passage, to describe marriage Kafka uses superlatives: "Das Äußerste," "Das Höchste." The writer remains in the lowlands, in the realm of closeness and nearness ("eine anständige *Annäherung*" in the first passage; here "Ich will es *näher* zu erklären versuchen"); but he navigates his unsure way dwarfed by the outward magnificence of the social institution of marriage. If it were possible for the writer-bachelor to marry, he would be on an equal footing with the father (literally, of equal birth – "ebenbürtig"). Because marriage leads to the grounding of a family, the writer-turned-husband would participate in the natural processes of biology and history. But it is precisely this move that Kafka recognizes as impossible, unrealizable, as unreal as a fairy tale ("Es ist zu viel, so viel kann nicht erreicht werden . . . Das wäre allerdings märchenhaft"). Of especial interest is the fundamental dichotomy between *Geschichte* (history) and *Märchen. Geschichte* is a causal sequence of real events that one can choose to memorialize or forget: *Geschichte* is the temporal setting and the mode of existence of both families and nations. *Märchen*, on the other hand, is the hypothetical, fictive mode of the writer-bachelor; it is the mode of storytelling, of magic transformation, of the Brothers Grimm and Scheherazade. It would be *märchenhaft* for Kafka, the creator of modern *Märchen*, to be reconciled with history. What is it that makes the writer-bachelor not susceptible to assimilation into family history? Kafka answers the question in a striking simile: "It is as if a person were a prisoner, and he had not only the intention to escape, which would perhaps be attainable, but also, and indeed, simultaneously, the intention to rebuild the prison as a pleasure dome for himself."

Writing is not simply a flight from the father: it is also a metamorphosing process, whereby one's prison becomes a castle. Or, to use Kafka's language, whereby the locks (*Schlösser*) on one's body become a pleasure-monument (*Lustschloß*). The transformation process, the escape mechanism, Houdini's secret key, are within language itself, within the significant potential of the word *Schloß*, and its derivatives.[23] On the level of the signified, Kafka's account of his plight is without positive solution. To marry would seem to be the only way to independence and freedom, yet it is also "in the closest relation" (*in engster Beziehung*) to the father, so that all efforts to escape the existential prison are evidence of "madness" (*Wahnsinn*). Yet, on the level of the signifier, when the very word for closure – *schließen, Schloß* – is *opened*, is liberated, is allowed to flee across contextual boundaries, Kafka's writing assumes the magical dimension of the *märchenhaft*, in which all family relations, including the all-powerful "engste Beziehung" to the father, are drained of historical-biological continuity and re-built (*umgebaut*) within the logic of the storyteller. Kafka's "place in the sun" will always be very small, because the father's solar energy radiates far and wide, but the writer does have his own "not very comforting" territories, and these are not affected by (enclosed within) the existential prison of marriage. Here, then, in appropriately *unheimlich* terms, is Kafka's Oedipal topography:

> But we being what we are, marrying is barred to me because it is your very own domain [*So wie wir aber sind, ist mir das Heiraten dadurch verschlossen, dass es gerade Dein eigenstes Gebiet ist*]. Sometimes I imagine the map of the world spread out and you stretched diagonally across it. And I feel as if I could consider living in only those regions that either are not covered by you or are not within your reach. And in keeping with the conception I have of your magnitude, these are not many and not very comforting regions – and marriage is not among them. (*L* 115; *B* 176)

The question of territory or territoriality is, of course, central to all Kafkan fiction, the animal stories as well as the novels. Nowhere is it more pervasive, more developed, or more explicit, however, than in his final novel, *The Castle*, in which the protagonist, K., is a land-surveyor (*Landvermesser*). The semi-autobiographical quality of *The Castle* is clear enough (and I do not believe it necessary to trace a psychocritical scheme of the one-to-one correspondences that might exist between events and persons in Kafka's life and the imaginary pseudo-events and "characters" of the novel), but it should be noted here that *The Castle* is, in many ways, a monstrous expansion of the image of the father stretched out on the globe that we just saw in the *Letter*. A narrative expansion, but also a multiplication of the father, who is incarnated, successively, in the various unattainable paternal figures whose power emanates from the Castle: Count Westwest (its owner, symbolic incarnation of the culture and values of the setting sun), Klamm (often described in deific terms), Momus, Erlanger, and Bürgel. K.'s role is to measure the distances that separate the town from the Castle and himself from the luminous "truth" of the father, which he seeks in complete blindness.

More than any of Kafka's works, including *The Trial, The Castle* is a dreamlike repetition, a staging and restaging of the *unheimlich*, understood in Freudian terms: "that class of the frightening which leads back to what is known of old and long familiar." Like Proust's Venice, the anonymous town through which K. wanders is both strange and familiar, exotic and homelike. The "genies" who guide the protagonist are, in this case, young women toward whom K. harbors feelings of erotic dominance and coercive desire: it is through their mediation that he expects an "Open Sesame" into the all-powerful bureaucracy of the Castle. The impossibility of K.'s task (which echoes Kafka's own expressions of impossible achievement in the *Letter* – "Es ist zu viel, so viel kann nicht erreicht warden . . . Das wäre märchenhaft") is conveyed, from the very beginning, by the German title of the novel: *Das Schloß*. As in Proust's Venice, the underlying goal of the protagonist is to unlock doors, to enrich the treasure-house of his experience; but the German title tells us that the doors are *already locked*, the treasure-room closed to all desires of penetration and acquisition.

On a psychological level, the resonance of the title is only too clear: the novel will be an elaboration of the protagonist's personal (Oedipal) frustrations when faced with the multiple enigmatic appearances of the Castle. But if one assumes that the words *Schloß* and *schließen* not only relate to the human drama of an imaginary/pseudo-autobiographical hero, but also to the very nature of the novel's construction, if it is assumed that the theme of closure might apply to the problematics of fictional structure, then it is necessary to investigate the specificity of the novel's narrative organization. I turn now to an analysis of two passages from *Das Schloß* that illustrate the dialectic of openness and closure within the Kafkan novel. My purpose is not to be exhaustive, but to sketch in broad lines a possible approach to a rhetorical reading (and not a narratology) of Kafka's storytelling.

In the first passage, which occurs in the second of the novel's twenty-five chapters, we encounter K. in the earliest stage of his quest, when he still believes in the easy accessibility of the Castle. He has just arrived in the unidentified small town, has found a room at the inn, and has met a messenger, Barnabas, who is to "serve" him in his future undertakings as land-surveyor. In the evening Barnabas comes to K. and walks with him, arm in arm, through the snow and the darkness. While they walk, K. becomes so overcome with fatigue that he "lose[s] control of his thoughts":

> They went on, but K. did not know whither, he could discern nothing, not even whether they had already passed the church or not. The effort that it cost him merely to keep going made him lose control of his thoughts. Instead of remaining fixed on their goal, they strayed. Memories of his home kept recurring and filled his mind [*Immer wieder tauchte die Heimat auf und Erinnerungen an sie erfüllten ihn*]. There, too, a church stood in the market-place, partly surrounded by an old graveyard, which was again surrounded by a high wall. Very few boys had managed to climb that wall, and for some time K., too, had failed. It was not curiosity that had urged them on; the graveyard had been no mystery to them [*Nicht Neugier trieb sie dazu, der Friedhof hatte vor ihnen kein Geheimnis mehr*]. They had often entered it through a small wicket-gate, it was only the smooth high wall [*die glatte hohe Mauer*] that they had wanted to conquer. But one morning – the empty, quiet market-place had been flooded with sunshine – when had K. ever

seen it like that either before or since? – he had succeeded in climbing it with astonishing ease [*gelang es ihm überraschend leicht*]; at a place where he had already slipped down many a time, he had clambered with a small flag between his teeth right to the top at the first attempt. Stones were still rattling down under his feet, but he was at the top. He struck the flag in, it flew in the wind, he looked down and round about him, over his shoulder, too, at the crosses moldering in the ground; nobody was greater than he at that place and that moment [*niemand war jetzt und hier größer als er*]. (*C* 37–38; *S* 40)[24]

The passage as a whole is constructed on the effects of *Unheimlichkeit*. K. is, "in reality," in the unknown village, where he can see only dark outlines of buildings, but the village bears an uncanny resemblance to his home-town, and it is this likeness that triggers the remembrance of a former boyhood "triumph." The topographical analogy between the *unheimlich* present and the remembered past of the *Heimat* not only accounts for the logical coherence of the daydream, but also produces a reassuring effect in the protagonist, who, upon refocusing on his real situation, concludes:

The sense of that triumph had seemed to him then a victory for life [*das Gefühl dieses Sieges schien ihm damals für ein langes Leben einen Halt zu geben*], which was not altogether foolish, for now so many years later on the arm of Barnabas in the snowy night the memory of it came to succor him. (*C* 38; *S* 40–41)

In narrative terms, K.'s sense of reassurance, and even fortitude, derives from the belief that the "victorious," "triumphant" content of the daydream can *spill out* into the frame-story. Since it was possible, in childhood, to climb the wall successfully and return home safely, then it should be possible, now, to penetrate the walls of the Castle and ascertain its secret. The "wall" between the main narrative and the framed remembrance must disappear, or it must be easy to "climb," if K. is to affirm, with justification, that the childhood experience is like a "foot-hold" (*ein Halt*) that can give support to later undertakings.

The difficulty one has in following K.'s line of reasoning and in accepting his optimistic conclusion is that the structure of the framed experience does not resemble that of the frame: the triumphant memory is not simply the *Urbild* of the narrative that encloses it. All of K.'s efforts during the main body of the narrative are directed at overcoming obstacles, opening doors, lifting barriers, whereas within the childhood scene, the obstacle has *already* been overcome, for him and the other children as well: "It was not curiosity that had urged them on; the graveyard had been no mystery to them. They had often entered it through a small wicket-gate, it was only the smooth high wall that they had wanted to conquer." The young

K. does not climb the wall so that he can enter a secretive or taboo domain: what interests the daydreaming subject is surface, not depth, smoothness ("die *glatte* hohe Mauer"), not resistance, the wall *between* life and death rather than the hidden depth of being – the free circulation of the signifier rather than the anchor-weight of the signified.

The framed memory sequence relates to its narrative frame as a wish-fulfillment dream relates to waking life – not in the parallelism of a metaphorical or analogical totalization, but in the more complex, less comforting mode of a distorted mirror-concatenation of elements that cannot be reduced to one common denominator. What the daydream stages is, in fact, a radical impossibility for the Kafkan imagination: it represents K. as achieving his easy phallic victory (i.e., the "masculine" planting of the flag) within the power-radius of the father (expressed poetically by the pervasive light that floods the city square) – whereas we know, from Kafka's *Letter*, that the most the son can expect is to "crawl to a clean little spot on earth where the sun *sometimes* shines and one can warm oneself *a little*". Further, it is easy to see that the young boy's claim to be "greater" (or "bigger" – *größer*) than anyone else on earth at the ecstatic moment of his triumph stands in direct contradiction to the measured topographical scheme of the *Letter*, in which the father stretches out over the earth, while the son must seek small, hidden places for his own territorial space. In the end, the daydream cannot be integrated into the rest of the story or anchored within the logic of the enveloping narrative: it exists as a cyst, a resistant membrane within the textual substance.

When K.'s passive memory-associations of the *Heimat* cease, he discovers that he is not, as he had hoped, in front of the doors of the Castle, but on the threshold of Barnabas's home. Hoping, in his conscious will, to penetrate the secret (*Geheimnis*) of the Castle, he arrives, instead, at the *Heim* of his servant, where he meets Barnabas's two sisters – Olga and Amalia, both of whom play a major role later in the novel. This peculiar movement of the story, whereby the protagonist sets out to encounter the Castle, but is directed away from it toward new "home-like" (*heimlich/unheimlich*) locations and new characters, accounts for the spiral-like narrative structure of the novel, and no doubt for its final unfinished form. The Kafkan novel ironizes the threshold chronotope through repetition and displacement. K.'s problem is not that he has no thresholds to cross or that it is impossible to cross them, but that they are always the *wrong* passages, never opening out onto the Castle, constituting a series of infinitely replaceable, analogous openings – onto nothing.

There is one episode of the novel, however, that seems to stand outside of the sequence of "false opening" thresholds: it is the long section, told by Olga, that illustrates her family's decline (*C* 243–95; *S* 229–78). This part of *Das Schloß* is atypical not only because its linear form of presentation bears little resemblance to the fragmentary and repetitious constructions to be found elsewhere, but also because of its overt explanatory, clarifying function. This is the one point in the novel at which the reader is tempted to feel that s/he might, finally, gain some access to the mysterious social laws that govern the complex overlapping of town and castle, and ultimately, to the inner workings of the Castle's bureaucracy. In the telling of her story Olga in fact reveals to K. the hidden causes of certain actions and situations that had previously seemed enigmatic; but the final result of her story is not the kind of explanatory narrative closure that seemed to lie within the reader's horizon of expectations.

The first chapter of the section, entitled "Amalias Geheimnis" ["Amalia's Secret"], explains the source of the family's disgrace. Amalia, who had attended a social outing at which she had been introduced to a Castle functionary named Sortini, received a letter from him, the contents of which are not precisely described by Olga, but which, apparently, is full of urgent erotic requests and insults. Olga does take great pains, however, to describe in theatrical terms the moment at which Amalia received the letter, and her precise reaction:

> Next morning we were roused from our heavy sleep by a scream from Amalia . . . She was standing by the window holding a letter in her hand which had just been passed in through the window by a man who was still waiting for an answer. The letter was short, and Amalia had already read it, and held it in her drooping hand . . . I knelt down beside her and read the letter. Hardly had I finished it when Amalia after a brief glance at me took it back, but she couldn't bring herself to read it again, and, tearing it in pieces, she threw the fragments in the face of the man outside and shut the window [*und schloß das Fenster*]. That was the morning which decided our fate [*Das war jener entscheidende Morgen*]. (*C* 249; *S* 234)

As has been pointed out in the critical literature, Amalia's gesture of refusal is unique in a novel that depicts female characters as acquiescent and subservient to the dominant males of the Castle-hierarchy.[25] In effect, by refusing to respond to Sortini, by closing the window to his advances (by refusing his messenger-service), she breaks the cycle of epistolary exchange that defines the very essence of the Castle's sway. She chooses silence as her mode of being. This silence is not a passive defense, Olga tells us, but a way of living with the truth:

> I'm glad to say I understand Amalia better now than I did then. She had more to endure than all of us, it's incomprehensible how she managed to endure it and still survive . . . Amalia not only suffered, but had the understanding to see

her suffering clearly; we saw only the effects, but she knew the cause [*wir sahen nur die Folgen, sie sah den Grund*], we hoped for some small relief or other, she knew that everything was decided, we had to whisper, she had only to be silent [*sie hatte nur zu schweigen*]. She stood face to face with the truth and went on living and endured her life then as now [*Aug und Aug mit der Wahrheit stand sie und lebte und ertrug dieses Leben damals wie heute*]. (*C* 272; *S* 256)

It is tempting to see in Amalia's way of being a counter-example to that of K., and in her decision to unbind herself from the Castle a way out of the labyrinthine impossible quest pursued by K. and his letter-circulating servants. One must be careful about succumbing to such an interpretive temptation, however. One must not forget that this moment of metaphysical grounding emerges from the giddy, verbose declarations of Olga, whose trustworthiness is far from established; and it would be difficult not to perceive an ironical tone in the excessive claims and high-blown rhetoric of Olga: "sie hatte nur zu schweigen, Aug in Aug mit der Wahrheit stand sie." The silence of Amalia, her nearness to the Truth in whose shadow she lives and whose "protectress" she is, sound like an anticipation of the late Heidegger, but that is precisely the problem. In this pseudo-philosophical "sounding-like" one detects the quarter-tone discrepancy of literary-stylistic exaggeration.

The difficulty one has in settling on a coherent univocal interpretation of the Amalia episode stems from the narrative organization itself. The presentation of Amalia as silent Watcher over Truth can be persuasive only if we can believe in the truthfulness of Olga's narrative voice, only if, unlike the structure of the boyhood *Heimat* sequence, the narrative frame does not add a distortion-effect to the "picture" it encloses. The fact that Kafka chose to have Olga frame an explanatory account of origins and sources (the cause of the Barnabas family's social ruin and ostracism) does not mean necessarily that he, as author, believed in the possibility of narrative grounding or closure. In fact, at the very end of Olga's intervention, just as the narrator is about to take charge of the storytelling again, the linear narration (*Geschichte*) comes full circle, only to open out again to the infinite possibilities of the *märchenhaft*. In the end, Olga explains how Barnabas came to be K.'s messenger in the first place:

And now for the final confession: it was a week after your arrival. I heard somebody mentioning it in the Herrenhof, but didn't pay much attention; a Land-Surveyor had come and I didn't even know what a land-surveyor was. But next evening Barnabas – at an hour agreed on I usually set out to go a part of the way to meet him – came home earlier than usual, saw Amalia in the sitting-room, drew me out into the street, laid his head on my shoulder, and cried for several minutes. He was again the little boy he had used to be.

Something had happened to him that he hadn't been prepared for. It was as if a whole new world had suddenly opened to him, and he could not bear the joy and the anxieties of all this newness [*Es ist als hätte sich vor ihm plötzlich eine ganz neue Welt aufgetan und das Glück und die Sorgen aller dieser Neuheit kann er nicht ertragen*]. And yet the only thing that had happened was that he had been given a letter for delivery to you. But it was actually the first letter, the first commission, that he had ever been given. (*C* 294–95; *S* 277–78).

This revelation is a bitter one for K., who discovers, in a retrospective ironical illumination, that the messenger in whom he put his trust at the beginning of the story had had no previous experience in the delivering of messages. Although, in accordance with what the villagers say throughout *Das Schloß*, one might assume that the mode of epistolary communication was in use long before K.'s arrival, it is essential to note that, for Barnabas at least, it is the intervention of the land-surveyor in a land without surveyed bounds, an undiscovered, undifferentiated paradise of sorts, that causes a loss of innocence and a plunge into the alienation-effects of *the letter* (literariness) as such.

Olga's description of the moment at which Barnabas becomes a messenger ("es ist *als hätte sich* vor ihm plötzlich *eine ganz neue Welt aufgetan*") repeats the dramatic threshold-experience of Kafka the writer on the evening he composed "Das Urteil" ("Nur so kann geschrieben werden . . . mit solcher vollständigen *Öffnung* des Leibes und der Seele"), but in the mode of tragedy, or depression. The beginning of Barnabas's messenger service is an incipient enslavement to the scribal Law of the castle hierarchy;[26] the *opening* of body and soul to epistolary exchange involves both happiness and anxiety ("das Glück und die Sorgen aller dieser Neuheit"), which are distributed in an uncanny alternating rhythm. *Das Schloß* as novel undermines the naive optimism of the temporarily triumphant author of "Das Urteil" by staging a double irony: first, the doors of all houses and inns are open, yet *the* door – to the Castle – remains always closed; secondly, narrative closure is impossible in a novel whose framing devices are continuously exceeded by the negative unravelling energy of the episodes they contain. *Das Schloß* is the paradox of an open-ended narrative conveying a sealed message.

IV CROSSING THE THRESHOLD: THE FLIGHT OF THE SIGNIFIER

As innovative writers with distinct personal styles, Proust and Kafka developed their narrative gifts in directions that are unique and (in the neutral sense of the term) incomparable. Narrative form in *Das Schloß* is not the same as that of the *Recherche*; any rigorous comparative "narratology" of the devices and techniques of the two novels will yield results that simply confirm the irreducible individuality of each author. My purpose in this chapter has not been to deny that individuality, but to descend below the level of recognizable and classifiable narrative traits, in order to uncover the point at which narration originates in both writers, the threshold at which metonymical spacing (*espacement*) begins.

As I indicated earlier in this chapter, the very notion of threshold, break, crisis, or *coupure* is part of the drama of a writer's life as depicted in the account of his/her biographer. The crossing of the threshold, the passage through the existential *or* textual "wound" are seen as a liberation from anxiety – whether considered in traditional Oedipal terms or as the anxiety of literary influence. The writers themselves reinforce the idea that there is *one* threshold to cross – Kafka in his description of the exhilarating composition of "Das Urteil," Proust in his ecstatic representation of the madeleine episode. The major difference between the fiction-writers' description of the *coupure* and that of their biographers is that the former locate the precise moment of the break within the act of writing, whereas the biographers read "underneath" the dramatic staging of the episode and tell us readers what hidden forces are at work, what psychic configuration of energies subtends the observable textual facts.

My goal in reading isolated but mutually resonant juxtaposed passages from Proust and Kafka has been to demonstrate that the presentation of the threshold-experience – whether by biographers or creative writers – is a euphoric fiction masking a more complex truth: that the Kafkan and Proustian texts have several entryways and plural exits, which originate in the liberating linguistic potential of the signifier. For Proust, there is much poetry but no novel until the word "Balbec" splits into two opposed units – the cathedral town on the one hand, the beach resort on the other – causing the protagonist to travel between the two places as he attempts to unify them in his mind. With the *coupure* of the signifier "Balbec" Proustian topography originates: the *topos* as such is born of the displacements of the signifier. The novel after the opening of "Balbec" will be a continual, repetitious attempt to link separate "essences." The theme of travel, of movement through space, is the fictional equivalent of Proust's theory of linguistic transport: *metaphor*.

I have noted, as well, that one place in Proust repeats, resembles, or envelops another: Venice is a "transposed" Combray; Balbec is "Baalbek," East and West, the rising and the setting sun. Topographical conflation of this type makes of Proustian space a fictional working-out of Freud's "development towards an ambivalence": Venice is the exotic *and* the familiar, the *unheimlich* and a re-decorated *Heim.* For Kafka, the signifier *Schloß* flees across contextual boundaries. The very word for closure opens up narrative space, and creates for the son an uncanny landscape – of deserts, islands, cages, walled expanses, and underground passageways – in which he can escape and deaden the influence of the solar father. Yet, as in Proust, the *topos* that seems most *unheimlich* itself always contains reflections of home, so that the wanderings of K. are destined to be endless and futile.

The non-ending, impossible quest for hidden, unavailable truths makes of the *Recherche* before the thunderclap of *Le Temps retrouvé,* and of *Das Schloß* in its entirety, negative images of the traditional *Bildungsroman,* where enlightenment and self-discovery result from the search for meaning. It is easy enough to see in *Das Schloß* and in the twin volumes of *La Prisonnière* and *Albertine disparue* preludes to Beckett's trilogy or Céline's *Voyage au bout de la nuit* – especially if one reads them as existential allegories. In this chapter I have argued that there is also an allegory of the signifier, a coherent narrative in and of the signifier that accompanies, *en sourdine,* the formal effects and significant themes of the novels. Proust and Kafka lived with the discomfort of knowing that, in the realm of the *märchenhaft,* all is (unfortunately) possible. Place-names weave a poetic fabric whose threads can be unwoven; a prison is a potential castle, but a "castle" is also only a lock, which is, after all, only a *word* – site of the novel's infinite power of expansion, sign of an author's incurable but linguistically productive ambivalence.

CHAPTER 7

Textualizing immoralism: Conrad's Heart of Darkness *and Gide's* L'Immoraliste

I INTRODUCTION: UNCANNY TEXTUAL RESEMBLANCES

For this chapter, I have chosen to compare two novellas – or, perhaps more precisely stated, *récits*[1] – which have an exemplary status as Modernist texts: Joseph Conrad's *Heart of Darkness* (1899) and André Gide's *L'Immoraliste* (1902). Both works possess the inwardness characteristic of the Modernist era – Marlow's serpentine hesitations about the sense and value of Kurtz's life and pronouncements; Michel's tortuous self-analysis – while, at the same time, they exhibit a remarkable formal complexity and virtuosity of style. To use the terms that frame my analyses in this book: aesthetic brilliance envelops an ethical labyrinth. The mode of this envelopment will be the main topic of the current chapter.

If I have chosen to juxtapose Conrad to Gide in an essay that appears to be "comparative" in the most traditional sense of a comparative literature study – an examination of authors whose texts resemble each other in some thematic sense but who write in different languages and within different literary traditions – it is not so much because strong thematic similarities, in outweighing linguistic or cultural differences, allow me as critic to bridge a cultural gap that had previously been unbridged, but rather because *Heart of Darkness* and *L'Immoraliste* bear what can only be called an uncanny resemblance to each other, a resemblance that challenges the critic, that unsettles him or her as reader. The *récits* of Conrad and Gide say nearly the same thing, but not quite: they mirror each other, but with notable distortions; they are not-quite-perfect *Doppelgänger*. It is this strange, disquieting closeness which will stand at the center of my interpretive efforts.

In a nutshell (an image to which we shall presently return), the shared elements that motivate a comparison of these short canonical texts of literary Modernism are the problem of the referent; the novella as quest; pedagogical exemplarity; the pedagogical employment of narrative frames; and the issue of immoralism.

The problem of the referent

Both *Heart of Darkness* and *L'Immoraliste* are based upon the personal experiences of their authors: Conrad's seven-month assignment for the *Société Anonyme Belge pour le Commerce du Haut-Congo* in 1890, during which, as commander of a steamer, he voyaged into the depths of Belgium's (i.e., King Leopold's) central African preserve; and Gide's several trips to North Africa, including an important initiatory journey of sexual liberation with his friend Paul-Albert Laurens in 1893, and his honeymoon with Madeleine (with whom he was to have a problematic and notorious *mariage blanc*) three years later. The history of the critical reception of both novellas is a vacillation between interpretive schemes that "see the reality" underneath the artistic license and transposition, and other hermeneutic constructions that emphasize the texts' heavily inflected symbolism and distance from the experiential sphere. Is the referent of *Heart of Darkness* the particularity of Leopold's Congo, or is it the depth of the human psyche, the "unconscious" world of dreams, which has a general significance for all human beings?[2] Is the referent of *L'Immoraliste* the exotic Muslim world of eastern Algeria in its specificity, or the ruminations of the protagonist, which, like the reflections of La Bruyère or La Rochefoucauld, address themselves to the human community at large, beyond all limitations and borders? The spectrum of critical readings of both works is quite broad, with manifold variations on the theme of the vexed cohabitation of particularity with generality.[3]

The novella as quest

Even the least symbolically inclined of readers are obliged to recognize that the voyages of Marlow and Michel resemble those mythical quests in the Western literary tradition in which the hero, in search of an object, person, or idea that can give greater significance to his life, is eventually transformed.[4] As is the case in classical representations of the quest, there is a person or agent who serves as both model and mediator for the protagonist: just as Virgil is necessary for Dante, so is Kurtz for Marlow and Ménalque for Michel. The function of the model/mediator is both similar and different in the two Modernist novellas; and the notion of the model itself, as we shall see in due course, is complex and requires clarification.

Pedagogical exemplarity

There is a curious effect of specularity between what is at stake within the two texts – the relative dosage of particular and general meanings they contain; the exemplary character of the questing protagonists and their mediator-models – and what has happened to them as they have been received by their respective publics in the "outside" world of evolving literary history. Both texts are considered (and this is how I am considering them, unproblematically, for the moment) to be the best possible models, examples, or even archetypes of Modernist writing. They are much taught because of their purported exemplary character. In the terms of classical rhetoric, these short works, as individual samples, stand in a relation of metaphorical synecdoche to the whole of Modernism. Undergraduates read both *Heart of Darkness* and *L'Immoraliste* as representative works, and do so, increasingly, in editions which frame the original texts in a wealth of critical commentary.

Heart of Darkness has not only appeared in three different Norton Critical Editions (1963, 1971, 1988), but more recently in two successive editions of the Case Studies in Contemporary Criticism published by St. Martin's Press (1989, 1996).[5] The need for the continual updates mirrors the rapidity with which Conrad criticism has evolved, and the degree to which it reflects the chaotic diversity of contemporary criticism in general. In the case of Gide, the 1963 Macmillan Modern French Literature Series edition of *L'Immoraliste* edited by Elaine Marks and Richard Tedeschi is also a model of its kind: although it does not contain critical essays, it has a well-written introduction, exhaustive explanatory notes, and a full glossary. For countless undergraduate students of French in North America, this edition has been, for nearly four decades, the framework within which Gide's *récit* is read.

It is not a matter of indifference, I think, that Marks and Tedeschi chose *L'Immoraliste* as exemplary Gidian text because of its general or generalizable human significance, as is evident from the editors' pedagogical vocabulary, which all teachers will recognize:

> Though freer from a kind of direct "moralism" than *La Porte étroite*, for example, *L'Immoraliste* is a deeply ethical work. It raises those problems of responsibility and freedom, experience and understanding, ethics and action, truth and misrepresentation, and sincerity and rationalization which are of concern to us all. It is a book highly conducive to the best sort of classroom discussion.[6]

The American editors' introduction to *L'Immoraliste* is nothing less than an abbreviated classical credo in the ethical value of literature. This transcendental value is said to rise above and encompass the particularity of the aesthetic form – in this case, that of the novella or *récit* – chosen by the individual writer for the best possible expression of his ideas. If a literary work can have a properly pedagogical import, it is because its pages contain unmistakable references to the large issues of responsibility and freedom, experience and understanding, and so forth. In the particular case of *L'Immoraliste*, the text has value insofar as Michel's hesitation between his pious affection for Marceline and the seductive qualities of Ménalque's life-philosophy call forth, in the mind of the reader (and thereafter, in classroom discussion) the general problems of responsibility, sincerity, truth and misrepresentation. One of the questions that will arise from the analytical sections of the present chapter, is the following: what, if anything, *is lost* in this passage from the particular to the general, from the immanence of narrative form and rhetorical construction to the transcendence of general ideas? Do the teacher and the class salvage meaning at the expense of literature itself – that is, the literariness of the literary, that which marks the text as literary but without external appeal to the large abstractions which are traditionally assumed to lie "within" the text? Can a text *have value* if it does not incorporate, or if it only seems to incorporate within its representational modality, the questions of truth, responsibility, sincerity, etc.? In short: is there room for irony – irony not in its corrective or "mastered" guise as momentarily imagined by Kierkegaard the dissertation-writer, but irony in the radical German Romantic sense of textual negation and self-dissolution? To pose this question is to invoke another uncanny resemblance between *Heart of Darkness* and *L'Immoraliste*, namely, the techniques of narrative framing on which both texts are constructed.

On the pedagogical usefulness of narrative frames

The most striking similarity between the novellas of Conrad and Gide is their narrative *situation* – with this term taken in its strongest etymological sense, as what one would call, in French, *une mise-en-site*. At the beginning of *Heart of Darkness* we learn that Marlow, who is about to tell the story of his quest for the obscurely discoursing Kurtz, is one of a group of five men held together by "the bond of the sea" (*HD* 18).[7] He, along with three other men who have only the most shadowy of identities – the Lawyer, the Accountant, and the nameless narrator of the external frame – are the guests of the Director of Companies on board the *Nellie*, a "cruising yawl" (17) now at rest on the Thames. The moment described is one of hesitation between the light of day and the oncoming darkness, between movement and repose – in the Bakhtinian terms introduced in the previous chapter, a threshold-moment par excellence. Described in the second paragraph of the text as resembling an "idol" (18) and in the last paragraph of the story as a "meditating Buddha" (95), Marlow will relate his tale with an interesting blend of dispassion, objectivity, and "impressionistic" descriptions of African exoticism,[8] tempered with rare but important outbursts of frustration at his inability to communicate the ineffability of what he experienced in the "heart of darkness."[9]

Of crucial importance to the narrative organization of the novella is that Marlow's tale addresses itself to a group of four men who, in a fundamental sense, "stand for" the larger readership of the book. We readers today are in the same situation as that of Marlow's companions: we are bound together, perhaps not by love of the sea, but by a love of stories and storytelling. We are thus engaged and involved in Marlow's crepuscular act of remembering, and, in our capacity as implied interlocutors, share a certain ethical responsibility in making sense of these complex and obscure images. This is also the case in *L'Immoraliste*, where a group of three friends come together to hear Michel's story, which, like *Heart of Darkness*, is told at the threshold-moment of the crossing from day to night, on a terrace (the transitional place between inside and outside, domesticity and foreignness or danger) overlooking the stark North African landscape:

> we went up to the terrace, the view from which stretches away endlessly, and the three of us, like Job's three friends, waited there, admiring across the fiery plain the sudden decline of the day. (*I* 6)[10]

As is the case in *Heart of Darkness*, the word "we" occurs at the very beginning of Gide's text, at its outermost frame, thus inscribing the reader (or, in pedagogical terms, the classroom group) into the moral dilemma which is about to appear in the slow unfolding of the narrative. On an abstract structural level, the two texts are set up in the same way, in a way so close to equivalency that the belated reader/critic necessarily wonders whether Gide, whose text appeared three years after Conrad's, had not patterned his *récit* on the model provided him by his esteemed Polish/English colleague. Literary-historical evidence does not support this hypothesis, however. It would seem that Gide did not read *Heart of Darkness* until after his first visit to Conrad at Capel House in 1911, which means that the close resemblance in the narrative structures of the two novellas is a matter of pure (uncanny) coincidence.[11]

Beyond the similarities in narrative structure as such, there is one fundamental difference between the two texts, which is a matter of rhetorical intensity or, to use a word notoriously difficult to define, of *tone*. Whereas the exterior narrator of *Heart of Darkness* says "We four *affectionately* watched [The Director of Companies] as he stood in the bows looking to seaward" (17; my emphasis), then evokes "the bond of the sea" (18), thereby establishing an atmosphere of calm and harmonious camaraderie, the tone of the first pages of *L'Immoraliste* is much more urgent, evoking danger, risk, and, with the allusion to the book of Job, the problem of divine judgment and retribution against human failings. The friends come together not during a logical pause in the natural rhythms of a river estuary, but because Michel, having fallen into a state of dejection, perhaps abjection, has lost all reference-points (*points de repère*) that might keep him attached to the norms and expectations of social discourse and action. The friends respond to a "pact" they had made as adolescents to help each other in times of distress (*I* 4).

The similar-yet-different quality of the two novellas emerges from the subtle distinction between "the *bond* of the sea" and the *pact* of human friendship. The bond is transpersonal; it envelops the individual human within a larger natural entity – an entity to which the human being responds intuitively. Seamen go to sea out of a love for the sea which they do not (need to) understand – *le coeur a ses raisons que la raison ne connaît pas*. The pact, on the other hand, is a human invention to defend against what nature can inflict on a person in the form of that person's "fate." Whereas Marlow's tale begins with his interlocutors being merely curious, perhaps merely interested in spending an evening of narrative diversion, Michel's confession, from its first words, has a menacing quality to it which, according to the exterior narrator's analogy, resembles the African desert in its "fiery" quality.

Because the rhetorical tone of the two stories is so different, because Michel's narrative is above all self-justification (despite all Rousseauesque protestations to the contrary) while Marlow's is the expression of amazement and admiration for the enigmatic Kurtz, the potentially interactive quality of the narrative set-up remains problematic in both cases, but differently problematic. Both stories, because of their narrative structures, hold out the promise of dialogue. The friends surrounding Marlow and Michel could, hypothetically, respond to the stories they are hearing, just as undergraduates could, *de jure*, respond to the teacher in the discussion of a text "highly conducive to classroom discussion." The interesting problem is that, in both cases, this interaction does not, *de facto*, take place. Both tales are set up as dialogues but function as monologues. Michel engages his interlocutors/readers in a labyrinth of morally complex acts the concatenation of which is impossible to break, thus rendering dialogic interventions, in their momentary character, difficult to formulate and sustain. And the very lack of specificity of Marlow's "Africanist discourse"[12] leaves his listeners very little common ground from which to respond or object to his symbolic diction. One has to wonder whether the creation of a community of readers implicit in the narrative modalities of both texts can be conceived of as resulting from a bond or a pact, and whether either form of relation can account for the textual praxis of these Modernist fictions.

Immoralism

The fundamental ethical question posed by both texts is that of immoralism – understood in Nietzschean terms as the stance assumed by the superior individual who, having rejected the introverted and sickly morality of *Ressentiment* espoused by the priestly caste, has gone "beyond good and evil." (These ideas can be found in the text which is itself entitled *Beyond Good and Evil* [1886], but are perhaps most cogently and systematically expressed in *The Genealogy of Morals*, written in 1887). But whereas Nietzsche develops his ideas on immoralism discursively throughout his late works, in an aphoristically executed arrangement of theme and variations, Conrad and Gide *textualize immoralism*: that is, they create characters who incarnate immoralist philosophies and, most importantly, live those philosophies within their respective texts. It is perhaps not an exaggeration to say that the vital principle of both *récits*, that which drives them forward narratively, is the self-actualization of immoralist characters as it affects or "infects" other characters and the reader him- or herself. Kurtz is the center, however hollow or blank, of *Heart of Darkness*. His active influence is everywhere present, from his reputation in the Outer and Central Stations, to the effect of his powerfully devious essay-cum-footnote concerning the "Suppression of Savage Customs" on the Harlequin, to his haunting of Marlow's mind throughout the story – not to speak of the results of his "civilizing" mission as it plays itself out, monstrously, on the inhabitants of the villages surrounding the Inner Station.

In the case of *L'Immoraliste* the situation is, once again, the same yet slightly different. The story is centered on Michel's actions, thoughts, and inner consciousness, and he is the immoralist referred to by the tale's title, the man who destroys his wife as he gains his own freedom from moral strictures. At the same time, however, whereas it is Marlow who tells the story of Kurtz from the outside perspective of a fascinated and increasingly wary observer, it is Michel who tells his own story, and who is himself at least momentarily influenced by another character – Ménalque – who, in his own way, lives a life "beyond good and evil."[13] Michel is thus a character who, in the gradual process of constructing himself, must face external influences, whereas Kurtz, whom we meet after it is too late, so to speak, after he is completely formed as a character, is presented as a closed surface, as an individual imprisoned in his own dangerous conceptions.

Despite these important differences, when the reader reaches the conclusion of both novellas, he or she is faced with protagonists to whom, in the most fundamental sense, one can no longer appeal in the name of anything conventionally moral, fictional characters whose development has taken them toward what Gide calls, at several points in his story, the *inhuman.* The inhuman is that which lies outside the boundaries of human discourse and action, outside the border-lines traced by ethical thought. In narrative terms, the inhuman appears as *the unframable,* that which, by its transgressive force, negates the separation between inside and outside on which framing as such is predicated. But how does one *read* the inhuman in or "beyond" novellas which are so obviously structured on the principle of framing devices? This is a question which is answerable only if we attempt to analyze, with some care, the praxis of narrative framing in both *récits.* It is to that task that I now turn.

II INSIDE AND OUTSIDE: NARRATIVE AND MEANING IN *HEART OF DARKNESS*

It is a critical commonplace that "the point" of *Heart of Darkness* is the encounter between Marlow and Kurtz, the moment at which the enigmatic master of the Inner Station, having been found after the travails of a long journey, begins his veiled discourse. On this view, the narrative movement of the tale has a pre-established telos: the narrative itself exists only as a means to the end of Kurtz's opaque revelations, and indeed, abolishes itself once his words have been uttered. It is perhaps not without significance that once Kurtz dies there is no gradual or detailed account of the journey back, but rather a brusque, transitionless textual "jump." The following is all Marlow has to say about the return navigation down the Congo and about the sailing back to Europe:

"No, they did not bury me, though there is a period of time which I remember mistily, with a shuddering wonder, like a passage through some inconceivable world that had no hope in it and no desire. I found myself back in the sepulchral city." (*HD* 88)

Marlow would thus seem to use his narrative with great skill but also with great *désinvolture* to express the meaning toward which the story moves. Once that meaning has been revealed, the narrative per se can collapse; it will have been only a prop, a theatrical device, a necessary but inessential element in the staging of a complex psychodrama – or, in spatial terms, the evanescent outside that can be discarded once the meaningful inside is opened up. The problem with this view, however, is that the exterior narrator of *Heart of Darkness* appears to contradict it, in a striking analogy which has been much commented upon in the critical literature. The analogy itself runs as follows:

The yarns of seamen have a direct simplicity, the whole meaning of which lies within the shell of a cracked nut. But Marlow was not typical (if his propensity to spin yarns be excepted), and to him the meaning of an episode was not inside like a kernel but outside, enveloping the tale which brought it out only as a glow brings out a haze, in the likeness of one of these misty halos that sometimes are made visible by the spectral illumination of moonshine. (*HD* 19–20)[14]

As J. Hillis Miller has pointed out in his essay "*Heart of Darkness* Revisited," it would seem that the narrator is performing an exact reversal of the traditional method of storytelling – that of the "yarns of seamen" in their "direct simplicity" – and in so doing, has inverted the categories of container (*contenant*) and contained (*contenu*). Whereas the entertaining stories we are used to hearing from men of the sea give us characters and narrative detail as an "inedible shell which must be removed and discarded so the meaning of the story may be assimilated," Marlow offers us a story in which "the meaning now contains the tale" (208). In the classical rhetorical terminology used by Miller, we pass from metonymical synecdoche (the kernel, the Rabelaisian *sustantificque mouelle*, is, in the critic's view, merely juxtaposed to the outer shell) to metaphorical synecdoche (the glow surrounds or contains the haze it "brings out," the moonshine envelops the misty halos in its spectral light). In philosophical terms, we move from the realm of contingency and chance association to a necessary relation. The "impressionist" and "symbolist" styles of Conrad would thus serve, in their evocative power, as guarantors of narrative necessity, with meaning standing outside of but in intimate relation to the tale which conveys it. But does the narrator say this unambiguously in this passage, and does the novella always, or even usually, depict meaning as that which lies beyond the vicissitudes of narrative framing?

A closer examination of the passage indicates that the neat oppositions between inside and outside, metonymical and metaphorical synecdoche, contingency and necessity, are not so neat in Conrad's own language. I would suggest, first, that for the seamen telling their tales, the relation between the shell and the cracked nut is in fact one of metaphorical synecdoche, or of necessary inclusion: the kernel and the shell are both parts of the same nut, made of the same essential natural ingredients; and the "simplicity" of the tale consists in the fact that meaning naturally resides within an outer shell which is easy enough to remove. It is interesting to note that if one uses the pedagogical examples which Miller proposes to illustrate the difference between the two forms of synecdoche – "I see a sail" for "I see a ship" is metaphorical because the sail is a part of the whole of the ship; "I drink a bottle" is metonymical because one drinks the liquid in the bottle, and the liquid has a different material composition from the glass which contains it – the relation of the kernel to the shell is clearly metaphorical, not metonymical, in Miller's own terms. The kernel relates to the shell as the sail relates to the ship, by a necessary link, not as wine relates to the bottle that merely happens to contain it. The fact that a human being must remove the shell to eat the nut's appetizing interior should not cause us to forget that both edible and inedible parts of the nut were formed during the same developmental process and, unlike wine and the bottle that contains it, are parts of the same naturally produced whole.

To further complicate the issue, to say that a glow "brings out" a haze, or that moonshine in some way "envelops" misty halos, is not to assert unambiguously that there is a necessary relation between these phenomena, or that the outside element truly *contains* the inside element as the whole of something contains its part. The glow and the haze, the moonshine and the misty halos, simply do not relate to each other according to the mode of part and whole. The word "sometimes" in the phrase "misty halos that sometimes are made visible" is also not terribly reassuring to the rhetorician or philosopher: what happens during "other times" – does the relation change? And if so, how? Finally – and here is where a question of logic disrupts the rhetorical scheme in a jarring way – what can one make of the very curious parenthetical remark in the sentence "But Marlow was not typical (if his propensity to spin yarns be excepted)"? The critics who read the passage, despite the significant divergences in their critical methodologies, are unanimous in one thing: *in not reading the parenthesis* – or, to be rhetorically correct, what is contained within the parenthesis. Absent the parenthetical comment, we can construct some kind of opposition between Marlow and other seamen, even though, as I have just indicated, that opposition is not easy to make in purely constative or neatly declarative terms. But with the parenthesis, we have something quite a bit more complicated.

The logical consequence arising from this phrase is as follows: although Marlow's storytelling is qualitatively different from that of his friends in that it inverts the relative positions of container and contained, it is still the spinning of a yarn, as are all narratives, however "impressionistic," "symbolic," experimental, or self-reflective. If we take the spinning of a yarn, or narrative possibilities in general, as the whole within which the methods of Marlow and most seamen are divergent parts, the parenthetical "aside," which has been ignored in the critical literature, now takes on an unsettling significance: it cancels out the theoretical assertions of the passage; it undermines the apparent solidity of the analogical scheme. The passage "works" only if Marlow is different from the other seamen, only if his storytelling is different from theirs. But if to narrate as such is always to spin yarns, of whatever variety, then Marlow, despite a contingent superficial distinctiveness in his mode of narration, *is typical because he also spins yarns*: he is typical at the level of necessity, or of "essences," to borrow from Proust. Even the narrator-performer who seeks distinction in the inventiveness of forms is just one other narrator-performer subsumed within the infinite extensiveness of narrative possibility, a transpersonal expanse within which all distinctions are leveled.

If one should accept this interpretation of the parenthetical insertion, the consequence for our overall understanding of the novella can be summed up as follows. We will need to see Marlow as a divided figure: first, as a remembered character possessing his own distinctiveness (his own individual way of being, his own personal "accent") who interacts with other characters within the story; and second, as a remembering consciousness subject to the general laws of narrative subsumption and thereby dispossessed of any fundamental distinctiveness *qua* narrator. In the early portion of the paragraph which concludes with the yarns of seamen / cracked nut analogy, the exterior narrator asserts that Marlow "did not represent his class" – he is not representative in that, unlike most seamen, for whom their ship is their home, the protagonist is a "wanderer" (*HD* 19). As character, not as narrator, therefore, it can be said of Marlow that he "was not typical" (*HD* 20). What I am suggesting here is something seemingly curious: that the undifferentiated flow of narrative exteriority, what Blanchot calls "le ruissellement du dehors éternel,"[15] envelops without mastering or, *strictu senso*, containing, the clearly delineated differentiations on which the dramatic content of the story is based. The novella is full of *untypical* personages, ranging from the "hollow" manager of the Central Station to the commedia dell' arte "phenomenon" of the Harlequin and the enigmatically discoursing Kurtz. They possess their own distinctiveness, but are immersed in the indistinction of narrative sameness.

The effect of this stark juxtaposition between an inside of dramatic conflict and theatrical oppositions and the indifferent narrative outside with which it cohabits but is incompatible, is that of uncanniness, *Unheimlichkeit.* Narrative exteriority, in other words, does not provide a home for that which it envelops yet does not, properly speaking, contain. And its undifferentiated "glow" often brings out the "haze" within the story, the areas of the story which are themselves not susceptible of integration within binary oppositions. Narrative exteriority necessarily *impinges upon* the system of distinctions and differences it envelops without containing, producing disjunctive moments in the text, moments of upheaval in which effective communication among characters, clear delineation among places, and relationality as such becomes problematic, if not impossible.

The entirety of *Heart of Darkness* is set up as a potential dialogue, at three essential levels: between Marlow the narrator and his interlocutors; between ancient civilized Europe and "blank" Africa; between Marlow the character and Kurtz. If the novella holds out hermeneutical possibilities for the reader, it is because the reader assumes there can and will be dialogic exchange at these levels, that relations of sameness and difference will allow for the construction of his or her interpretive grid. The problem, however, is that the narrative contract or *bond*, to use Marlow's expression, is, in fact, an unkept promise, a hypothetical framework which contains nothing, which yields nothing to the pressure exterted on it by the reader's interpretive efforts. The possibility of dialogue, which is nothing less than the potentiality within aesthetic form for the creation of an ethically grounded interpretive community, rests on the interlocutor's (or reader's) ability to *appeal to* a common ground on which both he and his partner in conversation stand. Yet Conrad, in what amounts to a devastating play on words undermining the very expression "common ground," has Marlow say the following about Kurtz, at the very beginning of their verbal "exchange":

"I had to deal with a being to whom I could not appeal in the name of anything high or low . . . There was nothing either above or below him and I knew it. He had kicked himself loose of the earth. Confound the man! he had kicked the very earth to pieces. He was alone, and I before him did not know whether I stood on the ground or floated in the air." (*HD* 83)

It is important to remember this evocation of Marlow's absolute, "groundless" and "floating" disorientation when, just five pages later, he asserts, with sudden (too sudden) confidence, that Kurtz's discourse amounted to "an affirmation, a moral victory paid for by innumerable defeats, by abominable terrors, by abominable satisfactions. But it was a victory!" (*HD* 88). Not only does Marlow have no proof or clear justification of what he has just said, but more importantly, he has no basis, no grounds, at the most primary level of communication, to assert anything whatever about Kurtz – the figure to whom he *bears no relation*. Marlow's "loyalty" to Kurtz is thus, properly speaking, pure nonsense: how can Marlow be the emissary of this personage, the repository for his "universal genius" (*HD* 89) when that genius is *not communicable*? The ethical basis of Marlow's posthumous companionship with the Inner Station's director is null and void, which is why his final lie to the "Intended" is both logical and necessary. Lying is the mode of apparent but unreal/fictional non-exchange, which is precisely the mode of the "relation" between the protagonist and the man he idolizes. Marlow's final lie makes him as untrustworthy as the man whose ideas he admires and represents to the world; Marlow ends by resembling, uncannily, the object of his admiration, the "remarkable man."

Just as the final resemblance of the initially differentiated characters of Kurtz and Marlow is "too close for comfort," in the same way the opposing poles of Europe and Africa on which the geographical symbolism of the story is based prove to be strangely similar in their uncanny qualities. Not only does Marlow use the term "uncanny" to describe one of the "fateful" women who, like one of the Parcae, knits menacingly in the Brussels office where he receives his appointment (*HD* 25), but he also describes the African soil in the same way when he emphasizes the lack of relation between the Europeans and their hostile environment: "We were cut off from the comprehension of our surroundings; we glided past like phantoms . . . The earth seemed unearthly" (*HD* 51). Just as Marlow cannot appeal to Kurtz, so the representatives of European civilization cannot find a hold on Africa. But the convoluted irony on which Conrad's tale is constructed can be paraphrased thus: it is not because Africa is different from Europe that it is dark and incomprehensible, but because it is part of the same extensive and undifferentiated uncanniness. At one of the novella's most dramatic moments, when the essence of Africa seems to express itself most menacingly (Kurtz has temporarily escaped from the steamer and attempted to return to the Inner Station, and Marlow must enter the jungle to find him), Marlow remarks:

> "I strode rapidly with clenched fists. I fancy I had some vague notion of falling upon him and giving him a drubbing. I don't know. I had some imbecile thoughts. The knitting old woman with the cat obtruded herself upon my memory as a most improper person to be sitting at the other end of such an affair." (*HD* 81)

The "obtruding" presence of the Brussels Parca is "improper" only if one goes by the assumption that Europe and Africa are, in their essence, polar opposites. From the unsettling narrative perspective of *Heart of Darkness*, however, it is the *same yarn*, if I may be permitted the pun, which stretches from Brussels into the Congo and which not only knits together the two places, but dissolves their separate identities into a fundamental and pervasive *Unheimlichkeit*. The critical debates that surround *Heart of Darkness*, and which focus *either* on the textually self-reflective "inside" (the novella as quest, as exploration of the unconscious mind) *or* on the real-world referential "outside" (the story as expression of the author's purported racism), presuppose, for their rhetorical effectiveness, that there are a discernible inside and a clearly delineated outside to which one can appeal for purposes of interpretive consensus. If, however, we are in a textual world which disrupts these distinctions, which *is* uncanniness in its generalized pervasiveness, we are *both* everywhere *and* nowhere. This very curious non-place not only does not allow for the equation of Africa with something like the primitive id and Europe with the locus of the clear-seeing ego, but it also evacuates the pathos with which a literal-minded political reading attempts either to condemn or to condone the content of Conrad's thought. Uncanniness is both within and without, in the "glow" and the "haze": as we have seen on several occasions in this book, it is *the unsurveyable* which readers inevitably and necessarily attempt to survey.

It is the very pervasive quality of uncanniness, its capacity to blur the boundaries of inside and outside, that calls into question the dividing lines which allow for differentiation at the level of narrative structure – in particular, for the clear-cut distinction, in *Heart of Darkness*, between the outer frame provided by the exterior narrator and the inner frame constituted by Marlow's tale of the search for Kurtz. Uncanniness, as disruption of narrative boundaries, is a modern response to the classical literary tradition, as embodied, for example, in Boccaccio's *Decameron* or Marguerite de Navarre's *Heptaméron*, where the listeners, who themselves become storytellers in their turn, are given the opportunity, as discussants, to judge the tale they have just heard for its moral as well as aesthetic merits. The exterior frame often functions as a control mechanism wherein a voice or voices of reasoned moderation engage in spirited dialogue with a storyteller who may have exceeded the bounds of decency or decorum. The reader of these tales becomes a virtual partner in the dialogue, and must choose among the various interpretive solutions offered, or else elaborate one of his or her own. The fundamental point, whatever the diversity of the stories' content or style, however tame or outrageous their premises, is that the personages discoursing at the exterior are active interpreters; and their interpretations enliven the framed text, engage with it actively.

In *Heart of Darkness* Conrad provides us with a framework which is, at the formal level of narrative technique, similar to what one finds in Boccaccio or Marguerite de Navarre. That is, Conrad sets up a formal apparatus which *could* function like its Renaissance models, and which has led no less perspicacious a critic than Ian Watt to affirm, in what I think can only be called the mode of wishful thinking:

> Marlow's memories of his lonely experiences on the Congo, and his sense of the impossibility of fully communicating their meaning, would in themselves assign *Heart of Darkness* to the literature of modern solipsism; but the fact that Marlow, like Conrad, is speaking to a particular audience makes all the difference; it enacts the process whereby the solitary individual discovers a way out into the world of others. (*Conrad in the Nineteenth Century*, 212)

At the level of textual praxis, however, this "way out into the world of others" is never realized. What is notable about the figures listening to Marlow is that they are merely listeners and never interlocutors. The narrative device of the external frame is just as hollow as Kurtz himself; like Kurtz, it is an empty shell "containing" a vacuous, seemingly "eloquent" monologic voice. The exterior frame merely "envelops" the primary narrative like a "glow," and, in its indistinct contours, effaces itself. Conrad not only silences the potential interlocutors; he makes them invisible as the night falls upon the voice of Marlow. Because the exterior frame cannot contain its inside, because, unlike in the Renaissance texts, there is no dialectic of interchange between the two, the exterior ends by mimicking the interior – and this, most strikingly, in what one might call *the infectious quality of idolatry as theme.*

In a nutshell (one more time): Kurtz, presented from afar as a kind of European god who has come to evangelize the natives with his Enlightenment culture, is revealed, progressively, to be an idol. Marlow, who declares emphatically, but, in Freud's language, with obvious *Verneinung*, "Mr. Kurtz was no idol of mine" (*HD* 75), in fact not only increasingly idolizes this "universal genius," but himself turns into an idol – interestingly enough, of Eastern provenance. All readers will remember the "meditating Buddha" of the story's final paragraph (95); the initial description of Marlow who, with "an ascetic aspect, and, with his arms dropped, the palms of his hands outwards, resembled an idol" (18); or, *curiouser and curiouser*, also in the novella's earliest pages, the evocation of the teller of tales as "a Buddha preaching in European clothes and without a lotus-flower" (21). Marlow is thus presented not only as an idol, which is to say, an empty or hollow god, but as a metaphysical cross-dresser who preaches with the wrong (culturally mismatched) accoutrements. From the very beginning, the "inside" of European culture and the "outside" of exotic Otherness display, with bogus theatricality, an *unheimlich* cohabitation. Inside *and* outside, here *and* there, reigns the fantasm of a transvestite blending and covering of contraries whose result, hermeneutically speaking, will be a radical textual undecidability.

What remains for the reader to do in these disconcerting, profoundly unsettling circumstances? Is there a way, despite the collapsing of frames and extensiveness of uncanniness, to read this text? Is there a reading of undecidable texts? An answer, perhaps the best one enunciated within Conrad's literary-historical moment, was proposed, with considerable wit, by Nietzsche in the preface to *Twilight of the Idols* (1888):

> Maintaining cheerfulness in the midst of a gloomy affair, fraught with immeasurable responsibility, is no small feat; and yet, what is needed more than cheerfulness [*Heiterkeit*]? . . . Another mode of convalescence [the "mode" previously mentioned was that of "war"] – under certain circumstances even more to my liking – is *sounding out idols* [*Götzen aushorchen*]. There are more idols than realities in the world: that is *my* "evil eye" for this world; that is also my evil *ear*." For once to pose questions here with a *hammer*, and, perhaps, to hear as a reply that famous hollow sound which speaks of bloated entrails – what a delight for one who has ears even behind his ears, for me, an old psychologist and pied piper [*Rattenfänger*] before whom just that which would remain silent must become outspoken [*gerade Das, was still bleiben möchte, laut werden muss*].[16]

The way to remain "cheerful" in the midst of interpretive "gloom" is to come to a double understanding. First, the search for truth, meaning, authenticity, for gods and universal geniuses, is doomed from the start because there are "more idols than realities in the world." And second (logically following from this first realization), since one is faced with an essential hollowness, one's interpretive method should consists of *sounding out idols*, of using the hammer (i.e., tuning fork) to bring out the resonance inhabiting that hollowness. *Heart of Darkness*, with apologies to Ian Watt, is a tale of modern or Modernist "solipsism," in which the promise of community is not kept; yet even the most forbidding and apparently unreachable of empty spaces resonates with and because of its emptiness. There may be no dialogue or interlocution in Conrad's novella, but there is a semantic resonance, to which the reader who has "ears even behind his ears" must attempt, however unsuccessfully, to be attuned. And once the tuning fork touches the string, the reverberating tones are everywhere, within and without the instrument: they do not call for or necessarily permit a dialogue in the same register, but they are released toward the possibility of a responsible listening.

III FRAMING MORAL DANGER: *L'IMMORALISTE*

Like Kurtz in *Heart of Darkness*, the protagonist of Gide's *récit* is an immoralist insofar as he has "kicked himself loose of the earth," insofar as his life-philosophy and actions appear groundless, relationless, morally unredeemable and socially irrecuperable. Michel is that individual who, at the end of his story, poses the greatest of possible threats to society, not so much because he has committed specific reprehensible criminal acts for which a court of law could condemn him, but because he may no longer, in any sense, be a part of the greater whole of the human community: no synecdochic relation of any kind, metaphorical or even metonymic, can be applied to him. As his wife Marceline says to him in the final stages of her agony: "Vous aimez l'inhumain" (*L'Imm* 468). The entirety of *L'Immoraliste* is the gradual narrative progression toward the category of the inhuman, toward that which lies "beyond good and evil" in the Nietzschean sense. The fundamental difference between the texts of Conrad and Gide, as I have noted, is that the reader encounters Kurtz after he has become inhuman, and can only recognize, belatedly, the external effects of that going-beyond. Marlow presents us with disquieting signifiers pointing to the signified "inhumanity," such as the footnote "Exterminate all the brutes!" on the treatise for the Society for the Suppression of Savage Customs, and the "round carved balls" (*HD* 68) on sticks serving as a fence for Kurtz's domain and which turn out to be human skulls. We infer from these signs that Kurtz has become inhuman; we perform what Ian Watt has called the "delayed decoding" of a text that shows us, in a first movement, the sheer unfamiliar appearance of things, followed by Marlow's (or the reader/interpreter's) differed understanding of what motivates that appearance.[17] In Gide's story, on the other hand, we see not Michel-the-immoralist, but rather how Michel *becomes* an immoralist. It is Michel himself who obligingly provides us with all the interpretive tools necessary to condemn him. The narrator-protagonist often explicates how the signs of his increasing personal liberty and detachment from social norms can only be understood as representing his voluntary exile from the human community, from its shared system of conventions and values.

In the case of Gide's highly structured and symmetrical *récit*, narrative is not the more or less transparent envelope containing a message that can be called *immoralisme* or *l'inhumain*; rather, the movement or progression of this narrative is, in and of itself, immoral and inhuman. In its slow unfolding, in its gradual development, Michel's narrative engages the reader with the becoming of immoralism, a becoming from which the reader cannot, at any precise point, extricate him- or herself. At the end of the story, in our final return to the external frame, we hear:

> Michel remained silent for a long time. We too said nothing, each of us struck dumb by a strange uneasiness [*pris chacun d'un étrange malaise*]. We felt, alas, that by relating it, Michel had somehow legitimized his action. Not knowing where to object to it, in his gradual accounting, made us almost . . . accomplices. We were somehow involved in it [*Nous y étions comme engagés*]. He had completed his story without a quaver in his voice, without an inflection or a gesture to reveal that any emotion whatever disturbed him, either because he took a cynical pride in not seeming moved, or because a kind of reticence kept him from moving us by his tears, or because he simply wasn't moved [*soit enfin qu'il ne fût pas ému*]. I can't distinguish in him, even now, what is pride, or strength, or aridity, or reserve [*Je ne distingue pas en lui, même à présent, la part d'orgueil, de force, de sécheresse ou de pudeur*]. (*I* 169; *L'Imm* 470–71)

What the external narrator is evoking here is that most *unheimlich* of moments in literature – when aesthetics becomes inseparable from, indistinguishable from, ethics; when aesthetic form, in other words, loses its capacity to contain, envelop, or frame the moral energy (no longer) "within" it. *Unheimlichkeit* emerges in the "strange uneasiness" (*étrange malaise*) one feels as a listener, and in the unusual combination of disorientation or dislocation and interpretive involvement. The reader feels himself to be caught up in a text in which he is increasingly uncomfortable, in which logical or hermeneutic distinctions as such have become impossible to make. Hence the series of "either-or" (*soit que . . . soit que*) hypotheses concerning Michel's motivations; hence the listener's quandary relating to the roles which such character traits as "pride, or strength, or aridity, or reserve" might play in the weaving of the narrative threads. Since we readers, like Michel's friends, hear the totality of the story from beginning to end, and are aware of the degree to which the protagonist has left behind his sense of solidarity with his fellow humans, we are likely to opt for the most extreme of the hypotheses: namely, that Michel "simply wasn't moved" by his own story. And it is the neutral term *sécheresse* (translated nicely by Richard Howard as "aridity," evoking a correspondence with the desert environment in which the tale is told) which best renders the state of mind of the narrator, not pride, strength, or reserve (*pudeur*), all of which convey an unmistakable moral content. The ultimate irony of the text is that Michel, who ends his quest for authenticity in a location beyond morality as such, in an area drained of all ethical reference and vocabulary, has managed to "infect" his readers with feelings of guilt. The moral ideas and sentiments which Michel no longer has now possess the reader and continue to exercise their influence within the reader's interpretive consciousness. Nature abhors a vacuum: that which is expelled from Michel is not lost, but is ingested by his uneasy listeners, who have been forced, throughout the *récit*, to inhabit the unhomely arid home provided them by their erstwhile friend.

The resistance of the threatening ethical content of *L'Immoraliste* to aesthetic domestication or enclosure has disturbed Gide's readers from 1902 until the present. A detailed history of the story's critical reception would show that, until the advent of structuralism and narratology, most readers found it difficult to take seriously the framing devices, which were considered to be artificial and contrived "guardrails" borrowed, for the sake of convenience, from the classical tradition.[18] Gide himself, stung by the violently negative reactions of some of his closest writer-friends to the first printing of the book,[19] inserted, for the second edition, a prefatory statement which itself acts as an additional framework beyond that provided by the fictional friends on the terrace, and which appears to serve the purpose of an authorial guarantee against the text's moral disruptions and dangers. It is as if Gide, rereading his own work in the light of contemporary readings of it, had retroactively realized that the immoralist philosophy of his protagonist needed additional containment:

if the floodwaters break over one dike, another must be constructed. It is the juxtaposition of this belated *addendum* to the passage I have just analyzed on the moral "engagement" or "complicity" of Michel's friends in the framed narrative which will reveal both the aesthetic and the ethical tensions on which *L'Immoraliste* as literary work is predicated.

Gide begins his prefatory remarks with an image which amounts to a variation on the textually self-reflective comparison between the cracked nut and the "yarns of seamen" in Conrad's novella. Gide compares his *récit* to a plant, a colocynth, which, native to the Mediterranean region, bears a bitter and purgative fruit:

> I offer this book for what it is worth [*Je donne ce livre pour ce qu'il vaut*]. It is a fruit full of bitter ash, like those desert colocynths which grow in parched places and reward one's thirst with only a more dreadful scalding, yet upon the gold sand are not without a certain beauty. (*I* xiii; *L'Imm* 367)

Like Baudelaire's celebrated title-image *Les Fleurs du Mal*, the container (*contenant*) here is aesthetically pleasing (the beauty of the flower in its exteriority set against the background of the golden sand), but the contained (*contenu*) is ethically threatening (the "scalding" taste of the flower's inside "ash," with its evocation of infernal privations and torture). However dramatic the contrast between outside and inside, however uncomfortable the cohabitation of the lovely flower and its bitter fruit, it is important to emphasize that Gide is not in this context questioning the separation of the two domains or suggesting that they in any way overlap or overflow each other's boundaries. Unlike Conrad, Gide remains within the classical representation of literary meaning as being contained by the narrative form which conveys it on a temporal line. *L'Immoraliste* will be disturbing in its contents, "hard to swallow," but the author appears confident, here, in the capacity of his text in its carefully crafted form to contain the protagonist's morally equivocal ideas within its envelope.

As the passage develops, Gide emphasizes the quasi-Flaubertian "indifference" or "neutrality" with which he has told his tale, and warns his readers against the temptation of searching, within the *récit*, for the author's own definitive morally grounded opinion of Michel's actions: "But I wanted to write this book neither as an indictment nor as an apology, and I have taken care not to pass judgment" (ibid.). The text offered to the public by André Gide, as now illuminated by this explanatory preface, presents itself as purely constative in its tone. If there are marks within the story by which the reader can orient him- or herself toward a moral judgment of Michel, those marks exist at the literarily immanent level of hermeneutical interaction between text and reader, and cannot be seen as clues pointing to the author's own existential situation. The work of art, in the formulation of this preface, is not only self-contained in its isolation from its author's life; as aesthetic form, it also holds within itself, without excess or remainder, the moral content of the narrative, which it represents in the protagonist's interactions with the other fictional characters and allegorizes in his symmetrically organized journeys through geographically symbolic regions.[20] In Gide's aphoristic formulation: "To tell the truth [*A vrai dire*], in art there are no problems – for which the work of art is not the sufficient solution" (*I* xiv; *L'Imm* 367).

The "problems" to which Gide refers here are the moral lapses of the protagonist, in whom, according to the preface, a number of readers have seen only a "sick man" or a "strange case" (ibid.). By stating that the work of art can solve the moral problems it contains, Gide is alleging that *aesthetics possesses its own morality*. In telling the truth about Michel's lies, in residing within the aura of the truth and of authenticity, the work envelops and contains all acts of perversity and deviousness, removing their sting. *L'Immoraliste* as aesthetic whole is thus the generality within which the particularity or peculiarity of Michel as "case" can be successfully subsumed and neutralized. In Gide's words, his precipitous and superficial readers – those who have seen in Michel *only* a man who is "sick" in the moral sense – have "failed to see that some very urgent ideas of very general interest may nonetheless be found in [his drama]" (ibid.). These readers have tasted the fruit of the desert flower, have reacted with disgust to its taste, and have not sought the arduous truths behind or beyond its bitter flavor. This thought leads Gide one step farther in his argument, a rather unfortunate step which illuminates with brutal clarity the author's defensive posture. Indeed, in the penultimate paragraph of the preface, having castigated his contemporary readers, Gide appeals to those readers of the future who will have the requisite insight to understand the complexity of his moral vision:

> But the real interest of a work and the interest taken in it by the public of the moment are two very different things. One may without too much conceit, I think, prefer the risk of failing to interest the moment by what is genuinely interesting – to beguiling momentarily a public fond of trash [*On peut sans trop de fatuité, je crois, préférer risquer de n'intéresser point le premier jour, avec des choses intéressantes – que passionner sans lendemain un public friand de fadaises*].[21] (*I* 20; *L'Imm* 368)

At the end of the preface, we are left with one concrete problem that we, as readers, need to solve: namely, what is the nature of the moral problem or problems that inhabit the text? What is the moral danger against which the *récit* seems compelled to erect multiple frames? Why must the author himself intervene in his work in order to defend its aesthetic integrity? What is it about the story's troubled hero, or anti-hero, that causes such consternation among the reading public?

Perhaps the most pervasively described and consistently disturbing trait of Michel throughout the *récit* is his tendency toward dissimulation, which manifests itself as a capacity to live a double life – on the one hand, the seeking out of amorous adventures and ethically suspect activities on the margins of society; on the other hand, the swearing of everlasting devotion to the woman he "loves," in the belief that he is capable of doing both at the same time, that his life can and does "contain" these extremes. In one of the rare moments in which Michel addresses himself directly to his interlocutors, we have the following pathos-infused rhetorical flourish:

> Oh, perhaps you think I didn't love Marceline. I swear, I loved her passionately [*Je jure que je l'aimais passionnément*]. Never had she been, and never had she seemed to me, so lovely. Illness had refined and actually exalted her features. I almost never left her now, surrounded her with continuous care [*l'entourais de soins continus*], protected, watched over her every moment of the day and night . . . When sometimes I left her for an hour to take a walk by myself in the country or in the streets, a loving anxiety, a fear she might be bored, quickly brought me back to her . . . I would return, my arms filled with flowers, early garden flowers or hothouse blossoms . . . Yes, I tell you I loved her dearly [*Oui, vous dis-je; je la chérissais tendrement*]. But how can I express this – that insofar as I respected myself less I revered her more – and who's to say how many passions and how many warring thoughts can cohabit in a man? (*I* 150–51; *L'Imm* 460)

The passage as a whole is built upon a desperate and wishful rhetoric of self-persuasion. One senses that Michel swears his love for Marceline so insistently, so "loudly" to his listeners, because he himself remains unpersuaded of the authenticity of his sentiments. The repetition of "Je *jure* que je l'aimais passionnément" and "Oui, *vous dis-je*, je la chérissais tendrement," is a quintessential example of Freudian *Verneinung* whereby the very emphatic quality of the speaker's tone points to his anxious insincerity. The words "Je jure que" and "Oui, vous dis-je" are referentially oriented formulae by which Michel temporarily removes himself from the inner frame of his story (in Emile Benveniste's terms, the past-tense *histoire* he is relating in its regular temporal unfolding)[22] in order to emerge, brusquely, in the "real time" of the concrete narrative situation (the terrace, the friends), thereby drawing attention to the enunciative present of his *discours*. It is when Michel breaks the frame that encloses the *histoire* as such within his *discours* that the moral complexity of the narrative erupts with the greatest force. It is precisely when moral contradiction or duplicity (expressed here in the mathematical proportionality of the phrase "insofar as I respected myself less I revered her more") is revealed in its most dangerous form that the aesthetic frame is least able to contain it.

Rather than "solve" the problems it contains, Michel's narrative, in its moments of greatest moral crisis, *dissolves*, leaving the reader to ponder the unanswerable general question, worthy, in its pithy formulation, of the pen of a seventeenth-century *moraliste*: "and who's to say how many passions and how many warring thoughts can cohabit in a man?" This is by no means the kind of general question Gide the preface-writer had in mind when he insisted upon the fundamental human significance of Michel's particular drama. The passage from the particularity of Michel's relation with Marceline to the generality of the "warring thoughts" inhabiting "man" is accomplished in a moment of extreme textual disjunction, and is, in fact, the *excuse* by which the protagonist attempts, quite lamely, to justify his own unjustifiable dissimulations. We have entered the moral labyrinth of speech-act theory, in which confessional discourse and the making of excuses collapse the text's purported aesthetic self-sufficiency and engage it in the referential realm of moral undecidability. The signals by which Michel tries to envelop his "love" for Marceline in the beauty of an aesthetic envelope ("Je jure que," "Oui, vous dis-je"), like the flowers with which he overwhelms her,[23] are protestations masking (badly) a sadistic desire to destroy her, to be rid of her stifling presence, protestations whose transgressive moral dimension cannot be tamed by any tale, however artfully told.

Gide's retroactive imposition of a preface as outside frame or containing vessel thus runs up against the subversive potential of the text's "inside," which resists final enclosure or domestication. In other words, the story's particularity, its irreducible moral complexity, cannot be subsumed within an aesthetically elaborated generality. The author's pleas for us readers to see in Michel's drama something more than a "bizarre case," something that transcends his individuality, are not convincing when set against the text's destabilizing rhetorical energy. *In particular*, we are being asked to see Michel's homosexual tendencies as part of a greater whole, as one element among others that can be subsumed within the general notion of immoralism. In this view, homosexuality, or, more precisely, *pédérastie*, the love of young boys, is no more or less important within the aesthetic totality of the text than those other health- or life-enhancing drives (Freud's *Triebe* applied to a Nietzschean philosophy of self-affirmation) that turn Michel away from Marceline and from his moral responsibility toward her. The question is, however: is this what the text says; is this what the text in fact *performs*? Is the impulse toward homosexuality merely one among other impulses in this particular text?

The answer to this question is, I think, an unequivocal No, and is conveyed by the *récit* in unmistakable fashion, in what might be called *an unframing device*. In the letter addressed to "Monsieur D.R., Président du Conseil" by which Michel's friends attempt to argue for the protagonist's reinsertion into society despite what his narrative will soon reveal about his past actions and current abject status, there is one interesting detail that risks going unnoticed and that might seem to be, at first glance, a mere concession to the fiction-writer's allegiance to verisimilitude: namely, the remark, inserted into the description of Michel's house and its setting: "A Kabyl child ran away as we approached, scrambling over the wall without a word" ("Un enfant kabyle était là, qui s'est enfui dès notre approche, escaladant le mur sans façon") (*I* 6; *L'Imm* 370). This same child reappears in the last paragraph of the story, as Michel breaks the spell of his now-finished *histoire* to address his friends directly. Although the first words of his peroration are in the mode of despair and urgency – "Drag me away from here; I can't leave of my own accord. Something in my will has been broken" (*I* 170) – his final musings revolve around the young Kabyl boy, named Ali, whom he prefers, for intimate companionship, to Ali's sister. It is she, says Michel, who laughingly "claims he's what keeps me here more than anything else. There may be some truth in what she says . . . " (171).

Ali is the detail, the particular, the unenclosable object of desire whose narrative function is that of frame-breaking. The wall he climbs so naturally and without fuss (*sans façon*) is the barrier set up, defensively, between the outside and the inside, the general and the particular. He is, simultaneously, that energy which exceeds frameworks of all kinds, and also, that individual who "keeps me here more than anything else," who represents an antidote to the protagonist's melancholy. He is both a Proustian *être de fuite* in his narrative function, and also the individual, the one and only individual, who establishes the possibility of staying, of dwelling. Irrecuperable, but also the promise of a future recuperation beyond the margins of society's framed permissibilities.

IV FRAMES: HUMAN AND DIVINE

Both *Heart of Darkness* and *L'Immoraliste* are cautionary tales which relate, underneath their portraits of immoralist characters, what might be called *the dangers of generalizing from the stance of admiration*. Marlow admires Kurtz for his eloquence and his "genius," but the particular words of Kurtz's discourse reveal nothing but emptiness, nothing but a moral vacuum. Michel admires Ménalque's pseudo-Nietzschean life-philosophy in its rhetoric of exaltation, but in applying this doctrine to the particularity of his relations with Marceline, he destroys her. Kurtz is said, on several occasions, to be a "remarkable man"; and Gide chooses, for the biblical passage that provides the first true frame of his story, a verse from Psalms 139 which reads: "Je te loue, ô mon Dieu, de ce que tu m'as fait créature si admirable." What both novellas perform is a radical undermining of the words "remarkable" and "admirable," a draining and desiccation of their moral meanings. Kurtz is "remarkable" only in the sense of someone who imprints an image of excess or *démesure* on one's eyes, not in the moral sense of someone worthy of our admiration. In the same way, Michel's actions are "admirable" only in the sense of causing our wonder or amazement, not in the sense of meriting our moral adhesion. The King James translation of the Psalms verse is worth quoting, as a final impetus for reflection: "I will praise thee; for I am fearfully and wonderfully made." There is no wonder without fear, no general example for human conduct that does not always contain its dangerous specificity. "Man" himself *is* danger, understood as that entity which is unframable by any text – unless it be God's own.

It is not without significance, I think, that the thirteen verses leading up to the Psalmist's praise of God for his "wondrous" creation relate, admiringly *and* fearfully, the impossibility of human escape from the infinite framework constructed by the Almighty. Following is the very exemplar of narrative framing which, in its sublime majestic inclusiveness, might well serve as dissuasion against all merely human attempts to contain the sinuous paths of moral progress and regress within the beautiful "glow" of an aesthetic envelope:

PSALM 139 (VERSES 1–14)

To the chief Musician. A Psalm of David

O LORD, thou hast searched me, and known me.
Thou knowest my downsitting and mine uprising, thou understandest my thought afar off.
Thou compassest my path and my lying down, and art acquainted with all my ways.
For there is not a word in my tongue, but, lo, O LORD, thou knowest it altogether.

Thou hast beset me behind and before, and laid thine
hand upon me.
Such knowledge is too wonderful for me; it is high, I
cannot attain unto it.
Whither shall I go from thy spirit? or whither shall I
flee from thy presence?
If I ascend up into heaven, thou art there; if I make my bed in hell,
behold, thou art there.
If I take the wings of the morning, and dwell in the uttermost
parts of the sea;
Even there shall thy hand lead me, and thy right hand
shall hold me.
If I say, Surely the darkness shall cover me; even the
night shall be light about me.
Yea, the darkness hideth not from thee; but the night
shineth as the day: the darkness and the light are
both alike to thee.
For thou hast possessed my reins: thou hast covered
me in my mother's womb.
I will praise thee; for I am fearfully and wonderfully
made: marvelous are thy works;
and that my soul knoweth right well.[24]

CHAPTER 8

Fishing the waters of impersonality: Virginia Woolf's To the Lighthouse

I PLUMBING THE DIARY'S DEPTHS

As readers of Virginia Woolf, we are fortunate to possess the literary treasurehouse of her five-volume, 1,700-page *Diary*, which not only illuminates the constellation of her family relations, friendships, and literary contacts (including the communal intellectual setting of Bloomsbury), but also contains, contemporaneous with and in counterpoint to her creative writing as it evolved, her own literary self-evaluations: her uncompromising descriptions of her travails, of her efforts at overcoming the technical limitations of narrative fiction as she had inherited it from the Victorians, and, perhaps most interestingly, her passionate evocations of those moments of elation in which she considered she had achieved aesthetic success. Precisely because Woolf was so intellectually honest and capable of a sober-minded, continual self-criticism, these moments emerge from the surrounding landscape (or better, for reasons that shall become clear presently: seascape) in dramatic fashion, as a triumphant rising-above-the-waves, as a bursting-forth of fluid energy, as an uncontainable overflow which carries along the writer in its wake. Thus her ecstatic entry of 23 February 1926, in which Woolf describes her feelings of being happily submerged in the writing of *To the Lighthouse*, the novel I shall be focusing on in this chapter:

> I am now writing as fast & freely as I have written in the whole of my life; more so – 20 times more so – than any novel yet. I think this is the proof that I was on the right path; & that what fruit hangs in my soul is to be reached there. Amusingly, I now invent theories that fertility & fluency are the things: I used to plead for a kind of close, terse, effort . . . I live entirely in it [*To the Lighthouse*], & come to the surface rather obscurely & am often unable to think what to say when we walk round the Square, which is bad I know. Perhaps it may be a good sign for the book though. (*DW* III, 59)[1]

To describe what separates *To the Lighthouse* (1927) from *Jacob's Room* (1922) and *Mrs. Dalloway* (1925), Virginia Woolf makes use of a clear-cut opposition between the "close, terse, effort" that characterized the earlier works and the "fertility & fluency" of her current project, the implication being that fertility and fluency are the signs or, one might say, symptoms, of a writing style which elaborates itself in a natural flow – in the French expression, *un style qui coule de source.* In terms of Woolf's own literary-historical background and baggage as Modernist writer, this would mean an overcoming of Symbolist aesthetics, of the "blanche agonie" represented by the Mallarméan white page and the writer's doomed efforts to overcome his or her stylistic impotence. Modernism would thus constitute an "advance" over Symbolism in its refusal of excessive, overwrought stylistic artifice, and in its adherence to the laws of nature, or even, the body. The fluidity of writing is a sure sign of the writer's being attuned to an inner rhythm, to which she releases herself willingly, allowing it to dictate the ebb and flow of her sentences.

However relevant such considerations might be to an examination of the crucial turn from Symbolist aesthetics to Modernist writing praxis, it must be kept in mind that Virginia Woolf does not express herself here in theoretical or rigorously conceptual terms, but metaphorically, and also playfully: "*Amusingly*, I now invent theories that fertility & fluency are the things." The "theories" come after the *fact* of writing itself and are expressed with ironical detachment. It is as if Woolf, in the very moment of her aesthetic triumphalism, were compelled to express some degree of caution about the force, or perhaps even the danger, of such fertility and fluency – qualities which derive from a submerging of self underneath the surface of everyday life. When she says that she "come[s] to the surface *rather obscurely*," it is as if, in the act of writing, she had been in contact with a formidable darkness, the remnants of which cannot easily be discarded, even when confronted with the light of (every)day. Even the apparently life-affirming expression "what fruit hangs in my soul is to be reached there," most probably derives (as the *Diary*'s editors obligingly indicate) from Shakespeare's *Cymbeline*, from lines which have a cautionary resonance: "Hang there like fruit, my soul, / Till the tree die!" (v v, 262). The taking of the "right path" and the reaching of that fecundity and fruitfulness which characterize Woolf's new style are threatened, hemmed in by obscurity and death, insofar as these are the forces lurking underneath the surface both of "life" and of an achieved fluid and "natural" style.

Although all of Virginia Woolf's novels can be said to contain personal reminiscences and transpositions of her friendships and social interactions, it is clear that *To the Lighthouse* is the most directly autobiographical, not only in the author's view, but also according to her family and contemporary readers. The line between fiction and autobiography is tenuously thin in this novel, and it is the very thinness of this evanescent and shifting boundary that accounts, I think, for the mixture of emotions, for the properly uncanny sensations experienced by the author as she vacillates between feelings of aesthetic mastery and intimations of darkness and death. Not only has she allowed her childhood experiences in St. Ives (Cornwall) to inform, quite transparently, the novel's imagined summerhouse in the Isle of Skye (Hebrides), but she has permitted her liaison with Vita Sackville-West to permeate the book, to seep through every aspect of Lily Briscoe's love for Mrs. Ramsay, and even to serve as a double or mirror for the new stylistic values she prizes:

> Vita having this moment (20 minutes ago – it is now 7) left me, what are my feelings? . . . She is not clever; but abundant & fruitful . . . Oh & mixed up with this is the invigoration of again beginning my novel [*To the Lighthouse*], in the Studio, for the first time this morning. All these fountains play on my being and intermingle. (*DW* III, 57; 19 January 1926)

Woolf's feelings of invigoration derive from the ways in which a lived relationship of reciprocated love can *intermingle* with the act of writing, can become consubstantial with it. Abundance and fruitfulness are both in Vita's body (after being in her *name*, of course: Vita the giver of life) and in Virginia's new style of composition. The realization of this consubstantiality produces the powerful image of "fountains play[ing] on my being." In the limited context of this particular diary entry, the eroticized surrender of the self to the play of rushing waters is unambiguously pleasurable. The being-as-body gives itself over to the spray of water without fear; the inviolability of the self's inner recesses is not threatened; there is playing-*on*, not playing-in.[2] Furthermore, fountains, as opposed to whirlpools, for example, are notable for their upward thrust; the water lying under the fountains' play is mere residue for recycling, and has no significance in itself. What causes fear is that which is hidden from view under an expanse of water, that which comes to the surface without apparent cause, producing an effect of uncanny fragmentation, of a haunting of life by death. Thus, Virginia's artistic accomplishment of making her mother live again in *To the Lighthouse*, highly praised by Vanessa, is mixed with an "upsetting" feeling. The rising to the surface of the mother in fiction is a terrifying haunting:

> The book [*To the Lighthouse*]. Now on its feet so far as praise is concerned. It has been out 10 days – Thursday a week ago. Nessa enthusiastic – a sublime, almost upsetting spectacle. She says it is an amazing portrait of mother; a supreme portrait painter; has lived in it; found the rising of the dead almost painful. (*DW* III, 135; 16 May 1927)

If the newly appeared novel is so successful as a work of art, it is because it has risen from the past as an artefact of memory and has encapsulated that past in a rigorously "true-to-life" fictional transmutation. It is doubtless no coincidence that Vanessa the painter should see the novel in the terms of her own art form – namely, as a "portrait." The power of the portrait derives not only from its resemblance to Julia Stephen "herself," but from the fact that Vanessa has had to *live within its frame*, has felt herself enveloped in the narrative design which renders with painful accuracy the reality of the family past. Now it may be true that the best-known theories of what we today call "High Modernism" – Joyce's "epiphanies," Woolf's own "moments of being," Proust's *souvenirs involontaires* – are based upon the instantaneous encapsulation of the depth of experience through memory's form-giving and symbolizing functions. What these theories do not state, but what Joyce, Woolf, and Proust in their very different ways illustrate in the praxis of their writing, is that the recovery of the past brings with it the re-enacted pain of loss and bereavement. The "exagmination" we as readers are forced to perform of Joyce's late work brings to the surface the death that has always inhabited life, the ghostly returns of repressed cultural memory that rise to the surface of the everyday and tear the fabric of habitual activity. The atemporal ecstasy of the first major occurrence of Proust's involuntary memory – the madeleine episode – is undercut considerably by a later occurrence, the so-called *intermittences du coeur*, in which the narrator, in the mundane act of tying his shoe, not only "sees" his dead grandmother but is compelled to relive his ambivalent relation with her, to experience once again, or rather, for the first time, her death. In the same way, the aesthetic "success" of Mrs. Ramsay as character – the fact that she resembles so closely her model, Julia Stephen – is at the same time, in experiential or existential terms, a fall into *Unheimlichkeit.*

To the Lighthouse depicts better, more "faithfully" than any other book, Virginia Woolf's home environment, the domestic haven in which she lived. At the same time, however, in making the dead rise, it thrusts the reader into the domain of the un-homelike, the alive-but-also-dead region of the uncanny. In the elliptical diary entry of 16 May 1927, we slip from the sublime ("Nessa enthusiastic – a sublime, almost upsetting spectacle") to the uncanny ("has lived in it; found the rising of the dead almost painful"). Whereas in the experience of the sublime, in its Kantian formulation, human reason, after an initial un-settling, does indeed return to itself, so that, once the power of nature is given its due, the separation between self and nature, inside and outside, is restored; the uncanny always presupposes the "intermingling" and interpenetration of inside and outside, self and other, life and death. An uncanny work of art, such as *To the Lighthouse*, always appears the most "lifelike" of all works, but only in order to *take the reader in*, to erase aesthetic distance and enclose and enfold him or her within an infinitely expansive discursive space. Reading becomes a kind of drowning, whereby the reader's consciousness is invaded by foreign waters[3] – a far cry, apparently, from the benign fluency and fluidity Woolf imagined as the founding qualities of her newly discovered style.

If the Modernist writer is not only the conscious creator of new forms that go beyond or overturn the tenets of Symbolist poetics and the conventions of the Victorian novel, but also the individual human who, in life and art, recognizes the force of the uncanny, the question arises: how can one come to terms with, or how can one find an adequate defense against, the dispossessing energy of *Unheimlichkeit*? To open oneself completely to the ghostly exterior is to risk annihilation, the submerging of subjective consciousness underneath the leveling effects of what Virginia Woolf herself, in her diary entry of 20 July 1925, calls "this impersonal thing" (*DW* III, 36) – i.e., the erosion of human individuality by the destruction of war, disease, and death, by the liquifying invasion of the house in the central section of *To the Lighthouse* entitled "Time Passes." It is not a matter of coincidence, I think, that this stylistically brilliant middle part of the novel's structure, in which characters die within parentheses, is itself placed within the larger parentheses of parts one and three, both of which focus on the detailed psychological depiction of highly differentiated characters, on their defeats and small triumphs as individuals. To borrow from the devices and terms of war, one might say that the second part of the novel is like the highly-concentrated explosive device that must be contained within a large diffusion-box: the function of parts one and three is to cushion the force of part two, to contain the destructive quality of uncanniness as death-within-life, as the death that permeates life just as the mists and moisture of the sea invade the house.

To guard against this invasion, therefore, the first method is that of narrative framing. The expedition to the Lighthouse, imagined but delayed in part one, does take place in part three, and its mere occurrence has been seen by a number of critics as proof of Woolf's faith in human endeavor. Whether it be Mr. Ramsay's successful landing at the Lighthouse or Lily Briscoe's completing of her painting, both activities are accomplished despite all odds and are concluded in a final, satisfying sense of repose after the expending of considerable effort. After tension, there is *détente*, and two of the novel's protagonists enjoy triumphs which may be small in scale, but which the narrator describes scrupulously and in great detail, with attention to their complexity and contextual meaning. In the end, it would seem, the individual does have his or her place on the earth, however restricted; and this sense of place emerges from the framing of death by life, of destruction by creation, of the uncanny by the final aesthetic conviction embodied in the tracing of a line at the center of a painting. This, at least, is what the overall narrative conception of *To the Lighthouse* suggests. Whether the reader is willing to accept such an interpretation depends upon his or her trust in the diffusing capabilities of the frames. The problem of the "stress" on the frames by the framed inner core is one to which I shall return in due course, in my discussion of the novel's inscription of the act of reading.

There is, beyond the possible large-scale narrative solution to the containment of the uncanny, a second avenue of approach which is not based upon the geometry of parentheses or frames, but rather on a highly coherent and cohesive use of metaphorical language – the language of catching, netting, and, in all senses of the word, *fishing*. If, in Virginia Woolf's *imaginaire*, water is both pleasurable, as a fountain playing on the body, and terrifying, as the dark element that can invade, overcome, and destroy the boundaries defining the limits of the self, then netting or catching a fish is the perfect image for the safeguarding of the self against the dangers of the unseen unknown: the fisherman penetrates the surface of the water and brings up from its depths one of its creatures, one of its hidden treasures, but is himself at a comfortable remove from its threatening undercurrents. With apologies to Carolyn Heilbrun, I wonder if it might not be possible to see in the thin thread of the fishing-line an irreverent Modernist variation on the theme of Ariadne's thread.[4] The line plunging into the unfathomable deep is both a connection to the loved and feared origin of all things (in Freudian terms, an umbilical chord leading back to the primordial maternal principle, to the primal uncanniness inhabiting the place from which we all come) and a protection against becoming lost in the labyrinth of human existence. The fishing-line or Ariadne's thread is solidly attached to a pole held by a figure who has reached dry land and is fishing *from the land into the water*; this figure has "already" emerged from the water, has evolved out of it, so to speak, and can speak of "catching" (or, in a variation on the same theme, "netting") even the most enigmatic of sea-creatures from the safety of the shore. Thus Virginia Woolf in her triumphant exclamations just after finishing *The Waves* (1931):

> Here in the few minutes that remain, I must record, heaven be praised, the end of The Waves. I wrote the words O Death fifteen minutes ago, having reeled across the last ten pages with some moments of such intensity & intoxication that I seemed only to stumble after my own voice . . . How physical the sense of triumph & relief is! . . . I have netted that fin in the waste of waters which appeared to me over the marshes out of my window at Rodmell when I was coming to an end of To the Lighthouse. (*DW* IV, 10; 7 February 1931)

The netting of the fish which appeared to Virginia Woolf only as an enigmatic "fin in the waste of waters" four and a half years prior to the completion of *The Waves* is a striking symbolic representation of closure, of the final artistic control that envelops the diverse narrative strands of what is perhaps her most technically challenging novel. The fish-as-fragment has been made whole by the aesthetic perfection of the new novel's polyphonic complexity. What was only a vague and strange vision has taken on consistency, has deepened and darkened into a work of art. The tone of the passage, like that of the *Diary* entries surrounding *To the Lighthouse*, is once again that of elation ("intensity," "intoxication," "relief").

Yet in the very moment of what Woolf describes explicitly and unmodestly as a "triumph," there is also a disquieting note of subjective dispossession in the phrase "having *reeled* across the last ten pages," as if the act of writing, even in the phase of its greatest apparent mastery and control, were, in its essence, a kind of inchoate stumbling. At the very instant of *reeling in* the fish, the writer of *The Waves reels across the page*, leaving the reader to wonder whether Woolf is the fisherwoman or rather the fish, which, in being brought up from the water, lurches violently this way and that, in the throes of the "Death" about which the narrator writes so eloquently. Put succinctly: when someone pens the phrase "Against you I will fling myself, unvanquished and unyielding, O Death!" (*The Waves*, 297), is the act of writing about death equivalent to a netting or envelopment of death's pervasive power? Or, to use biblical language, does writing about death remove the latter's "sting"? In the end, are the numerous expressions of physical and emotional elation contained in the *Diary* and summed up in the image of landing a fish merely the symptoms of the temporary sentimental delusion that insidiously takes over the writer when he or she is *emerging from writing*, and therefore *no longer really in writing*? If this should be the case, are those expressions of "triumph" that punctuate a number of important episodes in *To the Lighthouse* like a highly structured leitmotiv to be taken at face value or treated with interpretive skepticism? Are we to believe Woolf when she seems to assert, albeit with gentle irony, that Lily Briscoe has achieved her own personal artistic vision, and that the incompletely intrepid philosopher, Mr. Ramsay, in reaching the Lighthouse, has accomplished something of note? These are thorny issues indeed, and cannot be answered in a peremptory way, but, as a first approach to these questions as they are developed in the fabric of the novel, it may be useful to cite the *Diary* once more. This is from the entry for 30 September 1926, at the point at which Woolf sees "a fin passing far out" for the first time:

> One sees a fin passing far out. What image *can I reach* to convey what I mean? Really there is none I think. The interesting thing is that in all my feeling & thinking I have never come up against this before. Life is, soberly & accurately, *the oddest affair*; has in it the essence of reality. I used to feel this as a child – couldn't step across a puddle once I remember, for thinking, how strange – what am I? &c. *But by writing I dont [sic] reach anything.* All I mean to make is a note of *a curious state of mind.* I hazard the guess that it may be the impulse behind another book. (*DW* III, 113; my emphasis)

This passage can serve, in Woolf's own terms, as the "sober" antidote to the "intoxication" of the other passages we have read thus far. To borrow from the vocabulary of speech-act theory, Woolf writes here in a purely constative mode: and what she notes with dispassion is the strangeness, the oddity, or what I have been calling, via Freud and E. T. A. Hoffmann, the uncanniness of life itself. Life presents itself, when viewed with sobriety, as an odd thing against which one stumbles or trips, as a puddle over or around which there may be no obvious path, no possible bridge or even detour. And whereas in the previous passages we have analyzed, the act of writing appears as that which promises a containment of the explosive power of the uncanny, here we have the disabused statement "But by writing I dont reach anything" – devastating words indeed coming from the creator of a protagonist whose most notable achievement, since he has not reached R, is at least to have reached the

Lighthouse! But *what does it mean*, as Virginia Woolf would say, to reach the Lighthouse? An answer to these questions, however tentative, is only possible if one leaves the relative safety of the *Diary* as writer's haven for an invigorating plunge into the murky waters of the novel – notably those intertextual depths of *To the Lighthouse* in which the act of fishing as controlled reeling-in *and* intoxicated reeling-across-the-page is thematized with great virtuosity.

II WOOLF AND THE BROTHERS GRIMM, OR "THE INADEQUACY OF HUMAN RELATIONSHIPS"

Among the various intertexts that nourish *To the Lighthouse*,[5] none is more crucial to the reader's understanding of the character of Mrs. Ramsay or the nature of her relationship with her husband than the Grimm fairy tale entitled "The Fisherman and his Wife," which enters the novel early in part one, as a fragmented "scene of reading." As in Proust's depiction of this same literary primal scene in the opening pages of *A la recherche du temps perdu*, a mother (Mrs. Ramsay) reads to her son (James). But the intimacy of the moment is rendered precarious, just as it is in Proust, by the threatening presence of the father – in this case the insecure Mr. Ramsay, whose insistent demands for affection from his wife cause his son to hate him (a theme which will be pursued, to great mock-dramatic effect, in the concluding chapters of part three, during the expedition to the Lighthouse). Proust lessens the Oedipal tensions of his scene by removing the father, depicted initially as a gigantic but slightly comical Abraham figure, from the action: it is his disappearance from view that allows for the mother and son to be alone and for the act of reading to take place. With the father absent, the child Marcel can enter into what he himself imagines to be an inappropriate, "illicit" relation with his mother, and, prompted by the plot of the George Sand novel his mother is reading, *François le Champi*, can imagine, within the relative safety offered by fictional transposition, the overcoming of the taboo on incest. Marcel understands, even as a child, that this evening of reading, of envelopment within the mother's voice, is fragile, evanescent: such evenings will not be the rule and may not happen ever again, but the pleasure of the moment is intense, and the scene of reading, once it is established, is uniquely pleasurable and uninterrupted.

Woolf treats the same essential scene quite differently. It does not take place once within the narrative flow, but is fragmented into four discrete occurrences spread over four successive chapters (part one, chapters 7,

8, 9, and 10). As is the case in Proust, the embedded text shares obvious thematic affinities with the primary text,[6] but Woolf is far more coy than Proust in indicating to her reader what these affinities might be. It becomes, therefore, a matter of ethical responsibility for the reader to go back to the Grimm fairy tale and to open its pages again – in order to determine the degree to which the Modernist novel is enlivened, enriched, but also complicated by the "primitive" narrative of the folk's collective unconscious. I shall begin with an examination of each reference, however elliptical, to the Grimm intertext, with particular attention to the context in which these references occur, to what the surface of the primary text is concerned with as the Grimm tale rises from the depths to inhabit it briefly. In a second development, I shall return to "The Fisherman and his Wife" as narrative and analyze its structure and language, in an effort to explore the somewhat hidden currents in whose depths important differences from as well as clear resemblances to the frame-novel can be found. Virginia Woolf used the Grimm story as a sounding-board for *To the Lighthouse*, as a same-but-different *Doppelgänger* whose relation to its brother/sister-text is itself uncanny.

"The Fisherman and his Wife" in context

The first time we hear of "The Fisherman and his Wife" is in the seventh chapter of part one, in two casual phrases which are delivered, to borrow from theatrical language, in the mode of *a parte*. In the first of these allusions, enveloped in a long sentence to which we shall need to pay attention, we have: "she [Mrs. Ramsay] had only strength enough to move her finger, in exquisite abandonment to exhaustion, across the page of Grimm's fairy story" (*TL* 38).[7] One page later we learn the title of the fairy story, but the narrator provides no commentary on its content or significance to the novel's characters. The scene of reading itself is posed quite precariously within a larger, emotionally charged episode whose principle theme is Mr. Ramsay's demands for his wife's sympathy and her ability to soothe and placate him (not without considerable cost to the tranquillity of her own psyche, however). The "exhaustion" to which the first passage refers is the inevitable by-product of Mrs. Ramsay's successful efforts at calming her husband and restoring a sense of balance and harmony to their relationship. It is in this chapter that Virginia Woolf stages the "war between the sexes" in a particularly memorable way, by depicting the male of the species as hard and sterile and the female as life-giving and bountiful – a binary opposition which will subtend the entirety of the novel, thereby lending it an unmistakable feminist tinge, even though Woolf's explicitly feminist writings were to begin only in 1929, two years after *To the Lighthouse*, with the publication of *A Room of One's Own*. James is not only the addressee of the fairy tale, but also the witness to a scene which children should never see: namely, a metaphorically-phrased enactment of sexual consummation in which Mrs. Ramsay, who "seemed to raise herself with an effort, and at once to pour erect into the air a rain of energy, a column of spray" (*TL* 37), finds herself obliged to submit to her husband:

Standing between her knees, very stiff, James felt all her strength flaring up to be drunk and quenched by the beak of brass, the arid scimitar of the male, which smote mercilessly, again and again, demanding sympathy. (*TL* 38)

It is this plunging and smiting that exhausts Mrs. Ramsay, that robs her of her own energy but at the same time produces what can only be described as the happy exhaustion of post-coital bliss. The scene of reading and the text of the Grimm fairy tale are thus inserted into the larger framework of the sexual act, with James looking on "stiffly" as voyeur. This scenario is quite different from that of Proust, where the evening of reading separates the narrator's parents and prevents their physical intimacy while allowing the child a fantasized union with his mother. In Woolf's version, the act of reading can take place only after the father has had his violent pleasure with his wife. Of great interest in Woolf's mythic rendition of the male–female pairing is the apparently curious fact that the male, who is arid and self-centered, can nevertheless produce in the overwhelmed female what the narrator describes as "the rapture of successful creation":

Immediately, Mrs. Ramsay seemed to fold herself together, one petal closed in another, and the whole fabric fell in exhaustion upon itself, so that she had only strength enough to move her finger, in exquisite abandonment to exhaustion, across the page of Grimm's fairy story, while there throbbed through her, like the pulse in a spring which has expanded to its full width and now gently ceases to beat, the rapture of successful creation. (*TL* 38)

The reading of "The Fisherman and his Wife" occurs after the metaphorical transcription of sexual climax, in the moments directly following upon orgasm. The first, sexual invasion, of the female by the male, is followed by a second invasion – that of the reader and listener by the otherness of the text as it unfolds itself, as it gradually expands into the shared consciousness of both participants. The fairy story, like the physical union that preceded it in time, will have occasion, through the following chapters, to "expand to its full width" and eventually flow through the primary text. In her first presentation of the Grimm intertext, Woolf thus suggests the possibility that the act of reading, by following in the wake of a sexually expressed male–female conjugation, by participating in its "throbbing" energies, may somehow share the same properties: reading appears as a possible *analogon* to sexual union understood as a properly invasive force. As we continue our investigation of the appearances of the folk story within the novel we must see whether this analogous relation is merely the product of a momentary textual coincidence, or whether something more fundamental to Woolf's literary imagination is at stake in this early embedding of reading within the "whole fabric" of sexuality.

The seventh chapter of part one moves from the language of exhilaration and sensual fulfillment to Mrs. Ramsay's distinctly melancholy conclusion concerning "the inadequacy of human relationships" (*TL* 40). Once the fervor and energy of the initial section have subsided, Mrs. Ramsay's thoughts are haunted by the realization that the couple she forms with her husband is based upon the hiding of "small daily things" and upon her "not being able to tell him [Mr. Ramsay] the truth" (ibid.) about the aggravating material difficulties from which she would like to shield him, the unpractical philosopher. This particular chapter raises the problem of the stark contrast between the flimsy quality of instantaneous gratification and the longer-term ethical dilemmas which, when "papered over" and ignored, drive a wedge between husband and wife, make them into separate creatures. Woolf's male–female opposition is not without its complexity, in that the female, depicted in positive terms as fecund and also altruistic (she "serves" both her husband in sex and her son by reading to him), is also a dissembler and a manipulator, someone who creates harmony in her household at the expense of the telling of the truth. Mrs. Ramsay's harmony, in other words, is an aesthetic veil she throws over an ethical situation, a denial of the poverty, both physical and emotional, in which she lives but which she refuses to recognize. Here we begin to see, in shadowy form, Mrs. Ramsay as the Fisherman's Wife, but need to read further before the points of convergence between the folk tale and the novel become fully visible.

The second, quite cursory allusion to "The Fisherman and his Wife" occurs in the following chapter, as Mrs. Ramsay, once again reflecting upon "the pettiness of . . . human relations" (*TL* 42) and upon her own flaws of character, turns to the reading of the fairy tale for diversion, for relief from her pessimistic ruminations. For the first time, the narrator of the novel quotes from the embedded story; and the chosen passage, far from offering relief or diversion, corresponds directly to the ethical problems adumbrated in the conclusion to chapter seven:

"The man's heart grew heavy," she read aloud, "and he would not go. He said to himself, 'It is not right,' and yet he went. And when he came to the sea the water was quite purple and dark blue,[8] and grey and thick, and no longer so green and yellow, but it was still quiet. And he stood there and said – " (*TL* 42)

For readers of Woolf who remember their own mothers reading to them from the Grimm story, it is not difficult to recall that the Fisherman's plight consists of carrying out his wife's wishes despite his own moral reservations. The key phrase in the passage is the simple statement "It is not right." At one level, the message of the fairy tale, like that of most folk literature, is a conservative one: accept your place in society; do not ask for too much; for if you do, nature will take its revenge upon your excessive desires, upon your hubris. The ethical judgment "It is not right" is inseparable from the dictates of a feudal society, in which class hierarchies are immutable. At the same time, of course, "The Fisherman and his Wife" can be seen as a folk formulation of misogynist literature, in that it is the shrewish wife who is punished for her willfulness and "put back in her place," while the patient and long-suffering Fisherman, who deserves better than the woman he lives with, accepts the constraints of everyday reality and is thus the object of our pity rather than our scorn.

Perhaps the most obvious function of the embedded story, in its apparent one-to-one correspondence to the frame narrative (Mrs. Ramsay "is" the Fisherman's Wife; Mr. Ramsay "is" the Fisherman), is to demystify Mrs. Ramsay, to reveal beneath her idealized beauty and capacity to "compose" people into harmonious groups (as in the *Boeuf en Daube* episode) a much less admirable tendency to want too much and to run other people's lives. Her oft-repeated categorical imperative, "they [all people of marrigeable age] must marry," is based upon her own defensive desires, upon her steadfast unwillingness to question the solidity of her own marriage. Her directive "they must marry" is an interesting parody of Kant and of his celebrated proposition, in the *Critique of Practical Reason*: "So act that the maxim of your will could always hold at the same time as a principle establishing universal law."[9] The "maxim" of Mrs. Ramsay's will does not derive from a pure ethical thought, but rather from a coercive desire: other people *must* do what she does, not necessarily because they will find happiness in the married state (would this be the case for Lily Briscoe?), but because misery loves company. How far, one wonders, is Mrs. Ramsay's imperative from *Schadenfreude*?

Throughout *To the Lighthouse* there is a complex vacillation between what one might call the irruption of the ethical into the aesthetic, on the one hand, and the aestheticization of the real, on the other. Thus, whereas the first two passages containing references to the fairy tale emphasize the problem of ethical thought and action as it emerges from underneath the threatened intimacy of the reading situation in its contextual presentation (lying or dissembling in the first case; the creation of a falsely grounded imperative in the second), the third allusion to "The Fisherman and his Wife" is pure idealization, pure aesthetization. It comes in chapter nine of part one, where it is mentioned as part of an artistic vision, as an element among others that contributes to the beauty of a domestic scene. Here, Lily Briscoe is on the verge of criticizing the tyrannical qualities of Mr. Ramsay to Mr. Bankes, when she notices that the latter is overcome by "rapture" at "the sight of her [Mrs. Ramsay] reading a fairy tale to her boy" (*TL* 47). What has happened in this passage is that the ethical dimension of the text (the rightness or wrongness of Mr. Ramsay's actions as potential subject for the moral adjudication of Lily and Bankes) has quite simply disappeared, has been effaced by the blinding light of a Modernist Madonna-with-Child image. "Rapture" has covered over the ethical in favor of a beautiful representation. Significantly, at the very moment of this aesthetic epiphany, *the content of the fairy tale disappears from view, becomes submerged.* Whatever "The Fisherman and his Wife" can tell the reader about human relations, about hubris, and also about *To the Lighthouse,* has become invisible, has receded behind the closed cover of the book, has lost its title as well as its inner structure and meaning.

The very act of transforming the scene of reading into a subject for visual representation reduces the book – the means of interpretive transaction between addressor and addressee – to a prop, to an object whose intrinsic value is lost as it gains a new, completely different value within the aesthetic whole of a sentimental tableau. In economical terms, the question becomes: what precisely is lost and what is gained in this transformation? Does Bankes's "rapturous" reaction to the scene of reading – "that barbarity was tamed, the reign of chaos subdued" (ibid.) – indicate that the reign of beauty begins *only when we close the book*, only when we neutralize the *energeia* of reading as interpretive activity? Why is it that reading as act (rather than image or icon) must be neutralized? What kind of imperative lies behind or below this aestheticizing gesture? These are questions to which we shall return after an examination of the novel's fourth and final intertextual homage to "The Fisherman and his Wife."

It is in the tenth chapter of the novel's first section that the fairy tale is dealt with most completely, even though, once again, its reading is often interrupted by the comings and goings of the characters and by Mrs. Ramsay's reflections and musings. In this chapter Virginia Woolf continues to develop the narrative technique which is typical of the entirety of *To the Lighthouse*, namely, the alternation between outer events and inner thought – in this case, between the prolonged walk of Paul and Minta and what Mrs. Ramsay assumes is Paul's impending marriage proposal, on the one hand, and the reading of the story, on the other. Mrs. Ramsay thus ranges in her mind between the question of the young couple's marriage and her conveying of the ancient fable to James; and, if we are to believe the narrator, she does so effortlessly. The following passage is one instance of the mixing of the two narratives, in which the transition from the outer frame to the embedded folk tale is made with particular ease:

"And when he came to the sea, it was quite dark grey, and the water heaved up from below, and smelt putrid. Then he went and stood by it and said,

> 'Flounder, flounder, in the sea,
> Come, I pray thee, here to me;
> For my wife, good Ilsabil,
> Wills not as I'd have her will.'

'Well, what does she want then?' said the Flounder." And where were they [Paul and Minta] now? Mrs. Ramsay wondered, reading and thinking, quite easily, both at the same time; for the story of the Fisherman and his Wife was like the bass gently accompanying a tune, which now and then ran up unexpectedly into the melody. And when should she be told? If nothing happened, she would have to speak seriously to Minta. (*TL* 56)

The image of the bass running up unexpectedly into the melody seems to be, at first glance, nothing more than a graceful rhetorical ornamentation meant to convey via analogy the simple contrast between real life (human relationships, specifically marriage) on the one hand, and literary diversion (the Grimm tale) on the other. Just as the bass in some musical compositions can rise into the melody momentarily (obliging the unfortunate pianist to cross hands in some cases – an *unheimlich* moment for those who have experienced it in certain pieces by Schumann, for example), in the same way Mrs. Ramsay's distracted thoughts about "The Fisherman and his Wife" can overflow into her more concentrated preoccupations concerning the future of Paul and Minta. To pursue the musical analogy for a moment: all is well if the interruption is brief, if the bass then returns to "where it belongs"; but what if the relation between the bass and the melody is itself one of uncanny resemblance – what if the bass *is* the melody, or rather, is, so to speak, the unconscious significance of a melody that does not "know itself"? If we look at the *analogon* of the relation between bass and melody, namely the possible parallelism between the Grimm tale and the Paul–Minta liaison, we have precisely such a disturbing state of affairs. The unhappy relation between husband and wife in the embedded narrative, in which the wife "wills not what I'd have her will," is the precise prophetic expression of what Paul and Minta's marriage will become – a *dialogue de sourds*, a continual clashing of the wills which ends in failure. Hence the appropriateness of the apparently brusque narrative elision between the sentence, "Well, what does she want then? said the Flounder" and its sequel, "And where were they now?" "They" are Paul and Minta, but Paul and Minta *as unwitting imitators of the Fisherman and his Wife.* Outer frame and embedded tale fold into each other: they tell the same story of disoriented desire; they are textual *Doppelgänger.* The invasion of the melody by the bass is thus less innocent, far more consequential narratively and far more dangerous in its cautionary tone than Mrs. Ramsay would like to think.

The balance of the chapter continues its quasi-metronomic alternation between Mrs. Ramsay's meditations on Paul and Minta and the progressive unfolding of the fairy tale, whose conclusion is reached in the moment before the light in the Lighthouse flashes for the first time in the evening sky – the Lighthouse Mrs. Ramsay realizes her son will not visit on the following day. The embedded story concludes on the note of repose and resolution traditional in fairy tales: "And there they are living still at this very time" (*TL* 61), and is then enveloped by the larger narrative framework, by the imagery of directed light but also by the somber intuition that the expedition so hoped for by James will not take place after all. Thus the fairy story is both more significant and less powerful than its fictional readers imagine: more significant in that it reflects, with an uncanny light, the existential plight of the novel's characters; less powerful in that, at the same time, it has no effect whatever upon other events of the outside world, such as the vagaries of the expedition-halting weather. Imaginative literature says more about the world than we would like; it also does less to the world than we would hope. Such is the conclusion the reader of Woolf and the brothers Grimm might reach after following the "fin" of the fairy tale in the novel's "waste of waters". This is, however, just a first step. I propose now to look beneath the waves into the undercurrents, to go fishing in the ancient narrative for the strange combination of sameness and difference that unites and separates the font of folk wisdom from its Modernist appropriation, transformation, and redirection.

"The Fisherman and his Wife" as told by the Brothers Grimm

Like the majority of folktales collected by the Brothers Grimm, "The Fisherman and his Wife" is characterized by brevity, a simple and predictable narrative design, and a clear moral message delivered at the conclusion of the tale. For the limited purposes of my analysis, the story can be summed up as follows:

A fisherman goes down to the sea and catches a flounder, who turns out to be an enchanted prince. Taking pity on the metamorphosed human (who is possessed of speech and of a very reasonable discourse, including the practical advice that, being human underneath his gills, he would not taste very good), the fisherman throws him back and returns home to his wife with nothing to show for his daily work. In an amusing literarily self-referential moment, the wife, who must have read some fairy tales herself, knows that in this kind of literature enchanted princes are supposed to grant wishes: consequently, she instructs her husband to ask that their squalid hovel be transformed into a cottage. No sooner asked than granted: after making his request to the flounder-prince, the fisherman returns home and finds a cottage standing in the place of the hovel. As of now, the narrative pattern is established for the remainder of the tale: the fisherman, driven on by the insatiable greed or cupidity of his wife (in the German text, the word is *Gier*)[10] will continue to ask for ever-larger and more imposing dwellings to accommodate his wife's overweaning ambition (having acquired a castle, she becomes king, then emperor, then pope), until the woman, like so many fairy-tale figures, makes one wish too many, namely, to become "like God" ("wie der liebe Gott") (F 166) and control the rising and the setting of the sun. After the fisherman relays this wish to the flounder-prince, he returns home to find the original hovel in place of the castle. It is here that he and his wife have continued to live, up until "this day" ("Darin sitzen sie noch heute, bis auf diesen Tag") (ibid.).

Of course, this bare-bones presentation of the story's narrative structure does not do justice to its considerable charm, which is based, in large measure, on what might be called its "musical" mode of theme and variations. Thus, as the castle keeps getting larger and larger to reflect the increasingly prestigious rank and onerous duties of its female occupant, the descriptions become correspondingly lavish: the king's throne is high, but the emperor's is higher, and the pope's is so lofty as to be almost invisible from ground level; the respective retinues of these officials range from large to huge to gigantic; and the accoutrements of power (crown, scepter, papal staff) shine with the ever-increasing accumulation of precious stones.[11] The story as a whole, with its moral message of cupidity punished, of the human being struck down for wishing to become "like God," and with its descriptive emphasis on the palace's dizzying loftiness, is a folk variation on the biblical story of the Tower of Babel. At the same time – and herein lies the poetic originality of the Grimm tale – there is an interesting correspondence between the vertical upward thrust of the couple's home and the increasingly high and threatening waves out of which the flounder-prince rises to address the fisherman. As the waves grow higher, so does the castle. But there is an important difference here – a difference that will allow us, in a moment, to return to Woolf and to her fairy-tale-inspired novel. The castle, a product of culture and of human ingeniousnous, of *techné*, is merely the accumulation of one stone upon the other, of one ornament upon the other: the pope's abode is merely larger than the emperor's, but not different in kind; what is high simply becomes higher. In the case of the waves, however, what is deepest becomes highest. One fears the waves because, as they become stronger and more "unsettled," they churn up what lies at the bottom of the sea and bring it to the surface. The force of nature, of *physis*, exceeds the designs of *techné* not in the superficial terms of measurable height, but in the uncanny presentation of depths rising above heights. Whereas the narrator tells us with obliging precision that the emperor's throne is "two miles high" (F 163), the final description of the waves is both less precise and more overpowering in its apocalyptic tone:

> The houses and the trees were blown down, and the mountains quaked, and cliffs fell into the sea, and all of heaven became jet-black; there was thunder and lightning, and the sea threw black waves into the sky as high as church towers and mountains. (F 166)

What is it about the nature-versus-culture combat in "The Fisherman and his Wife" that fascinated Woolf? In what way does the elegantly simple progression of the folk tale hold a mirror to the Modernist writer's complex experimental narrative forms? Certainly it seems plausible to agree with the critics that Mrs. Ramsay is "like" the Fisherman's wife in her strong will and coercive desires. But Mr. Ramsay in no way resembles the humble and uncomplicated Fisherman, and there is apparently no flounder-prince in *To the Lighthouse*, at least not in immediately recognizable form. Further, the ironic, deflated tone of the fairy tale's conclusion would seem to have nothing in common with the triumphant double ending of the novel: Mr. Ramsay's successful landing at the Lighthouse, and Lily Briscoe's completed painting. One-to-one correspondences between specific characters and plot elements are therefore quite limited, much more so than in the case of the strong thematic connection between the characters and plot of *François le Champi* and the frame-tale of Proust's novel. I would suggest, however, that the deep, under-the-surface resemblances of the Grimm story to Virginia Woolf's narrative lie in two related areas: that of mediating structures and what can be called the triangle of desire, on the one hand; and of indirect, figural language on the other.

In *To the Lighthouse* Mrs. Ramsay is continually engaged in a combat of wills with her husband, and although her strategies of domination (for example, not saying "I love you" but indicating her affection in her own way at the end of part one: "For she had triumphed again. She had not said it: yet he knew" [*TL* 124]) are subtle in the forms they take, they emanate uniquely from her consciousness and are her own creation. In the Grimm tale, however, the Fisherman's wife accomplishes nothing by herself: she needs both her husband as messenger and the flounder-prince as enacter of her desires. It is the triangulation of desire that produces the metamorphoses of the hovel into cottage then castle. The male characters must be used; they must serve their "lady" for the vertical ascent of the home to take place, for the unsatisfied woman to create the dwelling of her never-ending dreams. At first sight, nothing of the sort exists in Woolf's novel, but only at first sight. In fact, Mrs. Ramsay's own kind of creation, her aesthetic "genre," so to speak – that of the harmoniously and cohesively organized group of humans into a fragile but beautiful community (the end-result of the *Boeuf en Daube* scene) – depends upon a similar, but somewhat masked mediation. Because Mrs. Ramsay takes credit for the social harmony she has worked so hard to achieve, it is easy enough to repress the fact that it is the cook, not Mrs. Ramsay, who prepared the delicious meal;[12] and the cook, like the fisherman and the flounder-prince, is merely used and obtains no credit for her own labors.

Let us now proceed a step farther – an admittedly perilous step since it involves entry into the troubled waters of what years ago would have been termed the "biographical fallacy." Let us assume that Virginia Woolf herself does not stand outside her book at the safe remove of aesthetic distance, but finds herself implicated in the fable of mediated desire which unites, beyond all superficial differences, Mrs. Ramsay with the fisherman's wife. What is it that the fisherman's wife and Mrs. Ramsay achieve in their respective homes? How do they transform their dwellings; how do they metamorphose their surroundings? By the addition of ornamentation, of decoration, to the actual bareness in which they are destined to live. It should not be forgotten that the fisherman's wife *never moves*: there is no medieval equivalent to a real estate agent in her story. The hovel becomes a cottage which becomes a castle which becomes a hovel again, *in the same place*. The flounder-prince's mode of discourse is that of the peformative; word becomes deed immediately according to the logic of tropic displacement. The castle simply replaces the cottage according to the laws of metaphorical substitution, of metamorphosis in the sense of *Verwandlung*. This means that, as the house grows out of all human proportion, its walls become incrusted with more and more jewels. There is an increasingly overwhelming but also stifling sense of over-decoration: the "magnificent ornaments" (*prachtvolle Verzierungen*) (162) make one forget the hovel underneath, the hovel to which one must return once the enchantment is broken. In the same way, the *Boeuf en Daube* scene is preceded by the ritual act of Rose's choosing her mother's jewelry; and when Mrs. Ramsay descends the stairway, the narrator compares her to a "queen who, finding her people [i.e. her "subjects"] gathered in the hall, looks down upon them, and descends among them, and acknowledges their tributes silently" (*TL* 82). The dinner itself is a transformation of the quotidian into an atemporal epiphany taking place under the aegis of Neptune, god and guardian of the sea – a quiet Neptune placated by the flower-offering placed as centerpiece on the dinner-table (*TL* 97).[13]

At an allegorical level, both "The Fisherman and his Wife" and *To the Lighthouse* tell the story of craftswomen, of mistresses of *techné*, who, using servant intermediaries, temporarily veil the emptiness of their existence with brilliant decoration. The question is: can one not say that this is the case for all artists, and for Woolf in particular, who, bringing back to life her father and mother and family life, is also "guilty" of fabricating *Verzierungen*, of weaving a brilliant rhetorical tapestry to cover the bare walls of past reality? Does there not lurk in the mind of the intellectually honest artist the suspicion that the flowers of rhetoric, like those of Rappaccini's garden, are the false creations of artifice, and that the carefully constructed aesthetic structure is really a vain attempt to veil reality itself – an attempt that can be punished for its hubris, for its transgression against ethics, *ethos* being understood in its original meaning as the home. As in Kierkegaard, the only place for the ethical life is the home, the home *as it is*, not as metamorphosed into the false semblance of aesthetic seductiveness.

The sea is beautiful on its surface. As the ageless background against which human endeavor deploys itself, it remains calm and, most importantly, flat. Yet it can also churn and rise, threatening to engulf the intrepid fisherman who will not remain at its edge, but will venture into depths best left unexplored. The catching or netting which represents, in Woolf's imagination, the successful solving of an artistic problem, the achieved creation of the artwork as such, can only be imagined in this triumphant way if the catch itself is robbed of its power, if the flounder, the *Plattfisch* or flat fish, the aesthetic object, is flattened down and made to serve as an icon within the geometrical abstraction of a tableau, just as Mrs. Ramsay and James act as visual equivalents to the Madonna and Child. But the flounder, if we listen to his words, says quite explicitly to his would-be captor: "ich bin ein *verwünschter* Prinz" ("I am an enchanted prince") (F 158). This means that he has his own story which is and will remain completely invisible, completely unknown to us, like an enigmatic "fin in the waste of waters" which disappears from view. And behind that story, whatever it might be, there was a wish gone wrong, a wrongful wish, a desire for aestheticization which was morally transgressive. Enchantment (*das Verwünschen*) is, after all, merely the deviation of wishing (*das Wünschen*), the false turn taken by a wish as it spins out of control, as it transforms its author from human to inhuman creature, from prince to fish. This uncanny metamorphosis, more powerful than the formal beauty born of the writer's ornamentations, pushes apart the carefully constructed walls between life and art, between the sea and the shore, and thrusts the prince-become-fish into the whirlpool of invading waters.

III LIFE AND ART INTERMINGLED, OR PLUNGING INTO IMPERSONALITY

The story of "The Fisherman and his Wife" is based upon the suppression of a previous story which, although unavailable to the reader, must have been based upon the same laws of enchantment and disenchantment as the primary text. The flounder was once a prince; he must have lived in the kind of palace that the fisherman's wife, with his assistance, wills into existence and temporarily inhabits. The fate of the fisherman's wife relates to that of the prince according to a chiastic structure: the prince presumably began his life surrounded by the ornamentations of wealth and class, only to find himself "enchanted" (*verwünscht*), transformed, reduced into a flounder; the fisherman's wife begins in just such a flattened state, dwelling, according to the German text, not merely in a "hovel," but rather in an even more restricted space – "in einem Eimer" (158), in a proto-Beckettian trash can or dustbin, from which she gradually emerges and swells up to the magnificent heights of her emperor's throne. Thus the moral of the story is contained in the beginning before it is enunciated, again, at the end: if the fisherman's wife had paid attention to the flounder-prince's past, if she had "read" his life, she might have understood the futility of her willfulness and the inevitability of a return from the swollen state of excessive ornamentation to the flatness of bare-bones reality. The narrative entitled "The Fisherman and his Wife" springs from another narrative; and this previous literary source must be kept under wraps for the Grimm tale to unfold. The flounder-prince, despite the symmetry of his destiny with that of the fisherman's wife, is of interest to her only insofar as he can advance her cause, only insofar as he can be called up from the depths to serve her hubris.

A variation on this scenario provides the fundamental narrative structure of *To the Lighthouse*. Like the flounder-prince, Mrs. Ramsay has her own story (which, in Woolf's novel, is told in elaborate detail), but she must disappear or be "flattened" in the "Time Passes" section in order for Lily Briscoe to emerge as the second female protagonist and create her art. As is the case in the Grimm tale, where the flounder-prince and the fisherman's wife are unwitting *Doppelgänger*, in the same way what Lily accomplishes in part three of the novel is uncannily similar to what Mrs. Ramsay did in part one. The work of both women is described in exactly the same terms, as an ordering, an assembling, a bringing together of disparate elements into an aesthetically pleasing whole, the only difference being that Mrs. Ramsay exerts her efforts on individuals within social groups and Lily on the elements that compose a painting. And, like the fisherman calling the flounder from the depths of the sea to accomplish his wife's bidding, in the same way, at the emotional climax of part three, when Lily is about to finish her painting, she calls the name "Mrs. Ramsay! Mrs. Ramsay!" (*TL* 202) in acknowledgment of her beloved friend's ghostly apparition at the window. That Woolf, in repeating the theme of the call, must have had in mind "The Fisherman and his Wife" as literary intertext, is evident, I think, from a humorous *clin d'oeil* within the apparition scene itself:

> Suddenly the window at which she [Lily] was looking was whitened by some light stuff behind it. At last then somebody [Mrs. Ramsay] had come into the drawing-room; somebody was sitting in the chair. For Heaven's sake, she prayed, let them sit still there and not *come floundering out* to talk to her. (*TL* 201; my emphasis)

Ironically, of course, it is Mrs. Ramsay who, while living, while vital and substantial in her beauty, had assumed the role of the fisherman's wife, and who now plays insubstantial and ghostly flounder to Lily, the new fisherman's wife. Lily does not call Mrs. Ramsay back into what in English we would call "full-blown" existence, but rather into the purgatorial, death-in-life state of *Unheimlichkeit.* It is only as misplaced and displaced apparition that Mrs. Ramsay can fulfill her function as inspiration for the enchantments of Lily's art.

The deep moral, the moral from the depths, of both the Grimm fairy tale and the Modernist novel is that the same character, the same person or personage, can be alternatively fisherman and fish, addressor and addressee of the call, in control as aesthetic master or mistress and overwhelmed by the revenge taken on art as artifice by the powers of nature. The alternating rhythm whereby aesthetic beauty builds itself up only to be torn down should make us as readers of *To the Lighthouse* think seriously about the perhaps too-perfect double resolution of the plot. Does Mr. Ramsay's reaching of the Lighthouse mean that human effort is ultimately rewarded; that the drowned bodies Cam imagines, via "The Castaway," as lurking underneath their boat are neutralized by the Ulyssean journey, by the overcoming of time and weather in the successful expedition? Or can these dead bodies, summoned by some tempest, return to the surface and haunt not only the pages beyond the artificially closed borders of *To the Lighthouse*, but also the life of their author? And does Lily's triumph as artist and aesthetic theorist signify that the existential drama of her life has been solved? Does the tracing of a line down the center of a painting fully compensate for a life that, like that of the flounder, is flat and barren? Is Virginia Woolf's incipient feminism, in 1927, strong enough as conceptual barrier to hold back thoughts of human insufficiency in the face of *childlessness*? Remarkably, in the recent critical literature I have had occasion to read dealing directly with the relation of the Grimm story to Woolf's novel, no one mentions the one most obvious difference between the willful Mrs. Ramsay and the domineering fisherman's wife: the former has numerous progeny, whereas the latter has none. The ending of the fable, "Darin sitzen sie noch heute, bis auf diesen Tag," is the description of a sterile couple doing nothing, accomplishing nothing. And what, finally, is the origin of the cupidity, of the *Gier* that drives the fisherman's wife? The fairy tale provides a psychological explanation based upon the transformation and deviation of desire that could easily have disturbed Woolf, the reader of Freud. This is the moment at which, having become pope, the unsatisfied woman wants even more:

> "Dear wife," he [the fisherman] said, "now be content. Now you are pope. You certainly cannot become more than that [*Mehr kannst du doch nicht werden*]." "I will think that over," said the wife. Thereupon they went to bed, but she was not satisfied [*aber sie war nicht zufrieden*], and cupidity prevented her from sleeping; she kept thinking about what she wanted to become [*und die Gier ließ sie nicht schlafen; sie dachte immer darüber nach, was sie noch werden wollte*]. (F 165)

The transparent message beneath the text is that the woman, instead of making love (and children) with her husband, has transmuted her sexual desire into *Gier*, an emotion which, unlike lovemaking, never provides a release or any sense of calm. She will never know happiness or satisfaction (*Zufriedenheit*), but will always be driven on, indefinitely, to *become more*. She refuses the home, the values of *ethos*, in favor of the infinite metamorphoses, the seductive ornamentation, of her aesthetically charged imagination. How could Woolf, from what we know of her biography, have been insensitive to this stark and, by the cultural logic of our contemporary thinking, primitively, reductively, and violently unfair alternative: *either* be a mother and agree to stay (*bleiben*) within the ethical as the home-like; *or* choose the dangerous metamorphoses inherent in rhetorical language, in the literary as such, the domain of continual becoming, of *werden*, of *Wandlung* and *Verwandlung*. To choose the latter course is to invite the revenge of the ethical, to risk, beyond all Modernist fantasizing of aesthetic self-sufficiency as the "netting of forms," the feared final transformation of fisherman into fish, whereby one returns to the depths of the sea from which one came.

The theme of the fish and the fisherman was nothing less than a leitmotiv, not only in Woolf's writings,[14] but also in her life. Hermione Lee informs us that when Woolf began her affair with Vita Sackville-West in December 1925, shortly after *To the Lighthouse* had been begun, the sight of "Vita striding into the *fishmonger's* shop, wearing pink and pearls . . . became a kind of password to intimacy" (*VW* 480; my emphasis). In speaking of her amorous success with Virginia, Vita wrote of "having caught such a big silver fish" (*VW* 499); yet Vita also called Virginia a "fish" for her reserve and lack of overt sensuality (*VW* 589). It would seem that Virginia Woolf, encouraged by her friends and relatives, saw herself, in life, as both fisherman and fish: in her optimistic and aesthetically triumphant moments, as fisherman capable of netting images, as creator of new forms; but in her times of depression, as flattened, sterile, un-*vital* creature incapable of espousing life on its own terms, and in danger of being submerged by its exigencies.

Yet in some of Woolf's letters to fellow writers, interestingly, the capacity to be submerged *in writing* is a sign of the authenticity of one's work, whereas didacticism is equated with floating on the surface. In a letter to Elizabeth Bowen she says: "until we [contemporary writers] can write with all our faculties in action (even the big toe) but under the water, submerged, then we must be clever, like the rest of the modern sticklebacks" (*VW* 642); and to Stephen Spender: "your desire to teach and help is always bringing you up to the top when you should be down in the depths" (*VW* 653). It would seem, then, that except in those rapturously described moments of epiphany or "moments of being" in which Woolf imagined, like other Modernist writers, that the aesthetic artefact could enclose the essence of reality, in other, more demystified times of reflection she saw the writer's true habitat as being beneath the waves, in the eddies and whirlpools which threaten to rise above the surface and unsettle the ground on which the fisherman stands.

In her own way, then, Virginia Woolf, like Kafka, intuited, below and beyond the level surface of her aesthetic creed, that the territory of writing is unsurveyable, unmeasurable in its uncanny and fluid rising-and-falling. To be engaged in writing is not to dominate through aesthetic achievement, but to have fallen into the watery depths, to be caught in the kind of vertigo that Blanchot equates with the act of writing in its dispossessing essence.[15] It is perhaps no coincidence that, in an *acte manqué* that foreshadowed her imminent death by drowning, Virginia herself suffered a disquieting but also strangely exhilarating fall, in which her very sense of self was effaced, in favor of a Blanchot-like descent into impersonality. In November 1940, four and a half months before her death, she wrote what Hemione Lee aptly calls "an ominous note" to her friend Ethel Smyth, describing what occurred when she took a walk into the recently flooded fields around her house:

> Yesterday, thinking to explore, I fell headlong into a six foot hole, and came home dripping like a spaniel, or water rugg (thats Shakespeare). How odd to be swimming in a field! . . . how I love this savage medieval water moved,

all floating tree trunks and flocks of birds and a man in an old punt, and myself so eliminated of human feature you might take me for a stake walking. (*VW* 739–40)

What Virginia Woolf had known all along, *pace* her Modernist aesthetic stance – namely, that writing is a descent into the maelstrom, a losing of self to featurelessness, an espousing of the impersonal – became, in the final months of her life, the ghostly knowledge with which she wrestled before succumbing to its unhinging power. One of the last, untitled, fragments that has been recovered from her writings, dated just one month before her suicide, skirts the boundary-line between sanity and madness, offering a bizarre arabesque of water and fish imagery:

The woman who lives in this room has the look of someone without any consecutive [?] part. *She has no settled relations with her kind.* She is like a piece of seaweed that floats this way, then that way. For the fish who float into this cave are always passing through . . . She inhabits a fluctuating water world . . . constantly tossed up and down like a piece of sea weed [*sic*]. She has no continuity. *The rush of water is always floating her up and down.* (*VW* 742; my emphasis)

What had held together *To the Lighthouse* as work of art – those "bolts of iron" underneath its "feathery and evanescent surface" (*TL* 171), to use Lily Briscoe's language – is now gone. No undergirding remains for a world characterized uniquely by fluid indeterminacy, by time as limitless *passage*, by the ceaseless alternating rhythm of rising and falling – in short, by uncanniness as *the unsettled dimension without borders or limits* in which the technician of language "dwells" in uprooted movement. As all limits and all borders fade into featureless impersonality, the final revenge of the uncanny occurs, in the "unnatural" inversion whereby life imitates art. At the very end of her life, when she had no projects and could no longer write nor even read with any enthusiasm, Virginia Woolf scrubbed the kitchen floors, obsessively, willfully, energetically (*VW* 745). Perhaps without knowing it in her conscious mind, she was imitating what the fisherman's wife "should have done" instead of seeking the power and glory of literary decoration and ornamentation, instead of adding her own incrustations to the already incrusted palace of literary tradition. But it was too late to rewrite the fable; and in any case, had the fisherman's wife remained contentedly ethically at home, there would have been no beautiful story.

EPILOGUE

Narrative and music in Kafka and Blanchot: the "singing" of Josefine

The historical trajectory I have traced thus far, which leads from the Kantian sublime to Modernist textual elaborations of *Unheimlichkeit*, tells the story of the difficult points of intersection between aesthetic theory and practice, on the one hand, and ethical complexity and danger, on the other. If there is common ground between the sublime and the uncanny, it is that both are depicted, by philosophers and writers, as unsettling experiences in which the individual human subject, having set out to plot the territory of beautiful forms, encounters, within these forms, the moral labyrinth on which they are constructed. The various strategies of containment and envelopment whereby the aesthetic and the ethical alternately negate and destroy each other's pretension to dominance have been at the center of this book, from Kant to Woolf.

If I have decided to end the chronological survey of my study with Woolf, it is because, in my view, her encounter with the dispossessive energy of *Unheimlichkeit* structured not only her intimate psychological struggles, but also her literary production. Woolf's fall into impersonality is, in and of itself, a fall into the fundamental unhomeliness of literature, of the literary as such. Yet it would be a simplification, I think, to conclude that the only mode of encounter with the uncanny-as-literature is that of fear and anxiety, whereby the individual subject, having lost her bearings in a world of blurred boundaries, succumbs to madness and death. In the present essay, I shall suggest that there is, at the extreme edge of Modernism and in its legacy, a way of encountering *Unheimlichkeit* that goes beyond the polar oppositions of life and death and that stages the drama of uncanniness as life-in-death in a tone far different from that of existential pathos.

The previous chapter can be considered a logical conclusion to my historically based argument on the movement from the sublime to the uncanny: Woolf, with her watery death, closes off a chapter in European literary history. This epilogue, on the other hand, should be viewed as an opening outward, as a suggestion of what the contemporary inheritance of Modernist uncanniness might be. In what follows, I shall be comparing Kafka's textual practice to Maurice Blanchot's theoretical meditations on literature as impersonality – or what the latter calls, more precisely, neutrality (*le neutre*). The point of convergence *and* disjunction between Woolf and Kafka/Blanchot is the very notion of impersonality. For Woolf, to disappear into the impersonal is to lose one's self, one's creative individuality, and one's very life. For Kafka and Blanchot, the descent into *Unheimlichkeit*, by which the individual does indeed lose his or her identity, is a necessary process which opens up the dialogical domain of community. The late short stories of Kafka and Blanchot's *récits* and theoretical meditations examine the question of impersonality without pathos, without anxiety, with a calm indifferent tone worthy of close scrutiny.

If I were to stretch beyond the self-imposed limits of the present study, I would suggest, "in a nutshell," that the progression from Kant beyond Woolf to Blanchot might be characterized as the movement from the sublime to the uncanny to the impersonal. The metamorphosis of Woolf's impersonal into Blanchot's neutrality would have a lot to do with the passage beyond Modernism to contemporary experimental writings. To document and substantiate this lapidary formula would require, of course, another book.

I THEORY AND PRACTICE OF NARRATIVE UNCANNINESS

In his review of Blanchot's early "fantastic" narrative entitled *Aminadab*, Sartre found a resemblance between this strange tale and the uncanny fictions of Franz Kafka, but noted in passing that Blanchot himself denied, at that point, having read Kafka.[1] Whether Blanchot was being entirely forthcoming in his denial or merely coy, the resemblances between the mysterious tone of *Aminadab* and a certain Kafkaesque atmosphere are unmistakable. However, it is later in his career, when he had moved away from fantastic or allegorical narratives and begun to compose his concentrated, elliptical *récits* that Blanchot, in my view, came much closer to Kafka's essential concerns as a writer.[2] As the theoretician of *L'Espace littéraire* (1955), *Le Livre à venir* (1959), and *L'Entretien infini* (1969), as the writer of *Au moment voulu* (1951), *Celui qui ne m'accompagnait pas* (1953), and *L'Attente l'oubli* (1962), Blanchot distanced himself from the imitative atmospherics of the "Kafkaesque" and began to participate in the fundamental *Unheimlichkeit* of the narrative universe created by Kafka.

There is uncanniness in the *récits* of Blanchot, but there are also points of narrative convergence between Blanchot and Kafka that can only be called, themselves, uncanny. It is as if Blanchot, the surveyor of literary forms, had "returned home" in reading Kafka; but this home presents the strangest form of defamiliarizing familiarity, so that the encounter (*rencontre*, a crucial notion for Blanchot) of the latter-day writer and theoretician with his predecessor has none of the coziness of tranquil domesticity, but rather the expropriating dizziness of a confrontation with what Blanchot, in his "Kafka et l'exigence de l'oeuvre," calls "le ruissellement du dehors éternel" ("the streaming of the eternal outside").[3]

In the pages that follow, I shall be concentrating on the relation between the act of narration and a certain kind of music (or "song") in both Kafka and Blanchot. I shall be analyzing in some detail the last short story Kafka wrote, "Josefine, die Sängerin oder das Volk der Mäuse" ["Josephine the Singer, or the Mouse Folk"], completed in 1924, the year of the writer's death. It is my contention that this convoluted and, in some ways, self-destructive tale marks the culmination of an idiosyncratic narrative form that Kafka had been developing in the later years of his life, and that Blanchot was able to mine the considerable theoretical possibilities thereof better than any other contemporary writer. My analysis will unfold in three distinct stages. First, I shall concentrate on the initial paragraph of "Josefine" in a close reading, then move on to examine several of the interpretive problems raised in later sections of the text; second, I shall turn to some of the crucial theoretical distinctions made by Blanchot in his discussions of narrative fiction as they relate to Kafka (it is here that the points of encounter between the two writers reach the level of properly uncanny similarity); and finally, I shall discuss the enigmatic conclusion of "Josefine", in which the constitution of community is linked in a fundamental way to the effacement of the protagonist, to her disappearance in death. In the end, I shall suggest that Kafka's late story is founded on the notion of forgetfulness (*oubli*) as theorized and fictionalized by Blanchot.

II "JOSEFINE, DIE SÄNGERIN ODER DAS VOLK DER MÄUSE": THE TEXT AS NARRATIVE UNWEAVING[4]

Perhaps the best way to encounter a text as rich and as narratively unusual as "Josefine" is to plunge in *in medias res*. Following is the story's first paragraph, which contains, in a highly concentrated declarative (assertive) exposition, the essential elements of the narrative's eventual undoing:

Unsere Sängerin heißt Josefine. Wer sie nicht gehört hat, kennt nicht die Macht des Gesanges. Es gibt niemanden, den ihr Gesang nicht fortreißt, was um so höher zu bewerten ist, als unser Geschlecht im ganzen Musik nicht liebt. Stiller Frieden ist uns die liebste Musik; unser Leben ist schwer, wir können uns, auch wenn wir einmal alle Tagessorgen abzuschütteln versucht haben, nicht mehr zu solchen, unserem sonstigen Leben so fernen Dingen erheben, wie es die Musik ist. Doch beklagen wir es nicht sehr; nicht einmal so weit kommen wir; eine gewisse praktische Schlauheit, die wir freilich auch äußerst dringend brauchen, halten wir für unsern größten Vorzug, und mit dem Lächeln dieser Schlauheit pflegen wir uns über alles hinwegzutrösten, auch wenn wir einmal – was aber nicht geschieht – das Verlangen nach dem Glück haben sollten, das von der Musik vielleicht ausgeht. Nur Josefine macht eine Ausnahme; sie liebt die Musik und weiß sie auch zu vermitteln; sie ist die einzige, mit ihrem Hingang wird die Musik – wer weiß wie lange – aus unserem Leben verschwinden. (J 200–201)[5]

Our singer is called Josephine. Anyone who has not heard her does not know the power of song. There is no one but is carried away by her singing, a tribute all the greater as we are not in general a music-loving race. Tranquil peace is the music we love best; our life is hard, we are no longer able, even on occasions when we have tried to shake off the cares of daily life, to rise to anything so high and remote from our usual routine as music. But we do not much lament that; we do not get even so far; a certain practical cunning, which admittedly we stand greatly in need of, we hold to be our greatest distinction, and with a smile born of such cunning we are wont to console ourselves for all shortcomings, even supposing – only it does not happen – that we were to yearn once in a way for the kind of bliss which music may provide. Josephine is the sole exception; she has a love for music and knows too how to transmit it; she is the only one; when she dies, music – who knows for how long – will vanish from our lives. (JMF 360)[6]

The first paragraph of the story establishes the *dramatis personae*: there is one character called Josefine who stands out from the rest of her "race" (*Geschlecht*) as being talented in music, as being a singer, whereas the remainder of the group (we later learn they are "mouse folk"), being possessed only of a "practical cunning," seem unable to "raise themselves" (*sich erheben*) to the lofty heights of the musical as such. Kafka begins his narrative in the most classical way, with a dramatic opposition between the mass of the people, devoted to everyday life (*das Alltägliche*), and Josefine, servant of the sublime (the noun *das Erhabene*, the sublime, being derived from the verb Kafka uses here, *sich erheben*). The paragraph points to the eventuality of a tension between Josefine and the mouse folk: they are so different in their fundamental outlooks that the reader might easily imagine a conflict arising as the narrative develops, the kind of conflict that nourishes or even makes possible the differential movement of narrative itself. When we find out, in the latter stages of the tale, that Josefine is somewhat of a prima donna, critical of her audience's ignorance and capricious in the demands she places on the material conditions of her performances, it would seem that the dramatic potential of the first paragraph has been realized.

At the same time, however, in order for there to be the highest level of conflict, drama, pathos, there must be oppositional pressure exerted from both sides. Now it may be true that, late in the story, Josefine and her retinue attempt to gain special favors from the mouse folk as a whole (thereby proclaiming Josefine's difference from the multitude); but their efforts are met, not by polemic or contention, but by calm indifference – an indifference that emerges subtly in the first paragraph, where the narrator makes clear that the mouse folk's inability to "raise itself" to the level of music is no matter of great concern. The narrator, who speaks *for* the mouse folk (and this speaking-for is no innocent rhetorical gesture),[7] asserts not only that "stiller Frieden ist uns die liebste Musik" – i.e., that silence, rather than music in the usual sense, is most appealing to the mouse folk, but that, after all, it is not certain, not proved, that music leads to happiness. The conditional mode of the narrator's statement is worth noting, and is typical of the modality of the story as a whole: "auch wenn wir einmal – was aber *nicht geschieht* – das Verlangen nach dem Glück *haben sollten*, das von der Musik *vielleicht* ausgeht" ("even supposing – only *it does not happen* – that we *were* to yearn once in a way for the kind of bliss which music *may* provide").

From the very beginning of the story there is a fundamental narrative skepticism about music – about its "essence" – as well as an interesting indifference to the efforts of Josefine, both of which tend to complicate the assertive tone of the remainder of the paragraph. On the one hand, Josefine is presented as an exception, as a singer among non-singers, as someone who not only communicates with a transcendental beyond (*Jenseits*), but who is also capable of communicating it to the mouse folk: "Nur Josefine macht eine Ausnahme; sie liebt die Musik und weiß sie auch zu vermitteln; sie ist die einzige" ("Josephine is the sole exception; she has a love for music and knows too how to transmit it; she is the only one"). Thus it would appear that Josefine might mediate between the unmusical folk and "the power of song," that she might play a properly pedagogical role in her society. On the other hand, however, it is not clear from the first paragraph whether the mouse folk has enough interest in music or in the performance activities of Josefine to accept or receive this potentially mediated song. "Josefine" seems, at first glance, to be a fine parable of *Rezeptionsästhetik*; but the question is whether the artistic performance has any effect on its audience whatever.

The two key words of the paragraph may well be the first and the last: "unsere" ("our" as in "our singer, Josefine"), and "verschwinden" ("to disappear" – a verb that seems, in the first paragraph, to be a euphemistic replacement for the starker "to die" or "sterben," but that has a prophetic ring to it, in that Josefine, at the end of the tale, does indeed disappear, mysteriously and without a trace). Both words help to define the ultimate effect Josefine has on her community in the narrator's telling of the tale. The use of the first-person plural possessive adjective is unusual for Kafka: of the other longer stories, only the second version of "Die Abweisung" ["The Refusal"] begins with the word "unser" or "our," with all other stories being fairly evenly divided between a first- or third-person singular narrating voice. Although the use of the possessive form can allow for intimacy and complicity in narratives that emphasize the emblematic heroism of one member of a group, in the case of "Josefine" the possessive emerges progressively as a form of envelopment or containment whereby the protagonist's difference is gradually effaced and eradicated.[8] In the end, although Josefine has manifested her desire to be appreciated in her uniqueness, in the quality of her musicality, she is fated (by the leveling-effect, the driving in-difference of the narrative movement) to disappear, to vanish, along with her music – i.e., not to die a tragic or pathetic or perhaps "operatic" death. She becomes subsumed by the streaming multitudes of her ceaselessly proliferating people (with apologies to Blanchot: *le ruissellement du peuple éternel*), enveloped in a general forgetfulness.

At the conclusion of the first paragraph, the reader is left with two related questions: First, what *is* music according to this story? What is its significance, its content, its "inner essence?" Second, how will the narrator develop Josefine's relation to the mouse folk in the remainder of the story? What kind of narrative progression will characterize this tale? The first paragraph only alludes to "die Macht des Gesanges" – that is, the powerful effect of song rather than the essence of song; and the question of Josefine's mediating influence on the mouse folk is merely raised without being answered. At the very least, the text must, and does, stage some of Josefine's performances, and it is in the encounter of these performances, where protagonist and folk are united in a community, that the nodal points of the narrative are to be found.

The section of the story immediately following the first paragraph is devoted to the narrator's musings on the significance of music. But these reflections never focus on the musical as exterior object of disinterested contemplation: rather, from the very beginning of the narrative, it is clear that the phenomenon of music or musicality can only be understood in relation to the mouse folk and its interactions with Josefine. The first sentence of the second paragraph is crucial in this regard, as is its problematic translation by Willa and Edwin Muir (the reader will note in passing that, as of the second paragraph, the narrator begins to alternate between the first-person singular and first-person plural forms, the former being used to express private thoughts which may or may not correspond to the received opinions of the mouse folk as a community):[9] "Ich habe oft darüber nachgedacht, wie es sich mit dieser Musik eigentlich verhält" ("I have often thought about what this music of hers really means") (J 201; JMF 360). The translators not only have added the phrase "of hers" to the original text, but they have made the Kafkan idiom more precise than it originally is in this context. They have rendered the narrator's cautious and, it must be said, rather vague and inelegant phrase "wie *es sich* mit dieser Musik *verhält*" (which means something like "how things stand with this music," or "what is the case with this music") by "what this music of hers *really means*." What the Muirs have done is a very interesting case of what might be called translators' (or readers') wish-fulfillment: like all readers of "Josefine," they would like to know what the text is going to propose as the meaning of music; they wish to penetrate the essence of music, its interiority, and their wish is so strong that they mistranslate the Kafkan story, inserting the verb "to mean" where it does not exist, where it is notably absent. The narrator's verb phrase *wie es sich verhält* is, of course, connected to the word for relationship: *das Verhältnis* – and the issue of the story (issue in the sense of topic as well as the sense of ending or final point), from beginning to end, is the relation of the mouse folk to Josefine, who, in some sense, represents or incorporates the mysterious phenomenon of music.

As the story progresses, not only is the interiority of music increasingly inaccessible to what one might call "mouse-consciousness," but the question arises whether Josefine is actually singing, or whether she is merely piping – piping (*das Pfeifen*) being, in the narrator's pseudo-philosophical vocabulary, "die eigentliche Kunstfertigkeit unseres Volkes, oder vielmehr gar keine Fertigkeit, sondern eine charakteristische Lebensäußerung" ("the real artistic accomplishment of our people, or rather no mere accomplishment but a characteristic expression of our life") (J 201; JMF 361). The narrative proceeds in a cascade of descending logical hesitations that can be summed up as follows: Josefine is the singer of the unmusical mouse folk (J 200); but does she sing or does she pipe? (J 201–202); does her song enrapture her audience, or is it the silence that surrounds that song? (J 203); why does the mouse folk attend her performances in the first place when it is clear that this community is not only unmusical, but, in fact, incapable of unconditional devotion ("bedingungslose Ergebenheit kennt unser Volk kaum" [J 205])?

The first section of the text leads from a highly skeptical discussion of Josefine's supposed musicality (in German this would be "*angebliche* Musikalität") to an interesting development on the (almost-Heideggerian) theme of *care* (*Sorge*). As the text moves forward, it becomes evident that the nature of Josefine's vocal production (whether it be artistic singing or everyday piping) will not be solved, which leaves the philosophical question of the relation of art to life open, undecidable. At the same time, however, the very fact of Josefine's performances (i.e., the fact that they take place at all) gains increasing weight in the story. At the midpoint of the tale, the narrator reaches what might be considered an extreme point of skepticism when he asserts: "Es ist nicht so sehr eine Gesangsvorführung als vielmehr eine Volksversammlung" ("It is not so much a performance of songs as an assembly of the people") (J 207; JMF 367). But this is perhaps the essential turn or defining twist of the narrative line, in which the text reveals to the reader what had been present, *sotto voce*, from the beginning: namely, that the content of the performance and the meaning of the song are unimportant in their potential emptiness, but that the existence of the performance, its social reality, is the one fact that counts. It is at this point of the narrative that the title of the story – "Josefine, die Sängerin oder das Volk der Mäuse"[10] – becomes fully understandable. The story is about the mouse people as much as it is about Josefine; it is constructed on their mutual devotion (at the exact middle of the tale there is a comical sequence of paragraphs in which the narrator describes how the people is convinced that it must care for its beloved but demanding and not always pleasant Josefine, whereas she is just as certain that her job is to protect her people from the dangers of the outside world through the uplifting power of her song [J 205–207]).

The second half of the text can be characterized as Josefine's gradual disappearing-act. In the first section, the protagonist vanishes from the scene as the narrator describes in some detail the difficult existence of the prolific mouse folk and its curious "prematurely old" but also "ineradicably young" outlook (J 209).[11] In the second section, we learn of the various excuses for not performing and the demands for special treatment Josefine makes on the mouse folk (including her proposal not to work, in order to devote herself entirely to her art), all of which are qualified as illogical or dismissed out of hand since Josefine, after all, is no different from other mice in her questionable "singing," which may be nothing more than everyday piping (J 211–15). And finally, in four short paragraphs the narrator discusses her disappearance (J 215–16) – a section to which I shall return later.

Viewed as a structural whole, "Josefine" is the story of the disappearance of music and the unweaving of narrative. Put more precisely, one should say that the primary narrative, at its most literal thematic level, dismantles the protagonist's pretentions to musicality as sublime artistic activity, and in this gradual dismantling focuses increasingly on the power of the mouse folk to contain or even eradicate Josefine's defiant individuality. The envelopment or swallowing-up of music in the primary narrative produces a secondary meta-narrative which is about the unweaving of narrative as such. The text becomes self-referential in that it tells the story of its own undoing, of its own impossible construction. In "Josefine" Kafka has gone far beyond the pathos and high melodrama of earlier stories such as "Das Urteil" ["The Judgment"](written in 1912) and "Die Verwandlung" ["The Metamorphosis"](1913), both of which develop along a steady narrative line from an initial, clearly defined existential situation to a tragic conclusion. In negating pathos and *peripeteia* as such in his later fiction, in replacing the bourgeois family milieu with the strangeness of an animal kingdom, Kafka seems to be espousing what might be called a pure hypothetical narration, which is, in a sense, an anti-narration, or non-narration. And while there is a stylistic evolution away from narrative progression in the classical sense (a progression dependent upon the differentiation of the protagonist from his/her milieu), there is also a shift from the emphasis on an individual's struggles with a family group toward a delineation of the relations that compose a community.

At this juncture, I would like to leave the fictional universe of "Josefine" for a while and turn to some of Blanchot's theoretical writings on narrative – which deal in various ways both with the possibility of a pure narrative and with the relation of the aesthetics of storytelling to the ethical issues involved in the inclusiveness of community. The use of the possessive adjective "our" is not innocent; it may be violent; it is a speaking *for*, on the part of a narrator representing his folk, that is also a robbery of the individual's voice. One wonders if it is on the basis of that silencing of musicality that the community erects itself, or whether the voiding of "music" and the vanishing of the individual into the indifferentiation of the mass (the folk, the "race") is merely, allegorically stated, the quite natural and ultimately peaceful fate of the artist (who, of course, may be no artist at all) as she returns "home."

III MUSIC AND NARRATIVE IN BLANCHOT

I have suggested that the meaning of music or musicality remains an elusive blind spot in "Josefine," and that the question of music as such emerges only in conjunction with, in relation to, the narrator and the mouse folk who act as the protagonist's audience. In Kafka's story, the content of music is beyond the reader's apprehension, while the enactment of music is a constant *factum* in the lives of the mouse community. The various musical performances by Josefine punctuate the narrative rhythm of the story; the bringing together of the mouse folk around the heroine's singing constitutes the narrative *as* movement. Thus, any interpretation of "Josefine" must take into account the interactions and intersections of musicality with narrativity as fundamental themes.

Maurice Blanchot, whose interest in Kafka's storytelling has been constant throughout his long career,[12] has written two essays that have a direct bearing on the constellation of interpretive problems I have raised up to this point. The first of these, "Le chant des sirènes," is uncannily close to the universe of "Josefine" in that it stages the act of singing as performance within an exposition on the problematic of narrativity per se. The second, entitled "La voix narrative, le 'il,' le neutre," treats the question of narrative voice in a way that prolongs the insights of "Le chant des sirènes" and leads to the explicit thematization of the possibility of a "pure" narrative – a notion that Blanchot develops theoretically through a discussion of Flaubert and Kafka and that subtends his own experimental *récits* in their spectral abstraction. I shall discuss both of these short essays in themselves before determining the ways in which they apply to Kafka's aesthetics in general and to "Josefine" in particular.

"Le chant des sirènes"

The point of departure for Blanchot's theoretical meditation is the episode in *The Odyssey* in which Ulysses encounters the song of the Sirens, or rather, does not encounter it, since, making use of his habitual wiles, he stops his ears with wax and, by not hearing the enchanting singing, manages to survive the episode and move onward in his navigation. Blanchot is interested in the double-edged quality of this event/non-event, this moment of high dramatic intensity in which a difficult encounter both does and does not take place. He sees in Ulysses's victory over the Sirens the inevitable result of the hero's obstinence and prudence, which qualities allowed him to "take pleasure in the spectacle of the Sirens, without risk and without accepting the consequences, this cowardly, mediocre and calm pleasure, measured, as it befits a Greek of the decadent period who never deserved to be the hero of *The Iliad*" (CS 11).[13] But this "victory" is only apparent according to Blanchot, in that the encounter with the Sirens is an *attirance*, a magnetic attraction, that causes Ulysses to fall into narrative:

> Although the Sirens were defeated by the power of technique, which will always try to play without danger with unreal (inspired) forces, Ulysses did not escape so easily. They [the Sirens] lured him to a place into which he did not want to fall and, hidden at the center of *The Odyssey* now become their tomb, they enlisted him and many others in this happy and unhappy navigation, which is that of narrative [*le récit*], a song no longer immediate, but told, and rendered in the telling only apparently harmless, ode become episode. (CS 11–12)

Thus Blanchot interprets the moment of the encounter between Ulysses and the Sirens as an allegory of narrative in which the protagonist's adventurous triumph (he manages to move beyond the Sirens, and this moving beyond is the very forward rhythm that defines this epic in its essence as a successful return, through and beyond all perils, to the comforts of domesticity) is overturned in the very instant of the encounter: without knowing it, Ulysses, like so many others, has fallen into the narrative maelstrom. The song of the Sirens may not have been heard, but it becomes told ("ode" becomes "episode"),[14] and the loss of immediacy that accompanies the transformation or translation of song into narrative in no way destroys the power or authority of the *récit* as it develops from within this central *point de rencontre*.

At the heart of Blanchot's essay is one crucial theoretical distinction – between *roman* (novel) and *récit* (narrative) – a clear polar opposition that organizes his argument and that helps the reader to understand what is at stake in Blanchot's own narrative fictions. Blanchot does not deny the importance of Ulysses's ongoing adventures, nor does his emphasis on the absolute quality of the moment of encounter with the Sirens negate the power of the events that lead up to and beyond that moment. Rather, he chooses to distinguish between the flow of narrative events as a whole, which he calls *roman*, and the instantaneous explosive episode, which he designates as *récit.* These are the definitions in Blanchot's words:

With the novel [*roman*], it is the preliminary navigation that appears on center stage, that brings Ulysses up to the point of the encounter. This navigation is an entirely human story, it concerns human time, is linked to human passions, really takes place and is rich and varied enough to absorb all the power and all the attention of the narrator. (CS 12)

Narrative [*le récit*] begins where the novel does not go and yet leads through its refusals and rich negligence. Narrative is, heroically and pretentiously, the telling of only one episode, that of the encounter of Ulysses and of the insufficient and enticing song of the Sirens. (CS 13)

A work as vast as *The Odyssey* is thus an amalgam of the *roman* and the *récit*, a text in which the human time of the novelistic flow of events is occasionally interrupted by the episodic immediacy of a decisive encounter such as the Song of the Sirens. And when this interruption occurs, the story turns, or metamorphoses, from its everyday human appearance into a pure fictive construct. According to Blanchot, whereas the *roman* advances through what he calls "the desire to allow time to speak" (time understood here in its usual human dimension), the *récit*, on the other hand, "progresses thanks to this *other* time [*cet autre temps*], this other navigation which is the passage from real song to imaginary song" (CS 16). In the system of polarities that structures Blanchot's theoretical argument, all those qualities associated with the *roman* (human time, everydayness, the song in its reality) are both more understandable to the reader and also, quite evidently, less interesting to the critic than the more complex, nearly ineffable attributes connected to the *récit* (an *other* time, the fall into fiction, the song in its textual/imaginary recreation). What Blanchot has done is to organize an expository theoretical discourse in a classical way – by setting up contraries, dichotomies – in which each term appears to have a clear opposite. The problem, however, is that whereas an interpretive community might have a shared understanding of the meaning of "human time," the notion of an *other* time remains enigmatic; and it does not help to say that this *other* time is "the opposite of" human time, whatever that might mean. In the same way, the fall into fiction and the idea of an imaginary song are difficult to imagine: these notions hover, metaphorically (or turn, tropically), around a central inexpressible void that is the point of fascination of Blanchot the critic and writer of fictions. There is, within the experience of the Song of the Sirens (which, we have seen, is also a non-experience, a non-event), an abyss, a *béance*, and it is the magnetic attraction of this nothingness that causes the *récit* to coalesce, to take form. It is no surprise, given this scheme, that for Blanchot, like Kafka, the center of the song is not a plenitude, but a lack: "the enchantment [of the Sirens] awakened the hope and the desire of a marvelous beyond, and this beyond only represented a desert, as if the home region of music were the only place completely devoid of music" (CS 10). Narrative constructs itself around the nothingness of music, a nothingness that it attempts to metamorphose into an imaginary textual equivalent, or, in other words, a pure fiction.

"La voix narrative, le 'il,' le neutre"

Originally written in 1964, Blanchot's essay on narrative voice is perhaps his most explicit and (if such a term is ever appropriate for this writer) most systematic theoretical statement on narrative as such. It is in this text that the notion of a pure narrative emerges with greatest clarity, and it is no coincidence that this takes place within a discussion of Kafka's fictional works. Blanchot establishes, from the beginning of his argument, that the matter of narrative voice should not be confused with the naïve conception of writing as a transparent representation of an individual consciousness. Narrative always implies distance, and this distance entails the impersonality of what Blanchot, in this essay as well as elsewhere, calls *le neutre* (the neuter).

Crucial to Blanchot's conception of narrative is the subtle passage or, to use Michel Butor's term, "modification" that takes place in the literary-historical transition from Flaubertian aesthetics to the fictional praxis of Kafka. Although Kafka did admire Flaubert (who, along with Goethe, remained one of the Czech writer's constant references in his letters and diaries), Blanchot cautions against the temptation of enlisting Kafka as a mere follower of Flaubert. Whereas aesthetic distance or "creative disinterest" defines the position of the writer and reader vis-à-vis the work of art for Flaubert, this same distance "enters into" the texts of Kafka:

> The distance – the creative disinterest (so visible in the case of Flaubert since he must fight to maintain it) – this distance, which was that of the writer and the

reader facing the work, allowing for contemplative pleasure, now enters, in the form of an irreducible strangeness, into the very sphere of the work. (VN 178)[15]

It is within the "irreducible strangeness" of this interior narrative distance that the *neutre* constitutes itself and acts to overturn the centrality of subjective consciousness. Blanchot makes it clear that the neuter "il" does not simply replace the classical third-person singular pronoun, but calls it into question *as subject.* It is through the neuter "il" that the "other" (*l'autre*) speaks, but this "other" cannot be reduced to the mere opposite of the self. The neuter "il" can never be subsumed within a personalized narrative, a narrative tethered to the foundation of human time and events: it will always be outside the act or the subject in which it seems to manifest itself. Hence the narrative voice as such has no place in the work, but is the void around which the work constructs itself:

The narrative voice [*voix narrative*] (I do not say narrating voice [*voix narratrice*]) owes its voicelessness to this exteriority. A voice that has no place in the work, but that also does not dominate it from above ... the 'il' is not the notion of comprehensiveness according to Jaspers, but rather like a void in the work. (VN 181)

As was the case in "Le chant des sirènes," in which the distinction between *récit* and *roman* structured the theoretical argument, the essay on narrative voice is organized around the foundational opposition between *voix narrative* and *voix narratrice.* And since the *voix narrative* is the voicelessness of exteriority emanating from a central neutral void, since it has no definable place in human time and reality, it is the narrative voice of the *récit.* Although Blanchot never explicitly defines the *voix narratrice,* it seems clear that this narrating instance is the "opposite" of the *voix narrative,* and that it is the voice of the *roman* in the fullness of subjective consciousness. Jacques Derrida confirms this hypothesis when he states that, unlike the *voix narrative,* which has "no place" in its radical exteriority, the *voix narratrice* can be situated within the theoretical discourse of poetics precisely because it "derives from a subject who tells something, remembering an event or an historical sequence, knowing who he is, where he is, and of what he speaks."[16]

In philosophical terms, one would have to say that the notion of the *neutre* is an a-conceptual concept: it slips between the logical oppositions that organize rational or theoretical discourse. Thus, although once again Blanchot's argument is apparently based upon solidly-established polar oppositions, the *voix narrative,* being without location, *insituable,* cannot simply be called the contrary of the *voix narratrice,* the narrating voice of individual human subjectivity. That which is without location is without a ground, and in the void of its voicelessness it cannot merely be opposed to the centrality of a voice present-to-itself. This is why any definition of the *neutre* must necessarily take the apparent form of a logical paradox: since the neuter is neither this nor that, but somewhere (where?) in between, it cannot be approached by a logic of simple assertive distinction or differentiation. In this sense, the *neutre* is itself radically exterior to the reference points upon which discourse as logical continuity is constructed:

> the neuter word [*la parole neutre*] neither reveals nor hides anything. That does not mean that it signifies nothing (by pretending to abdicate meaningfulness in the form of nonsense); that means that it does not signify according to the manner in which the visible-invisible signifies, but that it opens within language an other power [*un pouvoir autre*], foreign to the power of enlightenment (or obfuscation), of comprehension or of misunderstanding. It does not signify according to the optic mode. (VN 183)

Just as in "Le chant des sirènes" Blanchot had spoken of an "other time" (*autre temps*) outside of human everydayness, here he alludes to the "other power" (*pouvoir autre*) opened up within language by the neuter word – a word which is foreign to the founding metaphorical principle of cognition: the "light-darkness" imagery by which Western thought expresses the accomplishments and frustrations of human understanding. What Blanchot calls, with admirable economy, the "optic mode," is the very horizon of our logical discourse, the ultimate limitation within which discourse as understandable human communication is inscribed. To write (or to read), according to the *voix narrative* as it opens up the strange space of the *récit*, is to find oneself beyond that horizon, in an *unheimlich* no-man's land, in the aridity of a desert which no land surveyor can encompass. And it is in this unlocatable "place," I would contend, that Blanchot's own *récits*, like Kafka's "Josefine," "take place.[17]

Kafka in the light of Blanchot

If Blanchot's theoretical meditations exhibit a certain relevance to the fictional praxis of Kafka, it is in their insistence upon two essential points: first, that at the center of narrative (understood rigorously as *récit*) lies a void, a nothingness, which is untranslatable in the terms of rational discourse but which generates the story in its radical exteriority; and second, that the *récit* as expression of the *neutre* is "voiceless," not attributable to a consciousness as human individuality and not subject to the laws of human time. The question that arises at this juncture is whether the writings of Kafka in some way correspond to these points, and if so, to what degree and in what manner. And, perhaps most crucially: *which* writings of Kafka are in proximity to Blanchot's theoretical concerns?

Because my book needs to reach closure, I will pass quickly over a subject that merits more detailed consideration, namely, the evolution of Kafka's prose style and narrative structures from the time of his first successful short story ("The Judgment," 1912). As I have suggested earlier, I think it could be demonstrated that the early stories, such as "The Judgment" and "The Metamorphosis," are constructed in a classical progression, a movement-toward-the-end that allows for melodrama and an ultimate tragic resolution. In Blanchot's terms, these stories would be the product of the *voix narratrice* and would differ from the aesthetics of the *roman* only in their concentrated length, only in the rapidity with which they move toward their respective resting-places. "The Metamorphosis" is really a short novel, quite untypical of the rest of Kafka's literary production in its clear tripartite structure, in its traditional theatricality. Most importantly, although Gregor Samsa is becoming an insect, he retains his very human consciousness, and the distance between his exterior appearance and his interiority produces a kind of irony that still derives from the aesthetic distance of Flaubert. In the case of "Josefine" – or "Forschungen eines Hundes" ["Investigations of a Dog"] (1922) or "Der Bau" ["The Burrow"] (1923) – however, the reader finds himself/herself immediately thrust into an animal world from which all human points of reference are absent. The *voix narratrice* cannot function because the human subjectivity of which it is the reflection, the full expression, is no longer on the narrative stage. My contention is that the literary evolution of Kafka can be formulated, in Blanchot's terms, as a gradual effacement of the *voix narratrice* in favor of the *voix narrative*, as a final victory for the *récit* over the *roman*. "Josefine" can be read as a textualization of Blanchot's theoretical points in that the protagonist's song is, in fact, a void, an emptiness, a problematic sound that may or may not "be" song; but this emptiness generates the entirety of the narrative movement, which can be defined as the impossible effort of the animal narrator to rationalize through logical discourse that which is already situated in the realm of the *neutre*. The point of the narrative is that what Josefine is producing is neither song nor piping, but something else – in Blanchot's terms, *un autre chant*.

The passage from the *roman* to the *récit*, from the human fullness of the *voix narratrice* to the animal squeaking of the *voix narrative*, could not have been an easy one for Kafka, who wrote with more anguish and less serenity than Blanchot. The final ruminations of the philosophical dog, the paranoia of the burrowing rodent, and the nervous exertions of the singing mouse are the end-result not of a theoretical meditation, but of a lived drama – Kafka's own. Blanchot senses this when, in his probing essay entitled "Kafka et l'exigence de l'oeuvre," he shows from a close reading of the *Tagebücher* [*Diaries*] that Kafka's intense involvement in Judaism (his learning of Hebrew and what may have been a more than passing interest in the Zionist question) brought religion into conflict with the exacting demands (*l'exigence*) of writing. For Blanchot, whose unique allegiance is to writing, Kafka's turn toward religion in his final days created an existential conflict from which the creator of the animal stories had difficulty disengaging himself. Proof of Kafka's ambivalence can be found in a haunting and much-cited diary entry from 28 January 1922, in which the real world (the domain of families, of biological fulfillment, and of achieved religious community) is contrasted with the "desert" in which the writer wanders endlessly:

> Why did I want to quit the world? Because "he" [my father] would not let me live in it, in his world. *Though indeed I should not judge the matter so precisely* [*So klar darf ich es jetzt allerdings nicht beurteilen*], for I am now a citizen of this other world, whose relationship to the ordinary one is the relationship of the wilderness to cultivated land (I have been forty years wandering from Canaan) . . . It is indeed a kind of Wandering in the Wilderness in reverse that I am undergoing: I think that I am continually skirting the wilderness and am full of childish hopes (particularly as regards women) that "perhaps I shall keep in Canaan after all" – when all the while I have been decades in the wilderness and these hopes are merely mirages born of despair, especially at those times when I am the wretchedest of creatures in the desert too, and Canaan is perforce my own Promised Land, *for no third place exists for mankind* [*denn ein drittes Land gibt es nicht für die Menschen*].[18]

There is a striking dissimilarity between the nostalgic and despairing rhetorical tone of this entry and the tranquil indifference of the mouse-narrator in "Josefine" – a dissimilarity that marks the separation between Kafka's unmediated thoughts as expressed in his diaries and the unearthly exteriority of his animal tales. In the passage quoted above, Kafka has set up an either/or alternative from which there is no escape, a polar opposition that exhausts all the possibilities, since we are told that, beyond Canaan on the one hand and the wilderness on the other, "no third place exists for mankind." Having been expelled from the world as "Promised Land" by his father, Kafka has been wandering in his own arid territories, unhappily and with sidelong wistful glances toward

Canaan. Now this expulsion into the outside, the beyond, reminds one of what happens to the dispossessed human subject when precipitated from the *roman* into the *récit*, from the domain of the *voix narratrice* into the voicelessness of the *voix narrative*. Yet what separates Kafka the human subject, author of the *Diaries*, from Kafka the writer, author of "Josefine," is that in the *Diaires* he has not found his way out of discursive logic, beyond pathos, beyond immediate existential despair.

As presented in the entry of 28 January 1922, the situation of the writer emerges as the mere logical opposite of the supposed happiness and fulfillment of ordinary humans, in which a note of self-pity is not absent. What Kafka achieves in "Josefine" is to move beyond an indulgence in differentiation (the representation of the artist as other, as sad foreigner, as outcast from society) toward a rhetoric of in-differentiation (Josefine may be singing, may be piping, is both same and different from all other members of the mouse folk). Yet it is just possible that the Kafka of the *Diaries* recognized the melodramatic tone of his rhetoric, that, to borrow from Proust's terminology, his *moi social* intuited what his *moi profond* was capable of achieving through writing.[19] This can be seen, I think, in a curious phrase that does not at first call attention to itself, a phrase like many others one finds in Kafka's writings that seems to express the writer's prudence in reaching a definite formulation, but which, in this case, may be more than a topos of modesty: "Though indeed I should not judge the matter so precisely" ("So klar darf ich es jetzt allerdings nicht beurteilen"). What is interesting here is the presence of a phrase that calls attention to the absolute quality of the polar oppositions structuring the remainder of the passage, and that calls into question the appropriateness of this very absoluteness. In other words: it may be that the Kafka of the *Diaries* recognized that the stark contrast of Canaan to the Wandering in the Wilderness is a theatrical simplification, the kind of trenchant distinction that makes possible structures like the Oedipal triangle and narrative order as such. Perhaps this kind of clarity is too clear; perhaps the act of judgment ("Das Urteil," *beurteilen*) necessarily contains within itself a categorical separation in the form of a cut (*Teil, teilen*) that is too neat. The evolution in Kafka the storyteller is from a transparent Oedipal allegory of banishment by the father in "Das Urteil" to the impossibility of sustaining a differential narrative and of making aesthetic judgments (the undecidability of Josefine's "song") in his final fictional work. There is a "third place," which is beyond the horizon of Canaan *and* the Wilderness, but it is not for humankind; it is for those animals vocalizing within the atopical space of the *neutre*.

IV COMMUNITY AND DEATH IN KAFKA AND BLANCHOT

At the end of "Josefine" the protagonist disappears; her song is lost for the mouse-people, who, in their practical slyness, will continue along their habitual path. The final four short paragraphs of the story are replete with the kind of logical hesitations and paradoxical formulations that have characterized the tale throughout, but in this case the narrator's language focuses almost exclusively on the problem of history ("Geschichte") as memory *and* forgetfulness. We are told, in the final sentence of the story, that since the mouse folk has no interest in history, Josefine, like the previous heroes and heroines of her race, is bound to be forgotten. Since we are in the realm of the *neutre*, however, since we are beyond the horizon of balanced polar opposites, this forgetfulness of Josefine should not be equated with her "tragic destiny." That is: forgetfulness is not the negative opposite of memory (memory understood positively as the capacity of a people to sustain through the interiorization of consciousness the essential life of its heroes). This is why the final paragraph of the narrative exhibits a Blanchot-like tranquillity:

Vielleicht werden wir also gar nicht sehr viel entbehren, Josefine aber, erlöst von der irdischen Plage, die aber ihrer Meinung nach Auserwählten bereitet ist, wird fröhlich sich verlieren in der zahllosen Menge der Helden unseres Volkes, und bald, da wir keine Geschichte treiben, in gesteigerter Erlösung vergessen sein wie alle ihre Brüder. (J 216)

So perhaps we shall not miss so very much after all, while Josephine, redeemed from the earthly sorrows which to her thinking lay in wait for all chosen spirits, will happily lose herself in the numberless throng of the heroes of our people, and soon, since we are no historians, will rise to the heights of redemption and be forgotten like all her brothers. (JMF 376).

The notion of "redemption" ("Erlösung"), which in a Judeo-Christian context would be linked to the preserving power of memory (when a people is redeemed, that is, "bought back," "ransomed" by a Savior, it is exonerated of its sin and allowed to continue, to further its existence and even, in certain scenarios, to obtain everlasting life), is here linked to the notion of forgetfulness. Josefine will be redeemed insofar as she is forgotten, insofar as her appeal for difference, her naïve belief in her identity as a "chosen spirit," are subsumed within the in-differentiating force of the masses. A detailed stylistic analysis of the verb tenses in the final section of the story would show that there is no precise moment, no dramatic point at which Josefine does, in fact, disappear. Rather, she slips between the interstices of the narrative texture: she has, so to speak, always been lost for the mouse folk.

In turning what the *voix narratrice* would have represented as the tragic end-point of death into an unlocalizable "disappearance," the *voix narrative* may have recovered the spectral and uncanny truth of death, its essential neutrality, its luminescent exteriority beyond the oppositions of light and dark, inside and outside. Although, as Heidegger would have it, I die my own death, which is mine and mine alone, there is an important dialogic relation between the one who dies or disappears and the one(s) who remain(s) behind; and it is in this relation and only in this relation that what we call "community" can arise. The relation that binds together Josefine and the mouse folk – an indifferent forgetfulness – may seem strange to the reader whose universe is that of the *roman*; but in the *récit*, this relation (*rapport*) has, in Blanchot's words, all the power and meaning of the secret, of mystery. Let me conclude with a fragment from Blanchot's *L'Attente l'oubli* (1962) that rewrites, in concentrated abstraction, the enigmatic ending of Josefine, the mouse singer, whose fate will have always been to disappear within her people, to lose what has always been lost – her precious identity:

> Nous n'allons pas vers l'oubli, pas plus que l'oubli ne vient à nous, mais soudain l'oubli a toujours déjà été là, et lorsque nous oublions, nous avons toujours déjà tout oublié: nous sommes, dans le mouvement vers l'oubli, en rapport avec la présence de l'immobilité de l'oubli.
>
> L'oubli est rapport avec ce qui s'oublie, rapport qui, rendant secret cela avec quoi il y a rapport, détient le pouvoir et le sens du secret. (87)

> We do not go toward forgetfulness, no more than forgetfulness comes to us, but suddenly forgetfulness has always already been there, and when we forget, we have always already forgotten everything: we are, in the movement toward forgetfulness, linked to the presence of the immobility of forgetfulness.
>
> Forgetfulness relates to that which forgets itself. And this relation, which renders secret that to which it relates, holds the power and the meaning of the secret.

Notes

1 BORDER CROSSINGS IN KANT

1 I do not wish to oversimplify the chronology of Kant criticism by suggesting that "only in recent years" have the Second and Third Critiques been granted their due. More than eighty years ago, in his important study entitled *Kants Leben und Lehre* (in German, 1918; English translation as *Kant's Life and Thought* by James Haden, 1981), Ernst Cassirer emphasized the importance of the later works, especially the *Critique of Judgment,* discovering in it the grounded and well-argued endpoint of the critical project. Perhaps more typical of the majority opinion of Kant scholarship is the judgment pronounced by *The Oxford Companion to Philosophy* (ed. Ted Honderich, 1995), which calls the *Critique of Pure Reason* "Kant's greatest masterpiece" (435), and describes the *Critique of Judgment* as "an extremely rich and important, if frequently perplexing work" (438). Whether the Third Critique is merely "rich and important," or whether it is also the cornerstone of the critical edifice as such is a major bone of contention in current Kant criticism.

2 For a variation on the Kantian notion of objects as conforming to our modes of knowing, see a later poetic formulation of a similar idea in Wordsworth's "Prospectus" to *The Excursion* (1814):

> How exquisitely the individual Mind
> (And the progressive powers perhaps no less
> Of the whole species) to the external World
> Is fitted: – and how exquisitely, too –
> Theme this but little heard of among men –
> The external World is fitted to the Mind. (l. 816–21;
> Wordsworth, *Selected Poetry*, 416)

The difference between Kant and Wordsworth in the description of the subject–object relation is subtle but important. For Kant, objects must *conform* to our modes of knowing, which means that they are subjected to our knowing, ruled by our conceptual apprehension of them. Wordsworth's vocabulary is less harsh: he speaks of a "*fitting*" of the Mind and the external World, a pure reciprocity in which neither Mind nor World achieves dominance.

3 References are to Immanuel Kant, *Critique of Judgment*, trans. and introduced by Werner S. Pluhar (Indianapolis: Hackett, 1987), abbreviated *CJ*; and *Kritik der Urteilskraft*, ed. Karl Vorländer (Hamburg: Felix Meiner Verlag, 1990), abbreviated *KU*.

4 On the importance of rhetoric and of linguistic play in general in Kant's works, and specifically, on the ways in which the materiality of the signifier undoes the claims to the phenomenal cognition of the aesthetic judgment in the Third Critique, see Paul de Man, "Phenomenality and Materiality in Kant," in his *Aesthetic Ideology*, 70–90.

5 The "fall" from the philosophical rigor of Kant to the simplifying dialectical manipulations of Schiller is a leitmotiv in Kant criticism. Paul de Man studies this "regression from the incisiveness and from the impact, from the critical impact, of the original [Kant]" in "Kant and Schiller," in *Aesthetic Ideology*, 129–55. De Man's rather unpolished statement (this article was delivered as a lecture, and the spoken style is everywhere apparent) – "So there is a total lack, an amazing, naive, childish lack of transcendental concern in Schiller, an amazing lack of philosophical concern" (141) – echoes the sentiments of a large number of Kant scholars. For a more sympathetic view of Schiller's contributions in the wake of Kantian philosophy, see Dieter Henrich, "Beauty and Freedom: Schiller's Struggle with Kant's Aesthetics." An excellent, philosophically rigorous presentation of Schiller's complex relations to Kant (in which Schiller is given his due as independent thinker) is to be found in Jacques Taminiaux, *La Nostalgie de la Grèce à l'aube de l'Idéalisme allemand: Kant et les Grecs dans l'Itinéraire de Schiller, de Hölderlin et de Hegel*. And finally, on the notion of "aesthetic morality" as such in its diverse Enlightenment manifestations, see the fine intellectual history of Robert E. Norton, *The Beautiful Soul*.

6 In this group are critics whose methodologies are quite divergent: Ernst Cassirer, Jean-François Lyotard, and Paul Guyer. In *Kant's Life and Thought*, Cassirer finds that the philosopher's analogy between the sublime and the moral law runs the risk of erasing the "special aesthetic character" and the "independent aesthetic value" of the sublime (330). In *Lessons on the Analytic of the Sublime*, Lyotard asserts that Kant's argument, if carefully read, does not allow for "any confusion, and even any continuity, between the ethical and the aesthetic. Their relation must be maintained by the critique in the form of an analogy" (213). By "analogy" here, Lyotard clearly means *only by analogy, by the weakness inherent in analogical argument*. And in *Kant and the Claims of Taste*, Guyer writes: "Beauty is a symbol of the morally good *only because* there is an analogy between aesthetic and moral judgment" (376; my emphasis).

7 One can include in this group Ted Cohen's subtle article "Why Beauty is a Symbol of Morality," as well as Paul Guyer's "Feeling and Freedom: Kant on Aesthetics and Morality" (1990), in which the author of the 1979 study *Kant and the Claims of Taste* modifies his earlier position by asserting: "The experience of beauty serves the purpose of morality most directly by improving our propensity for moral feeling" (140). In his 1994 essay

"Kant's Conception of Fine Art," Guyer goes even further in his now positive emphasis on the analogical relation between the aesthetic and the ethical when he states that Kant's "fundamental conceptions of morality become part of the experience of art without actually being part of the explicit content of individual works of art: his argument is precisely that the beautiful may serve as the symbol of the morally good because there are key analogies between the *experience* of beauty and the nature of moral motivation and judgment" (283; Guyer's emphasis).

8 The problem with the creating and reading of analogy extends beyond the issue of its relative aptness (i.e., whether a hand mill is the "best" analogon to a despotic state, given innumerable other illustrative possibilities). More crucial than aptness or appropriateness is the difficult question of the transparence or opaqueness of the analogical figure. In this case, for us as readers to understand that a hand mill corresponds to a despotic state, Kant must *tell us that this is so*, since the hand mill, on its own, could potentially call to mind many other supersensible entities. The hand mill, if displayed in the glass case of a museum, would need a descriptive tag, or *étiquette*, next to it, indicating what it symbolizes. Its creator, Immanuel Kant, needs to *point out its significance* for the analogy to be understandable.

9 On the question of ornamentation in Kant, and on the complex manipulations of the inside/outside polarity in paragraph 14 and beyond, see Jacques Derrida, "Parergon," in his *La Vérité en peinture*, 19–168.

10 The scholarly literature on Kant's theory of the sublime has reached colossal proportions, and, given the limited scope of my own inquiry, I shall not be engaging in any detailed way the far-reaching critical debates that have arisen around this topic in the last three decades. The reader wishing to pursue this discussion might begin his or her research, minimally, with the following: *Lessons on the Analytic of the Sublime* (the best close reading of Kant's sublime to date) and also *The Inhuman*, both by Jean-François Lyotard; *Of the Sublime: Presence in Question*, a collection of essays translated from the French by S. Librett that includes contributions by Jean-François Courtine, Michel Deguy, Eliane Escoubas, Philippe Lacoue-Labarthe, Jean-François Lyotard, Louis Marin, Jean-Luc Nancy, and Jacob Rogozinski; the careful historical account by Dominique Peyrache-Leborgne entitled *La poétique du sublime de la fin des Lumières au romantisme*; Paul Guyer's *Kant and the Claims of Taste*; and Frances Ferguson's *Solitude and the Sublime: Romanticism and the Aesthetics of Individuation*. For an elegant presentation of the history of the concept of the sublime, see Richard Macksey, "Longinus Reconsidered," in which the term is traced from its original use in Longinus through Burke and Kant up to Harold Bloom and Paul de Man.

11 The quintessential Modernist meditation on the problem that Kant raises here – that of the graven image (*Bildnis*), of the image as sign, metaphor, or sensible presentation of the Idea (*Bild*), and of the image as copy (*Abbild*), is to be found in Arnold Schoenberg's *Moses and Aaron* (1930–32). The fundamental theme of the opera is stated by Moses in Act 1, Scene 2: "Kein

Bild kann dir ein Bild geben vom Unvorstellbaren" ("No image can give you a picture of the unimaginable/unpresentable") (Karl Heinrich Wörner, *Schoenberg's "Moses and Aaron,"* Libretto, 118). The combat between Moses, man of thoughts (*Gedanken*) and Aaron, man of images (*Bilder*), is a directing theme of the opera as a whole.

12 The foray will be brief because my main interest, in this chapter, is the examination of the areas of contact or intersection between the aesthetic and the ethical in Kant, insofar as these nodal points are useful for my further analyses of Modernist texts. My purpose, therefore, is not to offer a survey, however concise, of Kant's ethical theory, which would need to be studied not only in the *Critique of Practical Reason* (1788), but also in the *Groundwork of the Metaphysic of Morals* (1785) and the *Metaphysics of Morals* (1797). I shall not be analyzing the Second Critique as it is often read – as a series of general propositions whose claims to universal validity need to be examined logically and tested against situations of possible ethical conflict in "real-life situations." Instead, I am interested in the rhetorical fabric of a text that seems, in its serious and univocal tone, to be based on the banishing of rhetoric from philosophical textuality.

13 References are to Immanuel Kant, *Critique of Practical Reason*, trans. and introduced by Lewis White Beck (New York: Macmillan, 1956), abbreviated *CPrR*; and *Kritik der Praktischen Vernunft*, ed. Karl Vorländer (Hamburg: Felix Meiner Verlag, 1990), abbreviated *KPrV*.

14 Kant's clearest statement on the notion of freedom in its "transcendental" sense runs as follows: "Now, as no determining ground of the will except the universal legislative form can serve as a law for it, such a will must be conceived as wholly independent of the natural law of appearances in their mutual relations, i.e., the law of causality. Such independence is called *freedom* in the strictest, i.e., transcendental, sense" (*CPrR* 28).

15 On seduction as "aesthetic action," see my discussion, in the following chapter, of Kierkegaard's "The Seducer's Diary," which concludes Part One of *Either/Or* (1843).

16 The words *Erhebung* and *erhaben* occur throughout the *Critique of Practical Reason* as a leitmotiv to characterize the "sublime" quality of the moral law and of our dutiful actions in its behalf. Perhaps the most notable occurrence of the word "sublime" used adjectivally is to be found in Kant's celebrated apostrophe to Duty, anglicized in the pathos of a quasi-biblical style in Lewis White Beck's translation: "Duty! Thou sublime and mighty name that dost embrace nothing charming or insinuating but requirest submission [*Plicht! du erhabener großer Name, der du nichts Beliebtes, was Einschmeichelung bei sich führt, in dir fassest, sondern Unterwerfung verlangst*], and yet seekest not to move the will by threatening aught that would arouse natural aversion or terror ... what origin is there worthy of thy noble descent which proudly rejects all kinship with the inclinations [*welches ist der deiner würdige Ursprung, und wo findet man die Wurzel deiner edlen Abkunft*], and from which to be descended is the

indispensable condition of the only worth which men can give themselves?" (*CPrR* 89; *KPrV*). It should be noted that Kant is seduced by the power of his own rhetoric in this passage, in that he refers to the "*noble* descent" of Duty. Kant has forgotten his own definition of the moral law as that which is clear and simple, democratically available to all people. Duty here is an aristocrat, a "world-traveller" of *Sittlichkeit.*

17 In the preface to his final work on ethical theory, *The Metaphysics of Morals*, Kant has nothing but scorn for those readers of his who, in his opinion, have not understood him, and who, in their criticisms, merely "quibble with words" (4). He uses the Greek term *logodaedalus*, in a pejorative sense, for such a class of people. One wonders, however, whether the study of literature must not always be located in the realm of the word-artificer, the craftsman whose effects, however masterful, partake always of some cunning. Joyce is not the only Modernist, or the only artist, who comes to mind when the *dédales* of artistic creation are evoked.

2 KIERKEGAARD: ON THE ECONOMICS OF LIVING POETICALLY

1 This phrase comes from the chapter "Irony after Fichte" in Søren Kierkegaard's *The Concept of Irony, with Continual Reference to Socrates*, edited and translated by Howard V. Hong and Edna H. Hong (Princeton: Princeton University Press, 1989), 297. Throughout this chapter references are to this edition, abbreviated *CI*.

2 For a concise exposition of these two influences on Kierkegaard, see the first two chapters of Sylvia Walsh's *Living Poetically: Kierkegaard's Existential Aesthetics*. I am indebted to Professor Walsh for her presentation of the central Kierkegaardian notion of "living poetically." For a more detailed analysis of the Hegelian intertext, see Niels Thulstrup's *Kierkegaard's Relation to Hegel*. Although it is universally admitted that Hegel and Hegelianism are clear and unequivocal targets of the Danish writer's criticism, Kierkegaard's debt to and struggle with Kant may be more profound than is usually assumed. On this point see Ronald M. Green, *Kierkegaard and Kant: The Hidden Debt*.

3 For a rhetorically sophisticated reading of Fichte's importance for the writings of Friedrich Schlegel in particular, see Paul de Man, "The Concept of Irony," in *Aesthetic Ideology*, 163–84.

4 See chapter five below for an interpretation of the abiding presence of the "beautiful soul" as constitutive poetic figure in late Romanticism and early Modernism.

5 Sylvia Walsh cites this passage in *Living Poetically*, but her summary of its content ("As Hegel sees it, then, romantic irony requires both poetic living and poetic productivity on the part of the artist" [56]) is quite flat and uninterpretive, in that it does not do justice to the rhetorical complexity of Hegel's ironization of irony.

6 This is not the only time Kierkegaard prophetically announces Flaubert. In a footnote to the section "First Love" in *Either/Or*, Part I, he writes: "It is altogether remarkable that there is no female counterpart to Don Quixote in all European literature. Is the age not yet mature enough for that; has not the continent of sentimentality yet been discovered?" (256–57). This "continent" comes into full view with the creation of Emma Bovary, some two decades after *Either/Or*.

7 The use of the term "hover" ("schweben") is, of course, not limited to the German Romantics. For a cogent and theoretically astute description of the "hovering" effects of the best poetry, see Coleridge, who admires Shakespeare's use of such phrases as "loving hate," "heavy lightness," "bright smoke," and "sick health" in *Romeo and Juliet* (I, i, 181–85). For Coleridge, these oxymorons are not Renaissance *préciosité*, but rather examples of the most sublime powers of the literary imagination. In these lines, we find "an effort of the mind, when it would describe what it cannot satisfy itself with the description of, to reconcile opposites and qualify contradictions, leaving a middle state of mind more strictly appropriate to the imagination than any other, when it is, as it were, *hovering between images*. As soon as it is fixed on one image, it becomes understanding; but while it is unfixed and wavering between them, attaching itself permanently to none, it is imagination ... The grandest efforts of poetry are where the imagination is called forth, not to produce a distinct form, but a strong working of the mind, still offering what is still repelled, and again creating what is again rejected; the result being what the poet wishes to impress, namely, the substitution of a sublime feeling of the unimaginable for a mere image" ("Lecture VII" [1811–12], in *Selected Poetry and Prose*, 458–59; my emphasis).

8 From a psychoanalytical point of view, one could argue that the transubstantiation is of necessity invisible, since to render it visible would be to indicate too clearly its origin in what could be termed its "primitive" substratum – in ritualistic cannibalism. Even if this unpleasant reminder were to be avoided by some form of artistic indirection, one could only imagine the depiction of the transubstantiation as a form of kitsch.

9 I shall deal with the late Romantic notion of aesthetic redemption in chapter four, in a discussion of works by Nietzsche, Baudelaire, and Wagner.

10 At the beginning of the third chapter of the *Philosophical Fragments* (1844), as he elaborates his distinction between Socratic truth and the truth of Christianity, Kierkegaard begins an examination of what he calls the "absolute paradox" with the following remarks: "one should not think slightingly of the paradoxical; for the paradox is the source of the thinker's passion, and the thinker without a paradox is like a lover without feeling: a paltry mediocrity. But the highest pitch of every passion is always to will its own downfall; and so it is also the supreme passion of the Reason to seek a collision, though this collision must in one way or another prove its undoing. The supreme paradox of all thought is the attempt to discover something

that thought cannot think. This passion is at bottom present in all thinking, even in the thinking of the individual, in so far as in thinking he participates in something transcending himself. But habit dulls our sensibilities, and prevents us from perceiving it" (29).

11 References are to *Either/Or: Part I* and *Either/Or: Part II*, both ed. and trans. by Howard V. Hong and Edna H. Hong (Princeton: Princeton University Press, 1987).

12 To illustrate Hegel's thesis on the internal *being* the external in the truest dialectical sense, the Hongs quote a passage from the *Wissenschaft der Logik* [*Science of Logic*] on p. 603 of their notes to part one of *Either/Or*: "The inner is determined as the form of *reflected immediacy* or of essence over against the outer as the form of being, but the two are only one identity. This identity is first, the substantial unity of both as a substrate pregnant with content, or the *absolute fact* [*Sache*], in which the two determinations are indifferent, external moments. By virtue of this, it is a content and that totality which is the inner that equally becomes external, but in this externality is not the result of becoming or transition but is identical with itself. The outer, according to this determination, is not only *identical* with the inner in respect of content but both are only *one fact*."

13 This is the enchanted place in which Tannhäuser experiences atemporal ecstasy (or, put differently, erotic imprisonment). Richard Wagner's opera *Tannhäuser* was completed in 1845, just two years after the publication of *Either/Or*. The final redemption of the protagonist in the Wagner drama is very un-Mozartian, and would not have pleased A, because this metaphysical cleansing introduces a strong dose of the ethical into the territory of the aesthetic.

14 On this point, see W. H. Auden's remark: "Don Giovanni's pleasure in seducing women is not sensual but arithmetical; his satisfaction lies in adding one more name to his list which is kept for him by Leporello" ("Balaam and His Ass," *The Dyer's Hand and Other Essays*, 119).

15 "The Concept of Irony," in *Aesthetic Ideology*, 169–70.

16 This term is a codeword in German Romanticism. The new art (poetry, criticism, painting, and also music) was aimed against bourgeois aesthetic values – as was the case, perhaps most notoriously and humorously, in Robert Schumann's invention of the "Davidsbündler" to do battle with the "Philistines." The Davidsbündler (Florestan, Eusebius and company) appeared not only in literary form, in Schumann's *Neue Zeitschrift für Musik* (first published in 1834), but also in his brilliant sequence of dances for the piano entitled the "Davidsbündlertänze" (1837).

17 In the Hongs' translation, the phrase "for the esthetic is not evil but the indifferent" renders quite literally the Danish original: "thi det Aesthetiske er ikke det Onde, men Indifferentsen" (*Enten-Eller* II, 179). Walter Lowrie used the term "neutrality" rather than "the indifferent" in his earlier Princeton University Press translation (original publication 1944; revised

by Howard A. Johnson in 1971) (II, 173). Both words place the aesthetic in the domain of the *neither/nor*, which is why, in the upcoming section of my argument, I draw a parallel between Kierkegaard's aesthetic theory and Blanchot's notion of *le neutre.*

18 I shall analyze Blanchot's essay "La voix narrative, le 'il,' le neutre" in some detail in the epilogue, in conjunction with the narrative pragmatics of Kafka's late fiction.

3 FREUD'S "DAS UNHEIMLICHE": THE INTRICACIES OF TEXTUAL UNCANNINESS

1 Kofman's argument for a "symptomal" reading of "Das Unheimliche" can be found in her *The Childhood of Art*, 6–8.

2 The critical literature on "Das Unheimliche" is by now quite extensive. The three articles which, it seems to me, remain to this day the most brilliant close readings of the essay are: Hélène Cixous, "Fiction and its Phantoms"; Sarah Kofman, "The Double is/and the Devil"; and Neil Hertz, "Freud and the Sandman" (in *The End of the Line*), all of which were first published between 1974 and 1979. More recent noteworthy interpretations include: Lis Møller, chapter five of *The Freudian Reading* (1991); Ruth Ginsburg's feminist analysis entitled "A Primal Scene of Reading" (1992); and Robin Lydenberg's "Freud's Uncanny Narratives" (1997), which has the singular merit of combining the best features of a review article of recent Freud criticism with genuine critical insights of her own.

3 Jacques Derrida has demonstrated that Freud gives a special "turn" to the very notion of speculation in the peculiar narrative fits and starts of *Beyond the Pleasure Principle*, and sees in the narrativizing of speculation a movement of excess which undermines analytical discourse as such (see "Spéculer – sur 'Freud,'" in *La Carte postale: de Socrate à Freud et au-delà*, 275–437).

4 References are to Sigmund Freud, "The Uncanny," in *The Standard Edition of the Complete Psychological Works of Sigmund Freud*, trans. James Strachey, vol. XVII (London: The Hogarth Press, 1955), 217–56, abbreviated TU; and "Das Unheimliche," in *Gesammelte Werke Chronologisch Geordnet*, vol. XII (London: Imago, 1947), 227–68, abbreviated DU.

5 On the "essence of literature" as a certain kind of falling, see my reading of Blanchot reading Camus: "Vertiginous Storytelling: Camus's *La Chute*," in *Of Words and the World*, chapter one.

6 References are to "The Sandman," in *Tales* of *Hoffmann*, trans. R. J. Hollingdale (London: Penguin, 1982), 85–125, abbreviated TS; and "Der Sandmann," in *Nachtstücke. Werke 1816–20*, vol. III of *E. T. A. Hoffmann: Sämtliche Werke*, ed. H. Steinecke and G. Allroggen (Frankfurt am Main: Deutscher Klassiker Verlag, 1985), 11–49, abbreviated DS.

7 On this point, see Peter Brooks's reading of *Beyond the Pleasure Principle* in his essay "Freud's Masterplot." Brooks writes: "Narrative always makes the implicit claim to be in a state of repetition, as a going over again of a ground already covered. . . . This claim to an act of repetition – 'I sing of,' 'I tell of' – appears to be initiatory of narrative. It is equally initiatory of *Beyond the Pleasure Principle*: it is the first problem and clue that Freud confronts" (97).

8 For an incisive feminist interpretation of the contrasting versions of the Sandman story provided by the mother and the servant woman, and for commentary on the latter's marginal or liminal role in the family, see Ruth Ginsburg's "A Primal Scene of Reading," 31–32.

9 For the reader of nineteenth-century American literature, the fortuitous physical arrangement pictured here – Nathaniel, as if by magic, transported to a place directly opposite the window of a beautiful but artificial creature – calls to mind a similar situation in Nathaniel (no comment) Hawthorne's "Rappaccini's Daughter" (1846), where the young protagonist, Giovanni, finds a room which overlooks the poisonous garden and from which he can spy on Beatrice. Like Spalanzani, Rappaccini plays with the laws of nature and produces unnatural offspring; and like Hoffmann's Nathaniel, Giovanni falls in love with a young woman who is not quite real (in the case of Hawthorne's imaginary universe, *no longer real*). An uncanny atmosphere reigns throughout "Rappaccini's Daughter," and although the word "uncanny" does not appear in the text, an English rendition of the French translation of "das Unheimliche" – *l'inquiétante étrangeté* – does appear, in an important expository section of the story. This passage through French is perhaps not so unusual in a text supposedly penned by a certain Monsieur de l'Aubépine ("aubépine," in French, meaning "hawthorn"):

> It was *strangely frightful* to the young man's [Giovanni's] imagination, to see this air of insecurity in a person [Beatrice] cultivating a garden, that most simple and innocent of human toils, and which had been alike the joy and labor of the unfallen parents of the race. Was this garden, then, the Eden of the present world? – and this man [Rappaccini], with such a perception of harm in what his own hands caused to grow, was he the Adam? (96; my emphasis).

Hawthorne's commentary on the scientist's garden, which turns out to be a chemically produced act of hubris and a diabolical inversion of Eden, reminds one, inevitably, of the perils of alchemy in "The Sandman."

10 For readers of German Romantic literature, E. T. A. Hoffmann's emphasis on Olympia's mechanical perfection *in dancing* is bound to evoke Heinrich von Kleist's suggestive and playful essay entitled "Über das Marionettentheater" (1810). In Kleist's rapidly traced cosmic vision, postlapsarian reflective man finds himself in an awkward middle position between the "grace" (*Grazie* or *Anmut*) of the puppet, on the one hand, and of godlike perfection, on the other. Like Hoffmann, Kleist bases his argument on a reversal of hierarchies: we readers of Kleist, like the inhabitants of post-Olympia

society in "Der Sandmann," are obliged to view human dancing as a poor, insufficient and unachieved mimesis of the puppet's or automaton's geometrically precise movements. For a clear overview of the position of Kleist's essay within German literary history, and for a discussion of the notion of *Anmut* in Kleist, Goethe, and Schiller, see Benno von Wiese, "Das verlorene und wieder zu findende Paradies: Eine Studie über den Begriff der Anmut bei Goethe, Kleist, und Schiller," in Walter Müller-Seidel, ed., *Kleists Aufsatz über das Marionettentheater*, 196–220. I discuss Schiller's use of the term *Anmut* in chapter five.

11 The question of victory and defeat in 1919 was not an abstract one. As an American citizen, Putnam had been, after all, on the winning side of World War I, whereas Tausk had actively participated in a losing effort. The concrete difficulty for Freud as leader of an international intellectual movement was to re-establish the forum for dialogue that had bridged national boundaries prior to 1914. It was of primordial importance that the unfortunate events of 1914–18 should not continue to separate an Ernest Jones from a Karl Abraham or a Sandor Ferenczi in the war's aftermath. Like his concerned contemporaries, Freud witnessed the redrawing of national boundaries with concern. In a letter dated 17 March 1919, he wrote to Ferenczi: "Today we learn that we are not permitted to join Germany, but must yield up South Tyrol. To be sure, I'm not a patriot, but it is painful to think that pretty much the whole world will be *foreign territory*" (quoted by Peter Gay in *Freud: A Life for Our Time*, 380; my emphasis). The problem of setting out upon foreign soil which structures "Das Unheimliche" thus also occupies Freud's thoughts as he considers a newly defined map of German-speaking lands.

12 Roazen, *Brother Animal*, 142; quoted in Hertz, "Freud and the Sandman," 116–17.

13 This and further citations from *Oedipus the King* are from David Grene's translation, in vol. II of the Centennial Edition of *The Complete Greek Tragedies* (Chicago: Chicago University Press, 1992), 9–76.

14 In his biography of Freud, Peter Gay writes: "In later life, Freud liked to call his daughter Anna his Antigone. It will not do to press this affectionate name too far: Freud was an educated European speaking to other educated Europeans and had raided Sophocles in search of a loving comparison. But the meanings of 'Antigone' are too rich to be wholly set aside. The name underscored Freud's identification with Oedipus, the bold discoverer of mankind's secrets, the eponymous hero of the 'nuclear complex,' the killer of his father and the lover of his mother" (*Freud: A Life for Our Time*, 442). Underneath the "affectionate name" of Antigone is the cruel fate of a woman who, through her father's sin, is expelled from society and branded as the unnatural, incestuous result of a criminal bond. One might be tempted to wonder (even if this be the kind of pure speculation which, according to Peter Gay, "will not do") if Freud felt some guilt about his psychoanalytical work having so absorbed his faithful daughter that the "quiet domestic happiness"

enjoyed by Clara at the conclusion of "The Sandman" (125) was denied her. In this sense, Anna, like Olympia or Rappaccini's daughter, becomes the artificial progeny of scientific hubris who looks, but *is not*, fully alive.

4 AESTHETIC REDEMPTION: THE THYRSUS IN NIETZSCHE, BAUDELAIRE, AND WAGNER

1 Percy Bysshe Shelley, *A Defence of Poetry*, in Shelley and Peacock, '*A Defence of Poetry*' and '*The Four Ages of Poetry*', 39–40.
2 I do not have the space to elaborate this large theme within the confines of this book. For a development on the poetic *hommage* in French Symbolist poetry, see my article "A Reading of Mallarmé's 'Hommage' (A Richard Wagner)."
3 This is no. 117 of the *Lyceum* aphorisms, quoted in Friedrich Schlegel, *Dialogue on Poetry and Literary Aphorisms*, 132. For a discussion of the status of the literary "fragment" in Schlegel, see Philippe Lacoue-Labarthe and Jean-Luc Nancy, eds., *L'Absolu littéraire: Théorie de la littérature du romantisme allemand*, 57–80.
4 Charles Baudelaire, "Richard Wagner et *Tannhäuser* à Paris," *Oeuvres complètes*, II, 793 (my translation).
5 Wagner is central to this chapter not "in himself," but *as figure*, insofar as he informs the writings of Nietzsche and Baudelaire. On the very question of Wagner as figure, see the incisive study of Philippe Lacoue-Labarthe, *Musica ficta: Figures de Wagner*. In this work, Lacoue-Labarthe concentrates on four "scenes" – readings of Wagner by Baudelaire, Mallarmé, Heidegger, and Adorno.
6 For a discussion of Nietzsche's views concerning a possible "music of the future," see Elliott Zuckerman, "Nietzsche and Music: *The Birth of Tragedy* and *Nietzsche Contra Wagner*." Zuckerman's conclusion reads as follows: "But if Nietzsche imagined the music of the future he imagined it, I think, as he imagined the music of the past, with tonality in his ears. As an historian, he failed to hear the ancient Dionysian as radically different from the great music of modern times. And as a prophet, he failed to prophesy the advent of a musical language that will be as radically different from tonality as tonality was from the music it replaced" (29).
7 In his informative article on the stages of Nietzsche's relation to Wagner, "Nietzsche und Wagner: Stationen einer Beziehung," Peter Wapnewski cites one of the last letters Nietzsche wrote to Carl Fuchs, just seven days before the onset of madness, as evidence of the philosopher's ambivalent attitude toward Wagner's music: "You cannot get around *Tristan*: it is a capital work and exerts a power of fascination that is without equal, not only in music, but in all the arts." Later in the same letter, Nietzsche admits that, in the opening section of *The Case of Wagner*, he alluded to Bizet only as "ironical antithesis" to Wagner: "What I said about Bizet should not be taken seriously" (quoted by Wapnewski, 422; my translation).

8 Quoted by Philippe Lacoue-Labarthe in the preface to his *Musica Ficta: Figures of Wagner*, xvi.

9 References are to "*The Birth of Tragedy*" *and* "*The Genealogy of Morals*," trans. Francis Golffing (New York: Anchor-Doubleday, 1956), abbreviated *BT*; and to *Die Geburt der Tragödie: Unzeitgemäße Betrachtungen I–IV*, vol. I of the *Kritische Studienausgabe*, ed. Giorgio Colli and Mazzino Montinari (Munich: dtv/de Gruyter, 1988), abbreviated *GT*.

10 Nietzsche's association of Dionysos with redemption has a mythical background: the story of the god's descent into Hades to release his mother, Semele, from the realm of the Shades. This story is alluded to in Hölderlin's magnificent poem "Brot und Wein," where Dionysos is further associated with the *Erlöser* of modern man, Jesus Christ. The structure of "Brot und Wein" is that of a movement from west (the *Abendland*, in particular the culturally reawakened Germany) to the east (the *Morgenland*, the Orient, the source of culture) and back to the west again. The *Festzug* of Dionysos is invoked in the context of this geographical symbolism. Thomas Mann also alludes to the Dionysian procession from east to west in the itinerary of the plague that progresses in that direction in *Death in Venice*, and Aschenbach's most fearsome dream is depicted as an irruption of Bacchic rites into the increasingly threatened rational calm of the artist's well-ordered universe.

11 For a detailed description of Nietzsche's eight-day "flight" from Bayreuth in August 1876, see Peter Wapnewski, "Nietzsche und Wagner: Stationen einer Beziehung," 410–11.

12 Giorgio Colli, "Nachwort" to "Richard Wagner in Bayreuth," *Die Geburt der Tragödie, Unzeitgemäße Betrachtungen I–IV, Nachgelassene Schriften 1870–1873*, 908–912. In the same vein, Peter Wapnewski describes *Richard Wagner in Bayreuth* as a collage or a palimpsest ("Nietzsche und Wagner: Stationen einer Beziehung," 412–16).

13 Walter Kaufmann, "Editor's Preface" to *Twilight of the Idols*, in *The Portable Nietzsche*, 463.

14 *Nietzsche Contra Wagner*, in *The Portable Nietzsche*, 680.

15 The original German texts of *Nietzsche Contra Wagner*, *The Case of Wagner*, *Twilight of the Idols*, and *The Antichrist* are quoted from vol. VI of the *Kritische Studienausgabe* ed. Giorgio Colli and Mazzino Montinari (Munich: dtv/de Gruyter, 1988).

16 For another example of this theme, see section 49 of *The Antichrist*: "The concept of guilt and punishment, the whole 'moral world order' was invented *against* science, *against* the emancipation of man from the priest … The concept of guilt and punishment, including the doctrine of 'grace,' of 'redemption,' of 'forgiveness' – *lies* through and through, and without any psychological reality" (*The Portable Nietzsche*, 630).

17 Baudelaire's evolution from a Romantic aesthetic of *correspondances* to the modernity of the uncanny cityscapes depicted in both the "Tableaux parisiens" and *Le Spleen de Paris* is not only to be understood in terms of an increased poetic self-reflectiveness, but also as a turn away from lyricism

conceived of as the internalized domain of a subjective consciousness. This point has been made both by Philippe Lacoue-Labarthe in *Musica ficta: Figures of Wagner* and by Barbara Johnson in her study of Baudelaire's prose poetry entitled *Défigurations du langage poétique: la seconde révolution baudelairienne.*

18 "Le Cygne" is one of Baudelaire's most discussed poems. During the past quarter-century, under the influence of Structuralism and a Formalist aesthetic in general, the poem has often been read in symbolic terms – "le cygne" being, essentially, "le signe." This kind of reading has been challenged by Richard Terdiman in *Present Past: Modernity and the Memory Crisis.* In a powerful reading that combines philological inventiveness with a thorough examination of the poem's historical context, Terdiman sets out to prove "that the relationship between the experience of dispossession 'Le Cygne' thematizes and the poem's reflection on the sign was intensely determined by Second Empire history" (106).

19 Both Richard Klein ("Straight Lines and Arabesques: Metaphors of Metaphor") and Barbara Johnson (*Défigurations du langage poétique*) read "Le Thyrse" in allegorical terms, as a poem about poetry, a figuration of the figural. An interesting counter-reading to those proposed by Klein and Johnson is that of Edward Kaplan (*Baudelaire's Prose Poems: The Esthetic, The Ethical, and the Religious in "The Parisian Prowler"*), who finds in "Le Thyrse" a demystification of "the tyranny of solipsistic imagination" (117). In a general sense, Kaplan's interpretation of the prose poems can be seen as a questioning of Johnson's strong emphasis on literary self-reflectiveness (to the exclusion of ethical and religious considerations).

20 I refer here to Edward K. Kaplan's translation, *The Parisian Prowler: Le Spleen de Paris/Petits poèmes en prose by Charles Baudelaire*, 129. I agree with Kaplan (who places the letter to Houssaye at the end of the sequence, in an appendix) that this convoluted dedication is less important theoretically than "Le Thyrse," and that Baudelaire's ambivalence toward an editor who both helped him into print and also wrote some very mediocre poetry makes of the letter a rather disingenuous exercise in false praise, certainly less centered on poetic theory or poetic writing than the poem to Liszt.

21 The only recent exception is that of Edward Kaplan, whose aforementioned *Baudelaire's Prose Poems* analyzes each of the works in sequence, with an eye toward Baudelaire's progression from solipsism toward the ethics of community.

22 Charles Baudelaire, "Le Thyrse," *Oeuvres complètes*, vol. 1, ed. Claude Pichois (Paris: Gallimard-Pléiade, 1975), 335–36; and "The Thyrsus," trans. Edward Kaplan in *The Parisian Prowler: 'Le Spleen de Paris/Petits poèmes en prose' by Charles Baudelaire*, (Athens and London: The University of Georgia Press, 1989), 86–87.

23 This and the next paragraph are Kaplan's creation (editorial decision). In the original French version of the poem, the second and final paragraph (which is Kaplan's fourth) begins with "Cher Liszt" ("Dear Liszt").

24 The three senses of the word *amalgam* given in *Webster's New Universal Unabridged Dictionary* are: "1. any metallic alloy of which mercury forms

an essential constituent part; 2. a native compound of mercury and silver found in fine crystals in mines; 3. a mixture of different things; combination; blend" (54). I have taken the figurative meaning of *amalgame* from *Le Petit Robert I*, 55. The quotation used to illustrate this sense of the word in *Le Petit Robert* is drawn from Victor Hugo: "L'amalgame et la superposition de toutes ces extravagances." One notes an interesting link between the literal sense of the word – a blend involving mercury – and the *mercurial* aspect of "extravagance." It could be that *Les Petits Poèmes en prose* are neither Apollonian nor Dionysian, but Mercurial (that is, of course, *hermetic*).

25 The citations in both German and English are taken from Richard Wagner, *Tannhäuser: Grand Romantic Opera in Three Acts by Richard Wagner* (New York: Rullman, 1925).

26 On this point, see the subtle analysis of Margaret Miner, whose book *Resonant Gaps: Between Baudelaire and Wagner* provides an overview of the Baudelaire–Wagner relation through a minute, step-by-step interpretation of "Richard Wagner et *Tannhäuser* à Paris." In her discussion of *Tannhäuser*'s conclusion, Miner writes: "In the Tannhäuser legend, this prophetic blossoming of the papal staff most immediately figures the Christian hope of redemption springing from Christ's death on the barren wood of the cross. In the context of *Richard Wagner*, however, the flowering staff also vividly calls to mind Baudelaire's famous description of a thyrsus in the prose poem 'Le Thyrse.' Like the pope's 'dried-up stick' [bâton desséché] bedecked with foliage, Baudelaire's thyrsus is also made up of a priest's staff [bâton hiératique] around which 'stems and flowers play and frolic with each other'. The priest in 'Le Thyrse' is of course Dionysos rather than the pope, but the prose poem and the opera text both explore the relations between spiritual discipline and sensual abandon" (123).

27 For a listing of the various meanings of *theoros* and *theorein*, see *Liddell and Scott's Greek-English Lexicon*, Abridged Version (London: Oxford University Press), 317.

5 THE "BEAUTIFUL SOUL": ALAIN-FOURNIER'S *LE GRAND MEAULNES* AND THE AESTHETICS OF ROMANTICISM

1 I quote from the translation by H. T. Lowe-Porter, in *'Death in Venice' and Seven Other Stories*, 13. The original version of the passage is as follows: "Und hat Form nicht zweierlei Gesicht? Ist sie nicht sittlich und unsittlich zugleich, – sittlich als Ergebnis und Ausdruck der Zucht, unsittlich aber und selbst widersittlich, sofern sie von Natur eine moralische Gleichgültigkeit in sich schließt, ja wesentlich bestrebt ist, das Moralische unter ihr stolzes und unumschränktes Szepter zu beugen?" (*'Der Tod in Venedig' und Andere Erzählungen*, 20).

2 See especially Marie Maclean, *Le Jeu suprême: Structure et thèmes dans 'Le Grand Meaulnes'*, for an excellent study of the novel's formal construction; Michel Guiomar, *Inconscient et imaginaire dans 'Le Grand Meaulnes'*, for an analysis of

the "unconscious" structures of the work; and, for an interpretation of *Le Grand Meaulnes* as "quest novel," Léon Cellier, *'Le Grand Meaulnes' ou l'initiation manquée.*

3 On this topic, see H.-A. Bouraoui, *Structure intentionnelle du 'Grand Meaulnes': vers le poème romancé.* Bouraoui contends that Alain-Fournier is attempting, in his own way, the same search for an aesthetics of the novel that characterizes Joyce's *A Portrait of the Artist as a Young Man.*

4 See the second half of Cellier's *'Le Grand Meaulnes' ou l'initiation manquée* and also Alain Buisine, *Les Mauvaises Pensées du Grand Meaulnes*, which I shall discuss below.

5 What the French call *critique génétique* has had major repercussions for the editing of texts, from the medieval to the modern periods. *Grosso modo*, the genetic critic questions and problematizes the notion of a "definitive" work, demonstrating instead that all texts have a history. What could be called the becoming-of-the-text, the *devenir textuel*, is the proper focus of study for the genetic critic. For an introduction to the field of *critique génétique* one may consult the series of essays edited by Louis Hay entitled *La Naissance du texte* (1989) and the synthetic study by Almuth Grésillon, *Eléments de critique génétique* (1994).

6 Especially notable in this category are the 1986 volume edited by Alain Rivière, Jean-Georges Morgenthaler and Françoise Garcia entitled *André Lhote, Alain-Fournier, Jacques Rivière. La peinture, le coeur et l'esprit. Correspondance inédite*; and the 1991 collection edited by Alain Rivière and Pierre de Gaulmyn called *Correspondance Jacques Rivière–Alain-Fournier.*

7 This entry from Gide's *Journal* is cited by Daniel Leuwers in the introduction to his edition of *Le Grand Meaulnes* (Paris: Livre de Poche, 1983), iii. All translations of French texts are mine.

8 In his correspondance with Jacques Rivière, Alain-Fournier often mentions the names of these writers, and seems conscious of the difficulties he is about to encounter in writing a novel that owes its existence to a certain poetic dream-quality and also to the conventions of novelistic realism. The following are two examples among many others cited in Herzfeld's edition of *Le Grand Meaulnes*:

> Yes, but how can I write it, this novel? . . . In searching I have found three categories of responses: There is Dickens. There are the brothers Goncourt. There is Laforgue. (263)

> For the moment, I would like to proceed from Laforgue, but in writing *a novel.* It's contradictory; but it would not be if one made of the characters of one's life, of the novel with its characters, dreams whose paths cross. . . . There are errors in dreams, false starts, changes of direction, and all of that lives, moves, meets, disengages, reverses itself. (340; Alain-Fournier's emphasis)

9 Buisine's book is on the way to offending many of the more pious specialists of Alain-Fournier's oeuvre, who do not appreciate certain incursions Buisine makes into the private life of the author of *Le Grand Meaulnes.* In particular, the analogy established by Buisine between the novelistic love-triangle

(Meaulnes – Yvonne – François) and the real triangle composed of Jacques Rivière, Isabelle Fournier/Rivière, and Henri Fournier, in which the critic suggests that François Seurel, like Fournier, was afraid of sexual relations and was jealous of his friend and his friend's wife – all of this cannot be pleasing to the defenders of the faith. Honesty compels one to admit that Buisine's analogy is more than convincing, but his formula – "Justement, ma soeur, elle a épousé mon meilleur copain" ("In fact, my sister, she married my best buddy") (*Les Mauvaises Pensées du Grand Meaulnes*, 112) – because of its schoolboy style, risks deterring some readers from a critical study which deserves close scrutiny.

10 References are to Alain-Fournier, *Le Grand Meaulnes*, ed. Daniel Leuwers (Paris: Livre de Poche, 1983); translations are my own.

11 The term *modernisme* is less commonly used and has a less precise significance in France than does the word *Modernism* in the Anglo-American tradition. In the Anglophone literary context, Modernism is associated, on the one hand, with a certain "religion of beauty" as theorized by Pater and Ruskin (and "imported" into France by Robert de la Sizeranne and Marcel Proust), and practiced, in quite diverse ways, by Eliot, Yeats, James, and the Joyce of *A Portrait of the Artist as a Young Man*; and on the other hand, with experimental formalism in general (Pound, the Joyce of *Ulysses* and *Finnegans Wake*, Virginia Woolf). For a solid recent study of the first tendency, see Leon Chai, *Aestheticism: The Religion of Art in Post-Romantic Literature*. For an excellent revisionist analysis of the aesthetic presuppositions of Modernism, see Perry Meisel, *The Myth of the Modern: A Study in British Literature and Criticism after 1850*. And for an interesting study of Modernism as experimental writing, notably of writing as "interruption," see Astradur Eysteinsson, *The Concept of Modernism*. Ross Chambers has argued for the existence of a specifically French Modernism in his book *Mélancolie et opposition: Les débuts du modernisme en France*.

12 The roots of the notion of the "beautiful soul" go back much further than the works of the German writers I shall be evoking here. As Robert E. Norton has pointed out in his account of the metamorphoses of the "beautiful soul" throughout the eighteenth century, the archaeological substratum of this concept is the ancient Hellenic idea of *kalokagathia* – the fusion of the beautiful and the good (see chapter three of Norton's *The Beautiful Soul: Aesthetic Morality in the Eighteenth Century*, 100–135). Norton's book is an admirable historical synthesis which goes far beyond the schematic account of the German incarnations of the "beautiful soul" that must suffice for my own interpretive purposes as I read *Le Grand Meaulnes* and the passage from Romanticism to Modernism. A more complete presentation of the "beautiful soul" in its eighteenth-century guises would have to include its most famous French-language representation – in Jean-Jacques Rousseau's *Julie, ou la Nouvelle Héloïse* (1761), where the heroine and Saint Preux are designated explicitly as "de belles âmes."

13 Friedrich Schiller, "Über Anmut und Würde," *Theoretische Schriften*, 370–71; my translation.

14 Friedrich Schiller, *On the Aesthetic Education of Man in a Series of Letters*, 110, 111–12; "Über die ästhetische Erziehung des Menschen, in einer Reihe von Briefen," 645, 646–48.

15 For a complete description of the origins of this friendship, and for a detailed report on the evolution of von Klettenberg's religious beliefs in their cultural and historical context, see the introduction by Heinrich Funck to the volume *Die Schöne Seele: Bekenntnisse, Schriften und Briefe der Susanna Katharina von Klettenberg*. Since the notion of the beautiful soul is based on a correspondence between the exterior beauty of a person and his or her moral qualities, the presence of Lavater behind the scenes in the "Confessions" is by no means a matter of coincidence. It is Lavater who developed the very precise system of physiognomy by which the examination of a person's features (the size and shape of the nose, ears, mouth, and, especially, the cranium) might open the door to his or her character. Balzac made ample use of Lavater's theories in his *La Comédie Humaine*.

16 On this point see Funck, *Die Schöne Seele*, 48.

17 Shortly after the publication of *Wilhelm Meister* in 1795, Goethe's mother writes to her son and observes: "You should be grateful that, after so many years, you were able to erect such a monument to the memory of the unforgettable Klettenberg; now she can still do good after her death" (Letter quoted by Funck, *Die Schöne Seele*, 5; my translation). In his letter of 17 August 1795 to Goethe, Schiller remarks that the "Confessions of a Beautiful Soul" should be understood "in its pure form" as "representation of beautiful morality [*Darstellung schöner Sittlichkeit*] or of the becoming-human of saintliness, and in this sense, [as] the only authentic aesthetic religion" (cited by Hannelore Schlaffer in her "Nachwort" to Johann Wilhelm von Goethe, *Wilhelm Meisters Lehrjahre*, 657; my translation).

18 See on this point Eric Blackall's judgment: "She [The Beautiful Soul] knows the attractions of the world but shrinks from them into a cultivation of the moral self and that only. She tells her story entirely from the standpoint of what she has persuaded herself to believe. It is a consistent – and, at times, frantic – piece of self-justification: and the statement at the end that she knows no pride is hardly convincing. Nevertheless it is an ordered world – but ordered only because it omits what is disruptive of its calm" (*Goethe and the Novel*, 129).

In an interesting psychocritical study of the "Confessions," Frederick Beharriell writes: "Goethe's intention from the first was to incorporate into the autobiography his own subtle exposé of the psychological roots of religiosity. In addition to the surface meaning, the perceptive reader was to find also a materialistic, psychological attack on, and explaining away of what Goethe had come to regard as fanaticism. And this was to be done through the words of the unsuspecting subject herself . . . Goethe seems, clearly, to be saying that this Beautiful Soul's pietism is a form of sexual neurosis, a sublimation, as Freud would later have said, of neurotically suppressed sexual energy" ("The Hidden Meanings of Goethe's 'Bekenntnisse einer schönen Seele,'" 41, 48).

19 Johann Wolfgang von Goethe, *Wilhelm Meister's Apprenticeship*, 248; *Wilhelm Meisters Lehrjahre*, 427.

20 On the issue of Novalis as "target" of Hegel's reflections, see the notes of Jean Hyppolite in his French translation *La Phénoménologie de l'Esprit*, vol. II, 186–89, as well as his detailed commentary on the paragraph on the "beautiful soul" in *Genesis and Structure of Hegel's 'Phenomenology of Spirit,'* 512–17; and Charles Taylor, *Hegel*, 194–95.

21 G. W. F. Hegel, *Phenomenology of Spirit*, 398, 400; *Phänomenologie des Geistes*, 462, 463.

22 Jean Hyppolite, *Genesis and Structure of Hegel's 'Phenomenology of Spirit,'* 517.

23 It goes without saying that the names of Schiller, Goethe, and Hegel represent only one "branch" of this reflection on and about Romanticism. As Jean-Luc Nancy and Philippe Lacoue-Labarthe have demonstrated in their magisterial presentation of the first German Romanticism, that of the brothers Schlegel and the *Athenaeum*, the dialectic of "creation" and of "chemical" reflection which inhabits Romanticism at its origins has produced what we call literary theory today (see *L'Absolu littéraire: Théorie de la littérature du romantisme allemand*).

24 Marcel Proust, *Le Temps retrouvé*, vol. IV of *A la recherche du temps perdu*, 490.

25 Rainer Maria Rilke, *Duino Elegies and The Sonnets to Orpheus*, 20, 22.

6 PROUST AND KAFKA: UNCANNY NARRATIVE OPENINGS

1 As will become apparent later in this chapter, the threshold-moments in Proust and Kafka combine an elision or abolition of chronological time with the creation of a fictional topography. With the beginning of narrative temporality, there is spatial differentiation and definition. For a discussion of the time–space continuum throughout the history of the novel, see Bakhtin's analysis of the *chronotope*, defined as "the intrinsic connectedness of temporal and spatial relationships that are artistically expressed in literature" ("Forms of Time and Chronotope in the Novel," 84). My study of the opening of narrative space in Proust and Kafka involves an examination of the *threshold chronotope*, which "is connected with the breaking point of a life, the moment of crisis, the decision that changes a life (or the indecisiveness that fails to change a life, the fear to step over the threshold)" (ibid., 248).

2 Painter's biography, published in two volumes in 1959 and 1965, remains an excellent study of Proust's life. Specialists of Proust generally agree, however, that this account has now been superseded by Jean-Yves Tadié's *Marcel Proust: biographie* (1996), which is both less speculative than Painter's study and richer in primary documentation.

3 For a close reading of "Das Urteil" which addresses the issue of the story's polyvalent significance (its "undecidability" and "abyss of meaning"), see the second chapter of Stanley Corngold's *Franz Kafka: The Necessity of Form*, entitled "The Hermeneutic of 'The Judgment'" (24–46). Corngold's book is important not only for its imaginative readings of individual Kafka

texts, but also for its contextualization of Kafka's writing within literary history.

4 The book *Figures III* (1972) is composed of two distinct parts. The first contains three essays that are related to each other only in a very loose thematic way, entitled "Poétique et histoire" (13–20), "La Rhétorique restreinte" (21–40), and "Métonymie chez Proust" (41–63). The second part, "Discours du récit" (67–273), is a self-contained expository development on narrative which was translated into English by Jane E. Lewin in 1980 as *Narrative Discourse: An Essay in Method*, and soon became one of the foundational texts of the field of narratology. The treatise provoked so much commentary that Genette, in 1983, published *Nouveau discours du récit* (English translation: *Narrative Discourse Revisited*, 1988) as a rejoinder to his critics and as a refinement of his theoretical terminology.

5 Genette's treatment of the polar opposition between the rhetorical figures of metaphor and metonymy owes a great deal to Roman Jakobson's groundbreaking article "Deux aspects du langage et deux types d'aphasies."

6 This is the somewhat inflated term used on the back cover of *Figures III* to advertise the book. Genette is much more modest, and also very conscious of the dangers of teminological inflation, in his excellent cautionary "Après-Propos" (269–73).

7 In his "Letter on Humanism" (1947), Heidegger reiterates in shortened and somewhat elliptical form what he had expressed in *Sein und Zeit* (1927), namely, that in a philosophical search for the pure experience of Being, one must free oneself from the utilitarian mode of thought as *techné* – "a process of reflection in service to doing and making" (194). Once philosophy becomes a mere means to the end of practical living or acting, speech itself falls under the technological imperative, which Heidegger describes as "the dictatorship of the public realm" (197). I am suggesting here that Genette's practical use of the *Recherche* as exemplification/illustration of narrative laws, despite its considerable intrinsic merit, cannot retain the analytical *nearness* to the source of Proustian rhetorical complexity that is achieved in "Métonymie chez Proust."

8 References are to *Remembrance of Things Past*, trans. C. K. Scott Moncrieff and Terence Kilmartin, 3 vols. (New York: Random House, 1981), abbreviated *RTP*; and *A la recherche du temps perdu*, 4 vols. (Paris: Gallimard-Pléiade, 1987–89), abbreviated *ALR*.

9 For an examination of the Venice episode in the light of its *avant-textes* in *Contre Sainte-Beuve* and *Jean Santeuil*, see my article "Proust's 'Venice': The Reinscription of Textual Sources."

10 I am referring here to Proust's brilliant stylistic study of Flaubert's revolutionary use of time (narrative temporality), "A Propos du 'style' de Flaubert." Proust wrote his essay as a polite but firm polemical rejoinder to Albert Thibaudet, who had declared, in his November 1919 *NRF* article "Une querelle littéraire sur le style de Flaubert," that Flaubert was a poor stylist and, therefore, not a great writer: "Flaubert n'est pas un grand écrivain

de race . . . la pleine maîtrise verbale ne lui était pas donnée dans sa nature même" ("Flaubert is not a great 'born writer' . . . he did not possess complete verbal mastery in its essence") (quoted in Marcel Proust, *Contre Sainte-Beuve*, 944, note 2).

11 Proust comments on this poem in "Sainte-Beuve et Baudelaire." The author of the *Recherche* was an admirer of Baudelaire's poetic depiction of cruelty, which he attempted to justify to his mother on purely aesthetic grounds in the imaginary dialogue of *Contre Sainte-Beuve*: "I understand that you only partially admire Baudelaire. You found in his letters, as in those of Stendhal, cruel remarks about his family. And he is cruel in his poetry, cruel with infinite sensitivity. His harshness is the more astonishing in that one senses that he felt acutely and deeply the sufferings he mocks with such nonchalance" (250; my translation and emphasis).

12 "Journées de pèlerinage" was first published in the *Mercure de France*, April 1900. Proust combined it with another essay, entitled "John Ruskin" (*Gazette des Beaux-Arts* [*La Chronique des Arts et de la Curiosité*], April–August 1900) to form the bulk of the translator's preface to *La Bible d'Amiens*. For critical assessments of the essays "Journées de pèlerinage" and "John Ruskin," see the first chapter of Walter Kasell's book *Marcel Proust and the Strategy of Reading*, entitled "The Pilgrimage: Proust Reads Ruskin" (18–30); Richard Macksey, "Proust on the Margins of Ruskin," and his excellent critical introduction to the volume *Marcel Proust On Reading Ruskin*; and the third chapter of my *The Reading of Proust*, entitled "Proust Reads Ruskin" (61–95).

13 See Proust's commentary on Ruskin's thematic or "polyphonic" use of the word *Sesame* at the beginning of the translator's notes to *Sésame et les lys*. Proust found as many as seven levels of meaning in the one word – an interesting (possible) foreshadowing of Vinteuil's Septet and the seven volumes of the *Recherche*.

14 No traces of the Phoenician colony of Baalbek remain today, but tourists who have explored the archaeological riches of the Middle East know that the Roman ruins of Baalbek are among the most impressive in the area, notably the temples to Jupiter and Bacchus.

15 The Venice section of *Albertine disparue* is everywhere tinged with the colors of *The Stones of Venice* (1851–53), Ruskin's powerful apocalyptic allegory of artistic and civic decline. But whereas Ruskin was concerned with depicting the public pride and ruin of the city, Proust's Venice is the site of the protagonist's private encounter with the retroactively revealed truth of Albertine's wayward existence. Venice is the third and final stage of Marcel's forgetting of Albertine, and the first step toward his discovery of an artistic vocation.

16 "The Uncanny," 220. As we saw in chapter three, the word "uncanny" translates the German "unheimlich," which is linked etymologically to words such as *Geheimnis* (secret), *Heim* (home) and *Heimat* (native-land). Thus the uncanny – the exotic, that which inspires fear or repulsion – is connected, through language, to that which is secretive, private, homelike.

17 My translation. This phrase, and the longer sentence that surrounds it, are, curiously, left out of the 1981 Moncrieff-Kilmartin translation, even though the sentence in its entirety is to be found in the 1954 Pléiade edition of the *Recherche* (III, 627).

18 Much of the theological criticism derives from the purported influence of Kierkegaard on Kafka. The first (and still in some ways most powerful, though debatable) assessment of the religious themes in Kafka's writings and of the turn toward religious thinkers in the author's later years can be found in Max Brod's *Biography*, chapter six. For a detailed textual study of "messianism" in *The Castle*, see W. G. Sebald. On existential/philosphical questions, see the works listed in the bibliography by Douglas Angus, Maurice Friedman, Judith Ryan, and Walter Sokel ("The Programme of K's Court").

For English-speaking readers of Kafka, the best overview of the complex Marxist debate on Kafka is contained in the collection of critical essays edited by Kenneth Hughes, *Franz Kafka: An Anthology of Marxist Criticism.* Readers with an antiquarian interest in politically motivated contextualizations of Kafka's writings will wish to consult Hughes's account of the Kafka conference held in Liblice (near Prague) in 1963, entitled "The Marxist Debate." See also Klaus Hermsdorf on the literary reception of Kafka in the erstwhile GDR; and Roger Garaudy on Kafka's "alienation."

Beginning in the late seventies, one can find creative and revealing psychocritical readings, including those by Charles Bernheimer (a structural *and* psychoanalytical juxtaposition of Flaubert and Kafka); Hartmut Böhme (on Kafka's "narcissism"); Margot Norris ("Sadism and Masochism in Two Kafka Stories"); Herman Rapaport (on the "relays of desire" in Kafka); and Walter Sokel ("Freud and the Magic of Kafka's Writing").

More recently, self-referential interpretations have grown by leaps and bounds, due to the influence of contemporary French critical thought, especially the writings of Lacan and Derrida. Notable readings of this sort include those by Marjanne Goozé, John Kopper, Henry Sussman, and Margot Norris (*Beasts of the Modern Imagination*).

19 It is a critical commonplace that Kafka's linguistic and cultural alienation affected, or even "produced" his sober, unadorned prose style. For an especially cogent analysis of Kafka's language as "minor literature," or literature of aterritorial intensification, see Gilles Deleuze and Félix Guattari, chapter three of *Kafka: Toward a Minor Literature.* For an assessment of the way in which Kafka treats the speech patterns of his fictional characters, see Marthe Robert, *The Old and the New*, especially the chapter entitled "Momus and Mockery."

20 I quote from the following: *The Diaries of Franz Kafka: 1910–1913*, trans. Joseph Kresh (New York: Schocken, 1965), abbreviated *D*; and Franz Kafka, *Tagebücher*, ed. Hans-Gerd Koch, Michael Müller and Malcolm Pasley (Frankfurt am Main: Fischer, 1990), abbreviated *T*.

21 The *Letter* was not only undelivered, but, because of its brutal frankness and accusatory tone, also undeliverable. It is intriguing to imagine how Hermann Kafka might have responded, had he received his son's message. Nadine Gordimer (whose fictional universe is more often South Africa than Central Europe) has attempted to recreate just such a response, in her excellent parody entitled "Letter from His Father." Although Gordimer lends Hermann Kafka a rather stiff, somewhat "literary" style, perhaps more in keeping with some of his son's fictional creations than with what is known of the Prague shopkeeper's expressiveness, the father's "answer" is an eloquent, brilliantly ironical rejoinder to the son's rather devious rhetoric of lamentation/self-justification.

22 References are to Franz Kafka, *Letter to His Father* (New York: Schocken Bilingual Edition, 1966), for the English translation (abbreviated *L*); and *Brief an den Vater*, ed. Joachim Unseld (Fischer, Facsimile Edition, 1994), for the German text (abbreviated *B*). The facsimile edition is interesting not only for its clear photographic reproduction of the letter in its original form (in which one notices, among other things, with what obvious fluidity the *Letter* was written – it contains very few corrections or false starts), but also for Joachim Unseld's informative "Nachwort" (187–238).

23 In pursuing the dual meaning of the word *Schloß*, I treat it as an *exemplum* of what Freud (following Karl Abel) called the "antithetical sense of primal words." For a good general discussion of Kafka's "primal words" and the connection to Freud's notion of psychological "ambivalence," see Marthe Robert, *As Lonely as Franz Kafka*, 153–57.

24 References are to Franz Kafka, *The Castle*, trans. Willa and Edwin Muir (Schocken, 1982) (abbreviated *C*); and to the paperback edition of *Das Schloß* published by Fischer in 1994 (abbreviated *S*). The 1994 edition, which is described on the title-page as "in der Fassung der Handschrift," is based upon the critical edition of *Das Schloß* established in 1981 by Malcolm Pasley (also published by Fischer).

25 Marjanne Goozé interprets allegorically (i.e., in the mode of textual self-reflection) Amalia's refusal to read: "The text, through the employment of subjunctive mood and extensive narrative layers, does not permit one to grasp the text as K. does Klamm's letters. If one attempts to interpret as K., one gets just as lost and confused as he. Kafka's text demands that the reader, like Amalia, actively question interpretation and even the form of the text itself" ("Texts, Textuality, and Silence in Franz Kafka's *Das Schloß*," 350).

26 *Das Schloß* is the story of what one might call the absent presence of the scribal law: writing, in the form of messages, delivered and undelivered, is infinite in its extension but impossible to localize, impossible for the land-surveyor to map. Kafka presents us with a quite different scenario in his short story "In der Strafkolonie" ["In the Penal Colony"], where writing appears with painful precision as an inscription on the body. Here, writing is again part

of the Law, but in this case we readers witness the "application" of the Law as writing in the form of a mad, mechanical cruelty.

7 TEXTUALIZING IMMORALISM: CONRAD'S *HEART OF DARKNESS* AND GIDE'S *L'IMMORALISTE*

1 I refer to André Gide's use of the term *récit.* In a diary entry of 12 July 1914, while retroactively examining the not-so-apparent affinities that relate the sulfurous *L'Immoraliste* to the much more pious *La Porte étroite* (1909) and to the playful tone of *Les Caves du Vatican* (1914), Gide distinguishes between *Sotie* (originally a medieval allegorical/satirical farce; in Gide's use of the term, a literary burlesque), *récit* (short narrative), and *roman* (novel in the classical sense): "Why do I call this book [*Les Caves*] *Sotie*? Why have I called the three preceding ones *récits*? To establish with clarity that these are not novels. Which explains why I concluded my prefaces with the designations *Soties, récits.* Until now I have only written *ironical* [Gide's emphasis] or critical books" (*Journal* I, 808; my translation). Ironical distance coupled with conciseness of narrative design characterize all of Gide's *récits.* In both *Heart of Darkness* and *L'Immoraliste* critical or ironical distance is maintained by a complex set of narrative frames – as we shall see in due course.

2 The first critical reading that emphasizes the role of dreams and the "unconscious" in *Heart of Darkness* is that of Albert J. Guerard, in his still-influential *Conrad the Novelist* of 1958, in which Marlow's quest-journey is described as a "night journey into the unconscious" (38). Subsequent interpretations of *Heart of Darkness* often owe more, consciously or "unconsciously," to Guerard than they are willing or able to acknowledge, including, perhaps most notably, Francis Ford Coppola's film *Apocalypse Now.*

3 Until the mid-1970s most readings of both *L'Immoraliste* and *Heart of Darkness* tended to stress the works' general appeal and to downplay those textual specificities which had a potential for controversy or embarrassment in the referential spheres of morality and politics (*in particular*, Gide's homosexuality as it is transposed, masked, alluded to in *L'Immoraliste*; and Conrad's ethnocentrically expressed anti-colonialism tinged with what, according to contemporary sensibility, would have to be called racism).

In her 1953 study *André Gide, l'Insaisissable Protée*, Germaine Brée asserts that homosexuality is only one of "numerous other repressed tendencies" in Gide's *récit*, and that its function in the text is an ancillary one – that of "revealing Michel's immoralism" (159–60). The *Verneinung* of the thematic centrality of homosexuality in *L'Immoraliste* is even stronger in Albert Guerard's *André Gide* (1951; rev. edn. 1969). More recently, the books of Emily S. Apter (*André Gide and the Codes of Homotextuality*, 1987), Patrick Pollard (*André Gide: Homosexual Moralist*, 1991), and Michael Lucey (*Gide's Bent: Sexuality, Politics, Writing*, 1995) emphasize the detailed textual inscription of homosexuality.

In the case of Conrad, whereas Ian Watt, in his 1979 masterwork *Conrad in the Nineteenth Century*, states matter-of-factly that *Heart of Darkness* is not primarily concerned with racial issues and "is not essentially a political work" (160), in 1988 Chinua Achebe condemns Conrad as a "thoroughgoing racist" (see "An Image of Africa: Racism in Conrad's *Heart of Darkness*," 257). In Ross C Murfin's 1996 edition of *Heart of Darkness*, Peter J. Rabinowitz warns against the ethical danger involved in over-emphasizing the purported general significance of the novella at the expense of the specificity of racism and colonialism (see "Reader Response, Reader Responsibility: *Heart of Darkness* and the Politics of Displacement," 143).

4 The most extended discussion of *Heart of Darkness* as quest is that of Jacques Darras, in *Joseph Conrad and the West: Signs of Empire*. In the case of *L'Immoraliste*, Michel's self-liberation occurs in North Africa after a long and difficult voyage south, following a bout with illness which itself has initiatory value.

5 Robert Kimbrough's third edition in the Norton series contains documents on the Congo in the heyday of King Leopold's rule; correspondence by Conrad on his experiences in the Congo; and several critical essays on *Heart of Darkness*, including excerpts from Ian Watt's *Conrad in the Nineteenth Century* and Chinua Achebe's polemic against Conrad's "racism." Ross Murfin's edition for the St. Martin's Press/Bedford Books series includes five critical essays, each of which is itself a model, an archetype of five different modern approaches to literary analysis: reader-response criticism; feminist and gender criticism; deconstruction; New Historicism; and cultural criticism. In Murfin's framework, the novice reader will not only discover an exemplary text of literary Modernism, but also exemplary readings of that text.

6 From the forward to *L'Immoraliste*, ed. Elaine Marks and Richard Tedeschi (New York: Macmillan, 1963), iii.

7 References are to *Heart of Darkness*, ed. Ross C Murfin, Case Studies in Contemporary Criticism, 2nd edn. (Boston and New York: St. Martin's Press/Bedford Books, 1996), abbreviated *HD*.

8 I borrow this term from Ian Watt, whose subtle discussion of the stylistic "impressionism" and "symbolism" (the two notions should not be confused, as Watt lucidly demonstrates) in *Heart of Darkness* is one among many strong interpretive moments in the fourth chapter of *Conrad in the Nineteenth Century*.

9 The most important of these outbursts, which in German rhetorical terminology is called *aus der Rolle fallen*, occurs toward the end of part one, when Marlow addresses his interlocutors thus: "[Kurtz] was just a word to me. I did not see the man in the name any more than you do. Do you see him? Do you see the story? Do you see anything? It seems to me I am trying to tell you a dream" (42).

10 References are to the excellent English translation by Richard Howard, *The Immoralist* (New York: Random House/Vintage Books, 1996), abbreviated *I*; and *L'Immoraliste*, in *Romans, Recits et Soties; Oeuvres lyriques* (Paris: Gallimard-Pléiade, 1958), abbreviated *L'Imm.*

11 The best comparative studies of Gide and Conrad, which deal with both biographical and textual issues, are those of Walter Putnam – both his book *L'Aventure littéraire de Joseph Conrad et d'André Gide* and his article "Marlow, Michel et le silence des sirènes," which describes the theme of narrative dissimulation common to both *Heart of Darkness* and *L'Immoraliste.*

12 I refer here to the important study of Christopher L. Miller entitled *Blank Darkness: Africanist Discourse in French*, and specifically to the chapter "The Discoursing Heart: Conrad's 'Heart of Darkness'" (169–83). "Africanist discourse," like the literature of Orientalism as described by Edward Said, is that language which the European inserts into the blankness or darkness of the exotic Other, that Other which is conceived to possess no speech of its own. As Miller says in a pithy formula: "If Africanist discourse had not existed prior to the advent of the modern novel, one would have had to invent it. There is a 'blank' in the science of narrating that can be filled with any figure one likes and that 'Africa' has been made to fill with its emptiness" (169).

13 Critical consensus has it that the Ménalque of *L'Immoraliste* is not to be confused with the character of the same name in *Les Nourritures terrestres* (1897), but is rather, at least in part, patterned on Oscar Wilde, whose wit and outrageous behavior were both fascinating and appalling to Gide. Ménalque's life-philosophy is certainly based in part on the famous Gidian notion of *disponibilité*, but it also has a Nietzschean flavor, notably in its emphasis on *active forgetting*. In his long nocturnal conversation with Michel, Ménalque states: "C'est du parfait oubli d'hier que je crée la nouvelleté de chaque heure" ("I create each hour's newness by forgetting yesterday completely") (*L'Imm* 436; *I* 111).

14 The passage on the tales of seamen and the cracked nut is one of those textual moments that calls for analysis and has certainly received its share of diverse interpretations. For Patrick Brantlinger, who shares Fredric Jameson's views on Conrad's "impressionistic" style as aesthetic obfuscation (see Jameson's reading of *Lord Jim* in *The Political Unconscious*), the narrator's appeal to "halos" and "moonshine" is a way of blinding the reader to more essential worldly (moral and political) concerns ("*Heart of Darkness*: Anti-Imperialism, Racism, or Impressionism?"). Peter Brooks interprets the same passage in narratological terms and finds that the analogy serves as a "warning that the structure of 'framed narration' used in *Heart of Darkness* will not in this instance give a neat pattern of nested boxes, bracketed core structures, nuts within shells" ("An Unreadable Report," 256). Certainly the most extensive, if not exhaustive, commentary on the cracked-nut analogy is that of J. Hillis Miller, in his essay "*Heart of Darkness* Revisited," to which I now turn.

15 Maurice Blanchot, "Kafka et l'exigence de l'oeuvre," 131. For an analysis of this expression in narratological terms, see my essay "Blanchot: Commentary, Narration, Reference."

16 *Twilight of the Idols*, in *The Portable Nietzsche*, 465–66; *Götzen-Dämmerung*, in the *Kritische Studienausgabe*, vol. VI, 57–58.

17 *Conrad in the Nineteenth Century*, 175.

18 See, for example, Germaine Brée, who in her 1953 study finds that the frame provided by the interlocutor-friends is without clear aesthetic grounds, and who writes of "the awkwardness of a beginning novelist" who was unable to "justify Michel's long oral confession" (*André Gide, l'Insaisissable Protée*, 167; my translation). More recently, two essays bearing the influence of narratology convincingly demonstrate the complexity of narrative framing in Gide's *récit*, a complexity that in no way betrays the lack of narrative skill of a "beginning novelist": Nathaniel Wing's "The Disruptions of Irony in Gide's *L'Immoraliste*" (1980) and Vicki Mistacco's "Reading *The Immoralist*: The Relevance of Narrative Roles" (1981).

19 Perhaps the most violently worded of these reactions by Gide's close acquaintances was that of Francis Jammes. Following are excerpts from a letter that would merit close psychocritical scrutiny, which I shall leave in the original French for its full effect to be appreciated, and which, for fear of muting its rhetoric of outrage, I shall not translate: "Ah! comme se fût écrié ton Philoctète: 'Je sens qu'autour de vous la nature est malade.' La charmille amoureuse y [dans ce roman] est un hôpital, le marié [Michel] un aliéné lamentable qui n'a même pas la force du vice, sadique et pédéraste en vain. Et comme il est bien situé dans cet abominable pays Biskri où le soleil semble un lange d'enfant mort-né, un cartilage de veau qui a séjourné dans un marécage! Ce livre . . . est un cri que l'on redoute d'entendre, le gémissement larvé d'un vieillard dans une cave, le sanglot d'un Rousseau lugubre. Ce sont de terribles limbes, ce n'est qu'un vagissement. Jamais ni la vie ni la mort n'*existèrent* moins qu'ici" (Letter of Francis Jammes to André Gide dated June 1902, reprinted in the "Notice" to *L'Immoraliste* in André Gide, *Romans, Récits et Soties; Oeuvres lyriques*, 1515–16).

20 For a detailed reading of the geographical symbolism in *L'Immoraliste*, see Paul A. Fortier, *Décor et dualisme: 'L'Immoraliste' d'André Gide* (1988).

21 It is in passages such as this that one regrets the heavyhanded arrogance of Gide the serious *auteur*. Stendhal also fantasized, repeatedly, about what readers would think of him a century or two after his death, but did so with the light touch of humor, and with the quizzical uncertainty of a man who knew he could not predict future fame.

22 See Emile Benveniste, "L'Homme dans le langage." Nathaniel Wing makes good use of Benveniste's theoretical terminology in the article I have previously cited, "The Disruptions of Irony in Gide's *L'Immoraliste*." Wing summarizes Benveniste's contrastive definitions as follows: "*Histoire* . . . refer[s] to the narrated 'events' situated by the narrator in the past and which constitute the content of the story to be related; *discours* . . . refer[s] to the act of narration in the fictional present" (84).

23 Just one page after Michel's self-justificatory direct address to his listeners, at the moment of our return to the inner frame of the *histoire*, the protagonist relates his buying-spree at a flower market on the Piazza di Spagna in Rome. He fills the hotel room with a profusion of bouquets, hoping to

cheer up his wife, only to be frustrated when she breaks into tears and says: "Those flowers – the scent makes me ill." Michel's reaction to his wife's physical frailty is to destroy the flowers, and to make the interesting "mental note": "If even this little bit of spring was too much for her! ..." (*I* 152).

24 I quote from the King James translation of the Bible (Cambridge University Press, 1988), 766–67.

8 FISHING THE WATERS OF IMPERSONALITY: VIRGINIA WOOLF'S *TO THE LIGHTHOUSE*

1 Here and elsewhere in this chapter, I refer to *The Diary of Virginia Woolf*, 5 vols., ed. Anne Olivier Bell, assisted by Andrew McNeillie (New York: Harcourt Brace/Harvest Books, 1977–1984), hereafter abbreviated *DW*.

2 Virginia Woolf's lifelong fear of penetration and invasion most probably began with one particular traumatic experience – the sexual assault upon her by her half-brother, Gerald Duckworth – which she describes unflinchingly at the beginning of her "Sketch of the Past" in 1939:

> There was a slab outside the dining room door for standing dishes upon. Once when I was very small Gerald Duckworth lifted me onto this, and as I sat there he began to explore my body. I can remember the feel of his hand going under my clothes; going firmly and steadily lower and lower. I remember how I hoped that he would stop; how I stiffened and wriggled as his hand approached my private parts. But it did not stop. His hand explored my private parts too. I remember resenting, disliking it – what is the word for so dumb and mixed a feeling? It must have been strong, since I still recall it. This seems to show that a feeling about certain parts of the body; how they must not be touched; how it is wrong to allow them to be touched; must be instinctive. (quoted in Hermione Lee, *Virginia Woolf*, 123)

In the writing of the present chapter, I have frequently, and always with profit, turned to Hermione Lee's recent biography *Virginia Woolf* (New York: Knopf, 1997), hereafter abbreviated *VW*.

3 In the twenty-third chapter of *Virginia Woolf*, Hermione Lee writes perceptively of the importance of the act of reading for the author of *To the Lighthouse*: "At the heart of the pleasure of reading is the delight in a free union, like a very intimate conversation or an act of love. That longing for loss of self, entry into an other, is one of the deepest plots of her books" (404). Woolf's own description of her reading of Proust emphasizes what might be called the erotics of reading, and serves as an interesting Modernist anticipation of Roland Barthes's *Le plaisir du texte*:

> Proust so titillates my own desire for expression that I can hardly set out the sentence. Oh, if I could write like that! I cry. And at the moment such is the astonishing vibration and saturation and intensification that he procures – theres [*sic*] something sexual in it – that I feel I *can* write like that, and seize my pen and then I *can't* write like that. Scarcely anyone so stimulates the nerves of language in me; it becomes an obsession. (cited in *VW* 404)

Hermione Lee informs us that Woolf was reading Proust while writing *To the Lighthouse* (*VW* 471). In a later development of this chapter, I shall discuss Woolf's "scene of reading" and compare it to Proust's own depiction of that same primordial or primal scene.

4 See the sixth chapter of *Hamlet's Mother and Other Women*, in which Heilbrun theorizes that Joyce, in his creation of the modern Daedalus, imitated the actions of Theseus by "forgetting Ariadne," whereas "Woolf's eyes turned, albeit metaphorically, to Ariadne, and the life she might make outside of the labyrinth-palace. While Joyce's characters remained in the ancient labyrinth, the world of the old cosmology, led more and more magically, with more and more Daedalean skill and artistry, through the mazes and passages of the old life, Woolf searched for Ariadne and, looking back through Ariadne to her mother, for the passion of Pasiphae, a daughter of the sun, who began, perhaps, a new cosmology subsequently lost in the triumph of the patriarchal culture founded by Theseus after his return to Athens" (70).

5 Although *To the Lighthouse* is not as heavily dependent upon intertextual sources as the works of Eliot or Joyce, nevertheless these literary-cultural echoes provide the novel with a certain effect of depth, a broadening of scope from the idyllic locale of the Isle of Skye. The by now very large corpus of criticism on *To the Lighthouse* includes some excellent studies of these influences. On the mythic undertones of the novel, see Anne Golomb Hoffman, "Demeter and Poseidon: Fusion and Distance in *To the Lighthouse*"; Carolyn Heilbrun, chapters six (on Ariadne) and ten (on Demeter and Proserpine) of *Hamlet's Mother and Other Women*; and Deborah Guth, "Virginia Woolf: Myth and *To the Lighthouse*." The allusions to Shakespeare and Tennyson have been amply commented upon by numerous critics, but the important intertextual presence of William Cowper's "The Castaway" (notably, the lines uttered as a pessimistic mantra by Mr. Ramsay: "We perish each alone: / But I beneath a rougher sea, / And whelm'd in deeper gulphs than he") had been only touched upon until the important detailed article of Roger D. Lund, "'We Perished Each Alone': 'The Castaway' and *To the Lighthouse*."

6 For the most part, the intertextual presence of "The Fisherman and his Wife" within *To the Lighthouse* is acknowledged in cursory fashion by critics, without regard to the context in which the fairy tale arises within Woolf's narrative. The consensus opinion – which, it seems to me, is convincing as far as it goes – is that the Grimm story is important in that it underlines Mrs. Ramsay's highhandedness and manipulation of people – the fundamental characteristics of the never-satisfied and domineering Fisherman's Wife. On this point, see, for example, chapter three of Maria DiBattista's *Virginia Woolf's Major Novels: The Fables of Anon*, 81–83. Although Hermione Lee also finds that the Fisherman's Wife anticipates Mrs. Ramsay in her willfulness, the biographer goes on to indicate that the folktale has polyvalent significant potential, that it contains "fluid possibilities" and "is not meant to serve as a definite analogy to the novel" (*VW* 127).

7 References throughout this chapter are to *To the Lighthouse*, with a foreword by Eudora Welty (New York: Harcourt Brace/Harvest Books, 1989), hereafter abbreviated *TL*.

8 In the Grimm story, the turning of the water's color toward the unsettling and violent hues of purple and dark blue echoes, in a painterly form of pathetic fallacy, the anger of God as it develops, with increasing ferocity, against a woman who wishes to be His equal. There is a subtle repetition of this color-motif in part two of *To the Lighthouse*, when the death and destruction of the Great War are evoked. English citizens going down to the beach during this time of distress for rest and introspection are reminded, by the passing of the occasional warship, of the events taking place across the Channel. This interrupted meditation occurs in the erasure of the sublime by the welling-up of bloody waters:

> There was the silent apparition of an ashen-coloured ship for instance, come, gone; there was a purplish stain upon the bland surface of the sea as if something had boiled and bled, invisibly, beneath. This intrusion into a scene calculated to stir the most sublime reflections and lead to the most comfortable conclusions stayed their pacing. It was difficult blandly to overlook them; to abolish their significance in the landscape; to continue, as one walked by the sea, to marvel how beauty outside mirrored beauty within. (133–34)

9 Immanuel Kant, *Critique of Practical Reason*, 30. See my discussion of this proposition in context, in chapter one.

10 My remarks on the Grimm fairy tale will be based upon the text "Von dem Fischer und seiner Frau" as translated from the Low German (Plattdeutsch) by Uwe Johnson. The story is included in the volume *Deutsche Märchen*, ed. Elisabeth Borchers (Frankfurt am Main: Insel, 1979), 158–66. References are to this edition, abbreviated F. English translations of the Grimm tale are mine.

11 This theme-and-variations technique based upon increasing size is not unique to "The Fisherman and his Wife," of course, but is part of the stock-in-trade of fairy tales. See, for example, Hans Christian Andersen's "The Tinder Box," in which the soldier searching for money must encounter three dogs: the guardian of the copper coins, whose eyes are as big as teacups; the guardian of the silver coins, whose eyes are as big as millwheels; and the guardian of the gold coins, whose eyes are as big as round towers ("The Tinder Box," *The Complete Andersen*, 1–7).

12 Even otherwise perceptive critics have fallen into this trap. Anne Golomb Hoffman, for example, asserts that Mrs. Ramsay "has labored long in the preparation" of the dinner ("Demeter and Poseidon," 190). For an analysis of the class bias that penetrates Woolf's treatment of servants in her novel, see Mary Lou Emery, "'Robbed of Meaning': The Work at the Center of *To the Lighthouse*."

13 Woolf returns to the Neptune motif humorously in the final chapter of the novel, when she compares Carmichael (who is pausing with Lily to observe

the successful landing of the expedition at the Lighthouse) to the god of the sea: "'He [Mr. Ramsay] has landed,' she [Lily] said aloud. 'It is finished.' Then, surging up, puffing slightly, old Mr. Carmichael stood beside her, looking like an old pagan god, shaggy, with weeds and the trident (it was only a French novel) in his hand. He stood by her on the edge of the lawn, swaying a little in his bulk and said, shading his eyes with his hand: 'They will have landed,' and she felt she had been right. They had not needed to speak" (208).

14 The image of fishing is not just a principal organizing image of *To the Lighthouse*; it also occupies center-stage in *A Room of One's Own*. Perhaps the most striking use of the image occurs near the beginning of the essay, when Woolf describes her first attempts at wrestling with the theme that has been proposed to her – "women and fiction" – and which she will take such a long time arriving at (the theme of "women and fiction," properly speaking, is the constantly deferred goal of Woolf's thought-expedition, her (and the reader's) longed-for Ithaca):

> The collar I have spoken of, women and fiction, the need of coming to some conclusion on a subject that raises all sorts of prejudices and passions, bowed my head to the ground. To the right and left bushes of some sort, golden and crimson, glowed with the colour, even it seemed burnt with the heat, of fire . . . There one might have sat the clock round lost in thought. Thought – to call it by a prouder name than it deserved – had let its line down into the stream. It swayed, minute after minute, hither and thither among the reflections and the weeds, letting the water lift it and sink it, until – you know the little tug – the sudden conglomeration of an idea at the end of one's line: and then the cautious hauling of it in, and the careful laying of it out? Alas, laid on the grass how small, how insignificant this thought of mine looked; the sort of fish that a good fisherman puts back into the water so that it may grow fatter and be one day worth cooking and eating. (5)

15 On this point, see the first chapter of my *Of Words and the World: Referential Anxiety in Contemporary French Fiction*, and also the epilogue to the present study.

EPILOGUE: NARRATIVE AND MUSIC IN KAFKA AND BLANCHOT: THE "SINGING" OF JOSEFINE

1 Jean-Paul Sartre, "*Aminadab*, ou du fantastique considéré comme un langage" (*Situations I*, 122–42).

2 For an excellent analysis of the five texts Blanchot explicitly designated as *récits*, see Brian T. Fitch, *Lire les récits de Maurice Blanchot*. In the second chapter of his book, Fitch discusses the distinction Blanchot makes between *roman* and *récit* – a distinction I shall be concerned with later in this epilogue.

3 Maurice Blanchot, "Kafka et l'exigence de l'oeuvre," originally published in 1958 and included in *De Kafka à Kafka*, 94–131; all translations from Blanchot are my own. Michel Foucault makes reference to the "ruissellement du

dehors éternel" in his essay "La penseé du dehors." For an English translation of this essay in conjunction with a translation of Blanchot's *Michel Foucault tel que je l'imagine*, see *Foucault/Blanchot*.

4 For reasons of economy I am focusing uniquely on "Josefine" in this epilogue. A more thorough examination of the multiple meanings of music for Kafka in his later writings would have to take into account the convoluted story written in 1922 entitled "Forschungen eines Hundes" ["Investigations of a Dog"]. In this tale, the canine narrator's investigations come into being after he witnesses a "musical" performance by seven dogs. The term "musical" must be used hesitantly because it is not clear, to the narrator or his readers, whether what is being performed takes place in the world of sound or in the domain of silence: "They [the seven great musical artists] did not speak, they did not sing, they remained generally silent, almost determinedly silent; but from the empty air they conjured music" ("Sie redeten nicht, sie sangen nicht, sie schwiegen im allgemeinen fast mit einer großen Verbissenheit, aber aus dem leeren Raum zauberten sie die Musik empor") ("Investigations," 281; "Forschungen," 183).

The narrator's conditional mode of discourse – his continual hesitations, within the story, between music-as-sound and music-as-silence – anticipate similar rhetorical moves in "Josefine," where the narrator cannot assert with any certainty whether the mouse folk "sings" or "pipes," or whether Josefine can be considered a singer or not. In my view, "Forschungen" is something like a long and undisciplined first draft of "Josefine."

5 Quotations from the original German are from "Josefine, die Sängerin oder das Volk der Mäuse," in *Gesammelte Werke*, vol. 4, ed. Brod (Frankfurt am Main: Fischer Taschenbuch Verlag, 1976), 200–16, abbreviated J.

6 For translations of the text into English, I shall refer to the version by Willa and Edwin Muir in *The Complete Stories* (New York: Schocken, 1971), 360–76, abbreviated JMF.

7 Most early critical readings of "Josefine" tended to emphasize the oppositional relationship between the heroine of the story and the mouse folk, while leaving in the dark the complex rhetorical position of the narrator. In recent years, this has changed. Thomas Vitzthum finds that "the narrator consciously and skillfully [uses] language to establish his art, or his artful irony, in opposition to Josefine's naïve singing" ("A Revolution in Writing: The Overthrow of Epic Storytelling by Written Narrative in Kafka's *Josefine, die Sängerin*," 275). Both Deborah Harter and Christine Lubkoll emphasize the crucial creative role of the narrator as historian of his people. Harter argues that the narrator is self-consciously concerned with his own craft as storyteller and that it is he who controls the destiny of the protagonist (see "The Artist on Trial: Kafka and Josefine, 'die Sängerin'."). According to Lubkoll, the male narrator attempts to "domesticate" the musicality of Josefine and to discredit her talents through descriptions of her "hysterical" mannerisms ("'Dies ist Kein Pfeifen': Musik und

Negation in Franz Kafkas Erzählung *Josefine, die Sängerin oder Das Volk der Mäuse*," 754).

8 Although "Josefine" is not commented upon as much as many of Kafka's earlier works, this story has been the object of increased critical interest in recent years. In my view the best close reading of the text is that of Margot Norris, "Kafka's 'Josefine': The Animal as the Negative Site of Narration," in *Beasts of the Modern Imagination*, 118–33. Norris's analysis is an excellent demonstration of the way in which the narrative movement of "Josefine" cancels itself out through the erasing of differences: "Narrative depends on the ability to sustain differences, and as Josefine's experience illustrates, it is impossible to maintain differences among the mice folk. The narrator, like Josefine, fails, and instead of being told, Josefine's story becomes negatively inscribed in this failure of the narration" (120).

9 On the alternation of pronoun forms, see Thomas Vitzthum: "Though the narrator identifies himself as one of the mouse-folk, he often seems much too outspoken, knowledgeable, and curious to be counted among their ranks. In fact, his confusing use of pronouns shows him to be sometimes one of them, sometimes not . . . Whereas in most cases the narrator does use 'wir' or 'unser' to describe his relation to the mouse-folk, he often seems to stand outside of or above the mouse-folk's tradition. He is the subverter of both the tradition and Josefine in that the very act of his writing undermines Josefine's position as Singer" ("A Revolution in Writing," 271–72).

10 It is only shortly before his death that Kafka added the second half of the title to his story. In his *Franz Kafka: Eine Biographie*, Max Brod reports Kafka's explanation of this addition in the following terms: "Solche Oder-Titel sind zwar nicht sehr hübsch, aber hier hat es vielleicht besonderen Sinn. Es hat etwas von einer Waage" ("Such 'or-titles' are certainly not very pretty, but in this case there may be a special meaning. There is something of a balance [or scales of justice] here") (quoted in Christine Lubkoll, "'Dies ist Kein Pfeifen'," 756; my translation). There is an interesting development on the juridical connotations of the image of the scales in Lubkoll's article.

11 Until now I have concentrated on narrative issues raised by "Josefine," and have (purposefully) not suggested who the protagonist and the mouse-folk might "symbolize" or "stand for." Given Kafka's well-documented interest in Judaism, Zionism, and the Hebrew language during the last six years or so of his life, Robert Alter's proposal to equate the mouse folk with the Jewish people in its historical reality is no doubt one of the more convincing symbolic options: "The mouse folk, leading as it does a constantly precarious existence, often in need of consolation, collectively childish yet prematurely old, haunted by a tradition of singing ('in the old days our people did sing') though fallen into an era of unmusicality, presents a whole series of correspondences to the Jewish people in its Diaspora history. Because of the analogy intimated between the real singing of the old days and the grandeur

of biblical Israel, the narrator's exposure of the true nature of Josephine's singing is not just a questioning of the possibility of sublime art but also a critique of the idea of transcendent language (Benjamin's or the Kabbalah's notion of Hebrew)" (Robert Alter, *Necessary Angels: Tradition and Modernity in Kafka, Benjamin, and Scholem*, 54).

12 Proof of this abiding interest can be found in the volume *De Kafka à Kafka*, which contains eleven essays by Blanchot on Kafka spanning a period of twenty-five years.

13 References are to "Le chant des sirènes," *Le Livre à venir* (Paris: Folio "Essais," 1959), 9–18, abbreviated CS. Translations of Blanchot are mine.

14 In fact, the narrative situation is more complicated than Blanchot's rapid description indicates. When Ulysses passes by the Sirens, what he does not hear is the Sirens' own narrative summary of the Trojan War, which they profess to "know" in its entirety and in its essence:

> We know all the pains that the Greeks and Trojans once endured
> on the spreading plain of Troy when the Gods willed it so –
> all that comes to pass on the fertile earth, we know it all!
> (*The Odyssey* 12. 205–7).

Thus it would be more accurate to say that we move from "episode" (the cryptic telling of the War in its fundamental meaning to us readers, but not to Ulysses) to "ode" to "episode." There is, within the Sirens' episode in *The Odyssey*, a *mise en abyme* of narrative itself which Blanchot does not initially "hear" before he passes on toward his own allegory of narrative.

15 References are to "La voix narrative, le 'il,' le neutre,' in *De Kafka à Kafka* (Paris: Gallimard "Idées," 1981), 171–84, abbreviated VN.

16 Jacques Derrida, *Parages*, 150; my translation.

17 Given the thematic parameters of this epilogue, and for reasons of discursive clarity, I have decided to focus on two of Blanchot's theoretical writings as they relate to Kafka's "Josefine," without reference to Blanchot's own fictional texts, those constructs of the *voix narrative* that defy the "optic mode" of critical analysis. The reader who would like to "see" the narrativizing of *le neutre* as radical exteriority might wish to read the passage in *Au moment voulu* (1951) in which the narrating voice finds himself/itself projected to the "outside of things." This section begins on p. 92 with the observation "je compris que je me trouvai là-bas, dans le froid léger, calme, nullement désagréable du dehors" ("I understood that I found myself over there, in the light, calm and in no way unpleasant cold of the outside") and concludes on p. 94 with the interrogative gesture: "Et qu'étais-je donc si je n'étais pas ce reflet d'une figure qui ne parlait pas et à qui personne ne parlait, seulement capable, appuyé sur la tranquillité sans fin du dehors, d'interroger, de l'autre côté d'une vitre, silencieusement le monde?" ("And so who was I if I was not this reflection of a figure that did not speak and to whom no one spoke, only capable, resting upon the infinite tranquillity

of the outside, of questioning the world in silence from the other side of a window?").

18 Franz Kafka, *Diaries 1914–1923*, 213–14; *Tagebücher 1910–1923*, 414; my emphasis.

19 For a development of the distinction between the writer's social self and his *moi profond*, see Marcel Proust, "La Méthode de Sainte-Beuve," 132–36.

Works cited

Achebe, Chinua. "An Image of Africa: Racism in Conrad's *Heart of Darkness*." In *Heart of Darkness*. Ed. Robert Kimbrough. 3rd edn. Norton Critical Edition. New York: Norton, 1988. Pp. 251–62.

Alain-Fournier. *Le Grand Meaulnes*. Ed. Alain Rivière and Daniel Leuwers. Intro. Jacques Rivière. Paris: Classiques Garnier, 1991.

Le Grand Meaulnes. Ed. Claude Herzfeld. Paris: Nizet, 1983.

Le Grand Meaulnes. Ed. Daniel Leuwers. Paris: Livre de Poche, 1983.

Alter, Robert. *Necessary Angels: Tradition and Modernity in Kafka, Benjamin, and Scholem*. Cambridge: Harvard University Press, 1991.

Andersen, Hans Christian. "The Tinder Box." *The Complete Andersen*. Trans. Jean Hersholt. New York: The Heritage Press, 1949. Pp. 1–7.

Angus, Douglas. "The Existentialist and The Diabolical Machine." *Criticism* 6 (Spring 1964): 134–43.

Apter, Emily. *André Gide and the Codes of Homotextuality*. Stanford French and Italian Studies 48. Saratoga: Anma Libri, 1987.

Auden, W. H. "Balaam and His Ass." *The Dyer's Hand and Other Essays*. New York: Random House, 1962. Pp. 107–45.

Bakhtin, M. M. "Forms of Time and Chronotope in the Novel." *The Dialogic Imagination: Four Essays*. Ed. Michael Holquist. Trans. Caryl Emerson and Michael Holquist. Austin: University of Texas Press, 1981.

Barthes, Roland. *Le Plaisir du texte*. Collection "Tel Quel." Paris: Seuil, 1973.

The Pleasure of the Text. Trans. Richard Miller. New York: Hill and Wang, 1975.

Baudelaire,Charles. "Richard Wagner et *Tannhäuser* à Paris." *Oeuvres complètes*. Vol. II. Ed. Claude Pichois. Paris: Gallimard-Pléiade, 1976. 779–815.

"Le Thyrse." *Oeuvres complètes*. Vol. I. Ed. Claude Pichois. Paris: Gallimard-Pléiade, 1975. 335–36.

"The Thyrsus." *The Parisian Prowler: 'Le Spleen de Paris / Les Petits poèmes en prose' by Charles Baudelaire*. Trans. Edward K. Kaplan. Athens and London: The University of Georgia Press, 1989. 86–87.

Beharriell, Frederick. "The Hidden Meanings of Goethe's 'Bekenntnisse einer schönen Seele.'" *Lebendige Form: Interpretationen zur deutschen Literatur*. Festschrift for Heinrich Henel. Ed. Jeffrey Sammons and Ernst Schürer. Munich: Fink, 1970. Pp. 37–62.

Benveniste, Emile. "L'Homme dans le langage." *Problèmes de linguistique générale.* Paris: Gallimard, 1966. Pp. 225–88.
Bernheimer, Charles. *Flaubert and Kafka: Studies in Psychopoetic Structure.* New Haven: Yale University Press, 1982.
Blackall, Eric. *Goethe and the Novel.* Ithaca: Cornell University Press, 1976.
Blanchot, Maurice. *L'Attente l'oubli.* Paris: Gallimard, 1962.
Au moment voulu. Paris: Gallimard, 1951.
"Le chant des sirènes." *Le Livre à venir.* Paris: Folio "Essais," 1959. Pp. 9–18.
"Kafka et l'exigence de l'oeuvre." *De Kafka à Kafka.* Paris: Gallimard "Idées," 1981. Pp. 94–131.
"La voix narrative, le 'il,' le neutre." *De Kafka à Kafka.* Paris: Gallimard "Idées," 1981. Pp. 171–84.
Bloom, Harold. "Freud and the Sublime: A Catastrophe Theory of Creativity." *Agon: Towards a Theory of Revisionism.* New York: Oxford University Press, 1982. Pp. 91–118.
Böhme, Hartmut. "'Mutter Milena': Zum Narzissismus-Problem bei Kafka." *Germanisch-Romanische Monatschrift.* NS 28 (1978): 50–69.
Bouraoui, H. A. *Structure intentionnelle du 'Grand Meaulnes': vers le poème romancé.* Paris: Nizet, 1976.
Brantlinger, Patrick. "*Heart of Darkness*: Anti-Imperialism, Racism, or Impressionism?" In *Heart of Darkness.* 2nd edn. Ed. Ross C Murfin. Case Studies in Contemporary Criticism. Boston and New York: St. Martin's Press / Bedford Books. 1996. Pp. 277–98.
Brée, Germaine. *André Gide, l'Insaisissable Protée.* Paris: Les Belles Lettres, 1953.
Brod, Max. *Franz Kafka: A Biography.* Trans. G. Humphreys Roberts. New York: Schocken, 1947.
Franz Kafka, Eine Biographie: Erinnerungen und Dokumente. New York: Schocken, 1946.
Brooks, Peter. "Freud's Masterplot." *Reading for the Plot: Design and Intention in Narrative.* New York: Random House / Vintage Books, 1985. Pp. 90–112.
"An Unreadable Report: Conrad's *Heart of Darkness.*" *Reading for the Plot: Design and Intention in Narrative.* New York: Random House / Vintage Books, 1985. Pp. 238–63.
Buisine, Alain. *Les Mauvaises Pensées du Grand Meaulnes.* Paris: Presses Universitaires de France, 1992.
Burke, Edmund. *A Philosophical Enquiry into the Origin of our Ideas of the Sublime and Beautiful.* Ed. and intro. J. T. Boulton. New York: Columbia University Press, 1958.
Cassirer, Ernst. *Kant's Life and Thought.* Trans. James Haden. Intro. Stephan Körner. New Haven: Yale University Press, 1981.
Cellier, Léon. '*Le Grand Meaulnes' ou l'initiation manquée.* Paris: Minard, 1963.
Chai, Leon. *Aestheticism: The Religion of Art in Post-Romantic Literature.* New York: Columbia University Press, 1990.
Chambers, Ross. *Mélancolie et opposition: Les débuts du modernisme en France.* Paris: Corti, 1987.

Cixous, Hélène. "Fiction and its Phantoms: A Reading of Freud's *Das Unheimliche* (The 'Uncanny')." *New Literary History* 7 (Spring 1976): 525–48.
Cohen, Ted. "Why Beauty is a Symbol of Morality." In *Essays in Kant's Aesthetics.* Ed. Ted Cohen and Paul Guyer. Chicago: Chicago University Press, 1982. Pp. 221–36.
Coleridge, Samuel Taylor. *Lecture VII. Selected Poetry and Prose.* 2nd enlarged edn. Ed. and intro. Elisabeth Schneider. San Francisco: Rinehart Press, 1971. Pp. 449–60.
Conrad, Joseph. *Heart of Darkness.* Ed. Robert Kimbrough. 3rd edn. Norton Critical Edition. New York: Norton, 1988.
Heart of Darkness. Ed. Ross C Murfin. 2nd edn. Case Studies in Contemporary Criticism. Boston and New York: St. Martin's Press / Bedford Books, 1996.
Corngold, Stanley. *Franz Kafka: The Necessity of Form.* Ithaca: Cornell University Press, 1988.
Darras, Jacques. *Joseph Conrad and the West: Signs of Empire.* Trans. Anne Luyat and Jacques Darras. London: The Macmillan Press, 1982.
Deleuze, Gilles. *Kant's Critical Philosophy: The Doctrine of the Faculties.* Trans. Hugh Tomlinson and Barbara Habberjam. Minneapolis: University of Minnesota Press, 1984.
Deleuze, Gilles and Félix Guattari. *Kafka: Toward a Minor Literature.* Trans. Dana Polan. Foreword Réda Bensmaïa. Minneapolis: University of Minnesota Press, 1986.
de Man, Paul. *Aesthetic Ideology.* Ed. and Intro. Andrzej Warminski. Minneapolis: University of Minnesota Press, 1996.
Allegories of Reading: Figural Language in Rousseau, Nietzsche, Rilke, and Proust. New Haven: Yale University Press, 1979.
Derrida, Jacques. *Parages.* Paris: Galilée, 1986.
The Post Card: From Socrates to Freud and Beyond. Trans. Alan Bass. Chicago: University of Chicago Press, 1987, Pp. 257–409.
"Spéculer – Sur Freud." *La Carte postale: de Socrate à Freud et au-delà.* Paris: Flammarion, 1980. Pp. 275–437.
La Vérité en peinture. Paris: Flammarion, 1978.
DiBattista, Maria. *Virginia Woolf's Major Novels: The Fables of Anon.* New Haven: Yale University Press, 1980.
Ellison, David. "Blanchot: Commentary, Narration, Reference." *Texte* 11 (1991): 215–48.
"Proust's 'Venice': The Reinscription of Textual Sources." *Style* 22 (Fall 1988): 432–49.
"A Reading of Mallarmé's 'Hommage' (A Richard Wagner)." *Yearbook of Comparative Literature* 42 (1994): 46–56.
The Reading of Proust. Baltimore: The Johns Hopkins University Press, 1984.
"Vertiginous Storytelling: Camus's *La Chute.*" *Of Words and the World: Referential Anxiety in Contemporary French Fiction.* Princeton: Princeton University Press, 1993. Pp. 25–43.

Ellmann, Richard. *James Joyce*. Rev. edn. New York: Oxford University Press, 1983.

Emery, Mary Lou. "'Robbed of Meaning': The Work at the Center of *To the Lighthouse*." *Modern Fiction Studies* 38 (Spring 1992): 217–34.

Eysteinsson, Astradur. *The Concept of Modernism*. Ithaca: Cornell University Press, 1990.

Ferguson, Frances. *Solitude and the Sublime: Romanticism and the Aesthetics of Individuation*. New York and London: Routledge, 1992.

Fitch, Brian T. *Lire les récits de Maurice Blanchot*. Amsterdam: Rodopi, 1992.

Fortier, Paul A. *Décor et dualisme: 'L'Immoraliste' d'André Gide*. Stanford French and Italian Studies 56. Saratoga: Anma Libri, 1988.

Foucault, Michel. "La Pensée du dehors." *Critique* 229 (1966): 514–42.

Foucault, Michel and Maurice Blanchot. *'Maurice Blanchot: The Thought from Outside' and 'Michel Foucault as I Imagine Him.'* Trans. Brian Massumi and Jeffrey Mehlman under the general title *Foucault/Blanchot*. New York: Zone Books, 1990.

Freud, Sigmund. "The Antithetical Meaning of Primal Words." *The Standard Edition of the Complete Psychological Works of Sigmund Freud*. Trans. James Strachey in collaboration with Anna Freud. Assisted by Alix Strachey and Alan Tyson. Vol. XI (1910). London: The Hogarth Press, 1957. Pp. 153–61.

"James J. Putnam." *Gesammelte Werke Chronologisch Geordnet*. Vol. XII (1917–20). London: Imago, 1947. P. 315.

"James J. Putnam." *The Standard Edition of the Complete Psychological Works of Sigmund Freud*. Trans. James Strachey in collaboration with Anna Freud. Assisted by Alix Strachey and Alan Tyson. Vol. XVII (1917–19). London: The Hogarth Press, 1955. Pp. 271–72.

"Über den Gegensinn der Urworte." *Gesammelte Werke Chronologisch Geordnet*. Vol. VIII (1909–13). London: Imago, 1943. Pp. 213–21.

"The Uncanny." *The Standard Edition of the Complete Psychological Works of Sigmund Freud*. Trans. James Strachey in collaboration with Anna Freud. Assisted by Alix Strachey and Alan Tyson. Vol. XVII (1917–19). London: The Hogarth Press, 1955. Pp. 217–56.

"Das Unheimliche." *Gesammelte Werke Chronologisch Geordnet*. Vol. XII (1917–20). London: Imago. 1947. Pp. 227–68.

"Victor Tausk." *Gesammelte Werke Chronologisch Geordnet*. Vol. XII (1917–20). London: Imago, 1947. Pp. 316–18.

"Victor Tausk." *The Standard Edition of the Complete Psychological Works of Sigmund Freud*. Trans. James Strachey in collaboration with Anna Freud. Assisted by Alix Stracey and Alan Tyson. Vol. XVII (1917–19). London: The Hogarth Press, 1955. Pp. 273–75.

Friedman, Maurice. "The Problematic of Guilt and the Dialogue with the Absurd: Images of the Irrational in Kafka's *Trial*." *Review of Existential Psychology and Psychiatry* 14 (1975–76): 11–25.

Funck, Heinrich. *Die Schöne Seele: Bekenntnisse, Schriften und Briefe der Susanna Katharina von Klettenberg*. Leipzig: Insel, 1912.

Garaudy, Roger. "Kafka und die Entfremdung." In *Franz Kafka: Eine Aufsatzsammlung nach einem Symposium in Philadelphia*. Ed. Maria Luise Caputo-Meyr: Berlin: Agora, 1974. Pp. 170–80.

Gay, Peter. *Freud: A Life for Our Time*. New York, Norton, 1988.

Genette, Gérard. *Figures III*. Paris: Seuil, 1972. Trans. Jane E. Lewin, under the title *Narrative Discourse: An Essay in Method*. Ithaca: Cornell University Press, 1980.

Gide, André. *Les Faux-Monnayeurs*. Paris: Gallimard-Folio, 1972.

The Immoralist. Trans. Richard Howard. New York: Random House / Vintage Books, 1996.

L'Immoraliste; *Romans, Récits et Soties; Oeuvres lyriques*. Paris: Gallimard-Pléiade, 1958. Pp. 365–472.

L'Immoraliste. Ed. Elaine Marks and Richard Tedeschi. Macmillan Modern French Literature Series. New York: Macmillan, 1963.

L'Immoraliste. Paris: Gallimard-Folio, 1989.

Journal. Vol. 1 (1887–1925). Ed. Eric Marty. Paris: Gallimard-Pléiade, 1996.

Ginsburg, Ruth. "A Primal Scene of Reading: Freud and Hoffmann." *Literature and Psychology* 38.3 (1992): 24–46.

Goethe, Johann Wolfgang von. *Wilhelm Meister's Apprenticeship*. Ed. and Trans. Eric A. Blackall in cooperation with Victor Lange. New York: Suhrkamp, 1983.

Wilhelm Meisters Lehrjahre. Ed. Hannelore Schlaffer. Munich: Goldmann, 1990.

Goozé, Marjanne. "Texts, Textuality, and Silence in Franz Kafka's *Das Schloß*." *MLN* 98 (1984): 337–50.

Gordimer, Nadine. "Letter from His Father." *Something Out There*. New York: The Viking Press, 1979. Pp. 40–56.

Green, Ronald M. *Kierkegaard and Kant: The Hidden Debt*. Albany: State University of New York Press, 1992.

Grésillon, Almuth. *Eléments de critique génétique*. Paris: Presses Universitaires de France, 1994.

Grimm brothers. "Von dem Fischer und seiner Frau." In *Deutsche Märchen*. Ed. Elisabeth Borchers. Intro. Wolfgang Koeppen. Frankfurt am Main: Insel, 1979. Pp. 158–66.

Guerard, Albert J. *André Gide*. 2nd edn. Cambridge, MA: Harvard University Press, 1969.

Conrad the Novelist. Cambridge, MA: Harvard University Press, 1958.

Guiomar, Michel. *Inconscient et Imaginaire dans 'Le Grand Meaulnes.'* Paris: Corti, 1964.

Guth, Deborah. "Virginia Woolf: Myth and *To the Lighthouse*." *College Literature* 11 (Fall 1984): 233–49.

Guyer, Paul. "Feeling and Freedom: Kant on Aesthetics and Morality." *The Journal of Aesthetics and Art Criticism* 48 (Spring 1990): 137–46.

Kant and the Claims of Taste. Cambridge, MA: Harvard University Press, 1979.

"Kant's Conception of Fine Art." *The Journal of Aesthetics and Art Criticism* 52 (Summer 1994): 275–85.

Harter, Deborah. "The Artist on Trial: Kafka and Josefine, 'die Sängerin'." *Deutsche Vierteljahrsschrift für Literaturwissenschaft und Geistesgeschichte* 61 (March 1986): 151–62.

Hawthorne, Nathaniel. "Rappaccini's Daughter." *Mosses from an Old Manse.* Centenary Edition. Columbus: Ohio State University Press, 1974. Pp. 91–128.

Hay, Louis, ed. *La Naissance du texte.* Paris: Corti, 1989.

Hayman, Ronald. *Kafka: A Biography.* New York: Oxford University Press, 1982.

Hegel, G. W. F. *Aesthetics: Lectures on Fine Art.* 2 vols. Trans. T. M. Knox. Oxford: Oxford University Press, 1975.

Phänomenologie des Geistes. Hamburg: Felix Meiner Verlag, 1952.

La Phénoménologie de l'Esprit. Trans. Jean Hyppolite. 2 vols. Paris: Aubier-Montaigne, n.d.

Phenomenology of Spirit. Trans. A. V. Miller. Foreword J. N. Findlay. Oxford: Oxford University Press, 1977.

Vorlesungen über die Ästhetik. Vol. XII of *Sämtliche Werke,* Jubiläumsausgabe in 20 vols. Ed. Hermann Glockner. Stuttgart: Friedrich Frommann, 1964.

Heidegger, Martin. "Letter on Humanism." *Basic Writings.* Ed and intro. David Farrell Krell. New York: Harper and Row, 1977. Pp. 193–242.

Heilbrun, Carolyn G. *Hamlet's Mother and Other Women.* New York: Columbia University Press, 1990

Henrich, Dieter. "Beauty and Freedom: Schiller's Struggle with Kant's Aesthetics." In *Essays in Kant's Aesthetics.* Ed. Ted Cohen and Paul Guyer. Chicago: The University of Chicago Press, 1982. Pp. 237–57.

Hermsdorf, Klaus. "Anfänge der Kafka-Rezeption in der sozialistischen deutschen Literatur." *Weimarer Beiträge: Zeitschrift für Literaturwissenschaft, Ästhetik und Kulturtheorie* 24 (1978): 45–69.

Hertz, Neil. "Freud and the Sandman." *The End of the Line: Essays on Psychoanalysis and the Sublime.* New York: Columbia University Press, 1985. Pp. 97–121.

Hoffman, Anne Golomb. "Demeter and Poseidon: Fusion and Distance in *To the Lighthouse.*" *Studies in the Novel* 16.2 (Summer 1984): 182–96.

Hoffmann, E. T. A. "The Sandman." *Tales of Hoffmann.* Trans. and intro. R. J. Hollingdale. London: Penguin, 1982. Pp. 85–125.

"Der Sandmann." *Nachtstücke. Werke 1816–20.* Vol. III of *E. T. A. Hoffmann: Sämtliche Werke.* Ed. Hartmut Steinecke in collaboration with Gerhard Allroggen. Frankfurt am Main: Deutscher Klassiker Verlag, 1985. Pp. 11–49.

Hölderlin, Friedrich. "Brot und Wein." *Werke and Briefe.* Vol. I. Ed. Friedrich Beißner and Jochen Schmidt. Frankfurt am Main: Insel, 1969. Pp. 114–19.

Homer. *The Odyssey.* Trans. Robert Fagles. Intro. and notes Bernard Knox. New York: Penguin, 1996.

Honderich, Ted, ed. *The Oxford Companion to Philosophy.* Oxford: Oxford University Press, 1995.

Hughes, Kenneth. "The Marxist Debate, 1963." In *The Kafka Debate: New Perspectives For Our Time.* Ed. Angel Flores. New York: Gordian, 1977. Pp. 51–59.

Hughes, Kenneth, ed. and trans. *Franz Kafka: An Anthology of Marxist Criticism.* Hanover: University Press of New England, 1981.

Husson, Claudie. *Alain-Fournier et la naissance du récit.* Paris: Presses Universitaires de France, 1990.

Hyppolite, Jean. *Genesis and Structure of Hegel's 'Phenomenology of Spirit.'* Trans. Samuel Cherniak and John Heckman. Evanston: Northwestern University Press, 1974.

Jakobson, Roman. "Deux Aspects du langage et deux types d'aphasies." *Essais de linguistique générale.* Paris: Minuit, 1963. Pp. 43–67.

Jameson, Fredric. *The Political Unconscious: Narrative as a Socially Symbolic Act.* Ithaca: Cornell University Press, 1981.

Johnson, Barbara. *Défigurations du langage poétique: la seconde révolution baudelairienne.* Paris: Flammarion, 1979.

Kafka, Franz. *Brief an den Vater.* Facsimile edn. Ed. Joachim Unseld. Frankfurt am Main: Fischer Taschenbuch Verlag, 1994.

The Castle. Definitive edn. Trans. Willa and Edwin Muir. With an homage by Thomas Mann. New York: Schocken, 1982.

Diaires: 1910–1913. Ed. Max Brod. Trans. Joseph Kresh. New York: Schocken, 1965.

Diaires: 1914–1923. Ed. Max Brod. Trans. Martin Greenberg with the cooperation of Hannah Arendt. New York: Schocken, 1965.

"Forschungen eines Hundes." *Gesammelte Werke.* Vol. v. Ed. Max Brod. Frankfurt am Main: Fischer Taschenbuch Verlag, 1976. Pp. 180–215.

"In der Strafkolonie." *Gesammelte Werke.* Vol. iv. Ed. Max Brod. Frankfurt am Main: Fischer Taschenbuch Verlag, 1976. Pp. 151–77.

"In the Penal Colony." *Franz Kafka: The Complete Stories.* Ed. Nahum N. Glatzer. Trans. Willa and Edwin Muir. New York, Schocken, 1971. Pp. 140–67.

"Investigations of a Dog." *Franz Kafka: The Complete Stories.* Ed. Nahum N. Glatzer. Trans. Willa and Edwin Muir. New York: Schocken, 1971. Pp. 278–316.

"Josefine, die Sängerin oder das Volk der Mäuse." *Gesammelte Werke.* Vol. iv. Ed. Max Brod. Frankfurt am Main: Fischer Taschenbuch Verlag, 1976. Pp. 200–16.

"Josephine the Singer, or the Mouse Folk." *The Complete Stories.* Ed. Nahum N. Glatzer. Trans. Willa and Edwin Muir. New York: Schocken, 1971. Pp. 360–76.

Letter to His Father/Brief an den Vater. Bilingual edn. Trans. Ernst Kaiser and Eithne Wilkins. New York: Schocken, 1966.

Das Schloß. In der Fassung der Handschrift. Frankfurt am Main: Fischer Taschenbuch Verlag, 1996.

Tagebücher. Ed. Hans-Gerd Koch, Michael Müller and Malcolm Pasley. Frankfurt am Main: S. Fischer Verlag, 1990.

Tagebücher 1910–1923. Gesammelte Werke. Vol. VII. Ed. Max Brod. Frankfurt am Main: Fischer Taschenbuch Verlag, 1976.

Kant, Immanuel. *Critique of Judgment*. Trans. and intro. Werner S. Pluhar. Foreword Mary J. Gregor. Indianapolis: Hackett, 1987.

Critique of Practical Reason. Trans. and intro. Lewis White Beck. New York: Macmillan, 1956.

Kritik der praktischen Vernunft. Ed. Karl Vorländer. Hamburg: Felix Meiner Verlag, 1990.

Kritik der Urteilskraft. Ed. Karl Vorländer. Hamburg: Felix Meiner Verlag, 1990.

The Metaphysics of Morals. Trans. and ed. Mary Gregor. Intro. Roger L. Sullivan. Cambridge: Cambridge University Press, 1996.

Kaplan, Edward K. *Baudelaire's Prose Poems: The Esthetic, The Ethical, and the Religious in 'The Parisian Prowler.'* Athens and London: The University of Georgia Press, 1990.

Kasell, Walter. "The Pilgrimage: Proust Reads Ruskin." *Marcel Proust and the Strategy of Reading*. Amsterdam: John Benjamins, 1980. Pp. 18–30.

Kierkegaard, Søren. *"The Concept of Irony, with Continual Reference to Socrates," together with "Notes of Schelling's Berlin Lectures"*. Ed. and trans. Howard V. Hong and Edna H. Hong. Princeton: Princeton University Press, 1989.

Either/Or: Part I. Ed. and Trans. Howard V. Hong and Edna H. Hong. Princeton: Princeton University Press, 1987.

Either/Or: Part II. Ed. and Trans. Howard V. Hong and Edna H. Hong. Princeton: Princeton University Press, 1987.

Either/Or. Vol. I. Trans. David F. Swenson and Lillian Marvin Swenson. Revisions and foreword Howard A. Johnson. Princeton: Princeton University Press, 1971.

Either/Or. Vol. II. Trans. Walter Lowrie. Revisions and foreword Howard A. Johnson. Princeton: Princeton University Press, 1971.

Enten-Eller: Et Livs-Fragment. Vol. II. Copenhagen: H. Hagerup's Forlag, 1950.

Philosophical Fragments. Ed. and trans. Howard V. Hong and Edna H. Hong. Princeton: Princeton University Press, 1985.

Klein, Richard. "Straight Lines and Arabesques: Metaphors of Metaphor." *Yale French Studies* 45 (1970): 64–86.

Kleist, Heinrich von. "Über das Marionettentheater." *Sämtliche Werke und Briefe*. Vol. II. Munich: Carl Hanser Verlag, 1965. Pp. 338–45.

Kofman, Sarah. *The Childhood of Art: An Interpretation of Freud's Aesthetics*. Trans. Winifred Woodhull. New York: Columbia University Press, 1988.

"The Double is/and the Devil." *Freud and Fiction*. Trans. Sarah Wykes. Boston: Northeastern University Press, 1991. Pp. 119–62.

Kopper, John. "Building Walls and Jumping Over Them: Construction in Franz Kafka's 'Beim Bau der chinesischen Mauer.'" *MLN* 98 (1983): 351–65.

Lacoue-Labarthe, Philippe. *Musica ficta: Figures de Wagner*. Paris: Christian Bourgois, 1991.

Musica Ficta: Figures of Wagner. Trans. Felicia McCarren. Stanford: Stanford University Press, 1994.

Lacoue-Labarthe, Philippe and Jean-Luc Nancy, eds. *L'Absolu littéraire: Théorie de la littérature du romantisme allemand*. Paris: Seuil "Poétique," 1978.

Lee, Hermione. *Virginia Woolf*. New York: Knopf, 1997.

Le Petit Robert I. Paris: Les Dictionnaires Robert, 1984.

Liddell and Scott's Greek-English Lexicon. Abridged Version. London: Oxford University Press, 1966.

Lubkoll, Christine. "'Dies ist Kein Pfeifen': Musik und Negation in Franz Kafkas Erzählung 'Josefine, die Sängerin oder Das Volk der Mäuse.'" *Deutsche Vierteljahrsschrift für Literaturwissenschaft und Geistesgeschichte* 66 (December 1992): 748–64.

Lucey, Michael. *Gide's Bent: Sexuality, Politics, Writing*. New York: Oxford University Press, 1995.

Lund, Roger D. "'We Perished Each Alone': 'The Castaway' and *To the Lighthouse*." *Journal of Modern Literature* 16.1 (Summer 1989): 75–92.

Lydenberg, Robin. "Freud's Uncanny Narratives." *PMLA* 112 (October 1997): 1072–86.

Lyotard, Jean-François. *The Inhuman: Reflections on Time*. Trans. Geoffrey Bennington and Rachel Bowlby. Stanford: Stanford University Press, 1991.

Lessons on the Analytic of the Sublime. Trans. Elizabeth Rottenberg. Stanford: Stanford University Press, 1994.

Macksey, Richard. "Introduction." In *Marcel Proust on Reading Ruskin*. Trans. and ed. Jean Autret, William Burford, and Phillip J. Wolfe. New Haven: Yale University Press, 1987. Pp. xiii–liii.

"Longinus Reconsidered." *MLN* 108 (1993): 913–34.

"Proust on the Margins of Ruskin." *The John Ruskin Polygon: Essays on the Imagination of John Ruskin*. Ed. J. D. Hunt and F. M. Holland. Manchester: Manchester University Press, 1982. Pp. 172–97.

Maclean, Marie. *Le Jeu suprême: Structure et Thèmes dans 'Le Grand Meaulnes.'* Paris: Corti, 1973.

Mann, Thomas. *'Death in Venice' and Seven Other Stories*. Trans. H. T. Lowe-Porter. New York: Random House / Vintage Books, 1989.

'Der Tod in Venedig' und Andere Erzählungen. Frankfurt am Main: Fischer Taschenbuch Verlag, 1990.

Meisel, Perry. *The Myth of the Modern: A Study in British Literature and Criticism after 1850*. New Haven: Yale University Press, 1987.

Miller, Christopher L. "The Discoursing Heart: Conrad's *Heart of Darkness*." *Blank Darkness: Africanist Discourse in French*. Chicago: The University of Chicago Press, 1985. Pp. 169–83.

Miller, J. Hillis. "*Heart of Darkness* Revisited." *Heart of Darkness*. 2nd edn. Ed. Ross C Murfin. Case Studies in Contemporary Criticism. Boston and New York: St. Martin's Press / Bedford Books, 1996. Pp. 206–20.

Miner, Margaret. *Resonant Gaps: Between Baudelaire and Wagner*. Athens and London: The University of Georgia Press, 1995.

Mistacco, Vicki. "Reading *The Immoralist*: The Relevance of Narrative Roles." In *Theories of Reading, Looking and Listening*. Ed. Harry R. Garvin. Lewisburg: Bucknell University Press, 1981. Pp. 64–74.

Møller, Lis. *The Freudian Reading: Analytical and Fictional Constructions*. Philadelphia: University of Pennsylvania Press, 1991.

Nietzsche, Friedrich. *The Antichrist. The Portable Nietzsche*. Ed. and trans. Walter Kaufmann. New York: Penguin, 1982. Pp. 565–656.

"The Birth of Tragedy" and "The Genealogy of Morals." Trans. Francis Golffing. New York: Anchor-Doubleday, 1956.

The Case of Wagner. Basic Writings of Nietzsche. Ed. and trans. Walter Kaufmann. New York: The Modern Library, 1992. Pp. 601–48.

Der Fall Wagner, Götzen-Dämmerung, Der Antichrist, Ecce Homo, Dionysos-Dithyramben, Nietzsche contra Wagner. Kritische Studienausgabe. Vol. VI. Ed. Giorgio Colli and Mazzino Montinari. Munich: dtv/de Gruyter, 1988.

Die Geburt der Tragödie: Unzeitgemäße Betrachtungen I–IV, Nachgelassene Schriften 1870–1873. Kritische Studienausgabe. Vol. I. Ed. Giorgio Colli and Mazzino Montinari. Munich: dtv/de Gruyter, 1988.

Nietzsche Contra Wagner. The Portable Nietzsche. Ed. and trans. Walter Kaufmann. New York: Penguin, 1982. Pp. 661–83.

Twilight of the Idols Or, How One Philosophizes with a Hammer. The Portable Nietzsche. Trans. and ed. Walter Kaufmann. New York: Penguin, 1982. Pp. 463–563.

Norris, Margot. "Kafka's 'Josefine': The Animal as the Negative Site of Narration." *Beasts of the Modern Imagination: Darwin, Nietzsche, Kafka, Ernst, and Lawrence*. Baltimore: The Johns Hopkins University Press, 1990. Pp. 118–33.

"Sadism and Masochism in Two Kafka Stories: 'In der Strafkolonie' and 'Ein Hungerkünstler.'" *MLN* 93 (1978): 420–37.

Norton, Robert E. *The Beautiful Soul: Aesthetic Morality in the Eighteenth Century*. Ithaca: Cornell University Press, 1995.

Of the Sublime: Presence in Question. Essays by Jean-François Courtine, Michel Deguy, Eliane Escoubas, Philippe Lacoue-Labarthe, Jean-François Lyotard, Louis Marin, Jean-Luc Nancy, Jacob Rogozinski. Translated and with an afterword by Jeffrey S. Librett. Albany: State University of New York Press, 1993.

Painter, George D. *Marcel Proust: A Biography*. 2 vols. New York: Random House, 1959 and 1965.

Peyrache-Leborgne, Dominique. *La Poétique du sublime de la fin des Lumières au romantisme*. Paris: Champion, 1997.

Pollard, Patrick. *André Gide: Homosexual Moralist*. New Haven: Yale University Press, 1991.

Proust, Marcel. *A la recherche du temps perdu*. 3 vols. Paris: Gallimard-Pléiade, 1954.

A la recherche du temps perdu. 4 vols. Paris: Gallimard-Pléiade, 1987–1989.

"A propos du 'style' de Flaubert," "Journées de pèlerinage," and "Sainte-Beuve et Baudelaire." *"Contre Sainte-Beuve," précédé de "Pastiches et mélanges" et suivi de "Essais et articles."* Paris: Gallimard-Pléiade, 1971. Pp. 586–600; 69–105; 243–62.

"La Méthode de Sainte-Beuve." *"Contre Sainte-Beuve" suivi de "Nouveaux Mélanges."* Pref. Bernard de Fallois. Paris: Gallimard, 1954.
Remembrance of Things Past. 3 vols. Trans. C. K. Scott Moncrieff and Terence Kilmartin. New York: Random House, 1981.
Proust, Marcel, trans. *La Bible d'Amiens.* Paris: Mercure de France, 1904.
Sésame et les lys. Paris: Mercure de France, 1906.
Putnam, Walter. *L'Aventure littéraire de Joseph Conrad et d'André Gide.* Stanford French and Italian Studies 67. Saratoga: Anma Libri, 1990.
"Marlow, Michel et le silence des sirènes." *Bulletin des Amis d'André Gide* 31 (October 1993): 613–29.
Rabinowitz, Peter J. "Reader Response, Reader Responsibility: *Heart of Darkness* and the Politics of Displacement." *Heart of Darkness.* 2nd edn. Ed. Ross C Murfin. Case Studies in Contemporary Criticism. Boston and New York: St. Martin's Press / Bedford Books, 1996. Pp. 131–47.
Rapaport, Herman. "An Imperial Message: The Relays of Desire." *MLN* 95 (1980): 1333–57.
Rilke, Rainer Maria. *"Duino Elegies" and "The Sonnets to Orpheus."* Bilingual edn. Trans. A. Poulin, Jr. Boston: Houghton Mifflin, 1977.
Roazen, Paul. *Brother Animal: The Story of Freud and Tausk.* New York: Knopf, 1969.
Rivière, Alain, Jean-Georges Morgenthaler and Françoise Garcia, eds. *André Lhote, Alain-Fournier, Jacques Rivière: La peinture, le coeur et l'esprit. Correspondance inédite (1907–1914).* 2 vols. Bordeaux: William Blake and Co., 1986.
Rivière, Alain and Pierre de Gaulmyn, eds. *Correspondance Jacques Rivière – Alain-Fournier.* Paris: Gallimard, 1991.
Robert, Marthe. *As Lonely as Franz Kafka.* Trans. Ralph Manheim. New York: Harcourt, Brace, Jovanovich, 1982.
The Old and the New: From Don Quixote to Kafka. Trans. Carol Cosman. Foreword Robert Alter. Berkeley: University of California Press, 1977.
Rousseau, Jean-Jacques. *Julie, ou la Nouvelle Héloïse.* Paris: Garnier-Flammarion, 1967.
Ruskin, John. *The Stones of Venice.* Vols. IX, X and XI of *The Works of John Ruskin.* Ed. E. T. Cook and A. Wedderburn. 39 vols. London: George Allen, 1903.
Ryan, Judith. "'Eigentlich, aber noch eigentlicher': Some Epistemological Problems in Franz Kafka." *Festschrift for Ralph Farrell.* Ed. Anthony Stephens, H. C. Rogers, and Brian Coghlan. Bern: Peter Lang, 1977. Pp. 108–19.
Said, Edward. *Orientalism.* New York: Columbia University Press, 1978.
Sartre, Jean-Paul. "*Aminadab*, ou du fantastique considéré comme un langage." *Situations I.* Paris: Gallimard, 1947. Pp. 122–42.
Schiller, Friedrich. *On the Aesthetic Education of Man in a Series of Letters.* Trans. and intro. Reginald Snell. New Haven: Yale University Press, 1954.
"Über Anmut und Würde." *Theoretische Schriften.* Vol. VIII of *Werke und Briefe.* Ed. Rolf-Peter Janz. Frankfurt am Main: Deutscher Klassiker Verlag, 1992. Pp. 330–94.

"Über die ästhetische Erziehung des Menschen in einer Reihe von Briefen." *Theoretische Schriften.* Vol. VIII of *Werke und Briefe.* Ed. Rolf-Peter Janz. Frankfurt am Main: Deutscher Klassiker Verlag, 1992. Pp. 556–676.

Schlegel, Friedrich. *Dialogue on Poetry and Literary Aphorisms.* Ed. and trans. Ernst Behler and Roman Struc. University Park: The Pennsylvania State University Press, 1968.

Sebald, W. G. "The Law of Ignominy: Authority, Messianism and Exile in *The Castle.*" *On Kafka: Semi-Centenary Perspectives.* Ed. Franz Kuma. New York: Harper and Row, 1976. Pp. 42–58.

Shakespeare, William. *Romeo and Juliet.* The New Folger Library. Ed. Barbara A. Mowat and Paul Werstine. New York: Washington Square Press, 1992.

Shelley, Percy Bysshe, and Thomas Love Peacock. *"A Defence of Poetry" and "The Four Ages of Poetry."* Ed. and intro. John E. Jordan. New York: Bobbs-Merrill / The Library of Liberal Arts, 1965.

Sokel, Walter H. "Freud and the Magic of Kafka's Writing." In *The World of Franz Kafka.* Ed. J. P. Stern. New York: Holt, 1979. Pp. 145–58.

"The Programme of K's Court: Oedipal and Existential Meanings of *The Trial.*" *Kafka: Semi-Centenary Perspectives.* Ed. Franz Kuma. New York: Harper and Row, 1976. Pp. 1–21.

Sophocles. *Oedipus the King. The Complete Greek Tragedies.* Vol. II. Trans. David Grene. Chicago: The University of Chicago Press, 1992. Pp. 9–76.

Tadié, Jean-Yves. *Marcel Proust: biographie.* Paris: Gallimard, 1996.

Taminiaux, Jacques. *La Nostalgie de la Grèce à l'aube de l'Idéalisme allemand: Kant et les Grecs dans l'itinéraire de Schiller, de Hölderlin et de Hegel.* The Hague: Martinus Nijhoff, 1967.

Taylor, Charles. *Hegel.* Cambridge: Cambridge University Press, 1975.

Terdiman, Richard. *Present Past: Modernity and the Memory Crisis.* Ithaca: Cornell University Press, 1993.

The Holy Bible, Containing the Old and New Testaments. Cambridge: Cambridge University Press, 1988.

Thulstrup, Niels. *Kierkegaard's Relation to Hegel.* Trans. George L. Stengren. Princeton: Princeton University Press, 1980.

Vitzthum, Thomas. "A Revolution in Writing: The Overthrow of Epic Storytelling by Written Narrative in Kafka's *Josefine, die Sängerin.*" *Symposium* 47 (Winter 1993): 269–78.

von Wiese, Benno. "Das verlorene und wieder zu findende Paradies: Eine Studie über den Begriff der Anmut bei Goethe, Kleist und Schiller." In *Kleists Aufsatz über das Marionettentheater: Studien and Interpretationen.* Ed. Walter Müller-Seidel. Berlin: Erich Schmidt Verlag, 1967.

Wagner, Richard. *Tannhäuser: Grand Romantic Opera in Three Acts.* Libretto. New York: Rullman, 1925.

Walsh, Sylvia. *Living Poetically: Kierkegaard's Existential Aesthetics.* University Park: The Pennsylvania State University Press, 1994.

Wapnewski, Peter. "Nietzsche und Wagner: Stationen einer Beziehung." *Nietzsche-Studien* 18 (1989): 401–23.

Watt, Ian. *Conrad in the Nineteenth Century*. Berkeley and Los Angeles: University of California Press, 1979.

Webster's New Universal Unabridged Dictionary. New York: Simon and Schuster, 1972.

Wing, Nathaniel. "The Disruptions of Irony in Gide's *L'Immoraliste*." *SubStance* 26 (1980): 76–85.

Woolf, Virginia. *The Diary of Virginia Woolf*. 5 vols. Ed. Anne Olivier Bell. Assisted by Andrew McNeillie. New York: Harcourt Brace / Harvest Books, 1977–84.

A Room of One's Own. Foreword Mary Gordon. New York: Harcourt Brace / Harvest Books, 1989.

To the Lighthouse. Intro. Eudora Welty. New York: Harcourt Brace / Harvest Books, 1989.

The Waves. New York: Harcourt Brace / Harvest Books, 1989.

Wordsworth, William. *Selected Poetry*. Ed. and intro. Mark Van Doren. New York: The Modern Library, 1950.

Wörner, Karl Heinrich. *Schoenberg's "Moses and Aaron."* With the Complete Libretto in German and English. Trans. Paul Hamburger. London: Faber and Faber, 1963.

Zuckerman, Elliott. "Nietzsche and Music: *The Birth of Tragedy* and *Nietzsche Contra Wagner*." *Symposium* 28.1 (Spring 1974): 17–32.

Index

Abel, Karl, 252 n. 23
abstraction, and the sublime, 15
Achebe, Chinua, 253–4 n. 3, 254 n. 5
action, moral, in Kierkegaard, 48
actualization
  in Hegel, 28
  in Kierkegaard, 33–4
adolescence, *Le Grand Meaulnes* as novel of, 114, 115–16
adventure novel, *Le Grand Meaulnes* as, 115, 116–17, 118
advice, and moral law, 17–18
Aeschylus, and Nietzsche, 93
aesthetics
  bourgeois, 43, 237 n. 16
  ethical dimension of, 88–9
  in Freud, 55–6, 63, 68, 77
  in Gide, 176–81
  in Hegel, 26–9
  as indirect discourse, 10–11
  ironical, 26, 30–6, 50
  in Kant's *Critique of Judgment*, 3–12, 19, 22, 87
  in Kant's *Critique of Practical Reason*, 18–19, 23, 87
  in Kierkegaard, v, ix–x, 24–6, 35–6, 39–44, 45–50
  and nature, 5–6, 15–16, 17, 59, 186
  in Nietzsche, 92–3, 98
  and philistinism, 43, 237 n. 16
  pre-ethical, 40–4, 88
  and the sublime, ix, 12–15, 19, 98
  Symbolist, 18–19, 186
  as text, 8
  and the uncanny, ix, 87, 133, 211
  in Woolf, 186 7, 190, 198, 204–5, 209–10
  see also ethics; redemption; Romanticism; uncanniness
Africanism, in Conrad, 165, 255 n. 12
Alain-Fournier *see Grand Meaulnes, Le*
alchemy, and the uncanny, 69–70, 71–2, 239 n. 9
alienation *see* alterity
Alter, Robert, 262–3 n. 11
alterity
  in Blanchot, 224
  in Conrad, 134
  in Freud, 56
  in Gide, 134
  in Hegel, 127–8
  in Kafka, 147–8, 156
  and the uncanny, 134
ambivalence, in Proust, 157–8
analogy
  in Freud, 75
  in Kant, 8–11, 22, 232 n. 6, 232–3 n. 7, 233 n. 8
Andersen, Hans Christian, "The Tinder Box", 259 n. 11
antinomy, and aesthetics, 11
Apollo, and Dionysos, 89, 92–5, 98, 101, 114
Ariadne, and Woolf, 190–1, 259, n. 4
art, as deception, 15–16
artifice
  and nature, 59–61, 70–3, 81, 84, 202–5, 207
  and perfection, 73–4, 125–6, 130, 239–40, n. 10
Auden, W. H., 237 n. 14
authenticity
  in Gide, 177, 179–80
  in Kierkegaard, 33
autobiography, and fiction, 187–9

Bakhtin, M. M., 163, 248 n. 1
Balzac, Honoré de, *La Comédie Humaine*, 247 n. 15
banality, and Hoffmann, 64, 65–6
Barthes, Roland, 257 n. 3
Baudelaire, Charles Pierre, 50, 90
  and Alain-Fournier, 117
  and Hugo, 102
  and Liszt, 90, 102–9, 112
  and Nietzsche, 111–12

and Proust, 250 n. 11
and Romanticism, 242–3 n. 17
and the thyrsus, x, 90, 101–12
and Wagner, 90, 108–10, 112, 241 n. 5
writings
"Le Cygne", 102, 243 n. 18
Les Fleurs du Mal, 102, 178
"Le Mauvais Vitrier", 39
"Les Petites Vieilles", 141
Les Petits Poèmes en prose, 102, 111, 244 n. 24
"Richard Wagner et *Tannhäuser* à Paris", 90, 108, 244 n. 26
"Les Sept Vieillards", 63
Le Spleen de Paris, 102, 242–3 n. 17
"Tableaux parisiens", 1–2, 242–3 n. 17
"Le Thyrse", 102–12, 243 nn. 19, 20
Bauer, Felice, 46
beauty *see* aesthetics
Beck, Lewis White, 234–5 n. 16
Beckett, Samuel, 158
Beharriell, Frederick, 247 n. 18
Bell, Vanessa, 187–9
Benveniste, Emile, 180, 256 n. 22
Bizet, Georges, *Carmen*, 91–2, 98, 241 n. 7
Blackall, Eric, 247 n. 18
Blake, William, 88
Blanchot, Maurice, 170, 209
and Kafka, x–xi, 212–13, 219–20, 223, 225–8
and *le neutre*, 47, 212, 223–6, 237–8 n. 17, 263–4 n. 17
and music and narrative, 220–8
and the uncanny, 47, 212–13
writings
Aminadab, 212
L'Attente l'oubli, 212, 230
Au Moment voulu, 212, 263–4 n. 17
Celui qui ne m'accompagnait pas, 212
"Le Chant des sirènes", 220, 221–3, 224, 225
L'Entretien infini, 212
L'Espace littéraire, 212
"Kafka et l'exigence de l'oeuvre", 213, 227
Le Livre à venir, 212
"La voix narrative, le 'il', le neutre", 220, 223–5
blindness theme, in *Oedipus the King*, 80, 82–3
Bloom, Harold, 53
Boccaccio, Giovanni, *Decameron*, 173
borders
in Freud, 53, 240 n. 11
in Hegel, 3
in Hoffmann, 71
in Kant, 3, 5–6, 13–14, 22
in Kierkegaard, 47
in Woolf, 210
Bouraoui, H.-A., 245 n. 3
Bowen, Elizabeth, 209
Brantlinger, Patrick, 255 n. 14
Brée, Germaine, 253 n. 3, 256 n. 18
Brod, Max, 251 n. 18, 262 n. 10
Brooks, Peter, 239 n. 7, 255 n. 14
Buisine, Alain, 117–19, 131, 245–6 n. 9
Burke, Edmund, 14
Butor, Michel, 223

Cassirer, Ernst, 231 n. 1, 232 n. 16
castration theme
in Freud, 61, 68
in *Oedipus the King*, 83
Céline, Louis-Ferdinand, 158
Cellier, Léon, and *Le Grand Meaulnes*, 117–19, 121, 129, 131
Chagall, Marc, 108
choice, in Kierkegaard, 47–8
Christianity
in Kierkegaard, 24–5, 32–3, 36, 48–51
in Nietzsche, 101
chronotope, threshold, 153, 248 n. 1
Cixous, Hélène, 53, 54
Classicism, German, 121–2
closure
in Freud, 57, 65, 77
in Hoffmann, 65–6
in Kafka, 146–7, 149, 151, 155–6, 158
in Woolf, 191
cognition
in Kant, 4–5, 7, 231 n. 2
in Wordsworth, 231 n. 2
Cohen, Ted, 232 n. 7
Coleridge, S. T., 236 n. 7
Colli, Giorgio, 96
command, and the sublime, 15, 17
community
in Blanchot, 212, 220
in Kafka, 212, 213, 217–20, 230
Conrad, Joseph
and Gide, 159, 163, 255 n. 11
and immoralism, 165–6, 175–6, 182–3
and irony, 171–2
and narrative framing, 162–5, 166–75
and threshold-moment, 163
and the uncanny, x, 134, 159, 162, 163, 170–4
see also Heart of Darkness
consciousness
and the beautiful soul, 127–8, 129
in Blanchot, 224, 225–6

consciousness (*cont.*)
in Hegel, 3
in Proust, 137–44
containment, 211
in Conrad, 167–70
in Freud, 65–6
in Gide, 177–8, 181
in Kafka, 216
in Proust, 140, 141–2
in Woolf, 192
content, and form, 11–12
contradiction
in Kant, 7
in Nietzsche, 93
and Romantic irony, 236 n. 7
conventionality, and the uncanny, 66–7, 73
Coppola, Francis Ford, *Apocalypse Now*, 253 n. 2
Corngold, Stanley, 248–9 n. 3
Cowper, William, "The Castaway", 207, 258 n. 5
criticism, literary, 90, 106
genetic, 115–16, 245 n. 5
of *Heart of Darkness*, 161, 167–9, 172, 254 n. 5
of *L'Immoraliste*, 177
of Kafka, 262 n. 8
psychocriticism, 145, 147, 150, 251 n. 18
of *To the Lighthouse*, 207, 258 n. 5, 259 n. 12
Critique of Judgment (Kant), 3–16, 231 n. 1
and aesthetics, 3–12, 19, 22, 87
and analogy, 8–11
and ethics, 6–9, 15–16, 19, 22
and Kierkegaard, 25
and nature, 5–6, 15–16, 17
and Romanticism, 5, 25
and the sublime, 6, 11, 12–14, 87, 233 n. 10
and textuality, 8
Critique of Practical Reason (Kant), 5, 6
and aesthetics, 18–19, 23, 87
and ethics, 16–19, 23, 87, 197
and nature, 19

Dante Alighieri, xii, 160
Darras, Jacques, 254 n. 4
de Man, Paul, 42, 232 n. 5
death
and Freud, xi, 52, 66–7, 74–5, 77–9, 83–4
and Hoffmann, 66–7, 74
and Kafka, xi, 213, 230
and Woolf, 186–7, 189–92, 207, 211
debt *see* guilt
deceit, and art, 15–16, 18, 45, 69–70, 73
Deleuze, Gilles, 4–5
Derrida, Jacques, 224, 238 n. 3, 251 n. 18
design, in Kant, 11–12
Deutsch, Helene, 78
dialectic
in Hegel, 3, 93
in Kierkegaard, 36, 50
in Nietzsche, 91–4, 97–100, 101
in Schiller, 122–3, 128
dialogue, in *Heart of Darkness*, 164–5, 170–1, 173–5
Dickens, Charles, and Alain-Fournier, 117
difference, in Kafka, 262 n. 8
dignity, moral, 122, 128
Dionysos
and Apollo, 89, 92–5, 101, 114
Goethe as, 99–101, 102, 106, 110, 111
Liszt as, 1–2, 106–7, 110
and redemption, 94–5, 100, 242 n. 10
and the *thyrsus*, x, 91, 92, 99, 102, 106–7
Wagner as, 95, 100
discipline, and form, 113
discourse
confessional, 181
and ethics, 50
indirect, 10–11
distance
aesthetic, 189, 204, 223–4, 226
ironical, 253 n. 1
and poetic sympathy, 89–90
domesticity
and ethics, 45–6, 49, 87, 181, 205, 210
and the uncanny, 70
Don Juan, and seduction, 26, 40–2
Doppelgänger
and Conrad and Gide, 159
and Freud, 56, 76–84
and Hoffmann, 72, 73, 75
and Oedipus, 80, 82
and Proust and Kafka, xi
and Woolf, 194–201, 206
see also doubling
doubling
as uncanny, 53, 56, 59, 63, 72–3, 75, 76–9, 82–3, 94
see also Doppelgänger
dreams, in *Heart of Darkness*, 160, 253 n. 2
drives
in Freud, 52, 77–9, 83, 181
in Rilke, 132
in Schiller, 123, 128–9
duality *see* polarity
Duckworth, Gerald, 257 n. 2
duty
in Kant, 18, 234–5 n. 16
in Schiller, 122–3

earnestness
in Hegel, 28–9, 33, 45
in Kierkegaard, 43–4, 50
economics, and ethics, 44–5, 48–9
ego, in Fichte, 27–9
Either/Or (Kierkegaard), 36–51, 71, 236 n. 6
and ethics and aesthetics, 24–6, 45–51, 87
and immediacy, 40–2
and irony, 29, 46
and moral value, 43–5, 48–9
and narrative framing, x, 38–40, 42–4
and the poetic life, 26, 33, 41–2
Eliot, T. S., 246 n. 11, 258 n. 5
ennoblement, and the sublime, 12, 13, 22
ethics
and aesthetics, 6–13, 15–19, 27, 175–9, 232 n. 5
and categorical imperative, 17
as discursive, 50
as domestic, 45–6, 49, 87, 205, 210
and economic metaphors, 44–51
in Gide, 175–82, 183
in Hegel, 27
in Hoffmann, 73–4
and immoralism, 159–84
in Kant's *Critique of Practical Judgment*, 6–9, 12–13, 19, 22, 87
in Kant's *Critique of Practical Reason*, 16–19, 23, 87, 197
in Kierkegaard, v, ix–x, 24–6, 32, 35–6, 39–44, 45–9, 205
and moral beauty, 121–8
and narrative framing, 40
and nature, 87
and philosophy, 89
and poetic imagination, 88–9
and Romantic irony, 32–3
and the sublime, ix, 12–15, 19, 87
textual, 37–8
and the uncanny, ix, 73–4, 133, 176–7, 211
in Woolf, 196–8, 205
Euripides, and Nietzsche, 93, 94
exemplarity, in Conrad and Gide, 161–2
existentialism
Christian, 24–5, 47–8
and irony, 36
and Kafka, 145, 251 n. 18

faculties, human, and aesthetics, 3–6
fallacy, biographical, 204
feminism, and Woolf, 195, 207
Fichte, Johann Gottlieb, 25, 27–9, 128
fiction
and autobiography, 187–9
and Freud, 56–8
and irony, 32, 42
and reality, 42
figuration
in French Symbolism, 39
in Hoffmann, 71
in Kierkegaard, 34–5, 49, 71
"The Fisherman and his Wife" (Grimm brothers), 193–201, 202–8, 210
fishing imagery, in Woolf, 190–3, 205, 208–10, 260 n. 14
Fitch, Brian T., 260 n. 2
Flaubert, Gustave, x, 30, 139, 220, 236 n. 6
and banality, 64
and Kafka, 223, 226
and time, 139, 249–50 n. 10
forgetfulness, in Kafka, 213, 216, 229–30
form
and content, 11–12
and ethics, 113–14, 131–2
formalism
in Kant, 11
and Modernism, 243 n. 18, 246 n. 11
Foucault, Michel, 260–1 n. 3
Fournier, Henri *see Grand Meaulnes, Le*
framing, 87
in Conrad, 162–5, 166–75
and frame-breaking, 182
in Freud, 65, 75, 76–9
in Gide, xi, 162–5, 166, 175–82, 183, 256 n. 18
in Hoffmann, 65, 73, 75
human and divine, 182–4
in Kafka, 152–6
in Kierkegaard, x, xi, 38–40, 42–4, 45
and pedagogical usefulness, 162–5
in Proust, 203
in Woolf, 190–9
France, and Modernism, 246 n. 11
freedom
and ethics, 17, 48, 123, 234 n. 14
and irony, 30
and nature, 5–6
and poetic licence, 56–8, 64
Freud, Anna, 83, 240–1 n. 14
Freud, Sigmund
and aesthetics, 55–7, 63, 68, 77, 123
and ambivalence, 157–8
and Hoffmann, 58, 61–3, 64–75, 79, 83, 87
and Kafka, 146
and literary style, 67, 68
and narcissism, 17, 63
and primal words, 252 n. 23

Freud, Sigmund (*cont.*)
and the uncanny, ix, xi, 39, 52–84, 143–4, 192, 250 n. 16
and unconscious motivation, 65, 67
and Woolf, 208
writings
Beyond the Pleasure Principle, 52, 67, 75, 238, n. 3
Drei Abhandlungen zur Sexualtheorie, 65
Inhibitions, Symptoms, and Anxiety, 52
The Interpretation of Dreams, 52
"Das Unheimliche", x, 52–8, 61–3, 64–7, 73–5, 77–9, 83, 250 n. 16
see also drives; framing; Oedipus complex; Oedipus figure

Gay, Peter, 240–1 n. 14
generality and particularity
in Conrad, 160, 162, 172–4
in Gide, 160, 182
Genette, Gérard, 135–7, 145
genius
in Baudelaire, 102–3, 104–8, 109–12
in Conard, 174
in Goethe, 125–6
Geschäft, and indirection, 10
Gide, André
and aesthetics and ethics, 176–81
and Conrad, 159, 163, 255 n. 11
and immoralism, 165–6, 175–82
and *Le Grand Meaulnes*, 116, 117, 119, 131
and narrative framing, xi, 162–3, 166, 175–82
and threshold-moment, 163
and the uncanny, x, 134, 159, 176–7
writings
Les Caves du Vatican, 253 n. 1
La Porte étroite, 253 n. 1
see also L'Immoraliste
Goethe, Johann Wolfgang von
and the beautiful soul, 124–7, 129–30
and irony, 124–5
and Kafka, 223
and Kierkegaard, 35–6
and Nietzsche, 99–100, 102, 106, 110, 111
writings
Wilhelm Meister's Apprenticeship, 124–7, 129, 131, 247 n. 17
Wilhelm Meisters Wanderjahre, 126
goodness *see* ethics
Goozé, Marjanne, 252 n. 25
Gordimer, Nadine, 252 n. 21
grace, aesthetic, 122–3, 124, 128
Le Grand Meaulnes (Alain-Fournier), x, 114–21
as adventure novel, 115, 116–17, 118
and the beautiful soul, x, 120–1, 129–32, 133
France and Germany in, 117–18
and Modernism, x, 131
as novel of adolescence, 114, 115–16
as quest novel, 115, 118
and Romanticism, 117–18, 119, 121, 128–32, 133
summary and commentary, 114–19
and the uncanny, 130, 133
Grimm, Jacob and Wilhelm, "The Fisherman and his Wife", 193–208, 210
Guerard, Albert J., 253 nn. 2, 3
guilt
in Freud, 78–9
in *Le Grand Meaulnes*, 133
in Kierkegaard, 44, 46, 48–9
in readers, 177
Guyer, Paul, 232 n. 6, 232–3 n. 7

harmony, in Kant, 7–8
Harter, Deborah, 261 n. 7
Hawthorne, Nathaniel, "Rappaccini's Daughter", 239 n. 9, 240–1 n. 14
Hayman, Ronald, 135, 137, 145
Heart of Darkness (Conrad), 18–19, 159, 253 n. 1
and Conrad criticism, 161, 254 n. 5
and immoralism, 165–6, 175–6, 182–3
and the inhuman, 175–6
and irony, 171–2
and narrative framing, 162–5, 166–75
and pedagogical exemplarity, 161–2
and problem of the referent, 160, 253 n. 3
as quest novel, 172, 254 n. 4
and threshold-moment, 163
and tone, 164
and the uncanny, 162, 163, 170–4
Hegel, Georg Wilhelm Friedrich
and aesthetics, 26–9
and the beautiful soul, 127–8, 129–30
and dialectic, 3, 93
and irony, 25, 27–9, 31, 128
and Kierkegaard, 25, 29, 30, 32, 39, 44, 50
and Romantic irony, 26–9, 30–1
writings
Aesthetics, 26–7, 32
The Phenomenology of Spirit, 27, 127–8, 129
Hegelianism, and Kierkegaard, 25, 45
Heidegger, Martin, 30, 132, 137
and Kafka, 155, 230
and Nietzsche, 92
writings
"Letter on Humanism", 89, 249 n. 7
Sein und Zeit, 249 n. 7
Heilbrun, Caroline, 190, 258 n. 4

Hertz, Neil, 53, 78–9
Herzfeld, Claude, 115, 245 n. 8
Hoffman, Anne Golomb, 259 n. 12
Hoffmann, E. T. A.
  "Der Sandmann", x, 58, 59–63, 64–75, 77, 79–84
  and intellectual uncertainty, 61–2
  and irony, 29, 35, 58
  and narrative framing, 65
  and the uncanny, ix, 56, 58–63, 64–74, 75, 87, 192
  and unconscious motivation, 65
Hölderlin, Johann Christian Friedrich, 122, 242 n. 10
Hollingdale, R. J., 60
Homer, *The Odyssey*, 221–2
homosexuality, and Gide, 181–2, 253 n. 3
Houssaye, Arsène, 102, 109
Howard, Richard, 177
hubris
  and Freud, 55–6
  and Hoffmann, 70
  and Oedipus myth, 81
  and Woolf, 197–8, 205
Hugo, Victor, 5, 98, 102, 244 n. 24
Husson, Claudie, 116
hypotyposis, in Kant, 8
Hyppolite, Jean, 129

Idealism, German, 121–2
idolatry, in *Heart of Darkness*, 174–5
image
  as sign, 14, 233–4 n. 11
  and the sublime, 14–15
imagination
  imaginative sympathy, 87–91, 111
  and the sublime, 14
  and the uncanny, 69–70
immanence, literary, 178–9
immediacy, aesthetic, 40–2
immoralism
  in Conrad, 165–6, 175–6, 182–3
  in Gide, 165–6, 175–82, 183
L'Immoraliste (Gide), 46, 159, 253 n. 1
  and ethics, 161–2, 163, 165, 176–81
  and immoralism, 165–6, 183
  and literary criticism, 161, 254 n. 5
  and narrative framing, 162, 163–5, 175–82, 183
  and pedagogical exemplarity, 161–2
  and problem of the referent, 160, 253 n. 3
  as quest novel, 160, 254 n. 4
  and threshold-moment, 163
  and tone, 164
  and the uncanny, 162, 163, 176–7
imperative, categorical, 17, 25
impersonality
  in Blanchot, 212, 223
  in Woolf, 134, 209–10, 211–12
incest theme, in Proust, 193
indifference
  and aesthetics, 46–7, 215, 227–30
  and ethics, 113–14, 131–2, 178
indirection, in Kant, 10–11
individuation, in Nietzsche, 94
inhuman, the
  in Conrad, 175–6
  in Gide, 166, 175
inside/outside
  in Conrad, 167–70, 172–4
  in Gide, 166, 178–81
  in Hegel, 3
  in Hoffmann, 69–70
  in Kant, 11, 21–2
  in Kierkegaard, 39, 42–3, 237 n. 12
  in Woolf, 199
intertextuality
  and Freud, 54
  Romantic, 89, 114–28
  and *To the Lighthouse*, 193–207, 258 n. 5
irony
  and aesthetics, 50, 26, 30–6
  in Conrad, 171–2
  controlled, 35–6
  and ethics, 32–3
  in German Romanticism, ix, 25, 26–9, 58, 63
  in Goethe, 124–5
  in Hegel, 25, 27–9, 31, 128
  ironical distance, 253 n. 1
  in Kafka, 153, 155–6, 226
  in Kierkegaard, 25–6, 29, 30–6, 42, 46, 50, 162
  and negativity, 30
  and pedagogical exemplarity, 162
  poetics of, 32–3
  Socratic, 30, 32
  and the uncanny, 58, 62–3, 70

Jakobson, Roman, 136, 138, 249 n. 5
James, Henry, and Modernism, 246 n. 11
Jameson, Fredric, 255 n. 14
Jammes, Francis, 256 n. 19
Jentsch, E., 56–8, 61–3
Johnson, Barbara, 111, 242–3 n. 17, 243 n. 19
Jones, Ernest, 76–7
Joyce, James, 20, 235 n. 17, 258 nn. 4, 5
  and Modernism, 188, 246 n. 11
  writings
  Finnegans Wake, 246 n. 11

Joyce, James (*cont.*)
A Portrait of the Artist as a Young Man, 245 n. 3, 246 n. 11
Ulysses, 246 n. 11
Judaism, and Kafka, 227, 262–3 n. 11
judgment
aesthetic, 12–13
and analogy, 9–10
in Gide, 178–9
in Goethe, 125–6
in Kafka, 228
and nature and freedom, 5–6
and understanding and reason, 5
in Woolf, 197

Kafka, Franz
as a bachelor, 46, 147–50
and banality, 64
and Blanchot, x–xi, 212–13, 219–20, 223, 225–8
and Flaubert, 223, 226
and Freud, 146
and Goethe, 223
and irony, 153, 155–6, 226
and Kierkegaard, v, 251 n. 18
and music, 213–20, 261 n. 4
and Proust, xi
and the sublime, x, xi, 214
and the threshold-moment, 134–5, 145–8, 153, 156, 248 n. 1
and the uncanny, x, 133–4, 144–56, 158, 212–13
writings
"Die Abweisung" ("The Refusal"), 216
"Der Bau" ("The Burrow"), 226
Brief an den Vater (Letter to His Father), 147–50, 151, 252 nn. 21, 22
The Castle, 150–7, 158, 251 n. 18, 252–3 n. 26
"Forschungen eines Hundes", 226, 261 n. 4
"A Hunger-Artist", 146
"In the Penal Colony", 146, 252–3 n. 26
"Josefine, die Sängerin oder das Volk der Mäuse", 213–19, 220, 225–8, 229–30
"The Judgment" ("Das Urteil"), 135, 145–6, 156, 157, 219, 226, 228, 248–9 n. 3
"The Metamorphosis" ("Die Verwandlung"), 66, 219, 226
Tagebücher (Diaries), 145, 227–8
The Trial, 150
Kant, Immanuel
and aesthetics and ethics, ix–x, 6–9, 16–23, 73, 87–8, 128
and the beautiful soul, 122
and borders and limits, 3, 5–6, 13–14, 22
influence of, 122
and Kierkegaard, 34, 235 n. 2
and literary style, 7–8, 19–23
in Nietzsche, 100–1, 106, 111
and the sublime, ix, xi, 6, 12–14, 58, 87, 211
writings
Critique of Pure Reason, 3, 5, 19, 231 n. 1
Groundwork of the Metaphysics of Morals, 234 n. 12
The Metaphysics of Morals, 234 n. 12, 235 n. 17
see also Critique of Judgment; Critique of Practical Reason
Kaplan, Edward, 103, 243 nn. 19–21, 23
Kaufmann, Walter, 96
Kierkegaard, Søren, 24–51
as a bachelor, 46
and ethics and aesthetics, v, ix–x, 24–6, 35–6, 39–40, 45–51, 87, 205
and Hegel, 25, 29, 30, 32, 39, 44, 50
influence of Kant on, 34, 235 n. 2
and irony, 25–6, 29, 30–6, 42, 50, 162
and Kafka, v, 251 n. 18
and literary style, 26, 45
and narrative framing, x, xi, 38–40, 42–4, 45
and paradox, 36, 49–51, 236–7 n. 10
and the uncanny, 39, 58
writings
The Concept of Anxiety, 24
The Concept of Irony, x, 24–5, 29, 30–6
Fear and Trembling, 24, 49
Philosophical Fragments, 24, 36, 49, 51, 236–7 n. 10
Repetition, 24
see also Either/Or
Kimbrough, Robert, 254 n. 5
Klein, Richard, 243 n. 19
Kleist, Heinrich von, 239–40 n. 10
Klettenberg, Susanna Katharina von, 124–5, 247 nn. 15, 17
Kofman, Sarah, 52–3, 64, 66

Lacan, Jacques, 251 n. 18
Laclos, Pierre Choderlos de, *Les Liaisons dangereuses*, 17–18
Lacoue-Labarthe, Philippe, 241 n. 5, 242–3 n. 17, 247 n. 23
Laforgue, Jules, and Alain-Fournier, 117
language
of philosophy, 89
of poetry, 89
and primal words, 149, 252 n. 23

Laurens, Paul-Albert, 160
Lavater, Johann Kaspar, 124, 247 n. 15
law, moral, 87
and Kant, 6, 15, 17–18, 19, 22
and Kierkegaard, 25
and pure reason, 17
as universal, 17–18, 19
Lee, Hermione, 208, 209, 257 n. 2, 257–8 n. 3, 258 n. 6
Leuwers, Daniel, 115, 245 n. 7
life, ethical, in Kierkegaard, 48
life, poetic/aesthetic
in Hegel, 27
in Hoffmann, 71
in Kant, 18
in Kierkegaard, 26, 32–3, 41–2, 48
Liszt, Franz
and Baudelaire, 90, 102–9
Lohengrin et Tannhäuser de Richard Wagner, 108–9
and Wagner, 98, 108–10, 112
literary theory
and narratology, 134–7
and Romanticism, 89–91, 112, 248 n. 23
literature
and criticism, 90
as impersonality, 212
and indirect discourse, 10
and the uncanny, 52–3, 56–8, 64, 211
love, and ethics, 88
Lowrie, Walter, 237–8 n. 17
Lubkoll, Christine, 261 n. 7, 262 n. 10
Lyotard, Jean-Francois, 232 n. 6

Mallarmé, Stéphane, 186
"Le Démon de l'analogie", 39
Mann, Thomas, *Death in Venice*, 113–14, 131, 242 n. 10
Marks, Elaine, 161
Marxism, and Kafka, 145, 251 n. 18
maxims, 14, 17–19, 21, 197
memory
in Kafka, 151–3, 229
in Proust, 131, 136, 188
in Woolf, 188
metaphor
in Baudelaire, 109
in Conrad, 167–8
in Kant, 9–10
in Kierkegaard, 44–51
and metonymy, 81, 136–7, 140–1, 144, 157, 167, 175
in Nietzsche, 93–4
in Proust, 138–41, 157
and synecdoche, 9, 161, 167–8, 175
in Woolf, 190, 195
metonymy
and metaphor, 81, 136–7, 140–1, 144, 157
and synecdoche, 167–8, 175
Miller, Christopher L., 255 n. 12
Miller, J. Hillis, 167–8, 255 n. 14
Miner, Margaret, 244 n. 26
mirroring *see Doppelgänger*; doubling
model, in quest novels, 160, 182–3
Modernism
and Romanticism, ix, 5, 121, 131, 133, 246 n. 11
and spontaneity, 20
and the uncanny, ix–x, 53, 133–4, 211–12
see also Conrad, Joseph; Gide, André; Kafka, Franz; Proust, Marcel; Woolf, Virginia
motivation
narrative, 120
unconscious, 65, 67
Mozart, W. A., *Don Giovanni*, 40–1
Muir, Willa and Edwin, 217
Murfin, Ross C, 254 n. 5
music
in Blanchot, 220–8
and immediacy, 41
in Kafka, 213–20, 261 n. 4
in Kierkegaard, 40–1
and narration, 213, 221–3
in Nietzsche, 91–3, 98
see also Wagner, Richard
mythology, in Nietzsche, 93–5, 100, 232 n. 10

Nancy, Jean-Luc, 248 n. 23
narcissism, 17–18, 29, 63
narration, and music, 213
narrative
in Blanchot, 219–28
in Gide, 253 n. 1
and immediacy, 41
and literary freedom, 56–8
and narrative voice, 59, 220, 223–6, 228, 230
and repetition, 67, 239 n. 7
and uncanny openings, 133–58
unweaving of, 219
narrative framing *see* framing
narrative theory, 136
narratology, 177, 256 n. 18
and rhetoric, 134–7, 157
narrator, role, 215–19, 220, 261 n. 7
nature
and the aesthetic, 5–6, 15–16, 17, 59, 186
and artifice, 59–61, 70–3, 81, 84, 202–5, 207
and ethics, 87
as purposive, 5–6

nature (*cont.*)
and the sublime, 14, 19
and the uncanny, 59, 71, 72
Navarre, Marguerite de, *Heptaméron*, 173
Nazi art, 88
negativity, and irony, 30
Neptune motif, in Woolf, 204, 259–60 n. 13
Nerval, Gérard de, *Sylvie*, 118–19, 120
Nestroy, Johann, *Der Zerrissene*, 65, 67, 75
neutrality
and the aesthetic, 46–7, 178, 212, 223–30
and Blanchot, xi
and Kafka, xi
Nietzsche, Friedrich
and aesthetics, 92–3, 98
and Goethe, 99–100, 102, 106, 110, 111
and immoralism, 165
and Kant, 100–1, 106, 111
and language of poetry, 89
and redemption, 91–101
and the sublime, 98
and the thyrsus, x, 90, 92, 94–5, 99, 111
and Wagner, 90, 91–3, 95–9, 101–2, 111, 241 n. 5
writings
The Antichrist, 96, 242 n. 16
Beyond Good and Evil, 165
The Birth of Tragedy, 89, 91–5, 100–1, 111
The Case of Wagner, 92, 96, 98–9
The Genealogy of Morals, 165
Nietzsche Contra Wagner, 96–8, 101
Twilight of the Idols, 96, 99–101, 174
Untimely Meditation: Richard Wagner in Bayreuth, 96
Norris, Margot, 262 n. 8
Norton, Robert E., 246 n. 12
nostalgia, in *Le Grand Meaulnes*, 129–30
Novalis (Friedrich von Hardenberg), 25, 27, 128

The Odyssey (Homer), 221–2
Oedipus complex, in Freud, 55, 61, 68, 83
Oedipus figure
in Freud, 63, 80, 83–4, 87
in Kafka, 150, 151, 228
in Proust, 193
in Sophocles, 80–3
Olsen, Regine, 30, 46
opening and closing, in Kafka, 146–7, 149, 151, 153, 156
Orientalism, 255 n. 12
ornamentation
in Kant, 11, 23, 233 n. 9
in Kierkegaard, 34
in Woolf, 199–200, 204, 206, 208, 210
otherness *see* alterity

Painter, George D., 135, 137
paradox
in Blanchot, 225
in Kierkegaard, 36, 45, 49–51, 236–7 n. 10
particularity and generality
in Conrad, 160, 162, 172–4
in Gide, 160, 182
Pascal, Blaise, 97
Pater, Walter, 246 n. 11
Peacock, Thomas Love, *The Four Ages of Poetry*, 88
perfection, and artifice, 73–4, 125–6, 130, 239–40 n. 10
Philistinism, in Kierkegaard, 43
philosophy
and direct discourse, 10
and ethics, 89
language of, 89
and psychoanalysis, 77
Socratic, 93, 94–5, 101
Pietism
and the beautiful soul, 122, 124
and Kant, 12
place, sense of, in Woolf, 190
place-names, in Proust, 138–44, 157–8
poetic, the *see* aesthetics; poetry
poetry
and ethics, 88–9
and imaginative sympathy, 87–91
and literary criticism, 90
and religion, 33
Romantic, 27
see also Baudelaire, Charles; thyrsus
polarity
Apollonian-Dionysian, 89, 92–5, 98, 101
in Baudelaire, 105–9
in Blanchot, 221–2, 224–5
in Conrad, 171
in Hoffmann, 59
in Kafka, 228
in *Le Grand Meaulnes*, 114
in Modernism, 211
in Nietzsche, 96–7
in Woolf, 196
see also Apollo; Dionysos; inside/outside
politics, and aesthetics and ethics, 88, 102
Pound, Ezra, and Modernism, 246 n. 11
power, and irony, 29
Proust, Marcel
and Baudelaire, 250 n. 11
and incest theme, 193
and Kafka, xi
and memory, 131, 136, 188
and Modernism, 188, 246 n. 11
and reading theme, 193–4, 195
and Ruskin, 142, 143, 250 nn. 12, 13

and spontaneity, 20
and the threshold-moment, 134–5, 136, 137–44, 248 n. 1
and the uncanny, x, 133–4, 143–4, 158
and Woolf, 257–8 n. 3
writings
A la recherche du temps perdu, 119, 131–2, 136, 137–44, 157–8, 193, 203
La Bible d'Amiens, 141
"John Ruskin", 250 n. 12
"Journées de pèlerinage", 141, 250 n. 12
"Sainte-Beuve et Baudelaire", 250 n. 11
Psalms, and narrative framing, 183–4
pseudonyms, and Kierkegaard, 37–8
psychoanalysis
and Kafka criticism, 145, 147, 150, 251 n. 18
and *Le Grand Meaulnes*, 117
and philosophy, 77
and the uncanny, x, 52, 53–8, 61–3, 64–9, 74–5, 76
Putnam, James J., 75, 76–9
Putnam, Walter, 255 n. 11

quest novel
Heart of Darkness as, 160, 173, 254 n. 4
L'Immoraliste as, 160, 254 n. 4
Le Grand Meaulnes as, 118

Rabinowitz, Peter J., 253–4 n. 3
racism, and Conrad, 172, 253–4 n. 3
rationalism
and ethics, 88–9
and irony, 30
reading
in Proust, 15, 193–4
in Woolf, 190, 193–8, 257–8 n. 3
Realism, Soviet, 88
reason
and judgment, 5
and moral law, 17
practical, 13, 16–17
pure, 17, 20–1
and the sublime, 14
and the uncanny, 74, 83
récit, 159, 212
and *roman*, 221–3, 224, 225–6, 228, 230, 253 n. 1, 260 n. 2
see also Heart of Darkness; L'Immoraliste; narrative
reconciliation, in religion and poetry, 32–3
redemption
aesthetic, 35, 91
in Baudelaire, 112
and Dionysos, 94–5, 242 n. 10
in Kafka, 229
in Kierkegaard, 24–5, 48–9
in Nietzsche, 91–101
in Wagner, 110–11
referent, in Conrad and Gide, 159, 160
reflection, in Kierkegaard, 40–3
relationships, in Woolf, 196–8
religion
in Kafka, 145, 251 n. 18
in Kierkegaard, 24–5, 32–3, 36, 48–51
in Nietzsche, 101
and Oedipus, 80–1
and paradox, 50–1
and poetry, 33
remorse, in *Le Grand Meaulnes*, 118, 120–1, 129, 133
repetition compulsion, 52, 55, 58, 67–8, 74, 78, 83
rhetoric
in Conrad, 164
in Gide, 165, 180–1, 183
in Hegel, 27, 235 n. 5
in Kant, x, 7–8, 10, 21–2, 232 n. 4, 234 n. 12
in Kierkegaard, 26, 46, 49–50
and narratology, 134–7
and the sublime, 15, 234–5 n. 16
and subtlety, 23
in Woolf, 199, 204–5
Rilke, Rainer Maria, 132
Rimbaud, Arthur, 5, 71
Rivière, Jacques, 245 n. 8
Roazen, Paul, 78–9
Robbe-Grillet, Alain, 81
roman see récit
Romanticism
and *Critique of Judgment*, 5, 25
and ethics of the aesthetic, 88, 122
and intertextuality, 89
and irony, ix, 25–9, 30–2, 50, 58, 63, 70, 162
and Kierkegaard, 25–6, 29, 30–6, 49
and *Le Grand Meaulnes*, 117–18, 119, 121, 129–32, 133
and literary theory, 89–90
and the sublime, 53
and the *thyrsus*, 90–1, 101
and the uncanny, 62–3, 70
Rousseau, Jean-Jacques, 16
Julie, 37–8, 246 n. 12
Ruskin, John, 34, 135, 246 n. 11
and Proust, 142, 143, 250 nn. 12, 13
writings
Sesame and Lilies, 142
The Stones of Venice, 250 n. 15
Russia, and Soviet Realism, 88

Sackville-West, Vita, 187, 208–9
Said, Edward, 255 n. 12
Sainte-Beuve, Charles Augustin, 135
Sand, George, *François le Champi*, 193, 203
Sartre, Jean-Paul, 212
schematism, in Kant, 8
Schiller, Johann Christoph Friedrich von, 8, 232 n. 5
  and the beautiful soul, 122–4, 126, 128–9
  and Goethe, 125, 247 n. 17
  writings
    "Über Anmut und Würde", 122–4, 128
    Über die ästhetische Erziehung des Menschen, 122–4, 126
    Über naive und sentimentalische Dichtung, 122
Schlegel, August Wilhelm von, 25, 29, 31–3
Schlegel, Friedrich von, 25, 27, 29, 31–3, 90
Schoenberg, Arnold, *Moses and Aaron*, 233–4 n. 11
Schopenhauer, Arthur, 91, 95
Schumann, Robert, 35, 237 n. 16
seduction
  as aesthetic action, 17–18, 23, 234 n. 15
  and irony, 36
  value-free economics of, 40–4
self-love, 17–18
self-realization
  in Hegel, 27–8
  in Kierkegaard, 48
self-referentiality
  and Kafka, 251 n. 18
  in Romanticism, 29, 63
self-reflectiveness
  in Baudelaire, 102, 242–3 n. 17, 243 n. 19
  in Conrad, 172
  in Gide, 178
  in Kierkegaard, 42–3
  and the threshold-moment, 134–5, 252 n. 25
sensibility
  and aesthetic judgment, 12–14, 123, 126
  and the moral law, 17
sentimentality, and Romanticism, 4, 31
sexuality
  in Freud, 78
  in Woolf, 195–6, 208–9
Shakespeare, William, 35–6
  and Woolf, 258 n. 5
  writings
    Cymbeline, 186
    Romeo and Juliet, 236 n. 7
Shelley, Percy Bysshe, *A Defence of Poetry*, 88–9
signifier
  in Conrad, 175–6
  in Kafka, 145, 149, 153, 157–8
  in Proust, 138–42, 144, 157–8
  role of, xi–xii, 232 n. 4
  and the uncanny, 134, 138–42, 144, 145
Sizeranne, Robert de la, 246 n. 11
skyld see guilt
Smyth, Ethel, 209
Socrates
  and Apollo, 89, 94–5, 101
  and literary criticism, 106
  Socratic irony, 30, 32, 93
Solger, Karl Wilhelm Ferdinand, 25, 32
solipsism
  and Baudelaire, 243 nn. 19, 21
  of *Heart of Darkness*, 173, 175
  of *Le Grand Meaulnes*, 129–30
Sophocles
  and Nietzsche, 93
  Oedipus the King, 80–3
soul, "beautiful", 246 n. 12
  in Goethe, 124–7, 129–30
  in Hegel, 27, 127–8, 129–30
  in Kant, 122
  in *Le Grand Meaulnes*, x, 120–1, 129–32, 133
  in Schiller, 122–4, 128–9
speech-act theory, 181, 192
Spender, Stephen, 209
spontaneity, in Kant, 20
Stendhal (Henri Marie Beyle), 256 n. 21
Stephen, Julia, 187–8
Stevenson, R. L., and Alain-Fournier, 117
storytelling
  and Blanchot, 219–28
  in Conrad, 163–4, 166–70, 173
  and Freud, 56–8
  in Gide, 163–4
Structuralism, 177, 243 n. 18
style, literary
  and Alain-Fournier, 115
  and Baudelaire, 111–12
  and Conrad, 159, 167, 254 n. 8, 255 n. 14
  and Freud, 67, 68
  and Gide, 159
  and Kafka, 145, 156–7, 219, 226
  and Kant, 7–8, 19–23
  and Kierkegaard, 26, 45
  and Nietzsche, 99
  and Proust, 156–7
  Symbolist, 186, 189
  and Woolf, 185–7, 189
sublime, the, 11, 232 n. 6, 233 n. 10
  and aesthetics, ix, 12–13, 14–15, 19, 98
  and ethics, ix, 12–15, 19, 22, 87
  in Kafka, ix, 214
  in Kant, ix, xi, 6, 12–14, 58, 87, 211

and reason, 14
and Romanticism, 53
and the uncanny, ix, 53, 58, 211–12
symbolism
in Conrad, 160, 167–9, 171–2, 254 n. 8
geographical, 171, 179
in Gide, 160, 179
in Kant, 8–10, 18
Symbolism, French, 5, 186, 189
sympathy
imaginative, 87–91, 111
and intertextuality, 89
synecdoche, and metaphor and metonymy, 9, 161, 167–8, 175

taste
in Kant, 3, 6–7, 12, 16
in Nietzsche, 97–8
Tausk, Victor, 75, 76–9
techné
and aesthetics, 87, 204–5
in Heidegger, 137, 249 n. 7
and nature, 59–61, 70, 81, 202–4
Tedeschi, Richard, 161
teleology, and aesthetics, 5–6, 13
Tennyson, Alfred, 1st Baron, 258 n. 5
Terdiman, Richard, 243 n. 18
territory, in Kafka, 150
Thibaudet, Albert, 249–50 n. 10
threshold-moment, 134–7, 248 n. 1
and Conrad, 163
and Gide, 163
and Kafka, 133–4, 145–8, 153, 156, 157–8
and Proust, 136, 137–44, 157–8
thyrsus
and Baudelaire, x, 90, 101–12
definition of, 105, 106–7
and Nietzsche, x, 90, 92, 94–5, 99, 111
and Wagner, x, 90
Tieck, Johann Ludwig, 25, 29, 30, 32
time
in Blanchot, 222, 226
in Flaubert, 139, 249–50 n. 10
in Gide, 180
and irony, 32
in Kafka, 248 n. 1
in Proust, 131, 144, 248 n. 1
To the Lighthouse (Woolf)
as autobiographical, 187–9
and ethics and aesthetics, 196–8
and "The Fisherman and his Wife", 193–208, 210
and narrative framing, 192–9
and the uncanny, 210
and Woolf's *Diary*, 185–93
tone, in Conrad and Gide, 164
tragedy, Greek, 93–5
transfiguration, in Kierkegaard, 33–5
transformation
in Hoffmann, 71
in Kafka, 148–9
in Kierkegaard, 48
in Mann, 113
transubstantiation, in Kierkegaard, 33–5, 236 n. 8
Troyes, Chrétien de, *Perceval*, 118

uncanny, the
and the aesthetic, ix, 87, 133, 176–7, 211
in Alain-Fournier, 130, 133
and alchemy, 69–70, 71–2
in Blanchot, 47, 212–13
and borders, 53, 71
in Conrad, x, 134, 159, 162, 163, 170–4
and *Doppelgänger*, 56
and ethics, ix, 73–4, 133, 176–7, 211
in Freud, ix, xi, 39, 52–84, 143–4, 192
in Gide, 159, 162, 176–7
in Hoffmann, ix, 56, 58–63, 64–74, 75, 192
and the impersonal, 134, 211–12
as the inhuman, 134
and irony, 58, 62–3, 70
in Kafka, x, 133–4, 144–56, 158, 212–13
in Kierkegaard, 39, 58
and Modernism, ix–x, 53, 133–4, 211–12
and narrative openings, 133–58
and Oedipus, 82–3
in Proust, x, 133–4, 143–4, 158
and Romanticism, 62–3
and the sublime, ix, 53, 58, 211–12
in Woolf, x, xi, 134, 187–90, 192, 205, 207, 209–10, 211
uncertainty, and the uncanny, 61–2, 134
unconscious, in *Heart of Darkness*, 160, 172, 253 n. 2
Unheimlichkeit see uncanny, the
Unseld, Joachim, 252 n. 22

value, moral, in Kierkegaard, 43–51
Virgil (Publius Vergilius Maro), xii, 160
Vitzhum, Thomas, 261 n. 7, 262 n. 9
voix, narrative and *narratrice*, 224–5, 226, 228, 230

Wagner, Richard
and Baudelaire, 90, 108–10, 112, 241 n. 5
as Dionysos, 95, 100
and the *Gesamtkunstwerk*, 90, 91, 93

Wagner, Richard (*cont.*)
  and Liszt, 98, 108–10, 112
  and Nietzsche, 90, 91–3, 95–9, 101–2, 111, 241 n. 5
  and the thyrsus, x, 90
  Tannhäuser, 110–11, 237 n. 13
Walsh, Sylvia, 235 nn. 2, 5
Wapnewski, Peter, 241 n. 7, 242 n. 11
water, as theme in Woolf, 185, 187, 189–93, 199–201, 202, 204–5, 209–10, 211
Watt, Ian, 173, 175, 176, 253–4, n. 3, 254 nn. 5, 8
Wieland, Christoph Martin, 122
Wilde, Oscar, 255 n. 13
Wing, Nathaniel, 256 n. 22
wit, and irony, 29
Woolf, Virginia
  and aesthetics, 186–7, 190, 204–5, 209–10
  and Ariadne's thread, 190–258 n. 4
  and ethics, 196–8, 205
  and feminism, 195, 207
  and fiction and autobiography, 187–9
  and Freud, 208
  and human relationships, 196–8
  and impersonality, 134, 210, 211–12
  and memory, 188
  and Modernism, 186, 246 n. 11
  and "moments of being", 188
  and narrative framing, 190–9
  and Proust, 257–8 n. 3
  and the uncanny, x, xi, 134, 187–90, 192, 205, 207, 209–10, 211
  on writing, 191–3, 209–10
  writings
    Diary, 185–93
    Jacob's Room, 186
    Mrs. Dalloway, 186
    A Room of One's Own, 195, 260 n. 14
    "Sketch of the Past", 257 n. 2
    The Waves, 191
    see also To the Lighthouse; water
Wordsworth, William, "The Excursion", 231 n. 2

Yeats, W. B., and Modernism, 246 n. 11

Zuckerman, Elliott, 241 n. 6